PROFITABLE FOOD AND BEVERAGE MANAGEMENT: OPERATIONS

PROFITABLE FOOD AND BEVERAGE MANAGEMENT: OPERATIONS

ERIC F. GREEN, GALEN G. DRAKE,

AND

F. JEROME SWEENEY

Harris, Kerr, Forster & Company

Ahrens Series

J. Williams
Book Company
P.O. Box 783
Jenks, Oklahoma 74037

Library of Congress Cataloging in Publication Data

Green, Eric F
     Profitable food and beverage management: operations.

     (Ahrens series)
     Bibliography: p.
     Includes index.
     1. Food service management.   I. Drake, Galen G.,
joint author.   II. Sweeney, F. Jerome, joint author.
III. Title.
TX911.3.M27G73   658'.91'64795   77-25023
ISBN   0-930745-03-5

Portions of this work originally appeared in *Profitable Food and Beverage Operation, Fourth Revised Edition,* edited by Joseph Brodner, Howard M. Carlson, and Henry T. Maschal, also published by Hayden Book Company, Inc.

Printed in the United States of America

Preface

Since the publication of an earlier text, *Profitable Food and Beverage Operation*, also edited by partners of Harris, Kerr, Forster & Company, the food service industry has grown enormously. It is now one of the largest employers and revenue earners in the country. Provision of food service is now very big business, with all the responsibilities and obligations that that entails.

As many independent operators have been replaced by chains, franchisors, and conglomerates, the industry has become more organized and subject to controls at all levels of government. Energy shortages, truth in advertising, nutritional content of meals, health codes, and new wage and hour laws are only a few of the items that concern every operator today. Both small and large operators are glad of the services provided to them by the trade associations—federal, state, and local—in keeping clear of violations and abreast of developments. Thus food and beverage operators can no longer afford to concern themselves solely with their own operation's costs, revenues, and day-to-day circumstances. Pressures that were unknown in this industry ten years ago must be relieved, and they must be dealt with on a national, sometimes world-wide, scale.

Somewhat surprisingly, the industry has only begun to respond in a unified way to problems and pressures that are national in scope. We are asked by clients and associations within the industry to advise them on subjects which were unknown or of such little importance a few years ago that they were ignored by most operators. Research projects into the economic impact of the loss of the tip-credit and the effect of changes in the tax treatment of business entertainment expenses have been commissioned by national associations representing the interests of their membership.

Notwithstanding all these new developments, operators still have to deal with all the old questions as well. Controlling, purchasing, preparing, and merchandising as part of the profit-making effort are more important than ever. The big changes the operator must make are in approach: Operators must not only operate, they must manage as never before. Faced with so much new subject matter in writing for students and operators, the editors of this text divided it into two volumes, one on planning and one on operations. The companion volume, *Profitable Food and Beverage Management: Planning*, covers mainly strategy, design, accounting, legal questions, and energy management—topics of interest to all operators and students but particularly to managers and prospective investors.

This operations volume is more concerned with the day-to-day questions of production, storing, issuing, personnel, sanitation, and security—among other things. It is intended as a manual for operators and as an educational textbook for those entering the industry or taking school and college courses.

A book of this size can only touch on the technical aspects of nutritional values, cooking techniques, and merchandising. We believe, however, that it is comprehensive of all the topics with which a manager must be familiar today. The lengthy bibliography gives some indication of additional sources of information in this complex field.

In the preparation of this text we have been greatly assisted by our clients and the companies that have permitted us to use their material and illustrations. Their contributions are acknowledged in the text. Many of our staff have contributed their time and knowledge. Changed methods made necessary by increasing labor costs that have become apparent to all of us in our auditing and consulting work have been introduced, although the urge that accountants have for detail has not been forgotten.

A special word of thanks is due to Carol King and David Berins of our staff, whose line experience in food service operations was invaluable. We should like it to be known to them and others of our staff who have contributed much time and effort that we appreciate the opportunity to be a conduit for their thoughts. The editors hope that these new volumes will provide a sound basis for students and businessmen alike in making operations profitable.

ERIC F. GREEN
GALEN G. DRAKE
F. JEROME SWEENEY

Contents

PROFITABLE FOOD AND BEVERAGE MANAGEMENT: OPERATIONS

PART ONE

Food Management

1

INTRODUCTION TO OPERATIONS MANAGEMENT

In any business, managers must make many decisions during the course of each day. Experts in the field of management have analyzed the decision-making process and have identified three types of decisions: strategic decisions, made mostly by top management; tactical or administrative decisions, made by middle management; and operational decisions, made by line supervisors and lower level management.

Strategic decisions are concerned with establishing the overall long-range goals of the organization, determining by what means those goals will be met, what resources will be required to meet the goals that have been established, and how those resources are to be acquired by the organization. Resources include capital, labor, and technology or "know-how." In a food service organization, strategic planning could involve decisions on the types of restaurant or food service operations that the company might expand into, market segments to be served or geographic areas for expansion, and determining how such expansion will be financed.

Administrative decisions are usually the area of middle management and involve short-term planning to implement the decisions made by top management. Such plans may be in the form of originating annual and monthly sales goals, submitting budgets, finding and evaluating sites for expansion, developing training programs for managers and for hourly workers, developing specifications for the materials purchased, and negotiating purchasing contracts.

Operational decisions are made by lower level managers and first line supervisors. These are the individuals who are responsible for seeing that the specific tasks of day-to-day operations are carried out in an effective and efficient manner. Their tasks include forecasting the day-to-day sales to permit proper labor scheduling and food ordering.

There is no clear line separating these types of decisions. The manager of a chain restaurant is primarily concerned with operational decisions and, to some extent, administrative decisions. Although he spends much of his time in direct supervision of operations in his store, he may also prepare annual and monthly sales forecasts and budgets for his store and perform other administrative functions. The area supervisor sets goals for his assigned operations and sees that the company's standards are enforced and its policies are carried out. He may also contribute information to top management for strategic decision making by investigating a new market opportunity in his area, or by studying and reporting on some new legislation affecting his operations.

Profitable food and beverage management requires competence in all levels of decision making. For noncommercial operations, where the main objective is the provision of desired services within an established budget, similar managerial competence is just as necessary.

The companion volume to this text, *Profitable Food and Beverage Management: Planning,* deals with the general principles of management and with strategic planning in the areas of marketing, finance, and operating concepts. Administrative aspects of management are also discussed in the chapters, Planning for Profits and Managing the Business.

This text deals mainly with the management of materials and manpower—the largest part of the restaurant or food service manager's job. These two items—raw or partially prepared ingredients and labor—constitute the largest cost of any operation, costs that are largely variable in nature and that therefore can have the greatest effect on profitability. Other important parts of a manager's responsibility—housekeeping, safety, and security—are also covered.

2

MENU PLANNING

History and Development of Menus

The earliest menus that have been preserved are lists of foods served at banquets or dinner parties. Presumably they were working documents for the cooks and were not given to the guests. It was not until the development of public restaurants after the French Revolution that menus as we know them developed. The earliest ones were actually posters hung at the entrance of the restaurants, listing their wares. These developed into individual menus presented to the guest. Later, great efforts were made to decorate and enhance the menu cards. Today the menu is the primary merchandising medium of the restaurant. Occasionally we even find more attention being given to the embellishment and decoration of the menu than to the selection of the items offered. The menu may be chalked on a blackboard (or otherwise posted on the walls), handwritten on scrolls, or presented in every conceivable printed form: in a single card, double card, folded card, a many-paged book, or a newspaper; on individual slates; or even painted on bottles. This chapter deals with the selection and combination of the menu items. (Menu pricing and merchandising are discussed in *Profitable Food and Beverage Management: Planning.*)

Development of the Menu Format

The earliest menus, designed for banquets and parties, did not provide for much choice by the guest. Because this is still true for most banquet service, each component of the banquet menu must complement the others. The restaurant menu, on the other hand, usually provides the guest with some degree of choice regarding the different courses. Therefore, the emphasis in restaurant menu writing is to balance and coordinate the selections within each course rather than the courses themselves.

The number of courses and the offerings within each course have steadily decreased since the height of culinary achievement in seventeenth century France. A meal served at the court of Louis XV included "4 ollas and 8 lesser soups, 12 fish entrées, 32 entrées and 44 lesser entrées, 12 removes, 4 hors d'oeuvres before the king, 2 grands entremets; 32 roasts, 2 lesser roasts at the ends of the table, 2 little dishes before the king, 40 cold entremets and 48 hot entremets." Not all the dishes offered in the various courses were actually eaten by every guest. The ordinary guest had to content himself with dishes set near him. Only the royalty and the guests of honor had a complete selection.

In 1825 Brillat-Savarin described the menus of first-class restaurants as offering "12 soups, 24 side dishes [hors d'oeuvres], 15 or 20 entrées of beef, 20 entrées of mutton, 30 entrées of game or poultry, 15 or 20 entrées of veal, 12 dishes of patisserie, 24 dishes of fish, 15 roasts, 50 entremets and 50 desserts."

Tradition dies hard. Charles Ranhofer, Chef of Delmonico's in New York in the late 1800s, classified the following menu items in his treatise *The Epicurean,* first published in 1920 (see Fig. 2–1):

Oysters or clams
Soups: two, one thick, one thin
Hors d'oeuvres and relishes
Fish, often with potato or salad
Removes or releves [so called because they "relieved" the fish course]: roasts of smaller animals or smaller cuts of beef
Entrées, accompanied by vegetables
Punch or sherbet
Roasts of poultry or game
Cold dishes such as terrines, galatines, cold meats, or seafood
Entremets* or hot sweet dishes such as puddings, omelets, fritters, followed by cold sweet dishes such as jellies, charlottes, cakes
Desserts, cheeses, fresh and preserved fruits, frozen desserts, followed by coffee and cordials

In the classic French service, the meal was divided into three parts or "services." The first service, consisting of everything from soups to roasts, was placed on the table before the guests entered the room. Although heaters were used, the hot foods served later usually got cold before they were eaten. The second service included everything following the roasts up to the sweet dishes. The third service consisted of the sweets, ices, and fruits, along with the products of the pastry chef—that is, the desserts. Tables were decorated with elabo-

---

*"Entremets" (literally between the courses) originally referred to music or entertainment provided between the second and third services. Later it came to mean vegetable side dishes served during the entertainment, and eventually came to be synonymous with sweets or dessert.

La Réception

Avant l'Oeuvre

*Moet et
   Chandon Brut Impériale
Beaujolais Blanc
Lillet Blanc
Kir
Vermouth Cassis*

Le Beluga Malossol Caviar des Côtes d'Iran
de la Maison Romanoff sur socle de glace
Les Blinis
Le Saumon fumé de la Nouvelle Ecosse
La Mousse de foie d'oie frais
Les Barquettes de Grenouilles
La Gougère Bourguignonne
Les Escargots Vaudoise

Le Menu

Madère Sercial

Le Potage. "Le Grand Hochepot"
(Petite Marmite)

*Meursault Genevrières 1971
Louis Jadot*

La Terrine des Pêcheurs en gelée
Les Canapés Rouille

Ducru Beaucaillou 1962

Le Baron d'Agneau de Printemps Persillé
La Pomme de Terre Sarladaise
Les manges Tout

Le Granité au Limon

*Beaune Clos des Ursules 1953
Louis Jadot*

Le Fromage de Brie Couronné
La Salade du Kentucky
Parfumée à l'huile vierge et jus de citron

L'APOTHEOSE

*Niersteiner Riesling
Rehbach Auslese 1971
OB Frank Karl Schmitt*

La Pêche du Grand Maître
Corbeilles de Friandises

*Liqueurs
VEP Chartreuse
Cognac Bras d'Or
   Hennessy
Liqueur de Poire William -
   Dettling*

Café du Jumelage

DE LA FACULTE

Chef: Fritz Sonnenschmidt - Bruno Ellmer - Luc Brondel - James Heywood -
   Alfred Natale - André Bertin - Jean-Henri Salomon.

Bakeshop and Pastry Chefs: George Metropolis - Albert Kumin - Walter Schreyer.

Maîtres d' and Catering Directors: Bernard Rosenstein - Edmond Fontaine -
   Michel Bonnemort - Michael Bully - Stephen Beno - Bernard Splaver -
   John Dodig - Denis Powell.

Fig. 2-1A. Classical Menu. Prepared for a dinner of Les Amis d'Escoffier Society of New York, this menu included English language descriptions of the food to be served. *(Courtesy of Les Amis d'Escoffier Society of New York, Inc.)*

For the Perfect Enjoyment of this Dinner

KINDLY READ THE FOLLOWING DINNER RULES
OF LES AMIS D'ESCOFFIER SOCIETY OF NEW YORK, INC.

The aim of the "Les Amis d'Escoffier" Society of New York is to bring together members of the culinary profession and loyal friends who appreciate good food and good wines; men who believe in the adage "Live and Let Live": men who place sincere friendship above all else.

Dinner Rules

The napkin must be tucked under the collar. Persons under the influence of liquor will not be permitted to sit at the table.

The wines, carefully selected to accompany and enhance the delicacy of each course, must be drunk during the course for which they are intended. To enforce this ruling, the glasses — even if full — will be removed at the end of each course. Smoking is absolutely forbidden up to the time dessert is served. A person who smokes while eating does not deserve the title of "Gourmet."

A Warning

Since the "Les Amis d'Escoffier" Society is dedicated to the art of good living only, it is forbidden, under theat of expulsion, to speak of personal affairs, of one's own work or specialty, and more particularly to attempt to use the Society as a means of making business contacts. It is unnecessary to elucidate further upon this delicate subject which everyone understands. Furthermore, at these dinner-meetings reference will never be made on the subjects of: politics, religious beliefs, personal opinions of either members or gusts irrespective of their profession or social status.

◆ ◆ ◆

The Menu

The perfect planning of a menu which in itself is a summary of work and an expression of taste is more difficult to do than is generally understood. It is not a question of just listing a certain amount of dishes, but the task is to make the proper choice of food so as to create an orchestration of delicacy and flavor, which also applies to the wines served.

It can be said that the art of cookery is going through a test of survival due particularly to the lack of properly trained culinarians available and the high degree of commercialization in our kitchens.

These condition which are taxing the back-bone of the food industry is the "raison d'être" of Les Amis d'Escoffier Society of New York, Inc. and Les Amis d'Escoffier Society Foundation, Inc. The writer firmly believes that the are of cookery is here to stay. People today are more aware of good food than ever and they know they are not always getting it. This alone augurs well for the future. Discrimination is an attribute of our palate which is giving us the sense of taste for the greatest enjoyment in life.   J. D.

Fig. 2-1B. "Dinner rules" for the meal served on the opposite page. *(Courtesy of Les Amis d'Escoffier Society of New York, Inc.)*

rate *pièces montées*—display pieces made out of edible and inedible materials—portraying temples and other types of buildings, scenes, or animals, particularly birds and fish. Some of the pieces were intended to be eaten and constituted the dessert, whereas others were purely for decoration. Materials used included butter and lard, doughs, almond paste, icings, sugar, or any other ingredient that would create the desired effect. Chefs had to be architects, painters, and sculptors. The custom of the *pièce montée* continues in the tiered wedding cakes of today, although the decorations are apt to be of molded plastic rather than pastillage or sugar work. The carved ice figures sometimes found on a formal buffet table also originated in this period.

By the nineteenth century, classic cuisine had degenerated into a display of conspicuous consumption. The rise of a rich industrialist class permitted many to maintain an extravagant table that in earlier times only the wealthiest of the nobility could afford. Household chefs had to prepare great banquets which were more elaborate and more expensive than those given by their wealthy employers' peers. Monumental parties were a means of establishing social status for the commoners. It was during this period that good taste and artistic sensitivity were often sacrificed, along with sensibility in diet. The basic tenets of the classic cuisine—economical and artistic utilization of all foods—were lost.

As with any social institution that outlives its usefulness, the nineteenth century's ostentatious style of dining eventually gave way to a more moderate style that retains some of the vestiges of the classic French service. A modern banquet of Les Amis d'Escoffier follows the classic pattern, in moderation. Following an assortment of hors d'oeuvres come a soup, a fish course, entrée, ice, a cold meat dish with salad, cheese, sweets, and coffee. (See Fig. 2–2.)

The basic order of a modern meal—appetizer, soup, entrée with vegetables and salad, dessert, and coffee—can be seen as having its basis in classic French cuisine. With minor variation, it is the accepted pattern of eating in Western cultures.

A contrast to the Western method of service is the Chinese manner of dining, in which all dishes are placed on the table at once. The number of dishes increases with the number of people at the table. Individual bowls of rice are served, but the diners help themselves to all other dishes, which are sometimes placed on a lazy Susan in the middle of the table to facilitate service. Traditionally in China, soup is consumed throughout the meal.

A Chinese menu consists of a minimum of two dishes (in addition to rice) and increases with the number of guests, up to about eight. The items selected offer a variety of tastes, colors, and textures to avoid repetition. Method of preparation is also varied to facilitate service. Some dishes are "long-cooked," whereas others are "quick-

Le Dîner de Printemps

Avant L'Oeuvre

Apéritifs:
Piper Heidsieck
Vermouth
ou
Chablis Cassis

LE CAVIAR DE LA MER CASPIENNE SUR SOCLE
BLINIS DE SARAZIN ET LA TRADITIONNELLE GARNITURE
MILLE FEUILLES AUX ROQUEFORT
POMPONETTES DE LA MARQUISE
CANAPÉS TRICOLORE
ALLUMETTES AUX ANCHOIS
LA TARTE À LA MODE DE TROIS EPIS
RILLETTES DE TOURS

Le Menu

LE POTAGE GERMINY
LES PAILLETTES DORÉES

∽

Chablis Grand Cru
"Les Clos" 1964

LES HOMARDS À LA FRANÇAISE
LE RIZ PATNA EN PILAFF

∽

Château D'issan
(Cruse) 1961

LA SELLE D'AGNEAU PERSILLÉE PROVENÇALE
LES POMMES DE TERRE DAUPHINE
LES HARICOTS VERTS CRÈME GRATIN

∽

LE GRANITÉ AU PARFUM VILLENEUVE-LOUBET

∽

Ruchottes Chambertin
1961

LES DÉLICES DE BRIOCHE STRASBOURGEOISE
À LA GELÉE DE PORTO
LA SALADE BERGERETTE

∽

DE LA FROMAGERIE ODORANTE
LE BON BRIE ET LE ROQUEFORT DE FRANCE

∽

Taittinger
Brut La Française

LA PYRAMIDE DE FRAISES
SUR GLACE VANILLE
CARDINAL RICHELIEU

∽

LES PETITS PANIERS
AVEC LES MIGNARDISES
DU MAÎTRE PUJOL

∽

Armagnac

LE CAFÉ DE HAITI

CHARLES OHREL   MARCEL HAENTZLER
Directeur des Banquets   *Chefs des Cuisines*

Fig. 2-2. A banquet menu, courtesy of Les Amis d'Escoffier, follows the classic French meal pattern.

cooked" just before service, either by sautéing or by the stir-fry method.

Contemporary Menus

As the classic Western menu got smaller and smaller, restaurants began to specialize in certain types of dishes to limit their menus even further. There are numerous advantages to having a limited menu:

The Hemisphere Club

Appetizers

Little Neck Clams on the Half Shell 2.95	Coupe of Cut Fruits 1.25
Supreme of Pink Shrimp 3.25	Proscuitto and Melon 2.75
Smoked Salmon with Asparagus 1.50	Juice of the Day .85

Small Antipasto   2.25

Soups

French Onion Soup 1.10	Potage St. Germain 1.10
Cold: Cream of Avocado 1.10	Consomme, Diablotin 1.10

From Rivers and Seas

Prawns Fried In Ale Batter   5.95

Sauteed Dover Sole, Meuniere   7.95   Baked Striped Bass   6.50

The Chef's Specialties

Filet of Beef Stroganoff   6.75

Broiled Pork Chop with Apple Nuggets   7.75

Grillades

Calf's Liver Sauteed or Broiled with Crisp Onion Rings and Bacon   6.95

Sirloin Steak   9.50   A Trio of Lamb Chops   8.50

Delmonico Steak Sandwich   7.50   Chopped Sirloin Steak   5.75

Roast of the Day   8.25

Eggs & Omelets

Shirred Eggs with Sauteed Sweet Breads 4.25	Omelet with Mushrooms and Herbs 4.50
Eggs Benedict 5.25	Strawberry Omelet 4.25

A Service of Luncheon Vegetables

From the Cold Kitchen

Shrimp Salad, Green Goddess Dressing 5.95	The Club's Chef's Salad 4.95
Chicken Salad with Avocado 5.25	Melange of Fruit, Honey Dressing 5.25
Tartar Steak at Table Side 6.75	Hemisphere Club Sandwich 4.95
Seasonal Salad .85	Half Cantaloupe filled with Crabmeat 5.95

Spinach and Bacon Salad   .95

Desserts

Hemisphere Ice Creams and Sherbets 1.10	Hemisphere Cheese Cake 1.50
Marble Pound Cake .95 Viennese Biscuit Torte 1.35	Compote of Fruits 1.20
Cheese of the Day .95 Chocolate Bavarian Cream with Vanilla Sauce 1.10	

———

Pot of English Tea .70	Espresso .85
Pure Colombian Coffee .70	Milk .60

Fig. 2-3. A luncheon club menu. *(Courtesy of Restaurant Associates Industries, Inc.)*

1. Customers are not confused by numerous listings, and decision making is simplified.
2. Service is faster, since reading the menu and ordering take less time.
3. Less preparation is required.
4. Better quality controls can be exercised.
5. Waste is decreased.
6. Less space is required to store and prepare items.
7. There is less food to be purchased and controlled.

Figure 2–3 shows a contemporary menu from a fine luncheon club. It is quite limited in content when compared to the historically large classic French menu, but it still follows the same general format. Although a few clubs and restaurants have been able to create and maintain a reputation based on a very large menu, the current trend is to limit the number of offerings to those which are the most likely to sell.

Bun 'n' Burger provides an example of an extremely limited menu (Fig. 2–4). Like many other fast-food operations, it restricts its menu to hamburgers and cheeseburgers, the most popular foods in America, and a few accompanying items. Beverages are a necessity of the modern eating pattern. French fried potatoes and desserts are offered to increase check averages. The whole operation is geared to fast seat turnover, limited production requirements, a minimum of manpower, and efficient utilization of space. The Sirloin & Saddle, a table-service restaurant, offers a limited dinner menu (Fig. 2–5).

Delicatessens use an expanded menu as the pattern for their operations. A close look at the items, however, will reveal that many of them are made from a certain group of basic ingredients. Furthermore, this type of menu is usually offered all day long and, in some cases, around the clock. Therefore, it must satisfy different tastes at different times of day, whether it is for a meal or a snack.

Developing a Menu

Menu development must begin with a careful analysis of the market. The menu is one of the keys to a restaurant's successful operation. To the operator, it is the catalog of his product line and provides the basis for purchasing, production, staffing, and service. It is also his principal advertising medium and most persuasive sales representative. To the customer, the menu is a spokesman for the restaurant, reflecting its image and policies, promoting its products.

Fig. 2-4. A limited hamburger menu. *(Courtesy of Bun N'Burger International, Inc., New York)*

Menu Format

In theory, the nature and format of the menu—that is, the type and number of items in the various food categories—should be determined by market analysis before the operation is begun, and should be the basis for the designing and planning of the restaurant. In practice, however, the kitchen is often well advanced in planning before much thought is given to the menu. In effect, the factory is built before the product is engineered. Given this situation, the format of the menu must be limited by the production capacity of the kitchen.

The basic nature of the operation also helps to determine the menu format. For example, the menu for a steak house will be different from that for a fast-food drive-in or a school lunch program.

The number of menus required should be determined. Should there be one menu for all day, or one for luncheon and another one for dinner? Is a late supper menu required? A breakfast menu? An afternoon menu? Is a different format indicated for weekends? In

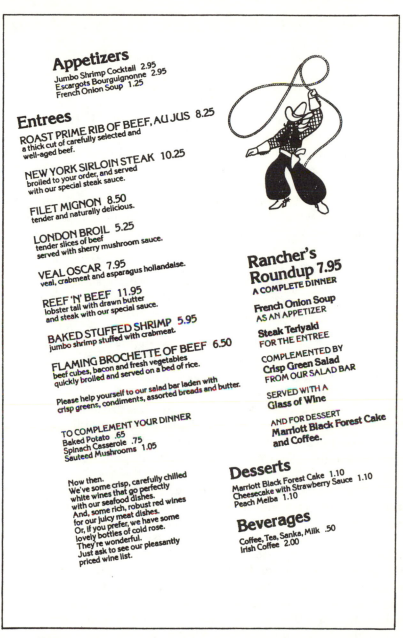

Appetizers
Jumbo Shrimp Cocktail 2.95
Escargots Bourguignonne 2.95
French Onion Soup 1.25

Entrees
ROAST PRIME RIB OF BEEF, AU JUS 8.25
a thick cut of carefully selected and
well-aged beef.

NEW YORK SIRLOIN STEAK 10.25
broiled to your order, and served
with our special steak sauce.

FILET MIGNON 8.50
tender and naturally delicious.

LONDON BROIL 5.25
tender slices of beef
served with sherry mushroom sauce.

VEAL OSCAR 7.95
veal, crabmeat and asparagus hollandaise.

REEF 'N' BEEF 11.95
lobster tail with drawn butter
and steak with our special sauce.

BAKED STUFFED SHRIMP 5.95
jumbo shrimp stuffed with crabmeat.

FLAMING BROCHETTE OF BEEF 6.50
beef cubes, bacon and fresh vegetables
quickly broiled and served on a bed of rice.

Please help yourself to our salad bar laden with
crisp greens, condiments, assorted breads and butter.

TO COMPLEMENT YOUR DINNER
Baked Potato .65
Spinach Casserole .75
Sauteed Mushrooms 1.05

Now then.
We've some crisp, carefully chilled
white wines that go perfectly
with our seafood dishes.
And, some rich, robust red wines
for our juicy meat dishes.
Or, if you prefer, we have some
lovely bottles of cold rose.
They're wonderful.
Just ask to see our pleasantly
priced wine list.

Rancher's Roundup 7.95
A COMPLETE DINNER

French Onion Soup
AS AN APPETIZER

Steak Teriyaki
FOR THE ENTREE

COMPLEMENTED BY
Crisp Green Salad
FROM OUR SALAD BAR

SERVED WITH A
Glass of Wine

AND FOR DESSERT
Marriott Black Forest Cake
and Coffee.

Desserts
Marriott Black Forest Cake 1.10
Cheesecake with Strawberry Sauce 1.10
Peach Melba 1.10

Beverages
Coffee, Tea, Sanka, Milk .50
Irish Coffee 2.00

Fig. 2-5. A limited dinner menu. *(Courtesy of Saddle Brook Marriott Motor Inn, New Jersey)*

multiple-outlet situations, such as in a hotel, the coordination of the various markets and planned operating hours should be considered. Will the same menu be offered in different places, or if not, can some

529768

of the items be duplicated? What about room service? Should children's menus be prepared?

The selling prices required, as indicated by market research, also have some bearing on the number and type of items to be offered. Should all the menu items be priced separately, that is, à la carte? Or should the whole menu be table d'hôte—one price for the complete meal? Or should the menu be a combination of à la carte and table d'hôte? The pricing policy will affect how the menu is written. (Menu pricing is discussed more fully in Chapter 8 of *Profitable Food and Beverage Management: Planning.* Finally, competing menus should also be considered in the format.

Table 1–1 is an example of a luncheon menu format from a medium-priced table-service suburban restaurant which has a clientele of shoppers and business people.

Varied versus Set Menu

Depending on the type of operation, menus may be either set (seldom changed) or varied (changed daily). A set menu is suited to an operation that caters to a transient market, whereas a daily menu is used when there is repeat patronage. A restaurant endeavoring to build a repeat clientele may offer a menu that is changed completely every day, or that has only certain sections or items changed to provide the desired variety. Certain standard items that are popular can, in themselves, develop repeat business. In Table 1–1, minute steak, shrimp cocktail, and certain sandwiches are set items, whereas all other items are changed daily. In institutions with captive audiences, a completely varied menu must be offered to avoid monotony. Many restaurants have fixed menus with clip-on sections for daily specials.

The preparation of a completely set menu is usually given careful thought and attention by management because it is an infrequent activity. Unfortunately, daily menu writing is often left to the discretion of a chef or cook who, because of the pressure of other duties, does not give it the consideration required. When menu writing becomes a day-to-day task, there is little coordination of items, and the selections can easily become confined to those few easiest to prepare or assumed to be favorites. There is a tendency to overproduce and offer the same item for several days, easing the work load but possibly being monotonous to the clientele.

The Cycle Menu

Good management practice requires that daily menu writing be approached systematically and in a businesslike way. One technique used is the cycle menu.

Table 2–1. Luncheon Menu Format—Mondays through Saturdays

Six Appetizers

One vegetable juice
One fruit juice (juice may be a shrub* or may be frosted for variety)
One fruit (combination or frosted for variety)
One other (anchovies, herring, chopped chicken livers, etc.)
Two soups, one thick, one thin
Shrimp cocktail

Seven Hot Entrées

One roast or solid meat, potato or vegetable, and salad
One fish, potato or vegetable, and salad
One poultry dish, vegetable, and salad
One meat substitute, vegetable, and salad
One lamb or veal dish, potato or vegetable, and salad
One stew (ground meat or meat extended dish), potato or vegetable, and salad
Daily: minute steak, French-fried potatoes, and salad

Three Salad Entrées

One protein type, such as chicken or seafood salad
One fruit salad plate
One mixed green combination bowl

Six Sandwiches

Cold sliced turkey
Cold sliced roast beef
Cold sliced ham and Swiss cheese
Quarter-pound hamburger with lettuce and tomato and French-fried potatoes
One open-face or special sandwich
One soup–sandwich combination

Eight Desserts	*Beverages*
Cake	Pot of coffee or tea
Fruit pie	Whole, skim, chocolate, or buttermilk
Soft pie	Hot chocolate
Fresh fruit	Iced tea or coffee
Sundae or parfait	Soft drinks
Ice cream or sherbet	
Hot fudge sundae	
Pudding or custard	

Other Considerations

1. Offer at least one beef entrée on each menu, in addition to minute steak.
2. Include an egg item on the Saturday menu.
3. Sometimes replace the potato with rice, biscuit, dumpling or noodles.
4. Occasionally use two vegetables in place of potato and one vegetable.
5. Offer a choice of two vegetables which are different from each other in color and texture. Be sure that at least one of the two is very popular.
6. Offer two salads, one fruit and one vegetable.
7. Specify the garnish to be used for each item.
8. During the summer, include one cold soup on the menu.
9. During winter, offer one hot sandwich (in addition to hamburger), and omit one salad entrée.

*A shrub, in this context, is made by adding acidulated fruit juice to iced water.

A cycle consists of a carefully prepared set of menus which are rotated according to a prescribed pattern. Cycles can be used even when the guest menus are printed and dated daily. The cycle has numerous advantages:

1. It can be planned to provide variety and interest, as well as balanced costs and work loads.
2. Once planned, it relieves both chef and management of day-to-day menu writing.
3. Through accumulation of a sales history, it provides a means for more accurate forecasting of sales and production requirements.
4. In operations with banquet or special party sales, function menus can be arranged to include items from the daily menu, thus coordinating the production and possibly expanding the banquet menu possibilities.

Depending on the market, a seven-day cycle may be appropriate so that a given menu will always be offered on the same day of the week. Many restaurants are renowned for having certain dishes on certain days of the week. Another operation may require a cycle with a larger number of menus in order to avoid repetition. An institution with a permanent population should use a longer cycle—one extending 28 days for example. Generally hospitals and hotels base the length of the cycle on the average length of stay per patient or guest.

Nutritional Considerations

The truth of the old adage "man is what he eats" is being reaffirmed by the current interest in health foods and good nutrition. The daily food plan (Table 2–2) was devised to provide a simple guide for planning nutritious meals. The plan includes four basic food groups and specifies the quantities of food in each group that will provide a foundation for a well-balanced diet. Most people eat more than the specified amount of those foods, and they also consume foods not listed, such as fats, oils, sugar, and unrefined grain products. Those unlisted foods are frequently combined with other foods to provide variety and enhance appeal.

Caloric content is another important factor in menu planning. The amount of calories each person requires daily depends on the amount of physical exercise he gets, the body weight he wishes to maintain, and the climate.

Nutritional considerations are a major concern when planning menus, especially in an institution with a captive population. The National School Lunch Program requires that the Type A school lunch provide at least one-third of the daily dietary requirements of children

Table 2–2. Daily Food Plan

Milk Group: Some milk daily—
Children . . . . .3 to 4 cups
Teenagers . . . . .4 or more cups
Adults . . . . .2 or more cups
Pregnant women . . . . .4 or more cups
Nursing mothers . . . . .6 or more cups
Cheese and ice cream can replace part of the milk.

Meat Group: Two or more servings—
Beef, veal, pork, lamb, poultry, fish, eggs, with dry beans and peas and nuts as alternates

Vegetable-Fruit Group: Four or more servings—
Dark-green or deep-yellow vegetable important for vitamin A—at least every other day
Citrus fruit or other fruit or vegetable important for vitamin C—daily
Other fruits and vegetables including potatoes

Bread-Cereals Group: Four or more servings—
Whole-grain, enriched, restored

10 to 12 years old. In hospital feeding, therapeutic menus must provide adequate nutrition within the restrictions of the diet ordered, although certain diets prescribed for a short term (such as for pre- or post-operative patients) may be lacking in some nutrients.

When a choice of foods is permitted on restaurant or institutional menus, management can offer the basic foods prescribed by the daily food plan and hope that the patron selects wisely. Care should be taken that the menu structure will permit a balanced selection and that the food is prepared in such a way that the nutritional content is maintained.

Writing the Menu

Although menu construction cannot be reduced to an infallible formula, too many of the menus presented to patrons today are simple listings of items selected because they are favorites of the menu writer, because a competitor offers the same items, or because tradition requires that certain offerings be included.

To be successful, the menus must reflect the eating habits and expectations of the restaurant's market. The tastes of customers are complex, varying from day to day and from season to season. No one person should be the menu writer if a truly representative menu is desired. The menu is far too important in determining the success or failure of an operation for personal biases to be reflected in it. Among those participating in the assembling of a successful menu for a large hotel will be (1) the maitre d', who will wish to include food preferences indicated by customer comments; (2) the chef, who will wish to assure proper utilization of equipment and distribution of the work load; (3) the purchasing agent, who will wish to assure the use of foods that are readily available at reasonable prices; (4) the food and beverage controller, who will calculate potential costs and also provide statistics on past customer preferences; and (5) a representative of management, who will coordinate the work of the entire menu-writing team.

All of the foregoing positions are usually found in a large hotel or restaurant. For an independent, small or medium-sized restaurant or the food service facility of a small motor hotel, the menu-writing team would be the manager, the chef, and the head waiter. In a hospital, the basic or "house" menu should be written by the dietitian, chef, and management personnel.

Sales Analysis

The starting point for menu construction for an established operation is a review of present performance—a sales analysis of each of the items listed on the menu. One method of accumulating these statistics is to have the food checker, cashier, or food and beverage controller use a menu to keep score of the number of portions sold of each menu item for each day of the week that it appears. Sales statistics can also be collected automatically (*Profitable Food and Beverage Management: Planning*, Chapter 13, Systems and Automation).

Actual tabulation of sales provides an objective, quantitative measurement not based on the personal recollections of the staff. That analysis will reveal actual customer eating habits and preferences and will quickly point up the items on the menu that have little appeal. It can show whether à la carte or table d'hôte listings are better sellers. The results of the analysis will permit the menu writer to make informed decisions about the items to be included on the menu.

The average sale per person or "average check" should be calculated for each meal period and reviewed against the menu price range. In that way, the price structure can be evaluated to see whether the right numbers of low- and high-priced items are offered.

Principles of Menu Writing

The sales analysis identifies the patrons' dining habits and food preferences. In combining those preferences into a daily menu, certain principles must be considered, such as menu variety, appearance, availability, balance of work load for both employees and equipment, utilization of by-products and leftovers, service requirements, and so on.

The Calendar and the Clock. The day of the week can influence dining preferences. Monday, for example, is often a budget day for people who have overspent during the weekend. Friday still remains a traditional fish day in certain areas. Paydays of nearby employers can affect luncheon sales. The hours and days of operation of shops and stores can also be a factor. During school holidays, the likelihood of an increase in patronage by children accompanied by a parent or other relative should be considered. Depending on the location and clientele of the establishment, Saturdays and Sundays may be days of peak volume, or they may be the slowest days of the week.

The time of year should be considered. In hot weather, people tend to eat lighter meals. Special attention should be given to sandwich plates, cold cuts, cold soups, and salad plates, which are popular during the summer and have a low food cost. Cold weather brings the need for more filling, hot foods, such as thick soups and stews.

Holidays afford an excellent opportunity for specialties that stimulate customer interest and create favorable comment. Thanksgiving, Christmas, and Easter have well-established culinary traditions. Other national and regional holidays offer the opportunity to create menus based on ethnic foods (St. Patrick's Day), sentiment (St. Valentine's Day), period foods (Washington's Birthday), or other selected subjects. Astute menu makers can take advantage of local civic, cultural, sports, or entertainment events to create special menus for the occasion. Off-beat "holidays," such as Pancho Villa's Birthday, also can serve as the basis for special promotion and a special menu.

The time of day should be considered. The need to offer standard breakfast items in the morning is obvious, but what about the rest of the day? Does a portion of the market have a living pattern different from that of the majority? Travelers are sometimes off schedule and want breakfast in the evening or supper in the forenoon. Work schedules are also a factor. Do employees in the neighborhood work on two or three shifts? Luncheon menus in resort areas may include some breakfast-type items for the late risers.

Other factors in the local market may call for special consideration. Theater-goers prefer a short, quick dinner or late supper. Shoppers may be looking for an afternoon snack. Commuters may want a snack with a five o'clock cocktail, and the working woman may want to take something home for the family dinner.

Appearance of the Food. Menu planning involves subtle merchandising. Eye appeal is vital in food merchandising because of the very personal association between the customer and the product. People enjoy their food because of what they see almost as much as because of what they taste. It is important, therefore, that every dish look as good as it tastes.

Good appearance is accomplished by paying attention to the details of color, texture, and shape. Color is an important factor in improving the appearance of food. The selection of a colorful garnish can enliven an entire plate. That traditional wedge of lemon served with a broiled or baked fish dinner not only enhances the flavor but also provides color contrast with the gray or brown of the fish. Grated parsley or a sprinkle of paprika adds further color interest to the plate. How much more appetizing a turkey sandwich looks if a leaf of lettuce is added and the sandwich is cut into three or four sections, speared with an olive on a frilly toothpick, and accompanied by a spoonful of cranberry-orange relish in a lettuce cup. In French cuisine each dish has a required "garniture," which is a basic part of the recipe. With a little imagination, colorful garnishes can be devised to make every plate distinctive. Cherry tomatoes, radish roses, a bit of watermelon pickle, a sprig of mint or watercress, or a galax leaf can add a special touch.

Color is also important in the combination of foods on a plate. When the menu lists an entrée with specified vegetables or salad, color becomes a major point in the selection of the accompanying items. Combinations such as carrots and sweet potato or cauliflower and boiled potatoes are obviously to be avoided. A broiled tomato looks better with a cheese rarebit than do buttered carrots. A green salad complements the red of a tomato-based pasta entrée.

Texture is another consideration of appearance. Mashed squash and whipped potatoes would be poor choices to accompany an entrée with a thick cream sauce or an escalloped casserole. A better choice would be crisp shoestring potatoes, broiled or fried tomatoes or broccoli spears, and a crisp green salad. It is probably not an accident that steak, green salad, and baked potato are a favorite combination. The soft, dry mealiness of the potato contrasts with the juiciness of the steak and the crispness of the salad. The addition of sour cream with chives or cheese with bacon to the potato provides another texture difference.

Shape is the third consideration in combining foods. Cucumber, for instance, is the same food whether it is in one chunk or cut into thin slices with the edges scored, but what a difference in appearance! Round, oblong, square, chopped, diced, big pieces or small—the detail of shape affects the appearance and appeal of the dish.

Flavor combinations should also be considered in combining foods. Bitter, salty, sweet, and sour are the basic taste sensations. The flavor of foods in combination should complement one another and not overwhelm. The delicate flavor of a fillet of sole is enhanced by a delicate white wine sauce or by browned butter sauce, parsley, and lemon juice, à la meunière. Fresh pineapple, oranges, or melons

provide a pleasant surprise with chicken salad. Strong-flavored vegetables harmonize with strong-flavored meats, such as corned beef with
cabbage. Certain flavor combinations are accepted and expected:
turkey and cranberry, lamb and mint, shrimp and cocktail sauce,
melon with prosciutto ham, ham with cheese. Consider the flavor
combinations of peach Melba. The tartness of the raspberry purée, the
sweetness of the peach, and the creaminess of the vanilla ice cream all
enhance one another, not only in taste but also in color, texture, and
shape.

The Market. Availability of foods in the market area in the desired
quantity and quality must be considered when planning menus.
Although most foods can now be obtained throughout the year,
seasonal and locally grown foods should be used as much as possible.
Their condition is usually better, and they are less expensive. Fresh
fruit and vegetables are often avoided because of the labor they require.
"Fresh fruit cup" too often consists of oranges and grapefruit right out
of a jar—a totally unimaginative offering. The guest who has just seen
a wide array of fresh fruit in the supermarket is justifiably disap-
pointed. The operator who can offer berries and melons or fresh
peaches and grapes, perhaps with sliced bananas, topped with a mint
sprig, has a distinct advantage over his less imaginative competitors.
Baked shad or shad roe, spring lamb, new potatoes, fresh asparagus,
and green apple pie are other examples of seasonal items that can be
offered to avoid monotony.

Delivery capability and frequency of delivery should be
considered, along with the state of delivery. If holding or processing,
such as ripening or butchering, is required by the restaurant before
the product is usable, sufficient time must be allowed before the item
is scheduled to appear on the menu.

The probable purchase price of a commodity should be
determined to avoid offering too many high-cost items.

Planning for Production Control. The items selected and offered in
combination should make it possible to control the quantities produced. For example, on a restaurant menu, certain items will be
prepared to order, whereas others will be made ahead of time. For
such dishes as stews and pot roasts, which take a long time to prepare,
a certain quantity is produced. If that quantity is all sold, the item is
removed from the menu. If not completely sold, the item becomes a
"leftover" and must be disposed of in the least costly manner, either
in the same or in a different form on subsequent menus (assuming the
quality of the product is maintained), or by being offered to employees
or staff, or by being thrown out. Some items may be remade if they run
out, such as creamed chicken mixtures or fricassees. Meat, sauce, and
garnishes can be prepared separately and combined as needed.

Ingredients left over can then be utilized in other dishes or freshly combined the next day. Cake layers, if they have no icing, can be frozen and assembled later. A good menu will balance the number of items that can be fully and partially controlled by being cooked to order with those items that are cooked completely in advance. Such a plan not only leads to a better food cost, but it also evens the work load on the preparation staff and the cooking equipment.

The Kitchen. The menu must be within the production capabilities and limitations of the kitchen. Too many dishes requiring the same method of cookery or preparation will overload a station. If everything is baked or roasted, the cook will probably set the oven temperature at top heat in order to get it all ready in time, and ignore quality considerations. If a large number of items require a steamer or steam kettle, the cook will start early and work fast, again with possible loss of quality. The expected sales mix (the proportion of total sales volume on each item) as well as the number of items should be considered. A grill or broiler that may be adequate for a small number of steak orders may be too small to handle a large number of hamburgers.

Although it is not advisable to write a menu entirely on the basis of the capability of the staff, some degree of thought should be given to the skills available. If the cooks cannot properly prepare a complicated item, it should be left off the menu until it is perfected, not just by one cook but by several.

Work loads should be balanced by station to permit optimum use of labor and to provide better service to the guest. Items requiring advance preparation should be scheduled when there is sufficient staff to do the work. For example, if on the weekends the operation is closed or has only a skeleton staff, the Monday menus should not require a lot of preparation. Friday menus for such an operation should be highly controllable, since leftovers could not be utilized for three days.

Service Requirements. The menu items and combinations of items should be selected for the most efficient service to the guest. If the tables are small or if the service staff uses arm service or very small trays, items requiring a number of side dishes should be avoided. Items that are prepared to order and require long waits should be avoided when a fast seat turnover is desired. Cafeteria entrées should be assembled beforehand so that they will have eye appeal and can be served with one motion to speed the line. Items that cannot be produced in large quantities, such as elaborate or flaming desserts, should not be offered on banquet menus. Some items that can be produced in quantity also may be unsuitable for banquet service if the labor required in assembling them and the length of the assembly time are too great. The temperatures of foods served together should be considered. For instance, if hot and cold foods are to be served on the same plate (not advisable on banquet service), the assembling must be done immediately before service. At a banquet, this could cause very slow service if the operation is not set up and staffed properly. Is the equipment adequate for keeping hot foods hot and cold foods cold? How much can be assembled or "plated" ahead, and how much must be done at the time of service? All these points will affect the pace of service and the quality of the food.

Price Ranges. The prices of the menu offerings should cover a range wide enough to attract patrons of the different income groups perceived as the target market. More importantly, the items and the expected sales mix of those items should produce a desired food cost. (Since pricing is a vital economic and image-building point, this topic is discussed fully in Chapter 8 of *Profitable Food and Beverage Management: Planning.*)

Utilization of By-products. Frequently the processing of a raw food item will yield salable by-products, depending on the form in which it is purchased. For example, if a beef tenderloin is butchered for orders of filet mignon, high quality hamburger meat and tenderloin tips will also be obtained, which can be used for such items as tenderloin tips, beef Stroganoff, and meatloaf or another ground beef item. Beef ribs will yield shortribs; poultry provides livers and gizzards. The menu must regularly provide for those items that can be prepared with these by-products. The amounts generated and the popularity of the by-product item will determine the frequency of the offering. A word of caution is necessary here. Where it is found that these by-product offerings do not sell, it may be better to alter the purchasing specification for the item in order to avoid buying unsalable merchandise. Although the cost per pound as purchased may be higher for a cut of meat with a little more trim, the resulting cost per serving may be lower.

Utilization of Leftovers. Because customer tastes are not static or precise, leftovers are inevitable whenever advance preparation is necessary. Adverse weather or other unforeseeable factors will also occasionally result in leftover food. A good menu will have some built-in provision for anticipated leftovers. If a roast of beef appears on one day's menu, a subsequent menu may feature barbecued beef sandwiches to dispose of the leftover roast. Hash or a croquette item utilizes cooked scraps and trimmings, as well as any leftover potatoes or dried bread. Other uses for scraps and trimmings are as flavorings for soufflés, omelets, and canapés, or as fillings for tea sandwiches. Sliced meats or unsauced poultry can be used on cold plates or cold sandwiches. Leftover stews or mixtures may be merchandized as an extra menu item if they have retained their quality. Forecasting to minimize leftovers is a science, but imaginative use of leftovers is an art.

Leftovers can be merchandized as "daily specials," but they must be of high quality, or regular guests will quickly learn to avoid the "specials." Items such as "Soup du Jour" and "Vegetables of the Day" provide some leeway. Entrées might be listed as "Daily Featured Luncheon" or "Chafing Dish Special," with members of the service staff telling the guest what the "specials" are. Menu clip-on cards, called "riders," can also be used, or the special items may be posted on a sign or blackboard.

Planning for Sales Control. The salability of any menu item is influenced by the competition of other items. That becomes an important consideration in forecasting and production planning, particularly when the menus are quite limited. The in-flight menu shown in Fig. 2–6 is an excellent example. Of the three entrées offered, one (tournedos) is far more popular than the others, thus simplifying the forecasting. If the three entrées were equally popular, the sales mix would be quite unpredictable.

Menu Planning by Computer

The computer is becoming an important tool in menu planning, particularly in hospitals and institutions where daily or cycle menus are used. Proposed menus can be evaluated by the computer much more quickly and thoroughly than by an individual. The following are some of the types of evaluation that computers now perform:

1. Cost analyses of proposed daily menus, showing costs per portion, projected consumption, and resulting daily food cost.
2. Variety evaluations, including the frequency of appearance of similar flavors or other characteristics, or frequency of use of specific recipes.
3. Nutritional analyses, determining the content of each meal combination for any number of specified nutrients.
4. Production capability or other constraint analysis. Limitations on production capability (such as equipment capacities), purchasing availability, item acceptability, or any other limitations can be built into the system.
5. "Best buy" alternatives, suggesting substitute items that will

PREMIERE CLASSE

FIRST CLASS

Sherry

Dubonnet   Campari

Manhattan   Gin Martini   Vodka Martini   Noilly Prat

Daiquiri   Bloody Mary   Screwdriver   Whiskey Sour

Tom Collins   Vodka Collins   Scotch   Bourbon   Canadian

Premium Beer   Gin   Vodka   Bacardi Rum

Mousse de Saumon, Sauce Bercy

Filet Mignon Grillé, Maître d'Hôtel

Grenadin de Veau Forestière   Suprême de Volaille Wellington

Pommes Dauphine   Légumes au Beurre

Salade Campagnarde

Dessert

Menthes

Café au Cognac ou Cointreau   Thé   Café Américain ou Décaféiné

Selected Red & White Wines

Champagne Brut

Bénédictine and Brandy

Drambuie   Bénédictine   Crème de Menthe   Grand Marnier

Cognac VSOP   Cointreau

Fig. 2-6. An in-flight menu planned to facilitate forecasting of passengers' preferences. *(Courtesy of Pan American World Airways)*

meet all nutritional, variety, production and other constraints at lowest possible cost.

A major reason for automating menu writing is to produce menus with the lowest possible food cost that will meet the criteria of nutritional content and acceptability. Other reasons include improving overall menu quality, freeing professional staff for other functions, and integrating menu planning with other automated subsystems (such as purchasing, production planning, and cost control).

Special Types of Menus

Breakfast

Since many patrons exercise a rather narrow choice in their breakfast selections, menu writers are apt to pay little or no attention to this meal and merely repeat the same choices every day of the year. A little variation, however, may do much for the volume of sales. French toast, for instance, lends itself to a variety of treatments and has enough substance to appeal to patrons who do not eat a light breakfast. It may be served with syrup, fruit, or preserves, or sprinkled with powdered sugar.

Pancake houses, which enjoy a great deal of popularity, have shown what imaginative fillings and toppings can do to make breakfast foods highly appealing. Different types of omelettes—ham, jelly, chives, green pepper, or cheese—also provide interesting variety. Fruit topping on cereals is extremely popular. It may become a meal in itself, sending the customers away satisfied and ready to try this same dish again.

Toast or sweet rolls may also be varied by providing toasted muffins containing nuts, fruits, or other flavorings. A plate of assorted tiny Danish pastries is a special touch. Fruit fritters, such as apple, pineapple, prune, banana, apricot, or pear, with syrup or a sauce, make an unusual breakfast dish.

A variety of juices, fruits, cereals, egg dishes, hot cakes, waffles, toasts, or sweet rolls may serve as a satisfactory base in a coffee shop. In a higher-priced dining room, additional and more substantial items may prove to be good sellers. Late risers sometimes prefer heavier breakfasts that will serve also as lunch. Some very early risers (particularly travelers) are ready for lunch when most people are eating breakfast. People who will be physically active during the day sometimes like small breakfast steaks and potatoes or steak and eggs. Resort dining facilities must appeal to a wide range of appetites in the morning, from that of the athlete to that of the late sleeper. Vacationers often like to try unusual items at breakfast. Some resorts even list "eye openers" from the bar on their breakfast menus.

When planning the breakfast menu, the characteristics of the dining room must be considered. A menu suitable for a coffee shop may not be effective in a formal dining room. Speed of preparation and service is an important factor in all breakfast operations. Even though a patron may seem buried in his newspaper, he has timed himself through habit for this morning ritual and may not tolerate delays in service. Vacationers may also have a schedule to meet. To speed ordering and service, some operators print their breakfast menu on place mats. This also eliminates the cost of printing separate menus.

A practice more widespread overseas than in the United States is the use by hotels of a combination menu and order form for room service breakfast. This form is left in each guest room during the day. After the guest fills out the form with his order and desired delivery time, he places it around the outside doorknob for collection during the night. Such pre-ordering enables the hotel kitchen to better coordinate breakfast room service. The Curaçao Hilton's combination breakfast menu and guest check is shown in Fig. 2-7.

Luncheon

Too often, the luncheon menu is simply a restricted dinner menu that does not conform to the changing pace of American life. Industrialization and urbanization have changed the traditional eating patterns in the United States, so that the main meal or dinner is consumed in the evening when the family is all assembled. Tradition-bound hotels and restaurants that persist in offering large portions of heavy foods at midday find their clientele drifting away. People who are health and weight conscious prefer light meals at noon. Most working people cannot afford the time for extended lunch periods, and many of them find that too much food at lunch makes them feel too full to work well in the afternoon.

Luncheon menus should offer light entrées such as soufflés, omelets, fish, and chicken, as well as extended dishes such as casseroles. In winter, the combination of soup and a sandwich is a very popular luncheon meal. In summer, salads, cold meat platters, and sandwiches are popular.

For some restaurants, the concentration of a high volume of business in the short lunch period causes severe problems. Luncheon guests are usually in a hurry and are reluctant to wait for a table in a crowded restaurant. Thus business can be lost because of slow turnover. This problem can be corrected by menu composition. If the customers can get their orders quickly, two objectives will be served: the guests will be pleased with the fast service, and the seats will empty faster, enabling more guests to be served and more sales to be made.

Brunch

Being a blend of breakfast and lunch, brunch is particularly popular on Sundays and holidays, when the normal work-a-day schedule does not hold. It is usually served from about mid-morning

ORDER YOUR BREAKFAST TONIGHT
PLEASE HANG THIS ORDER OUTSIDE
YOUR BEDROOM DOOR BEFORE RETIRING

Please Circle Items Desired and Indicate
the Number of Orders Required

ROOM NO._____   NO. OF PERSONS_____

SERVE BETWEEN _____ AND _____ A.M.

THE CONTINENTAL 2.75

Juices: ___Fresh Orange ___Tomato ___Pineapple
___Grapefruit Juice or ___Seasonal Melon

___Roll Basket or ___Toast
with ___Butter ___Jam ___Marmalade

___Fragrant Coffee with ___Milk, ___Cream
___Tea with ___Lemon ___Milk, ___Cream
___Pasteurized Milk

THE DUTCH WAY 4.50

Juices: ___Fresh Orange ___Tomato ___Pineapple
___Grapefruit Juice or ___Seasonal Melon

___Two Eggs ___Soft Boiled ___Medium Boiled
___Poached ___Fried ___Scrambled
with
___A Variety of Cold Meats and Dutch Edam Cheese

___Roll Basket with Dutch Breads,
Rusk and Deventer Koek
___Butter ___Jam ___Marmalade

___Fragrant Coffee with ___Milk, ___Cream
___Tea with ___Lemon ___Milk, ___Cream
___Pasteurized Milk

THE AMERICAN 5.50

Juices: ___Fresh Orange ___Tomato ___Pineapple
___Grapefruit Juice or ___Seasonal Melon

___Cold Cereal ___Hot Cereal with ___Milk, ___Cream
or
___Two Eggs: Soft Boiled ___Medium Boiled
___Poached ___Scrambled ___Fried
or
___Pancakes or ___Waffles with ___Syrup ___Jam

___Ham ___Bacon ___Sausages

___Roll Basket or ___Toast
with ___Butter ___Jam ___Marmalade

___Fragrant Coffee with ___Milk, ___Cream
___Tea with ___Lemon ___Milk, Cream
___Pasteurized Milk

Signature _____
Prices in N. A. Guilders, Plus 10% Service Charge.
M.A.P. guests are entitled to the Breakfast of their
choice at a Room Service Charge of One Guilder
per person

PRINTED IN U.S.A.   CURAÇAO HILTON

Fig. 2-7. A combination menu and ordering ticket for hotel room service. *(Courtesy of Hilton International)*

through the normal lunch hour and follows a regular breakfast format except that the main items are likely to be a combination of breakfast and lighter luncheon items. Brunch often lends itself to buffet service. Brunch menus need not be elaborate, but if properly designed, they can help to build substantial sales volume in what would otherwise be a slow sales period.

Tea

Afternoon tea is not an American institution, but the afternoon coffee break is becoming increasingly popular. Where there is a market for afternoon food service, the items offered are usually beverages and desserts, such as ice cream and pastries, as well as muffins and Danish pastries. A limited selection of sandwiches may be offered for persons who are eating a late lunch.

Dinner

Dinner is the most relaxed meal of the day for most people, and dinner guests are inclined to be more self-indulgent than other customers. The dinner menu should emphasize dining pleasure by offering a broader and more expensive selection of appetizers and soups and richer and more substantial entrées with emphasis on the "prepared to your order" items, followed by an attractive variety of desserts.

Although most diners will enjoy their meal at a leisurely pace, those people who may be in a hurry, such as travelers or theater-goers, should not be overlooked. Skilled menu copy can draw these guests' attention to fast service items or invite diners to notify their waiters of the need for special service.

Late Supper

Many restaurants located near evening entertainment facilities or transportation terminals have a great opportunity to build a supper business. The supper patron may at first be in the market only for "coffee and . . .," intending to spend a nominal amount, but may easily be persuaded to spend more, especially if the menu selections are enticing. Others may stop for a "night cap" and stay on for food, as well as beverages. Some popular supper items include sandwich specialties, pastas, cheese rarebits, pancake dishes, eggs and cheese, and small steaks. Pastries and soda fountain items can also be promoted.

Care should be taken that the supper menu is within the production capabilities of the staff. Late evening staffing is usually minimal and, therefore, unable to cope with an elaborate menu or menu items that are difficult to prepare.

In some areas, a market exists for all-night food service. A menu suitable for that market is similar to the late supper menu except that it may include more breakfast items. Toll-road feeders have found that there is some demand for breakfast items practically around the clock, and they offer a limited breakfast menu as part of their regular menu.

Holidays and Special Occasions

Holidays can be very busy times for family-oriented restaurants. Mother's Day is the biggest day of the year for the restaurant industry. Easter, Thanksgiving, Christmas, and New Year's Eve are also high-volume days. Local events may also generate occasional days of high sales volume.

Menus for holidays and special occasions must reflect the festive spirit which patrons expect, but of equal importance is staying within the production capability of the operation on those high-volume days. The menu should be simplified for ease of production and service. Usually a limited number of foods will be, by tradition, closely associated with each holiday.

When an unusually heavy volume of business is anticipated, some restaurants institute a reservations policy and schedule sittings for the meals. Since each sitting is served almost simultaneously, most or all of the food should be ready to serve, and menu items which must be prepared to order should be minimized. In this way, service is not delayed by to-order items, and the seats are vacated in time for the next sitting. The facilities for holding prepared food in the kitchen should be adequate for the quantities required.

The printed menu for a holiday does not have to follow the format of the regular menu. Since guests may want to take the holiday menu home as a souvenir, an inexpensive but attractive card, decorated in keeping with the occasion, can be ordered.

Children's Menus

"Where can we go with the children?" is a question that often precedes a family meal away from home. In addition to cost consideration, parents like to take their offspring where they know children are welcome. The operation that recognizes this and features menus specially designed for children increases its chance for a larger share of an important market. Merely to advertise "children's portions at half price" is to miss a valuable opportunity for sales promotion through menu merchandising. Children like to "study" the menu in the same way adults do, and there is no purpose in handing a child a regular menu, which is often unwieldy and incomprehensible, or at least confusing to the child. Colorful, junior-sized menus with copy written for young readers have proved successful in many restaurants. Games and puzzles may be included to help keep the child occupied until the food comes. If suitable menu items are offered, the child can often read his menu and make his own selection. Thus, eating out becomes a learning experience for the child.

Menu copy and design can encourage children to take their menus home. Perhaps the menu will end up in a toy chest or scrapbook, where it can serve as a constant reminder of the good time that was had at the restaurant and possibly prompt the child to suggest a return visit.

Drink and Wine Lists

All alcoholic beverages may be listed together on one separate card or on separate pages of the regular dining room menu. Sometimes the regular menu will include only selected drinks and wines, and a separate complete wine list will be available.

Drink lists for bars and cocktail lounges should name the brands that are available and give the prices of all drinks. Drinks are categorized as follows:

> Apéritifs and bitters
> Cocktails and other mixed drinks
> Highballs
> Cordials, liqueurs, and brandies
> Beers and ales
> Wines
> Nonalcoholic beverages

Long drinks may be listed separately from the cocktails, and highballs may be grouped by type of whiskey (such as bourbon, rye, Scotch, Canadian, and Irish). Specialty or featured drinks may be listed separately or promoted with table tents. Figure 2–8 shows a portion of a special drink menu from the Cerromar Beach Hotel. When folded, it can be used as a table tent. Figure 2–9 shows another form of table tent.

When a limited variety of food is served in a bar, the drink list may also be the food menu. After-dinner drinks can be merchandised in a dining room by listing them on a separate dessert menu.

Although patrons tend to order their "usual," without requesting a drink menu, atmosphere or theme bars that specialize in exotic concoctions should always present a menu to the guests so that they will know what unusual items are offered. This kind of operation was developed by Trader Vic, and most atmosphere bars still have a "South Seas" theme.

Wines may be listed on the dinner menu, on the drink menu, or on a separate wine list. Restaurateurs who take pride in having a good wine cellar usually prepare a separate wine list. Other operators have found that they sell more wine when the listings are included on the main menu. An operator must consider the degree of sophistica-

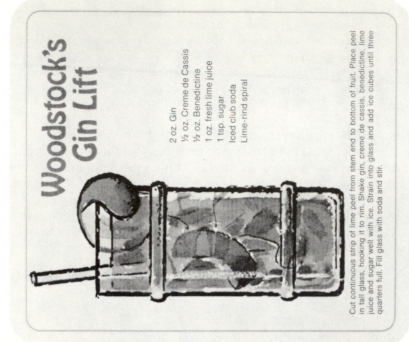

Woodstock's Gin Lift

2 oz. Gin
½ oz. Creme de Cassis
½ oz. Benedictine
1 oz. fresh lime juice
1 tsp. sugar
Iced club soda
Lime-rind spiral

Cut continuous strip of lime peel from stem end to bottom of fruit. Place peel in tall glass, hooking it to rim. Shake gin, creme de cassis, benedictine, lime juice and sugar well with ice. Strain into glass and add ice cubes until three quarters full. Fill glass with soda and stir.

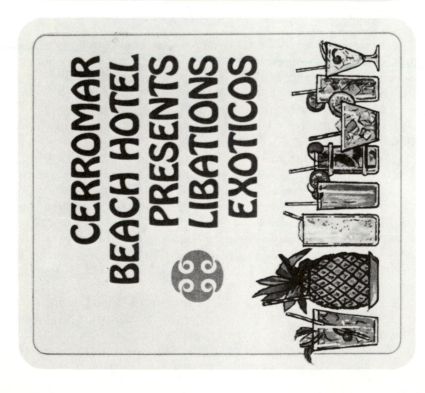

CERROMAR BEACH HOTEL PRESENTS LIBATIONS EXOTICOS

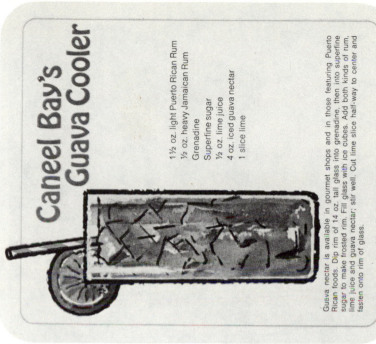

Caneel Bay's Guava Cooler

1½ oz. light Puerto Rican Rum
½ oz. heavy Jamaican Rum
Grenadine
Superfine sugar
½ oz. lime juice
4 oz. iced guava nectar
1 slice lime

Guava nectar is available in gourmet shops and in those featuring Puerto Rican foods. Dip rim of 14 oz. tall glass into grenadine, then into superfine sugar to make frosted rim. Fill glass with ice cubes. Add both kinds of rum, lime juice and guava nectar; stir well. Cut lime slice half-way to center and fasten onto rim of glass.

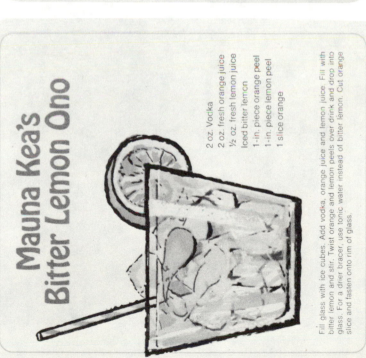

Mauna Kea's Bitter Lemon Ono

2 oz. Vodka
2 oz. fresh orange juice
½ oz. fresh lemon juice
Iced bitter lemon
1-in. piece orange peel
1-in. piece lemon peel
1 slice orange

Fill glass with ice cubes. Add vodka, orange juice and lemon juice. Fill with bitter lemon and stir. Twist orange and lemon peels over drink and drop into glass. For a drier bracer, use tonic water instead of bitter lemon. Cut orange slice and fasten onto rim of glass.

Fig. 2-8. Several pages from the drink menu of the Cerromar Beach Hotel, Dorado Beach, Puerto Rico. The drinks shown are specialties from various other hotels in the Rockresorts group. This menu is a booklet which can be stood up on the tables like a table tent. *(Courtesy of Rockresorts, Inc.)*

Fig. 2-9. A table tent drink menu from the Ala Moana Hotel, Honolulu. *(Courtesy of Design Unlimited Menu Consultants, Hempstead, N.Y., and Americana Hotels)*

tion of his particular market when developing a wine merchandising program. Listing wines by bin number relieves the guest of the need to pronounce foreign names. On some menus, a recommended wine is listed with each entrée.

Wine lists may be a single printed card or an elaborate book with removable pages. A cellar containing a number of different vintages and small quantities of rare wines requires an extensive menu which must be updated periodically. Such wine lists can have index tabs and devote up to a full page to each category of wine. A restaurant with a wine list long enough to fill a book will have only one or two hand-lettered copies for presentation to the guest on request. Other operations with a more limited selection of popular priced wines can have a printed wine list for each table.

Wine is growing in popularity and is available at popular, as well as high, prices in retail stores. Restaurant patrons are able to recognize and respond to good values.

3

Components of the Menu

Appetizers

Appetizers are the introductions to the meals and are supposed to enhance the appetite. They should be appealing to the eye, appetizing, and of the highest quality. The unpleasant aftertaste of an inferior appetizer may completely spoil the rest of an otherwise well-prepared meal. Depending on the menu format, there should be a balanced selection of appetizers in the following categories.

Juices

Juices fall into two categories: vegetable juices (such as tomato or vegetable blends) and fruit juices. Tomato juice is usually expected by the public and should be available even if it is not listed on the menu. To avoid waste, five-ounce cans can be purchased and kept chilled for individual servings. The selection of other vegetable juices could include tomato-clam juice, tomato-sauerkraut juice, or V-8 juice. Health-food bars offer freshly puréed cucumber, celery, and spinach juices. Tomato bouillon may be offered "on the rocks."

Fruit juice suggestions include grapefruit juice, pineapple juice, apricot nectar, apple juice or cider, grape juice, and cranberry juice. Shrubs or blends of juices are also good sellers. Low-cost blends of fruit punches can be made by diluting the heavy syrups of light-colored canned fruits and cutting the sweetness with lemon and lime juice. Some juices turn cloudy when blended with others, so small amounts should be tasted first.

There is a tendency to offer juices just as they come from the can, without making any attempt to add to their appeal. Juices should be served either hot or cold, not at room temperature. Adding a bit of crushed ice to the cold juice when it is served, or blending the juice with crushed ice will make a frappé. The glass may be served in a supreme dish with ice. Juices served hot sometimes border on thin soup. Suggestions for hot juice include mulled cider or wine, hot tomato juice with sour cream and chives, hot spiced apricot nectar, bloody Mary soup (with vodka), and hot spiced orange-tomato bouillon.

Juices should be garnished for merchandising appeal. Tomato juice is usually offered with a wedge of lemon, but can be made more appealing with a sprinkle of chopped parsley or some cheese straws on the side. Another suggestion is to serve a canapé or two with the juice to justify a higher selling price. Fruit juices can be topped with sherbet of a contrasting color and a mint sprig. A tart, light-colored juice may have a spot of grenadine in the bottom of the glass for color. Hot cider or nectar can be served with a stirrer of stick cinnamon.

Seafood and Shellfish

Shrimp cocktail is probably the best selling shellfish appetizer and is available in some form in practically every first-class restaurant. Clams and oysters on the shell are also standard items wherever they are available. Where fresh shell fish are not available, a variety of frozen and preserved fish and seafood can be offered. Frozen king crabmeat, shrimp and scallops, seafood mixtures, marinated or smoked herring, salmon or other fish, and caviar are examples.

Fruits

Starting a meal with a fruit is an American innovation, and fruit cocktail is one of the most popular appetizers. Grapefruit halves broiled or chilled, or melons in season are frequently listed. Mixed fruits unfortunately are often strictly canned products, but they can be improved by the addition of several fresh fruits. Color combinations and garnishing are important elements of the fruit cocktail. Parsley is not considered suitable for use with fruit dishes. Syrups of light colored canned fruits can be used, but the sweetness should be cut with lemon or lime juice. Bananas and peaches can be kept from turning brown with a solution of lemon juice and water, sweetened for taste. Some fruit combinations are Tropicale (bananas, oranges, pineapples, and coconut), peaches and grapes, jellied fruit mixtures, or fruits combined with meats, such as melon or fresh pineapple with prosciutto ham. In some market areas, a variety of imported and/or local fresh tropical fruits may be available to add variety to the menu. Fruit cocktails may be garnished with mint, fresh berries or ices of contrasting color, or flavored with wine, liqueur or extract for interest.

All fresh fruits should be served at the proper point of ripeness, well peeled and trimmed for ease of eating. A grapefruit is not properly sectioned by a few random passes of a paring knife, and the guest should not have to remove inedible membranes with his tableware. Similarly, fresh pineapple must be cored and sliced into bite-size pieces in the kitchen. Fresh grapes and cherries used in fruit mixtures should be seeded or pitted.

Hors d'oeuvres

The term hors d'oeuvres literally means "outside the main work"—that is, food served prior to the actual meal. A number of cuisines have a course similar to the French hors d'oeuvres—antipasto in Italy, smorgasbord in Scandinavia, or zakouska in Russia. An hors d'oeuvre is any small, tasty tidbit, preferably eaten with the fingers, although not necessarily. It may be hot or cold. A canapé is an hors d'oeuvre made with a bread base. Relishes, pickles and olives, and pieces of raw vegetables are also considered hors d'oeuvres. They may be served to the guest on individual plates, offered from a large tray, placed on the table in serving dishes, or displayed on a table for the guest to help himself.

Small stuffed tomatoes, individual quiches or tartlets filled with piquant mixtures, slices of cold meats, sausages or cheeses, pâtés, hard-cooked eggs with fillings or sauces, chilled cooked vegetables with sauces, or escargots are hors d'oeuvre suggestions. Hot hors d'oeuvres may be tiny cocktail sausages, bite-sized pieces of deep-fried seafood, vegetables, or mixtures, clams casino or oysters Rockefeller, hot canapés of crabmeat or other mixtures, or oysters with bacon. Hot hors d'oeuvres, of course, should be served both hot and fresh, or their whole appeal is lost.

Soups

If only one or two soups are offered, they are usually included with the appetizers. A more formal menu should list the soups as a separate course.

Soups are usually classified as "thick" or "thin." Where two or more soups are offered, the listings should be balanced between thick and thin soups. Thin soups are broths, bouillons and consommés, and may be served with a light garnish of rice, finely chopped vegetables, or any one of the many classic garnishes. A broth is brown or white stock taken from the stock pot with little or no clarification. Bouillon refers specifically to a dark, rich beef-based stock that has been clarified. Consommé is made from the lighter stocks, including veal and chicken, that have been clarified. Consommés are clear, with delicate flavoring. Meat and bones for bouillons are browned to develop a rich meaty flavor, while those intended for a consommé are put into the pot unbrowned. A few soups with a milk or cream base, such as oyster stew, are classfied as thin soups.

Thick soups may be classified as purées, creams or veloutés in the classic French cuisine. Purées usually refer to soups with a vegetable base, such as that of dried beans or peas. Nonstarchy vegetables may be used for a purée, but a thickening agent is required. Veloutés are made with rich creams and a white stock, usually of chicken, but sometimes of veal or seafood. A velouté made with shellfish is called a bisque. Cream soups are made with milk or cream and a white roux of flour and butter. Such thick soups as chowders, gumbos, stews, and chilies are not part of the classic cuisine. Escoffier would have classified them as "plain household cookery." Although they are a part of the modern repertory they are still considered somewhat plebian for a formal dinner. Being hearty and filling, they are suitable for a lighter meal or for service as a main course in themselves.

The following are examples of popular soups:

Onion Soup au Gratin, a dish of provincial France, is one of the most popular soups in American restaurants.

Manhattan Clam Chowder, New England Clam Chowder, and Philadelphia Clam Chowder are the best known of the various fish chowders that originated in different parts of the United States. These soups usually carry the name of their place of origin. Various oyster chowders are named for the Chesapeake and Eastern Shore areas. Louisiana and other Gulf states have their own rich chowders made from shrimp and other types of fish indigenous to the region.

Gumbo is a thick soup that has okra as a main ingredient. There are a number of different kinds of gumbo, including chicken gumbo, shrimp gumbo, and cabbage gumbo.

Pepperpot is a highly seasoned stew-type of soup. Philadelphia pepperpot features small cubes of tripe.

Minestrone is a heavy Italian vegetable soup containing macaroni. Grated Parmesan cheese should be served with it.

Borscht may be served as a clear soup, in which case it is a brilliant ruby red, or it may contain raw cucumber slices, boiled potatotes, shredded beets, diced carrots, cabbage strips, sour cream, or any combination of these. A description of the type of borscht being offered should be included on the menu.

Mulligatawny is a heavy curry-flavored soup that originated in India, but there are a number of variations of this soup, such as Chicken Senegal.

In certain circumstances, soups may be served chilled as well as hot. Cold soups are often welcome in hot weather. Vichyssoise is usually served cold, and other commonly offered cold soups are jellied madrilene or bouillon, consommé on the rocks, Spanish gazpacho, borscht, and Swedish fruit soup (a slightly tart soup made from dried fruits).

Entrées

Entrées can be classified by the main component: beef, veal, pork and ham, lamb and mutton, poultry, fish and shellfish, eggs, and meatless items. Game is also considered a separate category but rarely appears on menus in the United States except in a few exclusive restaurants or private clubs. Entrées can also be classified by method of preparation or presentation, such as roasted, grilled, broiled, fried, braised, stewed, in a casserole, or in a mixture.

Some restaurants specialize in items known to have wide appeal, such as steaks, hamburgers, or seafood. On a general menu, the entrées should be balanced to offer variety to the guest, a balanced work load for the staff and equipment, and a selling price range suited to the market. In an existing operation, the sales analysis will indicate patron preference, and should form the basis for the new menu.

Beef

Americans are beef eaters. According to a United States Department of Agriculture estimate, they consumed 3.2 billion pounds of beef in public and institutional eating places alone in 1969, twice the consumption of all other meats combined. The USDA study reported that 44 percent of all beef purchased by food services was in the form of ground beef or patties. Another 22.5 percent was purchased in the form of steaks, 12.6 percent as roasts, and 20.9 percent in other forms.

Hamburgers are a staple in the American diet. They may be "dressed up" with a wide variety of garnishes, relishes, different kinds of cheese, pickles, bacon, tomatoes, and lettuce, and double-decked on different types of buns or bread.

Steak is the second-largest seller in the beef category. The most tender cut is the tenderloin. Steaks cut from the tenderloin are called filet mignon, tournedos, or medallions of beef. A double filet mignon is a Châteaubriand. Steaks from the strip loin are a little less tender than the tenderloin, but have more flavor, and are equally popular. These steaks may be called strip steaks, New York steaks, or sirloin steaks. Porterhouse and T-bone steaks are cut from the short loin before the tenderloin is removed; they contain both the tenderloin muscle and the loin muscle. T-bones come from behind the porterhouse cuts, where the tenderloin muscle is smaller. Club steaks are cut from the end of the short loin and have no tenderloin muscle. Steaks can also be made from the top sirloin butt or from the ribs.

A general restaurant menu will usually offer a tenderloin steak, one or two sizes of strip steaks, and if butchering is done on the premises, a chopped steak to utilize the ends and trimmings. Institutional operations and restaurants offering lower-priced meals often used tenderized steaks from lower-graded animals or smaller portions in order to obtain a lower portion cost.

Roast beef is another standard menu item. Roast ribs of beef is probably the single most popular entrée offered. Technically, prime ribs should be only from USDA prime beef. "Prime" does not refer to the "first" ribs, since the ribs are numbered from the front to rear, and the cut referred to consists of the sixth through the twelfth ribs. The top sirloin and top round can also be dry roasted, although they are less tender than the rib eye. Whole tenderloin can be roasted and sliced but should not be cooked beyond the medium stage, because its lack of internal marbling makes it rather dry. A steamship or café round, consisting of the top and bottom rounds, bone-in, roasted rare and carved in view of the guest, can be effectively merchandised in low- or medium-priced restaurants or as a monotony breaker for an institutional audience.

Roasts and steaks taken from the most tender cuts of the beef are prepared with dry heat. The less tender cuts are prepared with moist heat and can be offered as stews, pot roasts, and braised steaks. Such dishes provide interest and variety in the menu and produce a good profit ratio. Practically every nationality has a different kind of stew. Sauces and garnishes are innumerable. Smoked, cured, and dried beef items can be merchandised effectively as corned beef, tongue, pastrami, and chipped beef.

Veal

Veal is from calves less than three months old. The best meat comes from animals about ten weeks old that have been milk-fed to produce firm white flesh. A pinkish tinge to the meat indicates that the animal has been grain or grass fed.

Because the supply is limited and prices are relatively high, veal consumption in the United States is very low. About half the veal purchased by public and institutional food services in the USDA study was in the form of steaks or cutlets. Veal cutlet Parmesan, wiener schnitzel, veal scallopini, and roast veal are the most frequently listed veal entrées. Other suggestions include braised breast of veal, stews and curries, veal chops, and Osso Bucco (cross-cut slices of the veal shank, including the bones).

Pork and Ham

Pork is considered a "heavy" meat and usually does not sell well in hot weather. Pork chops, roast loin of pork, roast fresh ham, broiled pork tenderloin, sauerkraut or beans with pork, and grilled sausages are good cold-weather sellers.

Ham, one of the most versatile of meats, offers the added advantage of having good shelf life. It can be carved on buffet lines for festive occasions, roasted and served hot or cold, or grilled to order. It combines well with many other foods to make combination entrées, such as cold meat platters or hot ham with cheese rarebit. Ham loaf or ham patties make good low-cost entrées and use up the trimmings and scraps when bone-in hams are used. To add variety, Canadian bacon can be substituted for ham in some dishes.

Lamb

Lamb is more popular on the East Coast than in other parts of the United States. Midwesterners eat very little lamb. The meat is thought to be "lighter" than pork or beef. Roast leg of lamb and lamb chops are the most frequently listed lamb entrées. Other lamb dishes include lamb stew, curry or shish-kabob, braised shoulder, or shepherd's pie. Braised lamb shanks are good sellers in some areas. Mutton is rarely available in the United States, and has virtually no demand.

Variety Meats

American consumption of offal or variety meats is very low compared with consumption in Europe. Beef and calf's liver and beef tongues have general acceptance, as do veal sweetbreads; but heart, kidney, brains, and tripe find little demand in this country, except in small communities of Europeans.

Poultry

Chicken ranks a close second to steak in popularity. It is considered more healthful and less fattening than beef and is lower in cost than any of the meats. Other poultry entrées include turkey, duck, cornish hen, and occasionally squab and pheasant.

The low cost and high popularity of chicken have given rise to fast-food chicken restaurants such as the Kentucky Fried Chicken chain. At the other end of the culinary spectrum, Larousse Gastronomique devotes 24 pages to recipes for chicken. Turkey is very much an American dish. It is no longer served only at Thanksgiving, and the availability of numerous processed forms has taken much of the labor out of the preparation and minimizes the waste. Once the cooked meat is removed from the bones, turkey can be used in mixtures and dishes in the same manner as chicken. Ducks and pheasant are usually roasted and served with sauce or dressing. Chicken livers and gizzards make a good luncheon entrée.

Fish and Shellfish

With the advent of economical air freight, no part of the country is more than a few hours from a major fish market. Patrons of first-class restaurants expect to find fresh fish on the menu. Most of the fish offered are salt-water fish, but in some areas, fresh-water fish may form the bulk of the supply. Fresh-water fish are milder in flavor than salt-water fish, which may influence the patrons' preferences in some localities.

In the 1969 USDA study, fish and shellfish purchases by public and institutional food services were estimated at about one billion pounds annually: 444 million pounds of fresh and frozen fish,

473 million pounds of fresh and frozen shellfish, and 84 million pounds of canned fish.

The most frequently purchased fish were haddock, cod, flounder, processed fish squares and sticks, perch, halibut, catfish, and swordfish. In the shellfish classification, shrimp was the best seller, followed by soft- and hard-shell clams, lobster, crabs, oysters and scallops, in that order. Tuna fish comprised about 75 percent of the canned-fish purchases. A first-class restaurant menu might include one or two sole dishes prepared in any one of a variety of ways, brook trout, whole lobster or lobster tails, a crab, lobster, or mixed dish, bay scallops, and perhaps red snapper or pompano. A cold salmon steak might also be offered. A seafood platter combining a variety of items and using a number of preparation methods can be a popular and profitable item.

Eggs

Eggs should not be regarded as only a breakfast dish. Many people are not heavy meat eaters at luncheon, and for them, eggs make a splendid substitute. Egg dishes are also well suited to late supper menus. Omelets and soufflés can be made with seafood, meats, vegetables, or many other flavorings and sauces. Cold plates can be made with deviled, jellied, or stuffed eggs.

Meatless Entrées

Since there are no longer any religious restrictions on eating meat on Friday, there is less demand for meatless entrées in restaurants. However, some people still abstain from eating meat on certain days, and others abstain altogether. Still others like a meatless dish occasionally just for variety.

Every entrée should contain some protein, since proteins are the basic building blocks of the body. In addition to meats, poultry, seafood, and eggs, protein can be found in milk and milk products, and to a lesser extent in dried beans, peas, lentils, nuts, and some cereals.

The following are a few examples of meatless entrées:

Pasta dishes, which may be served with a variety of meatless sauces such as cheese, mushroom, tomato, butter, and marinara.

Vegetable platters, composed of three or four of the du jour vegetables. The platters can include a stuffed egg, jellied salad or mousse, cheese strips, corn fritters, macaroni and cheese, or a fruit salad with cottage cheese to provide some protein.

Cheese dishes, such as Welsh rarebit, cheese strata, or cheese fondue.

Mushroom dishes, such as creamed mushrooms on toast.

Pizzas.

Quiches, which are custard pies with a variety of fillings.

Miscellaneous Entrées

Batter items, such as pancakes, waffles, crêpes, corncakes, and fritters, served with bacon, sausage or ham, or rolled with a filling, can be popular low-cost luncheon items. Frankfurters, sausages, and other wursts can also be used alone or in combination with other items for menu variety.

Cold plates are a good use of leftover roast meats. Combinations of cold beef, ham, turkey, veal, pork or lamb are possible, as well as of cold baked fish and shellfish.

Thick soups such as chowders, bouillons, and chilies can also be utilized as main dishes at luncheon, and are very good sellers on a cold day.

Salads

On the classic French menus, the salad was served after the roasts, with cold dishes and before the sweet dessert. Occasionally, one still finds the salad served between the main course and the desserts, but the place of the salad in the modern service is usually with the main course. Sometimes, if no soup or appetizer is served, the salad may be served as an appetizer. French cuisine classifies salads as "simple" and "combined." Simple salads contain only greens or other vegetables, while combined salads are more elaborate and contain meats, shellfish, fruits, and so on.

Appearance is primary in the appeal of a salad. The four "C's" of salads are "clean," "cool," "colorful" and "crisp." Ingredients should be selected with regard to color and textures. Garnishes should be compatible with the ingredients. Salads should never look wilted or "worked over." As with the appetizers, the guest should be able to eat the salad with his tableware and not have to peel, core, slice, or trim the ingredients.

A general rule is that fruits and vegetables should not be combined, but an exception is the Waldorf salad, made of apples, nuts and celery. Salad greens are also used to line a fruit salad.

Entrée Salads

The following are the basic types of entrée salads:

Mixtures of greens with some protein material included as a garnish. Usually this type is served in a large bowl. The greens may serve as a base for other ingredients as well.

Cold plates of solid meats, seafood, and/or cheese. These plates may be garnished with such cold ingredients as tomatoes, and potato or pasta salad.

Fruit plates or bowls. The fruits may be cut up in a mixture and served in a bowl, or they may be arranged on a plate. Protein garnishes such as cottage cheese, gelatin cubes, julienne cheese or cream cheese balls, or nuts may be used.

Combination vegetable plates. "Fancy" vegetables such as asparagus can be the focal point of a colorful salad plate garnished with hard-cooked eggs, tomatoes, or other vegetables. Tomatoes and artichokes can be stuffed with salad mixtures.

Cold plates having a base of jellied fruit or vegetables or mousse.

Cold plates or bowls with a salad mixture of chicken, seafood, or egg as the main ingredient.

Side Salads

The basic side salad is one of fresh greens, either of one kind or mixed. It may be garnished with other fresh vegetables, croutons, or protein material such as cheese, bacon bits, or grated egg. If only one salad is offered, it should consist of fresh salad greens.

There are many types of salad greens that can be used to vary the taste and color of the salad. Besides iceberg or head lettuce, there are romaine, leaf lettuce, chicory or curly endive, butter (Boston) lettuce, escarole, watercress, bibb, and fresh spinach. Dandelion greens, mustard greens, beet tops, and nasturtium leaves also can be used. Belgian endive is usually served separately because of the cost of this imported delicacy.

The side salad is intended to complement or enhance the main entrée, not overpower it. Thus, protein ingredients other than cheese and egg are usually omitted from the side salad, both to avoid overpowering the entrée and for reasons of cost. "Heavy" ingredients such as potatoes or pastas should not be used unless the entrée is "light." Where salads must be produced in any kind of quantity, they are usually kept simple to minimize the labor requirement.

In addition to mixed greens, the following types of side salads are popular with Americans:

Gelatin—either fruit or vegetable flavored. Mousses may be used.

Fruit—pieces of fruit garnished with cheese, nuts, preserves or other fruits, or mixtures of fruits.

Vegetable—potato salad, marinated cucumbers, beets or beans, slaws, tomatoes, and head lettuce. (The latter two salads are very popular and should be available even if they are not listed on the menu.)

Miscellaneous—macaroni salad.

Side salads may also be hot (such as Dutch lettuce or hot potato salad) or frozen (such as frozen fruit mousse), but side salads which are extremely sweet are usually reserved for festive occasions. Some restaurants take a work load off the kitchen and add merchandising appeal by installing self-service salad bars in the dining room. Pre-prepared salads may be displayed or the various ingredients may be set out, allowing the customer to use his ingenuity in assembling his own salad. This kind of salad is usually a mixture of greens with a variety of dressings and garnishes.

The four basic categories of salad dressings are French, mayonnaise, cream, and cooked. French dressing is a temporary emulsion of oil and vinegar with seasoning. Mayonnaise is a permanent emulsion of oil and vinegar stabilized by egg yolks. Cream dressings have as their base sweet, sour, or whipped cream. Cooked dressings are thickened with starch and egg yolks, and a much smaller amount of oil is used. When only one green salad is offered, the salad dressing can be distinctive, a merchandising asset to the restaurant. Using one of the four basic dressings, a "house dressing" can be developed, including a combination of herbs, spices, or other flavoring ingredients.

Sandwiches

The sandwich is a uniquely American menu item and the most popular luncheon main dish in the United States. Probably the most attractive feature of the sandwich is its convenience. A sandwich can be virtually anything edible, put between two pieces of bread or in a roll. In fact, one sandwich has even entered the realm of American folklore—the Dagwood. It contains not just anything, but everything!

For the purposes of menu writing, sandwiches can be categorized as follows:

Hot Sandwiches

Sliced meats. The meats may be in a closed sandwich to be eaten with the hands, or open-faced and covered with gravy or sauce to be eaten with a fork.

Broiled, grilled, or fried. "Main dish" items on bread or rolls, such as hamburgers, frankfurters, minute steaks, boneless chops, cutlets or patties, and eggs.

Toasted sandwiches. Toasted sandwiches include French-toasted, open-faced broiled, or closed grilled sandwiches. These usually include some kind of cheese that is melted.

Cold Sandwiches

Sliced meats and cheeses.

Fillings or mixtures.

Open-faced sandwiches, which may include sliced ingredients and/or fillings. A single slice of bread forms the base for the salad-like ingredients.

Fancy sandwiches, such as tea sandwiches and sandwich loaves.

Because the sandwich always seems to sell, there is sometimes a temptation to become careless in its preparation. The filling is shoved between two pieces of bread and slapped on a plate with only a wilted pickle chip, a few potato chips, or perhaps a little paper cup with a dab of coleslaw for a garnish. As with every other menu item, sandwiches can be attractively garnished and merchandised to increase sales. Butter or mayonnaise spread evenly and lightly over the bread will enhance the taste. Interest can be added in the way the sandwich is cut and arranged on the plate. Garnishes should be part of the arrangement, not just left to roll around on the plate. Thick sandwiches can be held together with fancy sandwich skewers, perhaps with an olive or cherry tomato. Corn relish, chow-chow, green tomato pickles, chutney, or spiced or fresh fruit can be used instead of the overworked dill pickle to garnish sandwich plates.

Vegetables

Except for the potato, vegetables are the stepchild of American cookery. In too many restaurants and institutions, vegetables die a slow steam table death, if they are not first killed by overcooking in the kitchen. The vegetables are often an afterthought on the menu, and sometimes they are not even listed at all.

A vegetable, broadly defined, is any plant that is eaten whole or in part, cooked or raw. The parts consumed may be the leaves, seeds, roots, tubers, bulbs, flowers, fruits, stems, or shoots of the plant. In common usage, however, certain fruits are not considered in the vegetable category. Furthermore, since potatoes have traditionally been such an important part of the diet, they often are listed separately from the other vegetables on the menu.

The restaurant that limits its potato offerings to "mashed or French" is missing a good competitive advantage. Potatoes may be fried, mashed, creamed, baked, boiled, or steamed. A variety of processed potato products are also available and easy to prepare. A few of the many potato dishes are listed below:

Whipped	Potatoes in jackets	Home-fried
Parlsey	Creamed	Hashed in cream
Rissolé	Escalloped	Pancakes
Browned	Long Branch	Steamed
Baked	Minute	au Gratin
Paprika	Pan roasted	French-fried
Bermuda	Duchess	Delmonico
Parisienne	Buttered	Julienne
Grilled	Roasted	O'Brien
Shoestring	Sauté	Cottage fried
Croquettes	Lyonnaise	Château

Potato substitutes provide variety. These include cereals (such as rice) and noodles and other pastas, which may be offered with a number of seasonings, spices and sauces.

Yams and sweet potatoes should be listed occasionally. They may be glazed, baked, or whipped. Sweets n' apples make a good accompaniment to a ham or pork dinner.

In planning the vegetables listings, there are a few guidelines that should be observed.

1. At least one green vegetable should always be offered.
2. Unless the number of vegetable offerings is very large, not more than one of the cabbage or onion families should be offered. Brussels sprouts, cauliflower, broccoli, turnips, and onions are all "strong" vegetables containing substances that some people cannot eat or do not like. Conversely, if the number of vegetables offered is restricted to one or two, use of these strong vegetables should be avoided.
3. Some vegetables are high in starch, namely peas, corn, lima beans, and other legumes. Listings from this group should also be limited to one per meal, unless a very large vegetable selection is offered.

Vegetable choices should provide a variety in color, texture, form, and method of cookery. Too often, the vegetables offered come straight from a can with no attempt to season or merchandise them. With a little imagination, dull vegetables can be avoided. For example, frozen green beans are available whole, regular cut, or French cut. For variety, Italian or flat beans can be used. They can be garnished with sautéed onions or fried onion rings, pimiento, mushrooms, or nuts, and served in cream or baked in cheese sauce. They can be seasoned with herbs or spices, such as beans Provençal with tomatoes and garlic.

Vegetable combinations can add menu interest. Instead of the usual mixed vegetables or peas and carrots, one can offer zucchini or eggplant with tomatoes, summer squash with green peas, tomatoes stuffed with green peas, turnips and peas, or Mexican or O'Brien corn. Combining vegetables with fruits is another way of transforming the ordinary into the unusual. For example, Brussel sprouts with red grapes, cabbage and apples, or beets and oranges. Cooked fruits can be used in the vegetable listings, and they are a good accompaniment for some of the lighter meats. Applesauce or fried apples are the most frequently used. However, fruits used that way should not be too sweet.

The method of preparation can add variety to the vegetable menu. Some suggestions are sautéed tomatoes, deep-fried cauliflower, braised lettuce, baked squash, corn pudding, or spinach soufflé. Sauces such as Hollandaise, vinaigrette, or lemon butter enhance the taste of vegetables, as do seasonings such as nutmeg in the spinach, dill on buttered peas, thyme on the green beans, and chives on carrots.

Desserts

The dessert should add the finishing touch to the meal, and if properly merchandised, it can be a highly profitable item. Although more and more operators are turning to purchased baked goods, "making your own" offers a competitive advantage.

In spite of a national weight consciousness, the all-American favorite dessert is apple pie. Ice cream and ice cream sundaes run a close second in popularity, followed by cheese cake and fruits.

Most desserts fall into the following categories: pies, cakes, pastries, fruits, ice cream and frozen desserts, puddings, and cheeses. As with all courses, desserts need garnishes too. Besides whipped cream and maraschino cherries, dessert garnishes include nutmeats, chocolate shavings or sprinkles, shredded coconut, cookie or cake crumbs, fresh, cooked, or candied fruit, candied flowers, icings, and sauces.

Pies

Pies may have a pastry or meringue crust, or a crust of cookie or cake crumbs. They may have two crusts, one bottom crust, or one top crust, as in deep-dish or lattice top pies. They may be flavored with nutmeats, cheese, or spices. Double-crust pies may be iced, and single crust pies may be topped with a streusel mixture. Fillings may be fruit, chiffon, cream, or custard. Other types of pies include frozen pies with a filling of ice cream or mousse, and Boston cream pie, which is actually a cake. Some pies have more than one filling, such as black-bottom pie with a layer of chocolate topped with a layer of rum chiffon, or a cheese layer topped with fruit. Tarts and turnovers are also in the pie category, as are cobblers and fruit grunt, a kind of deep-dish pie which is made with biscuit dough instead of pastry.

Cakes

Dessert cakes are usually leavened with baking powder or soda, or with air incorporated in the mixing. Babas, a sweet yeast dough cake soaked with rum, is one of the few exceptions. Cakes are categorized as those with butter or fat and those without fat. There are three types of cakes with fat: regular butter cake, chiffon cake using oil and beaten egg whites, and pound cake which uses only air for leavening. Of the nonfat cakes, angel cakes are made only with the whites of the egg, and sponge cakes are made with the whole egg. A torte is a rich multilayered cake of German origin. Cakes may be layered or formed in loaves, sheet cakes, or cupcakes. They may be served plain or covered with icing or glaze; they may be served with ice cream or sherbet, with fruit, with fillings or jellies, or made into petits fours. Icings may be butter cream, boiled or marshmallow, fondant or fudge. Royal icing is used for decorating.

Pastries

Pastries are usually individual portions of baked goods, rich and elaborately decorated. Tarts are individual pie shells often filled with a cream custard and topped with whole glazed fruit. Petits fours are bite-sized cakes, iced and decorated. Other items found on a pastry tray may include the following:

Eclairs and cream puffs. These pastries are leavened by steam. Their composition is similar to that of popovers and Yorkshire pudding except that sugar is added. Eclairs are formed long and thin with a pastry tube and are usually filled with a cream filling and frosted. Cream puffs may also be formed with a pastry tube into a round puffy or cabbage shape, which gave the dough its French name "choux paste." Cream puffs may be filled with ice cream, whipped cream, or custard filling, and they may be iced or served with a sauce.

Puff pastry. This pastry is used in a variety of ways, including Napoleons, cream horns or lady locks, palm leaves, millefeuille (thousand leaves) cake, or shells. The pastry is made by a long process of rolling and folding layers of butter between thin layers of dough to produce a tender flaky product.

Strudel. Strudel is a Hungarian product somewhat similar in effect to puff pastry. Strudel dough contains egg, and instead of being folded with butter, it is worked and stretched into a paper thin sheet that is then rolled up with a filling, usually of cheese, apple, cherry, meat, or poppyseed in the middle. The absence of butter and the incorporation of the egg produces a crust structure less tender than that of puff pastry but more suited to heavier kinds of filling. In some areas, strudel dough (as well as puff pastry) may be purchased ready to use, which saves considerable labor.

Individual babas au rhum. Babas are made in little molds and decorated with whipped cream.

Meringues shaped like swans or baskets. Meringues may be tinted delicate colors and served with a variety of fillings.

For banquets or special occasions, choux paste, puff pastry, or meringue may be made into a larger piece and displayed to the guests before the meal. Turbans or St. Honoré cakes are made of cream puff paste, as is a Croquembouche.

Fruits

At least one fruit item, preferably fresh, should be on the menu. Melons, grapefruit, and berries are the fruits offered most frequently. Broiled grapefruit with sherry is good on a cold day, and melon à la mode is a popular summer dessert. Other fresh fruits which can be offered are pineapple, grapefruit, peaches, pears, apples, plums, and grapes. Fresh fruits may be served whole or peeled, with syrup, and either singly or in combination with other fruits or with cheese. If fruit is served whole or unpeeled, a fruit knife should be included in the service.

A compote is one or more kinds of fruit cooked in a syrup. The fruits may be fresh or dried, and the syrup may be flavored or unflavored. Baked apples are another popular cooked-fruit dessert. Fruits may also be flamed and served alone or over ice cream.

Frozen Desserts

Frozen desserts include the following:

Ice cream. Custard made with cream, sweetened and flavored, to uniform consistency, and frozen.

Sherbet. Water-sugar syrup thickened with gelatin or egg white and whipped.

Ices. Water-sugar syrup that is whipped.

Mousse. Sweetened, flavored whipped cream thickened with gelatin. The mixture is not whipped.

Biscuit. Similar to a mousse but frozen in individual molds.

Bombe. A large round or conical molded dessert, usually with several layers of ice cream, sherbet, or mousse. It may be decorated.

Coupe. The French equivalent of a sundae, taking its name from the stem glass in which it is served.

Pies, cake rolls, or layer cakes. These can be made with frozen fillings. Ice cream can be used to top puddings that are warm, pies, cakes, or other baked goods. It can also be served in a meringue, pastry shell, or cream puff with sauce, or it can be rolled in coconut or nuts.

Puddings

Puddings originally were soft foods, either baked or boiled, and served as a main dish or side dish. Some were stuffed into sausage casings before being boiled. Except for a few side dishes such as corn pudding, puddings are now considered desserts. A few of the old suet-based puddings such as plum pudding and mincemeat are now steamed in molds and served on holidays.

The following are some of the sweet puddings:

Custards. Milk thickened with eggs and cooked.

Tapioca and cornstarch puddings. Milk or other liquid thickened with starch and cooked.

Soufflés, Whips or Chiffons. Beaten egg whites baked with flavoring.

Gelatins. Fruit gelatin, such as Bavarian or Spanish cream.

Whipped Cream Base. Rice cream, fruit fools (whipped cream and fruit purée).

Fruit Pudding. Usually made with some kind of cereal base or binder, such as apple crisp or brown Betty.

   Thickened Baked Puddings. Indian pudding or pudding-cakes.

Cheese

   Cheese, either alone or with fruit, provides a lighter finish to a big meal than does a sweet dessert. Cheese should be served at room temperature and accompanied by butter and toast or crackers. Popular dessert cheeses include blues such as Roquefort, Stilton, or Gorgonzola; soft ripened cheeses such as Brie or Camembert; semisoft cheeses such as Port du Salut or Bel Paese; and unripened cheese such as ricotta or cream cheese.

Beverages

   The United States is still a nation of coffee drinkers, even though the rate of per capita consumption has been declining since the early 1960s. Surveys by the Pan-American Coffee Bureau show that coffee drinkers consume about two and a half cups per day, down from a high of over three cups in 1962. About 80 percent of all coffee is consumed in the home, with consumption of the remainder divided between "at work" and "in eating places." Coffee consumption at work is a rapidly growing segment of the coffee market, having more than doubled between 1950 and 1971. Decaffeinated coffee enjoys a small but rapidly growing segment of the market.

   Other drinks in order of popularity are milk and milk products, fruit and vegetable juices, soft drinks, tea, and chocolate drinks. Lemonade and iced tea have become year-round sellers in many areas.

   It takes very little imagination to write three words "Coffee-Tea-Milk" at the bottom of a menu. Most customers will order a beverage regardless of how inadequate the listing, but a nicer impression is created if beverage descriptions are in keeping with the balance of the menu. If coffee or tea is served in a pot, it should be so stated. If whipped cream is served with hot chocolate or cocoa, that should also appear on the menu.

   Check averages can be increased by offering special blends of coffee and tea at premium prices. Espresso is gaining in popularity. Other specialty coffee drinks are mocha, cappuccino, Irish coffee, café brûlot, and coffee royale.

   Operators are recognizing the growing popularity of beer and wine as mealtime beverages, and even establishments such as snack bars and coffee shops are adding them to their menus. A choice of red or white house wines and domestic beer is sufficient for informal quick-service operations. Draft beer can be offered if space is available for the equipment. Imported brands can be profitable where there is a market for higher-priced beers.

4

FOOD PURCHASING

The character of the product and the resulting product cost begin with the purchasing of the raw materials. Although poor preparation practices may destroy the quality of a good product, good preparation practices cannot instill quality where it never existed. The best menu merchandising policies cannot compensate for purchasing that is not alert to new products, new markets, and new trends. And cost controls cannot be wholly effective in production or service if buying is inefficient.

Buying must always be judged by its overall effectiveness and never by price comparison alone. An item's purchase price is only as important as the item itself; it may be five cents less per pound or 15 percent cheaper by price but 30 percent more expensive in actual yield. The buyer should be interested in the lowest price only when the items are comparable in quality and yield. Good buying procedures provide a food operation with the products most suited to its merchandising policy at the most economical price.

"Buying" is not to be confused with "ordering." Buying involves making decisions and setting policies about what products to buy and how to buy them, approving the vendors to be used and determining the frequency of the purchases and the quantities to be bought. Ordering is a clerical activity which is done within the buying policy.

There are two approaches to commercial food buying: the needs of the operation and the availability of products on the market. When the food service operation is located at some distance from a food distribution point, the buyer may have to begin with what is available to him and make adjustments in the menu and preparation accordingly. When product availability is not a problem, the buyer first analyses the needs of the operation and searches out the products he needs. Most often, the products ultimately purchased are a compromise between need and availability. Whatever the approach, the food buyer should have some understanding of the market in which he is dealing.

Structure of the Food Market

The path of food products from the grower or producer to the end user is quite complex. Figure 4–1 shows the marketing channels taken by most food products. The route begins with the producers or growers, who sell their product to processors. Often, an intermediary (a concentrator) is necessary to gather the output of numerous, widely dispersed producers into transportable quantities. Concentrators may be grain elevators, receiving plants, or cooperative marketing organizations, such as Sunkist growers in California. Processors may be divided into primary processors such as flour mills and secondary producers such as bakers. Producers may use a food broker to sell their processed product. A broker is an independent sales agent who works on commission and does not take title to the goods. From the processor, the goods are shipped to major distribution centers and wholesalers around the country or region. The processor himself may maintain regional warehouses and act as wholesaler. The wholesalers are usually specialized according to the markets they serve—institutional or retail stores. Institutional distributors may be specialized even further, dealing only with top quality hotels and restaurants or specializing in a very few products or just one product.

Although the marketing channel may vary somewhat for different types of food products, the pattern shown in Fig. 4–1 generally applies. The restaurant or institutional buyer may buy the product at various stages in the channel. If he buys from a local farmer, he is buying from the producer. He may buy from a local or district office of the processor, or from a variety of wholesale distributors. He may even enter the channel farther down and buy a few items from a retail store, although this is usually a poor practice.

Marketing food products through channels is an enormous and costly task. Approximately 60 percent of the consumer food dollar goes to the cost of marketing, and about 40 percent goes to the farmer. Labor has always been the largest cost in marketing, with transportation second. Packaging is another cost that is increasing in importance.

Marketing cost has been viewed suspiciously by the consumer and food service operator alike as pure profit to many unnecessary middlemen; but these middlemen provide the following important services: storage, grading, and identification of products, transportation, transfer of ownership (buying and selling), packaging, advertising, and financing.

Storage

Because most food production is seasonal, storage is necessary. Storage also contributes to a more stable market price and provides a more even supply of the product to meet the year-round

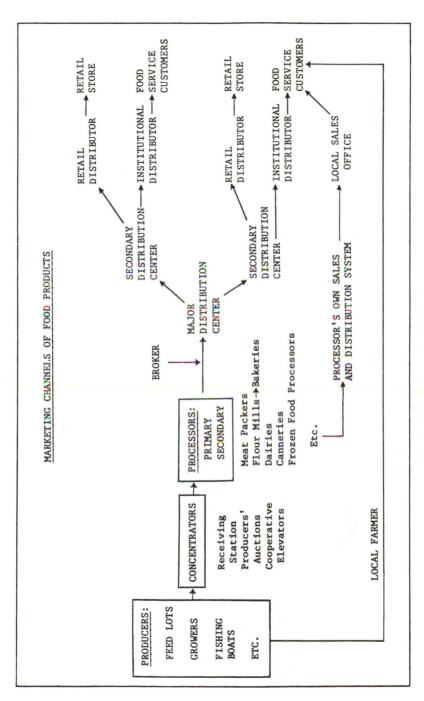

Fig. 4-1. Marketing channels of food products.

demand. It also evens out the supply of the product in the marketing channel.

Product Identification

The buyer must know the condition of the product being offered for sale: the degree of processing, the quality of grade, and the size. Without product identity standards, prices for like items in different markets cannot be compared.

Grading

The marketing process is facilitated by common standards of identification for products which can vary widely in quality. Before food grades were established, buyers or their agents had to inspect every purchase personally to determine quality. Grades also classify products according to use. The most widely used grading system is that of the federal government (see p. 58), although some industries have their own grades, as do some producing areas or states.

Transportation

Transporting the product from the producer to the end user is a process of concentration and dispersion. The product is gathered from many widely dispersed growers into transportable units that are then shipped to processors or to major distribution centers, and from there to secondary distribution centers and to end users.

Transfer of Ownership

For every producer to sell his product directly to the end user would be an impossibility. Marketing channels, therefore, provide a means for matching buyers and sellers and for establishing prices. These channels segregate buyers and sellers who are dealing in a particular type of product. They also eliminate the problem of identity of product when the product of one producer is mingled with the product of another, or when the product goes through some sort of processing. The marketing process also establishes the ground rules of the transaction, such as terms of payment, time and conditions of delivery, or means of transportation.

Packaging

Packaging may be done by the processor or by the concentrator, as is the case with fresh produce. In some cases, further packaging or repackaging is done at several stages in the marketing process. The first function of the package is to protect the product. The package also divides the product into convenient, countable market-sized units, and the outside may contain advertising, product information, or suggested uses.

Advertising Promotion and Product Information

Most food advertising is sponsored by food manufacturers and by producer organizations such as the Dairymen's League. Trade associations and government agencies, such as the Florida Citrus Commission, also sponsor advertising. Less than half the total funds spent on promotional activities goes for advertising in the mass media. The rest is spent for merchandising aids, public relations, consumer information, and administrative expenses.

Financing

Financing and risk taking occur throughout the marketing process. Farmers must finance their operations until the crop is harvested and sold. Processors spread the risk of price fluctuations by buying "futures" or "hedging." Wholesalers extend credit to their customers. All these operations represent a cost to the marketer.

Government Activities in the Food Market

Federal Government

The federal government maintains many programs that affect the food market in various ways, ranging from the economic impact of price supports to the regulation of trade practices of processors, to research and technical assistance programs for farmers.

The following are some of the programs and agencies which are of particular importance to the food buyer:

The Food and Drug Administration (FDA), Department of Health, Education and Welfare. The FDA attempts to protect the public health by keeping unsafe, impure, and unwholesome foods off the market. It does this by establishing reasonable standards of identity, quality and fill of container, and labeling requirements. Compliance with FDA requirements is mandatory, and is enforced by condemnation and seizure of harmful or unfit products, as well as injunction proceedings in Federal courts. FDA standards are usually minimal requirements to identify unfit or substandard products and remove them from interstate commerce. Most states have similar laws pertaining to food products that do not come under the jurisdiction of the FDA.

While FDA standards try to ensure the safety of the product, they do not provide a sufficient measurement of quality. Therefore, further definition of quality is necessary for the purposes of the food buyer.

Agricultural Marketing Service (AMS), Department of Agriculture. The AMS provides numerous food inspection, regulatory, and information programs:

Fig. 4-2. Federal inspection mark.

1. Standardization, inspection, grading, and classifying.
2. Inspection for wholesomeness, and truthful labeling.
3. Dissemination of market news and information.

   With the exception of the inspection of meats, poultry, and egg products, which is mandatory, the programs listed above are voluntary.

Inspection. The Wholesome Meat Act of 1967 and the Wholesome Poultry Products Act of 1968 supplemented earlier legislation pertaining to inspection. These acts now require all meat and poultry plants to be under an inspection program, either that of the U.S. Department of Agriculture (USDA), or a state operated program that meets USDA approval. Under the inspection program, diseased and unfit meat and poultry are detected and destroyed, the sanitary standards and practices of product handling and plant maintenance are overseen, and the use of harmful food additives is prevented, as is false and deceptive labeling.

   Products which are acceptable under the inspection program are given a federal inspection mark, such as the one shown in Fig. 4–2. The number of the plant is included. This inspection stamp indicates only that the product has been judged fit for human consumption at the time of inspection. It is not an indication of quality.

Grading. The USDA instituted its grading program because "some official yardstick for measuring quality was needed to give the consumer-buyer confidence in his purchase. . . ." Grades such as "U.S.

Fig. 4-3. Federal grade marks.

No. 1", "U.S. Choice" or "U.S. Grade A" have been developed for most of the important farm commodities.

The use of the USDA Grading Service by processors is voluntary, and is paid for by the processor who requests it. However, all products that are graded must first pass federal inspection. Official federal grade marks are usually in the form of a shield, as shown in Fig. 4–3. "Federal-State Graded" indicates that the grading was done under a cooperative Federal-State agreement.

The Federal grades are termed "quality grades" or "consumer grades." A separate grading system is used by the military, which purchases on the basis of "procurement" grades. A third type of grading, "yield grading," has been developed for beef and lamb. Yield grades reflect the difference in yields of boneless, closely trimmed cuts from the high value parts of carcasses of the same quality grade. For beef, these are the round, loin, rib and chuck. Yield grades are most applicable when purchasing whole carcasses, although they can be applied to some primal cuts. The major criteria in determining yield grades are the area of the rib eye muscle (taken at the breakpoint of the hindquarter and forequarter) in relation to the expected size for the particular carcass weight; the thickness of the fat covering over the rib eye; and the amount of kidney, pelvic, and heart fat.

USDA Acceptance Service. The Agricultural Marketing Service offers a special Acceptance Service for organizations buying large volumes of fresh and processed fruits and vegetables, meats and meat products, poultry and eggs, and dairy products.

Under this program, the buyer submits his own specifications to the service, along with the purchase order. Government specialists then examine the products at the plant and certify that they meet the buyer's specifications. Cartons are then sealed and stamped with a USDA Acceptance Stamp. (Fig. 4–4).

The USDA grader, in effect, "receives" the merchandise for the buyer. The cost of the inspection is borne either by the buyer or the seller, according to their contract. USDA graders will also assist the food buyer in writing the specification.

ACCEPTANCE STAMP
Fig. 4-4. Acceptance stamp.

Other Activities of the Federal Government. Other departments of the federal government also engage in activities that affect the food market in various ways. The United States Public Health Service (USPHS), acting in an advisory capacity, proposes model ordinances and legislation pertaining to milk, water supplies, and more recently, the shellfish industry.

Product standards development and grading of fresh and frozen fish, shellfish, and seafood products is done by the National Marine Fisheries Service, an agency of the Department of Commerce.

The National Bureau of Standards (NBS), also under the Department of Commerce, is concerned with standard weights and measures. It makes recommendations concerning such things as package sizes and product measurement.

The Federal Trade Commission (FTC) is charged with keeping competition both free and fair and to this end has established trade practice rules for a number of industries, including food processors.

The Internal Revenue Service (Department of the Treasury) has certain regulatory functions pertaining to the legal alcohol industry, whereas the Department of Justice is responsible for enforcement of federal liquor laws.

In addition to these activities, several departments and agencies have established food standards and specifications—the Department of Defense and the Veterans Administration for their own internal use, and the General Services Administration for the use of any other governmental agencies that purchase food for their own use.

State Governments and Others

In addition to the activities of the federal government in the food market, state governments, counties, and sometimes even municipalities may engage in activities pertaining to food marketing. States may require inspection of foods not intended for shipment in interstate commerce, since federal inspection is not generally mandatory for those commodities. A state that is a major producer of a certain commodity may have standards for that commodity. Laws pertaining to dairy products vary from state to state and may even vary among the counties of a state.

Metric System

The United States is the only industrialized nation in the world that has not yet adopted the metric system of weights and measures. Although conversion to the metric system has been discussed for many years, it appears now that some form of metric conversion legislation will be passed in the foreseeable future. The Department of Commerce is one agency actively supporting metrification because it believes that it is necessary to make United States products marketable in international trade.

The major effect of metrification in the food service industry will be in packaging of food and nonfood materials. The Department of Commerce foresees this conversion taking place over a long period of time. Initially, existing package sizes will be retained, with the contents additionally stated in metric measures. In most cases, the resulting measure will be an unwieldy fractional measure, and this in time will be replaced with new package sizes in standard metric units. This last step will come about gradually as existing packaging equipment is replaced.

During the conversion process, food buyers will have to be constantly alert to package sizes, weights, and measures to be sure that they are getting the best value and the amount of merchandise needed. In the long run, however, conversion to the metric system should eliminate much of the lack of standardization in food packaging.

The Food Buyer

The food buyer is not simply an order clerk, telephoning requests for purchases of items he has been asked to buy. Buying is a key function, requiring technical knowledge. To fill such a position effectively, the food buyer should be experienced in food operations. He must understand the workings of a kitchen and know what happens to food in production.

The food buyer should be familiar with market trends and be alert to new sources, new products, and shifts of market availabilities. He should know how prices paid in distribution and processing centers today will affect prices in his local market next week. He should be able to judge if a fair price was quoted by a dealer, based on current market reports.

The food buyer must understand the purveyor's operating situation and not spread his orders so thinly that no one dealer can make a profit on his business. He should be fair in his demands for service. Trucks and driver payroll expense represent major costs for the distributor. Too many small or emergency orders are costly for the distributor and he can only pass this cost back to the customer, where it belongs. It is unfair to expect the distributor to pay for the laziness, lack of planning, or inefficiency of the food buyer. A reputable distributor knows his products and his business and, of course, is in business to make a profit. Every customer is an investment in time, service, and money, and the dealer will do whatever is necessary to keep good customers. The overdemanding or unethical buyer can never best the purveyor. Sooner or later the purveyor will make up for it, or else refuse to do business. A reputable dealer expects to be competitive and respects good buying practice. His knowledge, confidence, and good will are valuable.

Who does the buying? In a study of hotel and motel purchasing policies conducted by the Cornell University School of Hotel Administration, the question was put "Who influences the selection of (food) purchases?" About half the food purchases were influenced by the chef, another third by the hotel manager, and about one fourth were influenced by the food manager. Others participating in the selection were the steward, the central office of a chain, and the purchasing agent. This study implies that few hotels have a full-time food buyer and that the buying function is not the exclusive domain of the chef.

In restaurants, food buying is most often done by the owner, manager, chef, steward, dietitian, or in a very large operation, by a purchasing agent. The latter position is most often found in the headquarters of a restaurant chain, although it can also be found in large, free-standing operations. Regional managers and supervisors of chain operations also participate in food buying.

In hospitals and institutions, food buying may be done by a dietitian or food manager, or it may be done by the institution's purchasing agent. In the latter case, the agent may purchase only nonperishables and supplies himself, and delegate the ordering of perishables to a member of the dietary staff. The purchasing agent does, however, participate in developing the purchasing specifications, procedures, and an approved vendor list for all foods purchased.

Some large companies or institutions may have a buying committee that makes decisions on new products or major purchases. The buying committee is usually composed of representatives of the production, marketing, advertising, and accounting or cost control office.

Determining Buying Policies

Except in areas where availability of product is a factor, the buying policies should be developed to fit the needs of the operation. Furthermore, the buying process itself should be as efficient and economical as possible. Much can be done throughout the operation to simplify the purchasing process and make it more efficient. The use of standardized or cyclical menus in conjunction with standardized recipes determines the number of items to be purchased, as well as the characteristics desired. With this information, standard purchase specifications can be developed for each product.

Standard menus, recipes, and specifications should not be regarded as inflexible. Rather, they provide a rational basis for evaluation and change. With a limited number of items for sale, the preparation and purchase of each item can be evaluated in depth and continually refined, which also gives the food buyer and other management personnel an opportunity to learn about and evaluate new products and techniques. When used in this manner, standardization accomplishes its purpose, which is to allow the greatest possible efficiency to be passed on to the customer in the form of quality and price, and to the operator in the form of added profits.

Whatever buying practice is used, purchase specifications must be developed for each product purchased. These specifications tell the purveyors exactly what product is required. They provide the buyer with a basis for comparing prices and for determining the acceptability of the merchandise that is delivered.

Formulating Purchase Specifications

The United States government defines a specification as a "statement of particulars in specific terms." Specification buying is, then, merely the utilization of such well-defined particulars in the purchasing of merchandise.

If properly used, a set of specifications will provide suitable buying standards for a particular operation and a common denominator of market bidding for the food buyers and purveyors. Purveyors' bids can be compared, since the purveyors are bidding on comparable merchandise. Specification buying also gives uniformity and consistency to purchasing and receiving that will help maintain a desired food cost.

The specifications currently in effect should be distributed to the various purveyors for their information and use. A set of specifications must also be available for use by the receiving clerk for inspecting incoming merchandise. Effective specification buying requires receiving by specification as well.

The usefulness of a set of specifications depends on how accurately the specifications were developed. In writing specifications, the purchaser should be guided by the results of actual kitchen tests of the products to be purchased, the planned use of the product, its merchandising suitability, final portion costs (rather than unit prices), and by the market conditions and availability. Trade and government standards concerning packs, grades, and varieties should be included.

Kitchen Tests

There are four types of kitchen tests:

Raw Food Tests. Raw food tests determine the best count and weight for fruits and vegetables—that is, a case of size 150 California oranges for use in salads should weigh at least 70 pounds net per crate.

Canned Food Tests. Canned food tests are made to check on the yields and actual cost of the different varieties of canned foods. In these tests, drained weight, count, quality, density and clearness of syrup, and uniformity of product are considered.

Butchering Tests. Butchering tests are cutting tests of the various wholesale units of meat, fish, and poultry as received. The butcher or the chef makes the tests to determine the actual portions obtained after waste, trim, and by-products have been considered.

Cooking Tests. Cooking tests often follow butchering tests, since they determine the final portion cost not only after waste and trim have been accounted for but also after cooking, slicing, and service loss have been considered.

Butchering and cooking test results can be used in several ways: to calculate portion costs, to calculate ratios and conversion factors for use in determining amounts to be purchased, to determine the best method of preparation, to determine purchase specifications and to test adherence to those specifications, and to check on employee adherence to standardized recipes and procedures in preparation. (See Chapter 6 for further discussion of how butchering and cooking tests are made, and the use of their results.)

General Conditions

A purchase specification usually has two parts: (1) the general terms or conditions of the transaction, and (2) the details or specifics concerning each product desired.

The general conditions state such things as the point and time of delivery, and the point where the buyer will take possession of the merchandise. General terms should include the responsibility for rejected merchandise, condition of merchandise at the time of delivery, required invoices and statements of account, and the schedule of payments. Other terms may include procedures for inspection and certification of quality, submission of samples, a performance bond or payment of late penalties by the seller, or conditions for contract cancellation in the event of nonperformance.

Food Purchasing Specifications

Below are examples of general conditions in the purchasing specifications of a large free-standing restaurant that buys on a continual basis according to needs.

Prices are to be F.O.B. delivered to The Example Restaurant, with merchandise off-loaded onto the receiving platforms at the rear of the Restaurant, located at 123 Main Street, Anyplace, New York.

Orders will be placed on the basis of the lowest bid for comparable merchandise and service, in a manner agreed upon by the purveyor and the buyer.

Deliveries will be accepted Monday through Friday, 6:00 A.M. to 2:00 P.M., and Saturday, 6:00 A.M. to 12:00 noon.

A *Delivery Ticket* or invoice must accompany each delivery. Tickets are to be signed by the receiver and one copy left with the receiver. All merchandise will be weighed, counted, checked, and inspected (as appropriate to the item) by the receiver in the presence of the deliveryman before signing the delivery ticket, unless prior arrangement has been made with the purveyor to accept the buyer's inspection after delivery.

A *Statement of Account* is to be rendered monthly. Statements should be sent to the attention of Mr. John Smith, Manager; The Example Restaurant, 123 Main Street, Anyplace, New York.

Bills will be paid weekly. All trade discounts will be taken.

Merchandise rejected must be picked up by the purveyor as quickly as possible. The buyer assumes no responsibility for such merchandise after notification has been given of its rejection. The amount of the rejected merchandise will be deducted from the invoice and a Request for Credit Memorandum will be sent to the purveyor.

Conditions of Merchandise:

1. All food merchandise must meet federal and state requirements of wholesomeness and fitness for human consumption. Food merchandise must be clean and wholesome, prepared, processed, and packaged in a safe and sanitary manner, and transported in clean, sound vehicles. All merchandise must be in the specified condition at the time of delivery.

2. All meats, prepared meats, meat food products, and meat by-products (as defined in Rules and Regulations of the U.S. Department of Agriculture Governing the Grading and Certification of Meats, Prepared Meats, and Meat Products) covered by these specifications must originate from animals which were slaughtered or from products which were manufactured or processed in establishments regularly operated under the continuous supervision of the 'Meat and Poultry Inspection Program (MPIP) of the United States Department of Agriculture (USDA) or under any other system of meat inspection approved by the Agricultural Marketing Service of the USDA.

3. All dairy products must be produced and handled in accordance with the best sanitary practices, and shall meet federal, state, and local regulations.

4. Frozen foods must be maintained and delivered in a solidly frozen state, and show no evidence of defrosting, refreezing, freezerburn, contamination, or mishandling.
5. Meats, poultry, fish, and sea food specified as "fresh" must be chilled to an internal temperature of not higher than 50° F. They must be held at suitable temperature (32°–38°F) and must be in excellent condition to the time of delivery.
6. Merchandise must be wrapped or packaged in a suitable manner so as to maintain the quality and wholesomeness of the product. Meat packaging must conform to USDA requirements as stated in the Institutional Meat Purchase Specifications.

Acceptability of any merchandise which deviates from the standards and specifications stated herein must be determined by Mr. John Smith, Manager, or Mr. Joe Jones, Chef.

Very large organizations may buy nonperishables only once a year, after the crop has been packed. In this case, the specification is usually written each year, and becomes a "Request for Bids." The general terms for this kind of purchase specification are even more detailed and specify such things as multiple delivery dates, warehousing requirements, and financing terms. The vast majority of food service buying, however, is done on a continuing, rather than an annual basis.

Specifics or Details of the Products Desired:
A specification should state the following:

1. The common or trade name of the products.
2. The grade or brand desired. Federal or trade grades may be specified.
3. The size of the container or the number of package units in a container.
4. The unit on which prices will be quoted.
5. Other information relating to specific products:

   a. Area of origin.
   b. Variety.
   c. Style of pack or cut.
   d. Size of pieces or count per can.
   e. Portion size.
   f. Condition (fresh, chilled, frozen, cured).
   g. Packing medium.
   h. Age.
   i. Type of package.

Now we turn to a discussion of specifications for purchasing specific commodities.

Meats

Meat specifications should state the name of the cut, style of cutting, grade, amount of fat covering permitted, size of the animal from which the cut should come, and the minimum and maximum weight range. The amount of aging required and the condition on delivery (fresh or frozen) should also be specified.

The United States Department of Agriculture, Livestock Division, has established institutional meat specifications for fresh beef, lamb, mutton, and pork; cured, cured and smoked; and fully cooked pork products; cured, dried, and smoked beef products; edible by-products; sausage products; and portion-cut meat products. The specifications for fresh meats are described and illustrated in two books published by the National Association of Meat Purveyors: *Meat Buyer's Guide to Standardized Meat Cuts* and *Meat Buyer's Guide to Portion Control Meat Cuts*. All the specifications are available from the U.S. Government Printing Office, Washington, D.C. In these specifications, use of the item numbers can greatly simplify the purchasing procedure. All that need be specified is the item number, grade, the weight range desired, condition (fresh or frozen), fat limitations, and any aging desired.

The meat grading system administered by the Department of Agriculture's Meat and Livestock Division is completely independent of the meat packing industry. Packers may use the system if they wish, and they bear the cost of the service. It is not mandatory that meat be federally graded, but a very high portion of the fresh meat bound for consumer use is so graded. Grading meats under federal standards is based on three fundamental characteristics: conformation, finish, and quality.

Conformation

Conformation applies to the general form and structure of the carcass, side, or cut of meat. It generally indicates the ratio of meat and fat or bone. It might be said that it is based on (1) build, (2) form, (3) shape, and (4) outline. In a U.S. Choice carcass of beef, the ratio of bone to the total weight of the carcass is from 16 to 19 percent. In a U.S. Good carcass this ratio will average 21 to 22 percent, whereas in the Commercial grades the ratio will run as high as 24 to 26 percent. This difference is balanced somewhat by the fact that the Prime carcass may have as high as 36 percent fat, as against approximately 21 percent in the Commercial grade.

Conformation or lack of conformation is very quickly seen when the carcass is judged. A Prime carcass will be blocky, thick, and well rounded, with well-fleshed ribs and full loins. The lower grades of meat will be thinner, more lengthy, and not so well curved, especially around the hip and shoulder joints.

In February 1976, conformation was dropped as a grading factor, but it remains important for retail value.

Finish

Finish generally refers to the finish on the outside of a carcass, but it can also mean the finish on the inside of the carcass. It refers to the amount, color, character, and distribution of fat on the outside and on the inside of the carcass in and around exposed bones. The amount of fat around the kidney also has a bearing on the grade, and the evenness of the fat over the carcass is considered.

Quality

Quality refers to the factors that make the cooked meat palatable and includes any of the elements of conformation and finish. Although there is no scientific basis for measuring quality, it is thought to be related primarily to the texture of the meat, the amount of connective tissue, and the consistency and flavor of the juices set free in the cooking process.

Table 4–1 shows the federal grades for the various kinds of meat.

Beef Grades

U.S. Prime is the highest grade of beef consistently available throughout the year. It is produced from young animals and is well marbled, with large amounts of fat and lean and a small amount of bone. The amount of fat helps to assure tenderness and contributes to a high degree of palatability. Most of the cuts from the round, loin, rib, and chuck are suitable for roasting and broiling. The revised grading standards introduced in 1976 reduced the marbling requirements both for Prime and Choice grades although eating quality was not lessened.

U.S. Choice is the grade most frequently available and most used by the buying public. While it does not have the marbling of the prime in the overall appearance of that grade, the very slight difference in eating quality between U.S. Choice and U.S. Prime grades of meat would be hard to recognize. For many restaurant uses, U.S.

Table 4–1. Federal Meat Grades

Beef	Veal	Lamb	Pork
U.S. Prime	U.S. Prime	U.S. Prime	U.S. No. 1
U.S. Choice	U.S. Choice	U.S. Choice	U.S. No. 2
U.S. Good	U.S. Good	U.S. Good	U.S. No. 3
U.S. Standard	U.S. Standard	U.S. Utility	U.S. No. 4
U.S. Commercial	U.S. Utility	U.S. Cull	U.S. Utility
U.S. Utility	U.S. Cull		
U.S. Cutter			
U.S. Canner			

Choice is preferable to U.S. Prime, since the additional fat covering which causes a carcass to be graded Prime must be trimmed off. Many buyers do not consider that the additional cost of the Prime is warranted.

U.S. Good, U.S. Standard, and U.S. Commercial are the next grades downward. Although these grades are not usually suitable for broiling or roasting, they provide a low-cost meat that is very acceptable in dishes that call for slow, long cooking. Some institutions use U.S. Good grade meat for steaks, tenderizing them to make them palatable. Under the 1976 rules U.S. Good was upgraded slightly.

U.S. Cutter and U.S. Canner are the lowest grades of meat and are usually not available to the food buyer. They are used principally in the manufacture of processed meat products.

Selected Grades refer to packers' brand names that indicate their own grades. These grades usually parallel the government grades. At times, meat that would not be graded Choice because of a small defect that does not affect its eating quality will be upgraded by the purveyor. He will do this to obtain a price closer to the Choice grade level rather than have it downgraded as Good and suffer the full price differential. An experienced buyer will often be able to get good value in upgraded beef by watching for such instances.

The same principles of conformation, finish, and quality determine the grading in pork and other meats. Since the variation in market hogs is less than in market beef, there has not been the same need for federal grading, and a larger proportion of the pork is graded as Selected, with packers' own grades.

Fish and Shellfish

Grading

There is no mandatory inspection program for fish products in the United States, but a voluntary inspection program was authorized in 1946. The original program was reorganized in 1974 under the Department of Commerce.

The program applies essentially to packaged and frozen products that carry the marks shown in Fig. 4–5. The mark reading "U.S.

Fig. 4-5.

Department of Commerce, Packed Under Federal Inspection" is given only to inspected fishery products and means that it has been statistically sampled and found to be of good quality. The Grade A Shield mark is given only to top quality products—ones that are uniform in size, free of blemishes and defects, and that possess a fresh flavor and odor.

Marketing

Fish and shellfish are marketed in four forms: fresh, frozen, canned, and cured. Fresh fish and shellfish are very perishable and should be kept well iced in transit. When buying whole fresh fish, look for firm flesh, freedom from odors, and scales clinging tightly to the skin. The eyes should be bright and clear, and the gills should be reddish pink and free from slime. There are seven market forms of fresh fish:

1. Whole or round, as it comes from the water.
2. Drawn. Only the entrails are removed.
3. Dressed or pan dressed. Scaled, eviscerated, and ready for cooking. Smaller fish may still have the head and tail left on, but the head, tail, and fins of larger fish are usually removed.
4. Steaks. Cross-sections sliced from larger types of dressed fish and ready to cook.
5. Fillets. Cuts from the sides of dressed fish, cut lengthwise away from the backbone. They are almost boneless and are ready to cook.
6. Butterfly fillets are two sides or fillets of a smaller fish, held together by the uncut belly skin. They are usually boneless and ready to cook.
7. Live. Some restaurants are also able to obtain live trout for dining room display and eventual cooking.

Fresh fish is plentiful in coastal regions, but express freight charges may make it too costly for some operations located some distance away from major fish markets.

Frozen fish is widely distributed and is available in many market forms, including almost all the forms described for fresh fish. In addition, fish may be frozen in blocks and cut into fish sticks or individual portions that may be breaded or unbreaded. Frozen fish should be stored at 10°F until it is ready to use, and it should not be refrozen once it is thawed. Table 4–2 shows the market forms of some of the most commonly used species of fish.

Tuna and salmon are the largest-selling canned fish. The specification for canned tuna fish should state the packing medium—oil, brine, or water; style of pack—solid (used for cold plates), chunk, flake, or grated; color—white, light, dark, or blended. Only Albacore tuna may be labeled as white meat. The country of origin may be specified also. Tuna is available in the following pack sizes: 6/66½ ounces (six cans of 66½ ounces per case), 24/13 ounces, 48/7 ounces, 48/3½ ounces. Canned tuna is not graded, but it must meet federal standards of identity. Salmon is marketed under several names depending on the species, including Chinook or King, Red Alaska, Sockeye, Medium Red, Pink, and Chum. Generally, the redder the meat, the higher the price. The specification should include the species desired, and the can size and pack. Salmon is packed 12/4 pound, 24/1 pound tall, 24/1 pound flat, 24/3¾ ounces. There are no federal standards of identity for canned salmon.

Fish may also be smoked or salted. Finnan Haddie is a haddock that has been salted and lightly smoked.

Shellfish are divided into two classifications: crustaceans and mollusks. Crustaceans include crabs, crayfish, lobster, and shrimp. Mollusks include clams, oysters, and scallops.

Shrimp are usually marketed frozen in five-pound boxes for food service use. There are a variety of market forms, including:

- Green—head off, shell on, uncooked.
- P & D—peeled and deveined, but not cooked.
- Cooked—peeled and deveined.
- Breaded—peeled except for the tail, and deveined.
- Butterfly—partially split, usually breaded.
- IQF—individually quick frozen, P & D, so they are loose in the package.
- Titi—tiny shrimp, more than 90 to the pound. May be cooked or raw.
- Pieces—broken pieces, peeled and deveined, used for cut-up dishes.
- Steaks—pieces frozen into blocks and cut into individual portions. Usually breaded.

In addition to the form desired, the specification should state the count, expressed as the number of pieces to the pound. Count categories per pound for shrimp are: 15 and under, 16–20, 21–25, 26–30, 31–42, and 42 and over. Federal government grades exist for frozen green and breaded shrimp.

Lobsters are marketed live and are also available as frozen lobster tails and canned lobster meat. Fresh meat and cooked in-the-shell are forms usually found only in producing areas. A specification for fresh lobster or lobster tails should state the size desired. Since these items are served by the piece but paid for by the pound, a small deviation in the specified weight can cause considerable variation in

Table 4–2. Comprehensive Species Chart

(Source: National Fisheries Institute)

Species	Other Names	Where Caught	Market Forms
Cod	Codfish, Scrod. (1½ lb. or less)	New England, Middle Atlantic, Pacific Coast, Iceland, England, Norway, Germany, Denmark, Canada	Drawn, dressed, steaks, fillets; fresh, frozen, salted, smoked. Breaded and precooked sticks and portions.
Flounder	Sole, Fluke	All U.S. coastal areas, Canada, Denmark, England, Iceland	Whole, dressed, fillets; fresh, frozen.
Greenland Turbot		North Atlantic, Greenland area; coast of Norway	Whole, drawn, fillets; fresh, frozen.
Grouper	Red, Black, Yellowfin, Speckled Hind, Gag, Scamp	South Atlantic, Gulf	Whole, steaks, fillets; fresh, frozen.
Haddock	Scrod (1½ lb. or less)	New England, Canada, Iceland, Norway, England	Whole, drawn, fillets; fresh, frozen, salted, smoked. Breaded and precooked sticks and portions.
Hake (See Whiting)			
Halibut		New England, Pacific Coast, Alaska	Drawn, dressed, steaks, fletches; fresh, frozen, smoked.
Ocean Catfish	Wolf Fish	North Atlantic	Fillets; frozen.
Ocean Perch	Rosefish, Redfish	New England, North-west Coast, Iceland, Germany, England, Norway, Canada	Fillets; fresh, frozen. Breaded fillets, portions.
Pacific Pollock	Alaska Pollock	Bering Sea, Northwest Pacific	Fillets, frozen; raw breaded and precooked breaded portions and sticks.
Pollock	Boston Bluefish	North Atlantic	Drawn, dressed, steaks, fillets; fresh, frozen, salted, smoked. Raw and precooked breaded sticks and portions.
Sea Bass (Black & White)		Pacific Coast	Steaks, fillets; fresh, frozen.
Common	Blackfish, Black Sea Bass	New England, Middle and South Atlantic	Whole pan-dressed, fillets; fresh, frozen.
Sea Trout Gray	Weakfish, Squeteagues	Middle and South Atlantic	Whole, drawn, fillets; fresh, frozen.
Spotted	Speckled Trout	Middle and South Atlantic, Gulf	Whole, drawn, fillets; dressed; fresh, frozen.
White	White or Sand Trout	Gulf	Whole, fillets; fresh, frozen.

Table 4–2. Comprehensive Species Chart (cont.)

(Source: National Fisheries Institute)

Species	Other Names	Where Caught	Market Forms
Snapper	Mangrove, Red Snapper, Yellowtail, Vermilion	South Atlantic, Gulf, Western Pacific	Whole, fillets; fresh, frozen.
Sole	Rex, Petrale, Sand, Grey, Lemon Sole	Pacific Coast, Alaska, Canada, Atlantic Coast, England, Holland, Belgium, Denmark	Whole, fillets, breaded portions; fresh, frozen. Stuffed. Stuffed breaded.
	Dover or English	England	
Whiting	Frostfish, Hake, Silver Hake	New England, England, South Atlantic	Whole, drawn, dressed, fillets; fresh, frozen; precooked portions and sticks.

the cost of this expensive item. Fresh lobsters should be alive when received and at the time of cooking. Crayfish are small crustaceans which look like small lobsters or large shrimps with claws.

Crabs may be the hard-shell varieties, such as the blue crab from the Atlantic, the Dungeness crab from the Pacific, or the Alaskan King crab. Soft-shell crabs are molting blue crabs that have lost their shells. Crabs may be marketed live in coastal areas, and King crab meat is available frozen in almost all parts of the country. In addition, fresh-cooked and frozen crab meat picked from the shell may be available. Federal standards for cooked crabmeat picked from the shell classify the meat as lump, flake, or claw. Claw is brownish in color, as opposed to white lump and flake meat, which comes from the body of the crab.

Clams and oysters purchased in the shell should have their shells tightly closed when received, indicating that they are still alive. Clams may be sold by the count, bushel, sack, crate, or pound. Littlenecks and cherrystones are small hard-shell clams eaten raw from the shell. Steamers are very small soft-shell clams. Chowders or sharps are larger hard-shell clams used for cooked dishes. Fresh clams are also sold shucked in gallons or No. 10 cans. They may also be frozen, and are available whole, minced, or as strips for frying. Oysters are available shucked. Clams and oysters are also available canned in various forms.

There are two types of scallops: sea scallops, which are usually marketed frozen in five-pound packages, and bay or cape scallops, which are usually marketed fresh in the producing areas. Bay scallops are smaller, sweeter and more tender than sea scallops, and they are usually higher priced.

Poultry

Poultry is classified as to "kind"—referring to the different species, such as chickens, turkeys, ducks; each kind is then divided into "classes."

Chicken

Rock Cornish Game Hen or Cornish Game Hen. A Rock Cornish game hen or Cornish game hen is a young immature chicken (usually five to seven weeks of age) weighing not more than two pounds ready-to-cook weight, which was developed from a Cornish chicken or the progeny of a Cornish chicken crossed with another breed of chicken.

Broiler or Fryer. A broiler or fryer is a young chicken (usually nine to twelve weeks of age), of either sex, that is tender-meated with soft, pliable, smooth-textured skin and flexible breastbone cartilage.

Roaster. A roaster is a young chicken (usually three to five months of age), of either sex, that is tender-meated with soft, pliable, smooth-textured skin and breastbone cartilage that may be somewhat less flexible than that of a broiler or fryer.

Capon. A capon is a surgically desexed male chicken (usually under eight months of age) that is tender-meated with soft, pliable, smooth-textured skin.

Stag. A stag is a male chicken (usually under ten months of age) with coarse skin, somewhat toughened and darkened flesh, and considerable hardening of the breast-bone cartilage. Stags show a condition of fleshing and a degree of maturity intermediate between that of a roaster and a cock or rooster.

Hen or Stewing Chicken or Fowl. A hen or stewing chicken or fowl is a mature female chicken (usually more than ten months of age) with meat less tender than that of a roaster, and nonflexible breastbone tip.

Cock or Rooster. A cock or rooster is a mature male chicken with coarse skin, toughened and darkened meat, and hardened breastbone tip.

Turkeys

Fryer-Roaster Turkey. A fryer-roaster turkey is a young immature turkey (usually under sixteen weeks of age), of either sex, that is tender-meated with soft, pliable, smooth-textured skin, and flexible breastbone cartilage.

Young Hen Turkey. A young hen turkey is a young female turkey (usually five to seven months of age) that is tender-meated with soft, pliable, smooth-textured skin, and breastbone cartilage that is some-what less flexible than in a fryer-roaster turkey.

Young Tom Turkey. A young tom turkey is a young male turkey (usually five to seven months of age) that is tender-meated with soft, pliable, smooth-textured skin, and breastbone cartilage that is some-what less flexible than in a fryer-roaster turkey.

Yearling Hen Turkey. A yearling hen turkey is a fully matured female turkey (usually under fifteen months of age) that is reasonably tender-meated and with reasonably smooth-textured skin.

Yearling Tom Turkey. A yearling tom turkey is a fully matured male turkey (usually under fifteen months of age) that is reasonably tender-meated and with reasonably smooth-textured skin.

Mature Turkey or Old Turkey (Hen or Tom). A mature or old turkey is an old turkey of either sex (usually in excess of fifteen months of age) with coarse skin and toughened flesh.

(For labeling purposes, the designation of sex within the class name is optional, and the three classes of young turkeys may be grouped and designated as "young turkeys.")

Ducks

Broiler Duckling or Fryer Duckling. A broiler duckling or fryer duckling is a young duck (usually under eight weeks of age), of either sex, that is tender-meated and has a soft bill and soft windpipe.

Roaster Duckling. A roaster duckling is a young duck (usually under sixteen weeks of age), of either sex, that is tender-meated and has a bill that is not completely hardened and a windpipe that is easily dented.

Mature Duck or Old Duck. A mature duck or an old duck is a duck (usually over six months of age), of either sex, with toughened flesh, hardened bill, and hardened windpipe.

Geese

Young Goose. A young goose may be of either sex, is tender-meated, and has a windpipe that is easily dented.

Mature Goose or Old Goose. A mature goose or old goose may be of either sex and has toughened flesh and hardened windpipe.

Guineas

Young Guinea. A young guinea may be of either sex, is tender-meated, and has a flexible breastbone cartilage.

Mature Guinea or Old Guinea. A mature guinea or an old guinea may be of either sex, has toughened flesh and a hardened breastbone.

Pigeons

Squab. A squab is a young, immature pigeon of either sex, and is extra tender-meated.

Pigeon. A pigeon is a mature bird of either sex, with coarse skin and toughened flesh.

Market Forms of Poultry

Ready-to-Cook Poultry. Most poultry is marketed in this form. It may be fresh or frozen.

Poultry Parts. These include halves, quarters, breasts, breasts with ribs, wishbones, legs, drumsticks, thighs, wings, and backs.

Poultry Food Products. These include raw and cooked poultry rolls and roasts, and specialty dishes containing poultry. Raw boneless poultry breasts and thighs are also included.

Live and Dressed. Poultry is seldom marketed live or dressed (head, feet and eviscera intact, blood and feathers removed) anymore.

Inspection and Grading

Under the Wholesome Poultry Products Acts of 1968, all poultry plants must be under either state or federal inspection.

Grades for poultry are U.S. Grade A, B, and C (Fig. 4–6). Grades are based on: (1) conformation; (2) fleshing; (3) fat accumulation under the skin; (4) freedom from pinfeathers; (5) freedom from exposed flesh, resulting from cuts, tears or broken bones; (6) freedom from discoloration of skin and from flesh blemishes and bruises; (7) freedom from freezing defects. In addition, raw poultry roasts and raw boneless poultry breasts and thighs may be graded U.S. Grade A if they meet the requirements. Ready-to-eat, dressed poultry and poultry parts that have passed federal inspection may also be graded.

A specification for poultry should include the kind, class, type (whether fresh chilled or fresh frozen), size or weight of the individual bird, market form, and grade.

Eggs and Egg Products

A specification for fresh eggs should include the grade, size of egg, and package size required. Fresh eggs are graded U.S. Grade AA or Fresh Fancy, A or B, depending on the height of the yolk, and the amount of spreading of the white when the egg is broken. The

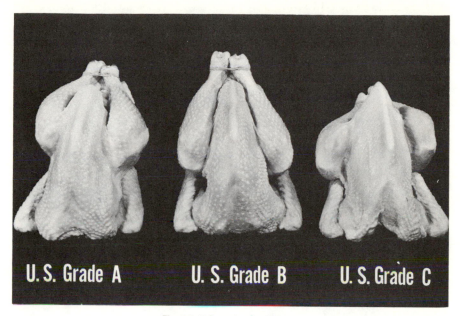

Fig. 4-6. U.S. grades for chicken.

condition of the shell is also a factor. Figure 4–7 shows the differences between the grades for eggs of the same size. The grade indicates the quality at the time of grading, and if eggs are mishandled, their quality can deteriorate rapidly. The grade may not apply at the time of use.

Size refers to the minimum weight per dozen (see Table 4–3). The size selected for fried and poached egg dishes depends on the desired portion size and cost. For cooking and scrambled eggs, the size giving the best value may be used. As a rule, if there is less than a seven cent price spread between sizes of the same grade, it is more economical to buy the larger size for this purpose. Eggs are usually marketed in 15 and 30 dozen cases for food service use.

Egg products are liquid, frozen, and dehydrated eggs, including separated whites and yolks, mixed whole egg, and blends of whole

Table 4–3. Size Categories for Eggs

	Min. Wt./Doz.	Min. Wt./30 Doz. Case
Jumbo	30 oz.	56 lbs.
Extra Large	27 oz.	50 lbs.
Large	24 oz.	45 lbs.
Medium	21 oz.	39 lbs.
Small	18 oz.	33 lbs.
Peewee	15 oz.	28 lbs.

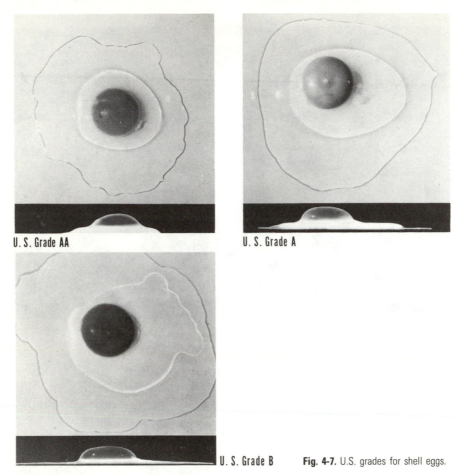

U. S. Grade AA

U. S. Grade A

U. S. Grade B   **Fig. 4-7.** U.S. grades for shell eggs.

egg and yolk. Egg products are often preferred to fresh shell eggs for cooking and baking because they have a longer shelf life and are less costly and less wasteful. Processing of all egg products must be under the continuous inspection of the Agricultural Marketing service of the USDA. The packages must show the inspection stamp shown in Fig. 4–8. Table 4–4 is a conversion table for frozen eggs.

Table 4–4. Conversion Table for Frozen Eggs

	Frozen Product	Shell Egg Equivalent
	(lb)	(No.)
Whole	1	9 eggs
Yolk	1	23 yolks
Whites	1	15 whites

**Official Egg Products
Inspection Mark**

Fig. 4-8. Official egg products inspection mark.

Milk and Milk Products

Federal standards of identity have been developed for cream, evaporated milk, sweetened and condensed milk, dry whole and nonfat milks, ice cream, sherbet, and frozen custard. As with all other identity standards established by the FDA, these standards are minimal requirements. Of more significance to the food buyer are the milk ordinances in effect in his state, county, or municipality.

The USPHS, in its advisory capacity, formulated a recommended Milk Ordinance and Code that has been adopted in many parts of the country. This code establishes standards and grades for various types of milk and milk products, including buttermilk, skim milk, cottage cheese, and frozen desserts, such as ice cream and sherbet.

The food buyer should be familiar with the following items when writing milk specifications:

Pasteurization is a process that kills harmful bacteria, leaving the product otherwise unchanged. The most commonly used method is to heat the raw milk to a temperature of 161°F for 15 seconds.

Homogenization breaks the butterfat into very small globules which will remain suspended in the milk, instead of separating.

Fortification is the addition of vitamins or other nutrients. The FDA specifies that milk fortified with Vitamin D must contain 400 U.S.P. units per quart.

Certified milk is milk that meets the standards for safety and quality of the American Association of Medical Milk Commissioners. It may be either raw or pasteurized, but is usually pasteurized. Very little certified milk is marketed today, since the milk ordinances now ensure safe milk.

Evaporated milk has had about half the water content removed under a vacuum.

Condensed milk is about one-third of its former volume, with 15 percent sugar added. Evaporated milk and condensed milk are not interchangeable.

The percentages of milkfat and total milk solids are defined by the FDA for evaporated milk and sweetened condensed milk. Table 4–5 shows the FDA standards for cream.

Table 4–5. FDA Standards for Cream

	Minimum Percentage of Milkfat
Light Cream	18%
Whipping Cream	30%
Heavy Whipping Cream	36%

Dry milks must meet standards of identity concerning wholesomeness, milkfat and moisture content, and other criteria. Nonfat dry milk may be graded U.S. Extra Grade or U.S. Standard Grade. Grades for dry whole milk are U.S. Premium, U.S. Extra, and U.S. Standard.

For other dairy products for which no U.S. Grade Standards have been established, a "Quality Approved" rating may be given. Federal standards for ice cream and related products are shown in Table 4–6.

Table 4–6. Federal Standards for Ice Cream and Related Products

	Milkfat		Total Milk Solids		Acid	Stabilizer	Weight per Gallon	Food Solids Per Gallon
	Min. %	Max. %	Min. %	Max. %	Min. %	Max. %	Min. Lb	Min. Lb
Plain Ice Cream	10	—	20	—	—	0.5	4.5	1.6
Fruit, Nut, Chocolate, etc.	8	—	16	—	—	0.5	4.5	1.6
Milk Sherbet	1	2	2	5	.35	0.5	6.0	—
Frozen Custard Egg Yolks 1.4%	10	—	20	—	—	0.5	4.5	1.6

Butter and Margarine

Butter is graded in terms of score, 100 points being considered a perfect rating. Such a rating is only theoretical, since under practical conditions, a 93 to 95 score is the best available. Scoring depends on flavor, color, body, salt content, and freshness. See Table 4–7.

Butter may be "sweet" or salted. It is available in 50- or 68-pound cubes, in one pound prints (packed 30, 32 or 36 pounds to the case), and in individual pats (cut 60, 72, or 90 pats to the pound,

Table 4–7. A Summary of Butter Grades and Scoring Characteristics

Score	U.S. Grade	Description
93 or above	U.S. Grade AA	Clean, highly pleasing flavor, fresh sweet cream base.
92	U.S. Grade A	Desirable flavor, clean, lacking somewhat in creamy flavor.
89-91½	U.S. Grade B	Fairly pleasing, though may contain slight off-flavor, sour taste.

usually packed 30 pounds per case). Individual pats are also available packaged with papers or individually wrapped.

Margarine may be an inexpensive substitute for butter for cooking and table use. It is graded and packaged much the same as butter.

Cheese

The USDA lists over 400 varieties of cheese in its *Cheese Varieties and Descriptions* handbook. Although it is very difficult to classify all varieties, cheeses are usually described as unripened or by their ripening agent—that is, by bacteria, by mold, by surface microorganisms, or by a combination of agents. They are also classified by the amount of aging. The longer the cheese has been aged, the harder it will be. This is owing to the amount of evaporation in the prolonged aging process. The following are examples of cheeses in the various classes (see also Fig. 4–9):

Very hard (grating)
1. Ripened by bacteria: Asiago old, Parmesan, Romano, Sapsago, Spalen.

Hard
1. Ripened by bacteria, without eyes: Cheddar, Granular or Stirred-curd, and Caciocavallo.
2. Ripened by bacteria, with eyes: Swiss, Emmentaler, and Gruyere.

Semisoft
1. Ripened principally by bacteria: Brick and Muenster.
2. Ripened by bacteria and surface micro-organisms: Limburger, Port du Salut, and Trappist.
3. Ripened principally by blue mold in the interior: Roquefort, Gorgonzola, Blue, Stilton, and Wensleydale.

Cheese	Origin	Consistency & texture	Color & shape	Flavor	Mode of serving
Asiago	Italy	Hard to hard grating; granular, tiny gas holes or eyes	Light yellow; cylindrical	Piquant, sharp in aged cheese	As such; as seasoning (grated) when aged
Bel Paese	Italy	Soft; smooth, waxy body	Slightly gray surface, creamy yellow interior; small wheels	Mild to moderately robust	As such (dessert); on crackers; in sandwiches
Blue	France	Semisoft; visible veins of mold, pasty, sometimes crumbly	White; marbled with blue-green mold; cylindrical	Piquant, spicy	As such (dessert); in dips, in cooked foods; in salads
Brick	United States	Semisoft; smooth, waxy body	Light yellow to orange; brick-shaped	Mild	As such; in sandwiches, salads
Brie	France	Soft; thin edible crust, creamy interior	Whitish crust, creamy yellow interior; medium and small wheels	Mild to pungent	As such (dessert)
Caciocavallo	Italy	Hard; compact, flaky	Light tan surface, light interior; tenpin shape, bound with cord	Sharp, similar to Provolone	As such; as seasoning (grated) when aged
Camembert	France	Soft; thin edible crust, creamy interior	White crusts, creamy yellow interior; small wheels	Mild to pungent	As such (dessert)
Cheddar (American)	England	Hard; smooth, firm body	Light yellow to orange; varied shapes and styles, with rind and rindless	Mild to sharp	As such; in sandwiches; in cooked foods
Colby	United States	Hard type but softer and more open in texture than Cheddar	Light yellow to orange; cylindrical	Mild	As such; in sandwiches; in cooked foods
Cottage	Uncertain	Soft, moist, delicate, large or small curds	White; packaged in cuplike containers	Mild, slightly acid	As such; in salads; in dips; in cooked foods
Cream	United States	Soft, smooth, buttery	White; foil-wrapped in rectangular portions	Mild, slightly acid	As such; in sandwiches; in salads; on crackers
Edam	Holland	Hard type but softer than Cheddar; more open, mealy body	Creamy yellow with red wax coat; cannonball shape	Mild, nutlike	As such; on crackers; with fresh fruit
Gjetost	Norway	Hard; buttery	Golden brown; cubical and rectangular	Sweetish, caramel	As such; on crackers
Gorgonzola	Italy	Semisoft; visible veins of mold, less moist than Blue	Light tan surface, light yellow interior, marbled with blue-green mold; cylindrical	Piquant, spicy, similar to Blue	As such (dessert)
Gouda	Holland	Hard type but softer than Cheddar; more open, mealy body like Edam	Creamy yellow with or without red wax coat; round and flat	Mild, nutlike, similar to Edam	As such; on crackers; with fresh fruit

Gruyere	Switzerland	Hard; tiny gas holes or eyes	Light yellow; flat wheels	Nutlike, sweetish	As such (dessert)
Limburger	Belgium	Soft; smooth, waxy body	Creamy white; rectangular	Robust, highly aromatic	In sandwiches; on crackers
Monterey (Jack)	United States	Semisoft; smooth, open texture	Creamy white wheels	Mild	As such; in sandwiches
Mozzarella (Pizza cheese)	Italy	Semisoft; plastic	Creamy white; rectangular and spherical	Mild, delicate	As such; in pizza and other cooked foods
Muenster	Germany	Semisoft; smooth, waxy body	Yellow tan or white surface, creamy white interior; small wheels and blocks	Mild to mellow, between Brick and Limburger	As such; in sandwiches
Neufchatel	France	Soft; smooth, creamy	White; foil-wrapped in rectangular retail portions	Mild	As such; in sandwiches; in dips; in salads
Parmesan (Reggiano)	Italy	Hard grating; granular, brittle body	Light yellow with brown or black coatings; cylindrical	Sharp, piquant	As such; as seasoning (grated)
Port du Salut (Oka)	Trappist Monks, France, Canada	Semisoft; smooth buttery	Russet surface, creamy yellow interior; small wheels	Mellow to robust, between Cheddar and Limburger	As such (dessert); with fresh fruit
Primost	Norway	Semisoft	Light brown; cubical and cylindrical	Mild, sweetish, caramel	As such, in cooked foods
Provolone	Italy	Hard; compact, flaky	Light golden-yellow to golden-brown, shiny surface bound with cord, yellowish-white interior; pear, sausage and salami shapes	Mild to sharp and piquant, usually smoked	As such; in cooked foods
Ricotta	Italy	Soft; moist and grainy, or dry	White; packaged fresh in paper, plastic or metal containers, or dry for grating	Bland but semisweet	As such; in cooked foods; as seasoning when dried
Roquefort	France	Semisoft; visible veins of mold, pasty and sometimes crumbly	White, marbled with blue-green mold; cylindrical	Sharp, spicy, piquant	As such (dessert); in salads; on crackers
Sap Sago	Switzerland	Hard grating; granular	Light green; small, cone-shaped	Flavored with clover leaves, sweetish	As such; as seasoning (grated)
Stilton	England	Semisoft; visible veins of mold, slightly more crumbly than Blue	White, marbled with blue-green mold; cylindrical	Piquant, spicy, but milder than Roquefort	As such (dessert); in cooked foods
Swiss	Switzerland	Hard; smooth, with large gas holes or eyes	Rindless blocks and large wheels with rind	Sweetish, nutlike	As such; in sandwiches; with salads

Fig. 4-9. Origin, characteristics, and mode of serving of commonly used natural cheeses. *(Courtesy of National Dairy Council)*

Soft

1. Ripened: Bel Paese, Brie, Camembert, Cooked, Hand, and Neufchatel (as made in France).
2. Unripened: Cottage, Pot, Bakers', Cream, Neufchatel (as made in the United States), Mysost, Primost, and fresh Ricotta.

Federal standards exist for a number of types of cheese, and grades have been developed for cheddar cheese and Swiss cheese. The grades for cheddar cheese are U.S. Grade AA, U.S. Grade A, U.S. Grade B, and U.S. Grade C. Swiss cheese grades are U.S. Grade A, U.S. Grade B, U.S. Grade C, and U.S. Grade D. Grading is based on flavor, body, and texture, and on the eye formation in the case of Swiss cheese. All graded cheese must be made in plants operating under the USDA regulations for sanitation and packing. In addition to Swiss and cheddar cheese, large quantities of processed cheese products are manufactured in plants under the USDA inspection.

Processed cheese is a mixture of natural cheddar cheeses blended with an emulsifier to keep the fat from separating out. Processed cheese is pasteurized to stop the curing action, and then it is poured into marketable-sized packages. The flavor of the processed cheese will vary according to the flavor of the original cheeses. Cheese food is similar to processed cheese, but it has added milk solids and other ingredients. The moisture content is often increased to give the product a spreading consistency.

To purchase the proper product, the food buyer should know the intended use of the cheese he buys. Some cheeses are interchangeable, others are not. The buyer should specify the type of cheese desired, the amount of aging desired, whether domestic or imported, and sometimes, the source of the milk (whether from cows, goats, or sheep). Except with processed cheese products, there is little standardization of package sizes. Some table cheeses are available in individually portioned packs.

Fresh Fruits and Vegetables

Specifications for fresh produce should include the grade, variety, size, packaging, and a statement of freshness. They may also include a requirement for partial preparation.

U.S. grades exist for practically all commonly used fresh fruits and vegetables, and some growing areas or states also have established grades for some specific commodities. U.S. Fancy and U.S. Nos. 1, 2, and 3 are the descriptions used by the USDA. Whatever the product, the grade selected should be suited to the intended use. The National Restaurant Association, the United Fresh Fruit and Vegetable Association, and the USDA all publish materials describing the various grade classifications of fresh fruits and vegetables, as well as other information of value to the food service buyer.

Specifications of variety or type is important and can affect the quality of the end product. Area of origin can also be important. For example, grapefruits may be pink or white, seeded or seedless. Different varieties of oranges are used for different purposes. Florida Valencias are usually used for juicing, whereas the California Navel and "Kid Glove" types make better table oranges. There are many varieties of apples—used in the food service in many different ways. Many types of onions and potatoes are marketed, and the food buyer must know the intended use in order to get the right kind.

Size is also related to the planned use of the produce. If a whole fruit or vegetable is to be served, the size selected directly affects the portion cost. When the fruit or vegetable is to be cut up, the size selected should produce the best yield as determined by kitchen tests. Size is usually expressed in number per case, with the smallest numbers indicating the largest size. Some commodities, such as asparagus, have names for the various sizes: colossal, jumbo, extra select. These names may vary from market to market, however.

Fresh produce is usually purchased by the carton, crate, or box; but for many products, there is little standardization of container size and fill. Figure 4–10 gives the approximate container net weights of the most commonly used containers for 99 commodities.

In addition to the grade classification, a statement of desired freshness should be included in any fresh fruit or vegetable specification. Because much deterioration can take place between the grading and the delivery to the final user, the buyer should specify that the produce must be up to the desired grade at the time of delivery. Wilted or decayed produce is seldom a bargain, regardless of the price. It may require several times the cost of the product in labor in order to trim deteriorated produce for use.

It may be more economical for food service operators to buy partially prepared produce than to have their own employees do the preparation. Pre-peeled potatoes, carrots, and onions are available in many market areas, and prepared lettuce and salad materials may also be available. Distributors dealing in large volumes can afford to use specialized machines to clean produce, and less bulk to transport reduces their delivery costs.

The best prices for fresh produce are usually obtained at the height of the season. Figure 4–11 shows the percentage of the crop coming to market in each month. Those products with fairly even year-round availability usually have the most stable prices.

COMMODITY	CONTAINERS	NET WEIGHT (lb)
Anise	Sturdee crt and wbd	40-50
	Crt.24	35-40
Apples	Ctn tray pk or cell pk	40-45
	Ctn blk	36-42
Apricots	Brentwood lug	24-26
	L A lug tight fill	27-30
Artichokes	7" deep ctn	20-25
Asparagus	Pyramid crt	32
	Ctn 16 1½ lb-pkgs	24
	2-lyr ctn	28-30
	1-lyr flat	14-18
Bananas	Ctn	20; 40
Beans, snap	Wbd crt	28-30
	Ctn	28-30
	Bu hmpr	28-30
Beets, bchd	Wbd crt 24 bchs	36-40
Beets, topped	Film or mesh bag	50
	1-lb bags in master	24
Berries (misc)	12 ½ pts on tray	5½-7½
Raspberries,		
Blackberries		
Blueberries	12-pt tray	11-12
Broccoli	Pony crt	40-42
	Ctn or crt 14 bchs	20-23
Brussels	Drum	25
sprouts	Flat 12 10-oz cups	7½-8
	Ctn	25
Cabbage	Crt or ctn	50-55
	Bag, mesh or paper	50-60
	Wbd crt	50
Cantaloupes	Jumbo crt 18-45	80-85
	Std crt	70-80
	Ctn 9, 12, 18, 23	38-41
Carrots, bchd	Ctn. 2-doz bchs	23-27
Carrots, topped	48 1-lb film bags in ctn	
	or wbd crt	50
	Bulk in mesh film lined bag	50
Casabas	Ctn 4, 5, 6	32-34
	Flat crt 5, 6	48-51
Cauliflower	Ctn 12-16 trimmed, wrpd	18-24
	Catskill or LI wbd crt	45-50
Celeriac	24 1-lb bags in master	24
	L A lug	30
	Sack	50
Celery, bchd	Fla wbd crt	55-60
	Calif wbd crate	60-65
Celery, hearts	12 film bags in ctn	24-28
	Wbd crts 24	30
Cherries	Calex lug	18-20
	Campbell lug	15-16
	Lug, loose pack	12-14
Chinese cabbage	Wbd crt	50
Coconuts	Burlap bag 40, 50	75-80
Sweet corn	Wbd crt	40-60
	Mesh or multiwall bag	45-50
Cranberries	Ctn 24 1-lb bags or boxes	24

COMMODITY	CONTAINERS	NET WEIGHT (lb)
Cranshaws	Ctn 4, 5, 6, 8	30-33
Cucumbers	1-1/9 bu wbd crt	55
	Bu bskt or ctn	47-55
	L A lug	28-32
	Ctn	26-30
Grnhouse	Ctn	8-10
Eggplant	Bu bskt or crt	30-34
	1-1/9 bu wbd crt	35
	L A lug 18-24	20-22
Endive-	Sturdee crt	30-36
Escarole	Wbd crt and ctn	30-36
	1-1/9 bu wbd crt	25-30
Figs	1-lyr tray	5-6
	2-lyr tray	10-15
Garlic	Crt and ctn	30
	Sack	50
	L A lug	20-22
Grapefruit,	4/5 bu ctn or wbd crt	42½
Fla	Bags 4, 5, 8, 20 lbs	
Grapefruit,	Ctn	32-33½
West	6 8-lb bags in master	48
Grapes, table	Lug or ctn	24-28
	Lug 16, 22, 24 wrpd bchs	22
Grapes, juice	Lug	36-44
Greens	Bu bskt or crt	20-25
Mustard	Bu bskt or crt	25
Turnip tops	Bu bskt or crt	25
Greens	1½- bu wbd crt	30-35
Honeydews	Ctn 4 or 5	29-32
	Flat crt	40-45
	Jumbo flat crt 6-8	45-50
Leeks	4/5 bu wbd crt	25-30
Lemons	Ctn	38
Lettuce,		
Bibb	12-qt bskt	5
Boston	Eastern crt 1-1/9 bu wbd	20-25
hothouse	Bskt (2 sizes)	5-10
Iceberg	Ctn	40-45
looseleaf	Var contrs 2-doz	20-25
Romaine	1-1/9 bu wbd crt	30
	Ctn 2-doz	35
	Bu bskt	25-28
Limes	Flat or ctn	10-11
	box or ctn	40-41
Mangoes	Flats var sizes	12-17
	Box or ctn	32-36
Mushrooms	Flat 12 4½-oz cups	4½-5
	Ctn 4 2½-lb bskts	10
	Ctn 8 2½-lb contrs	20-21
	4-qt bskt	3
	Var contrs of 1-lb ctns	*
Nectarines	Sanger lug or ctn 2-lyr	
	tray pk	19-22
	L A lug 2-lyr	22-29
	4-bskt crt	28-32

COMMODITY	CONTAINERS	NET WEIGHT (lb)	COMMODITY	CONTAINERS	NET WEIGHT (lb)
Okra	Bu bskt or crt	30	Prunes, fresh	NW prune lug	12; 15
	L A lug	18		½ bu bskt	28-30
	5/9 bu wbd flat	18	Pomegranates	Lug 2-lyr place pk	23-26
Onions, dry	Sack	50	Potatoes	Sack	100
	Ctn	48-50		Sack or ctn	50
	Film bags 1½, 2, 3, 5, 10-lb			5 10-lb sks baled	50
	in master contr	*		10 5-lb sks baled	50
Onions, green	Ctns 4-doz bchs	15-18	Radishes,	Ctn of 30 6-oz bags	11¼-11½
	Wbd crt 8-doz bchs	35-40	topped	Film bag, bulk	25
Oranges, Fla	4/5 bu ctn	45		12-qt bskt 30 6-oz bags	11¼-11½
	4/5 bu wbd box	45		Film bag, bulk	40
	Also 4, 5, 8, 20-lb consumer bags		bchd	Ctn or crt 4-5 doz bchs	30-40
Oranges,	Ctn	37½	Rhubarb	Case 10 5-lb ctns	50
West	8 5-lb film bags in			Ctn	20
	master contr	40		Western apple box	35
Oriental	L A lug	26-28	Spinach	Bu bskt or crt	18-25
vegetables	Wbd crt	20-22		Ctn 2-doz bchs	20-22
Papayas	Ctn	10		Wbd crt	20-22
Parsley	Bu bskt	21	Squash, small	Bu bskt or crt	40-45
	Ctn 5-doz bchs	21		1-1/9 bu wbd crt	44
	1-1/9 bu wbd crt 5-doz	21		½ bu wbd crt	21
Parsnips	Sack, film or mesh	50		Ctn or L A lug	24
	L A lug	30	Squash, large	Bulk bins, var sizes	900-2000
	Bu bskt	50	Strawberries	12 pt cups in tray	11-12
	Film bag	25	Sweet potatoes	Ctn	40
Peaches	½ bu wbd crt or ctn	23-28		Bu bskt or crt	50
	L A lug 2-lyr	22-29	Tangelos	Fla 4/5 bu ctn or wbd crt	45
	¾ bu ctn, wbd crt or bskt	35-42		Calif ctn	30
	Sanger lug 2-lyr	19-22	Tangerines	Fla 4/5 bu wbd crt	45
Pears	Western box, lug and			Calif ctn and lug	23-30
	tight-fill ctn	45-48		Fla ctn	30
	Ctn tight-fill	36	Tomatoes	Ctn or wbd crt	40
	L A lug or 2-lyr ctn	21-26		L A lug	30-34
Peas, green	Bu bskt or hmpr	28-30		Flats, ctns, 2-lyr	20-23
	Wbd bu crt	28-30		Lugs and ctns, 3-lyr	30-33
Peppers, chili	L A lug or ctn,			8-qt bskt	9-11
	loose pk	16-25		12-qt bskt	18-20
Peppers, sweet	Ctn	28-34	cherry	12 bskt tray	16-18
	1-1/9 bu crt	28-33	Topped root	Sack or bu bskt	50
	Bu bskt or crt	28-30	vegetables	Film or mesh bag	25
Persians	Ctn 4, 5, 6	*		L A lug	30
	Flat crt	35-50		1-lb bags, 24 per master	24
Persimmons	Lug 2-lyr tray pk	20-25	Turnips,	Sack	50
	Flat 1-lyr tray pk	9-12	topped	Mesh or film bag	24
Pineapples	Crt or ctn	35		L A lug	30
	1-lyr flat 4, 5, 6	18-20	bchd	Bu bskt or crt	29
	2-lyr flat 8, 10, 12	36-40	Watercress	Ctn 2-doz bchs	*
Plums	4-bskt crt	24-32	Watermelons	Var bulk bins	800-2000
	Sanger 2-lyr lug tray pk	18-22		Ctns 3, 4, 5	55-80
	L A lug or ctn loose	26-30			

Abbreviations: *weight not available; bchd bunched; bskt basket; bu bushel; crt crate; ctn carton; contr container; hmpr hamper; L A Los Angeles; lb pound; lyr layer; oz ounce; pk pack; pkg package; pt pint; sk sack; std standard; var various; wbd wirebound; wrpd wrapped.

Fig. 4-10. Container net weights for fresh fruits and vegetables. *(Courtesy of United Fresh Fruit and Vegetable Association)*

COMMODITY	% Jan	% Feb	% Mar	% Apr	% May	% June	% July	% Aug	% Sept	% Oct	% Nov	% Dec
Apples	11	10	10	8	6	3	2	3	10	15	11	11
Apricots					5	62	31	2				9
Avocados	11	11	11	11	9	7	6	6	5	6	8	8
Bananas	7	8	9	9	10	10	8	8	7	8	8	8
Blackberries					13	56	19	12				
Blueberries					2	32	39	23	4			
Cantaloupes	*	1	1	3	8	24	24	22	12	4	1	
Casabas						1	5	16	29	29	18	2
Cherries	*				14	39	42	4				1
Coconuts	8	6	8	5	3	3	4	4	11	14	18	16
Cranberries	1	1							6	21	49	22
Crenshaws				*	3	8	17	27	27	15	2	*
Figs, Fresh					1	15	8	29	24	19	4	*
Grapefruit	12	12	13	12	10	6	3	2	2	8	10	10
Grapes	3	3	3	3	2	6	10	18	19	15	11	7
Honeydews	2	5	7	6	3	7	14	22	21	12	1	*
Lemons	7	6	7	8	10	11	11	10	8	7	7	8
Limes	6	4	4	4	6	15	16	13	10	7	6	9

COMMODITY	% Jan	% Feb	% Mar	% Apr	% May	% June	% July	% Aug	% Sept	% Oct	% Nov	% Dec
Mangoes				2	19	39	29	10	1			
Nectarines		5				16	35	34	8			
Oranges, all	12	11	11	10	9	7	5	5	5	6	8	11
Oranges, West	9	9	10	10	9	7	7	7	7	8	6	11
Oranges, Fla.	15	15	14	11	10	6	2	1	*	3	10	13
Peaches	*	*	*		2	26	31	27	13	1		
Pears	6	6	7	6	4	1	6	15	16	15	10	8
Persians					*	5	15	29	31	19	1	*
Persimmons	1								2	41	39	17
Pineapples	8	9	12	14	15	17	7	4	2	3	4	5
Plums-Prunes	1	1	1		2	18	25	25	24	3		
Pomegranates									20	63	15	2
Raspberries					1	21	55	5	6	7	4	1
Strawberries	1	2	5	15	31	26	10	5	3	1	*	*
Tangelos	10									7	46	37
Tangerines	24	8	3	1							20	44
Watermelons		*	1	2	11	27	33	21	5	*		

*Less than 0.5 of 1% of annual total.
The table is based on unloads of fresh fruits in 41 cities as reported by the U. S. Department of Agriculture, and on import figures.

COMMODITY	Jan %	Feb %	Mar %	Apr %	May %	June %	July %	Aug %	Sept %	Oct %	Nov %	Dec %
Artichokes	6	7	12	23	15	5	4	3	4	6	9	8
Asparagus	*	2	20	33	28	15	1	*	*	1	*	*
Beans, Snap	5	5	6	8	9	13	12	11	10	8	7	6
Beets	4	4	5	5	7	13	15	13	12	11	7	4
Broccoli	10	10	12	11	9	5	4	3	6	10	11	9
Brussels Sprouts	14	9	5	2	1	1	1	2	11	19	20	16
Cabbage	9	8	10	9	9	10	8	7	8	8	8	8
Carrots	10	8	10	9	8	8	8	7	8	8	8	8
Cauliflower	9	7	7	7	5	5	4	5	11	19	14	8
Celery	9	8	9	9	8	7	7	7	8	9	10	9
Chinese Cabbage	9	8	7	6	8	8	9	11	9	10	11	10
Corn, Sweet	1	1	2	6	15	16	20	18	11	4	3	2
Cucumbers	4	4	5	9	12	14	14	10	8	8	8	6
Eggplant	8	6	7	8	7	8	9	12	12	8	8	8
Escarole-Endive	7	7	9	8	7	9	9	9	9	10	8	7
Endive, Belgian	5	15	15	14	11	4			4	10	9	15
Greens (misc.)	10	10	11	11	8	7	6	6	6	8	8	10
Mushrooms	10	9	10	10	8	7	5	5	6	8	10	11
Okra	*	*	1	4	11	19	23	21	12	7	3	1
Onions, dry, all	8	7	8	9	9	10	9	8	9	8	8	8
Onions, dry, Texas	*	*	6	32	30	14	11	6	1	*	*	*

COMMODITY	Jan %	Feb %	Mar %	Apr %	May %	June %	July %	Aug %	Sept %	Oct %	Nov %	Dec %
Onions, dry, New York	10	9	10	6	2	1	2	12	14	13	11	11
Onions, dry, California	2	2	1	1	9	21	23	14	9	8	7	3
Onions, Green	6	6	8	10	10	11	11	10	8	7	7	7
Parsley and Herbs	6	6	8	8	7	8	8	8	8	10	13	11
Parsnips	13	11	11	9	6	5	3	3	8	14	11	9
Peas, Green	7	8	9	15	13	15	13	9	5	3	2	2
Peppers, Sweet	7	6	7	7	8	10	10	10	10	9	9	7
Potatoes, All	9	7	9	9	9	9	8	8	8	8	8	8
Potatoes, California	4	4	4	3	10	26	24	11	5	3	3	4
Potatoes, Maine	11	11	16	19	16	9	2	*	*	1	5	9
Potatoes, Idaho	14	12	14	14	9	2	*	2	3	8	12	12
Radishes	6	6	8	9	11	12	11	9	8	7	7	7
Rhubarb	6	12	15	22	27	13	3	1	*	*	*	1
Spinach	9	8	10	10	8	8	6	5	7	9	9	8
Squash	7	5	6	7	8	9	10	9	10	11	11	8
Sweetpotatoes	9	8	9	7	4	2	3	6	10	12	17	13
Tomatoes, All	6	6	8	8	11	11	12	10	8	8	6	6
Tomatoes, Florida	12	10	14	16	23	8	*				4	13
Tomatoes, California	2	1	*	*	2	8	19	17	16	19	12	4
Tomatoes, Mexico	13	20	24	22	13	3	*	*	*	*	1	4
Turnips-Rutabagas	12	11	10	6	4	4	4	4	9	12	13	11

*Less than 0.5 of 1% of annual total
The table is based on unloads of vegetables in 41 cities in 1963-65 inclusive as reported by the U. S. Department of Agriculture.

Fig. 4-11. Monthly availability of fruits and vegetables expressed as a percentage of total annual supply.

Processed Fruits and Vegetables

Processed fruits and vegetables include canned and frozen products, dried or dehydrated fruits, and fluid, concentrated, or dehydrated juices. Fruit jelly and preserves are also included. Standards for these products are available from the Processed Products Standardization and Inspection Branch, Fruit and Vegetable Division, Agricultural Marketing Services, United States Department of Agriculture.

Specifications for canned fruits and vegetables should be written precisely, using the proper terminology. Considerable information may be required in order for the purveyors to identify exactly what is being requested. The following types of information should be included in a properly written canned fruit or vegetable specification:

1. *Proper Identification of the Product Required.* Federal standards of identity exist for most processed fruits and vegetables. The product desired can be automatically identified by the established name.
2. *Style.* Style refers to cut or shape, such as pineapple rings or chunks, mushroom caps or stems and pieces. Style also refers to characteristics of specified products, such as cream-style corn vs. whole-kernel corn.
3. *Size or Count.* Size frequently is expressed as number of pieces (such as peaches) per can or container, 30/35 meaning that there are 30 to 35 pieces in the can. Size for items such as peas may be expressed in terms of sieve size.
4. *Packing Medium, Density.* Fruits may be packed in water, or in sugar syrups of varying density, labeled light, medium, heavy, or extra heavy syrup. The intended use of the product will determine the desired density. Syrup density or sugar can be expressed in degrees Brix, for more exact definition of the product. The packing medium for vegetables may also be specified, such as olives in olive oil, or tomatoes in tomato juice. "Solid pack" has no added liquid.
5. *Specific Gravity.* Specific gravity should be specified for such products as tomato purée or tomato catsup.
6. *Variety or Type.* Variety refers to different types of fruits or vegetables within the generic class. Examples are Yellow Cling and Elberta Freestone Peaches, Italian Plum Tomatoes, and Round Regular Tomatoes.
7. *Source of Growing Area.* Some growing areas may produce a type or quality of commodity with special characteristics. For example, California tomato juice, or Hawaiian pineapple.
8. *Can Size and Pack.* The pack desired, whether it be cans,

glass or plastic jars, or packages, should be specified. Commonly used can sizes are shown in Fig. 4–12.

9. *Grade.* The basic USDA grades for canned fruits and vegetables are shown below:

> *U.S. Grade A—Fancy*—Excellent high quality foods. Practically uniform in size and very symmetrical. Practically perfect in every respect, color and texture. Succulent, tender. Represents the best of the crop. Fruits are usually packed in extra heavy syrup.
>
> *U.S. Grade B—Choice—Fruits; Extra Standard—Vegetables*—High quality foods, reasonably uniform in size. Reasonably good color and texture. Reasonably free from defects. Fruits are usually packed in heavy syrup.
>
> *U.S. Grade C—Standard*—Fairly good to good quality foods. Fairly uniform in size, color, and texture. Fairly free from defects. Fruits are usually packed in light syrup.
>
> *U.S. Grade D—Substandard*—Products that fail to meet the requirements of Grade C or the standard of quality outlined under the Pure Food and Drug Law.

10. *Point Score.* USDA grades are assigned on the basis of points. If a more precise statement of quality is desired than is indicated by the letter grades, then the minimum point score that is acceptable can be stated.

11. *Drained Weight.* The drained weight is the weight of the product after it has drained for two minutes. The procedure must be carried out in a prescribed manner, using specified types of sieves. Certain minimum drained weights are recommended in government standards, but drained weight is not a factor in determining grade.

12. *Brand.* In some cases, national brands are specified. However, the brand name itself is no guarantee of the desired quality or characteristics, although packing houses do try to maintain consistent quality in their advertised brands. National or advertised brands usually carry a higher price than private label merchandise. Frequently, merchandise of identical quality may be packed under a number of labels, including the nationally advertised brands. Therefore, the buyer should not limit himself to specifying by brand. He should state the desired characteristics of the product, and brand may be included, but the phrase "or equivalent" should be included to permit the purchase of comparable but lower priced private label merchandise.

The labels of cans or jars of identical size may show a net weight for one product that differs slightly from the net weight on the label of another product, due to the difference in the density of the food. An example would be pork and beans (1 lb.), blueberries (14 oz.), in the same size can.

Container			Products
Industry Term	Consumer Description		
	Approximate Net Weight (check label)	Approximate Cups	
8 ounce	8 oz.	1	Fruits, vegetables, *specialties
Picnic	10½ to 12 oz.	1¼	Condensed soups, small quantities of fruits, vegetables, meat and fish products, *specialties
12 oz. (vacuum)	12 oz.	1½	Used largely for vacuum packed corn
No. 300	14 to 16 oz.	1¾	Pork and beans, baked beans, meat products, cranberry sauce, blueberries, *specialties
No. 303	16 to 17 oz.	2	Fruits, vegetables, meat products, ready-to-serve soups, *specialties
No. 2	1 lb. 4 oz. or 1 pt. 2 fl. oz.	2½	Juices, ready-to-serve soups, *specialties, and a few fruits and vegetables

No. 2½	1 lb. 13 oz.	3½	Fruits, some vegetables (pumpkin, sauerkraut, spinach and other greens, tomatoes)
No. 3 Cyl.	3 lb. 3 oz. or 1 qt. 14 fl. oz.	5¾	Fruit and vegetable juices, pork and beans, condensed soup and some vegetables for institutional use
No. 10	6½ lb. to 7 lb. 5 oz.	12–13	Fruits, vegetables for restaurant and institutional use

*SPECIALTIES: Usually a food combination such as macaroni, spaghetti, Spanish style rice, Mexican type foods, Chinese foods, tomato aspic, etc.

SUBSTITUTING ONE CAN FOR ANOTHER SIZE—for institutional use

Approx.

1 No. 10 can equals.........7 No. 303 (1 lb.) cans
1 No. 10 can equals.........5 No. 2 (1 lb. 4 oz.) cans
1 No. 10 can equals.........4 No. 2½ (1 lb. 13 oz.) cans
1 No. 10 can equals.........2 No. 3 Cyl. (46 to 50 oz.) cans

HOME ECONOMICS—CONSUMER SERVICES
NATIONAL CANNERS ASSOCIATION

Fig. 4-12. Common container sizes. (Courtesy National Canners Association)

The following are several examples of well-written canned food specifications:

Cherries, 6/10 Dark, Sweet Bing, Pitted: U.S. Grade B (Choice); score: 80 or better; 275–300 count; in heavy syrup; Pacific Northwest Pack.

Peaches, 6/10 Yellow Cling Halves: U.S. Grade B (Choice); score: 80 or better; in heavy syrup; 30–35 count. Pie Peaches, Yellow Cling Slices: U.S. Grade C (Standard); score: 70 or better; solid pack, preheated.

Beets, Whole, 6/10 U.S. Grade A (Fancy); score 85 or better. Northwest Pack . . . #1 size—250/over count—M.D.W.*69 oz.

Tomatoes, 6/10 U.S. Grade B (Extra Standard); score 80 or better; drained weight 70 oz. minimum; California Pack, Plum Tomatoes (Italian style).

Tomato Puree, 6/10 U.S. Grade A (Fancy); score 90 or better; meet U.S. Standards for fill of container; California Pack. 1.07 Specific Gravity; Extra heavy concentration.

Frozen Foods

Frozen foods can cover a wide range from fully prepared convenience goods to raw, trimmed vegetables (see Fig. 4–13). All frozen foods should be maintained and delivered in a solidly frozen state. Frost or freezer burn is an indication of thawing and/or poor packaging and is reason to reject the merchandise. (Freezer burn is indicated by a dry white surface and is caused by dehydration of the surface tissues or cells).

Other Groceries

Herbs and Spices

Herbs and spices should be bought on the basis of strength, quality of flavor, and good color. Imitation spices should be checked carefully for strength of flavor. Herbs and spices should be purchased in small quantities because they tend to loose their aroma and flavor if stored too long. Some newer flavorings on the market are dehydrated vegetable seasonings such as onion, garlic, sweet pepper, celery, mint, and parsley flakes. These products can save considerable labor in the kitchen. Herb and spice specifications should include the form desired, such as whole, leaf, ground, or cracked.

---

*Minimum drained weight.

Extracts

Extracts are aromatic flavorings usually dissolved in some type of solvent, such as water or alcohol. Vanilla is the most commonly used extract, and it can be either pure, coming from natural sources, or imitation, being derived chemically in a laboratory. The chemical structure of the flavoring material is the same, regardless of the source. Like herbs and spices, extracts lose their flavor if stored too long, and should only be purchased in small amounts.

Flour

There are many types of flour available, and the buyer should specify the right flour for the intended use. Wheat flours are classified as "hard" to "soft," depending on the protein content. A soft or low protein flour produces a weak cellular structure and a tender crumb more suitable to cakes, whereas a hard flour is more suited to breads. A food service operation with a full bakery may require three or more types of flour: bread, cake and pastry flour, as well as some of the specialty flours such as cracked wheat or rye. Wheat flours are usually marketed in 100-pound bags.

Dried Vegetables: Peas, Beans, Lentils, and Rice

Nearly all peas and lentils and about one third of all the beans are officially inspected, but they are not usually graded. Federal and state grades do exist, however. Federal grades are based on shape, size, color, damage, and foreign material. There are special "hand-picked" grades for dried beans. They are U.S. Choice Handpicked, U.S. No. 1 Handpicked, U.S. No. 2 Handpicked, and U.S. No. 3 Handpicked. In other than handpicked grades, the grades for beans are simply numerical. Grades for dry peas and lentils are also numerical: U.S. Nos. 1, 2, and 3. Lima beans may be graded U.S. Extra No. 1.

Dried peas, both yellow and green, are usually marketed split, but whole peas are available. Dried black-eye peas are also available. The variety of bean should also be specified such as red, kidney, pea, navy, or lima. Dried lima beans are also bought according to size. Dried peas, beans, and lentils are marketed in one-pound packages, usually packed 24 to the case, and in 25- and 100-pound bags.

Standards for dried peas, beans, and lentils are available from the Grain Division, USDA's Marketing Service.

Rice may be graded on the basis of the presence of defective kernels (broken or damaged), mixed varieties that may affect cooking qualities, and objectionable foreign material. General appearance and color are also considered in grading milled (white) rice. There are six numerical grades for milled rice and four for brown rice.

	Sizes, Styles or Types	Package Size	Grades (U.S.)[1]	Remarks
Apples	Unsugared Sugared, with proportions of 5:1 or 7:1 Sliced, Diced	5,10,15,25 and 30 lb. cans Drained Weight of a 30 lb. Can: 5:1 mix – 20-23 lb. 7:1 mix – 21-25 lb. Unsugared – 26-28 lb.	A or Fancy C or Standard Substandard	May be soaked in brine or sulphur dip solution in processing. The process can effect the end product, depending on use.
Apricots	Unsugared Sugared, 5:1 or 7:1 Hand pitted preferred for dessert use	2-1/2, 5, 8-1/2, 10, 15, 30 and 32 lb cans	A or Fancy B or Choice C or Standard Substandard	Count: About 14 halves per lb. Ascorbic acid added to prevent browning.
Berries: Blackberries Boysenberries Dewberries Loganberries Youngberries and similar types	IQF (individually quick frozen) no sugar Sugared	10, 15, 20, 25, 28 and 30 lb. cans	A or Fancy B or Choice Substandard	

(1) Note: Grades expressed as U.S. Grade A or U.S. Fancy, except that products which fail to meet the requirements of the lowest grade classification are graded "substandard". The substandard classification was formerly known as U.S. Grade D.

	Sizes, Styles or Types	Package Size	Grades (U.S.)	Remarks
Blueberries	Small, wild or large, cultivated, mostly IQF, unsweetened	2-1/2, 5, 10, 20, 22 and 30 lb. cans	A or Fancy B or Choice C or Standard Substandard	Usually packed with added sugar - 5:1 ratio.
Cherries, R.S.P. (Red, Sour, Pitted)	Montmorency preferred for color	30 lb. cans, also 2-1/2, 6, 10 and 15 lb. cans. Drained weight of a 30 lb. can: 22-23 lbs. for high quality fruit	A or Fancy C or Standard Substandard	
Cherries, Sweet	Types: Light sweet, such as Royal Ann Dark sweet, such as Bing Styles: Pitted or unpitted		A or Fancy B or Choice Substandard	
Cranberries	IQF	1 lb. container, 24 lb. cases, 25 lb. cans	A or Fancy B or Choice C or Standard Substandard	
Grapefruit Sections	Pink or White	2, 2-1/2, 4 lb., also 6 and 15 lbs. Drained weight of 2 lb. package - 18-1/2 to 20 oz.	A or Fancy B or Choice Broken Substandard	Counts vary - 16-20 sections per lb. Usually packed without added sugar.

Fig. 4-13. Purchasing data for frozen fruits and juices.

	Sizes, Styles or Types	Package Size	Grades (U.S.)	Remarks
Melon Balls	Types: Cantaloupe – entirely Honeydew – entirely Mixed – Honeydew and Cantaloupe in various proportions Other types of melons used singly or in combinations	8 lb. cans, 48 lb. case	A or Fancy B or Choice Substandard	Ascorbic acid usually added to prevent oxidation (browning).
Peaches	Mostly Freestone types – such as Elbertas Halves, counts per 8-1/2 lb. can: 15/20, 20/25, 26/30 Slices Sugar or syrup added (syrup preferred) Ratios: 4:1 or 5:1	2-1/2, 8-1/2, 10, 15, 30 and 32 lb. cans Drained weight of 30 lb.can 4:1 or 5:1 syrup packed: 20-21 lbs. for high quality fruit	A or Fancy B or Choice C or Standard Substandard	
Pineapple	Styles: Whole slices, half slices Broken slices, crushed Tidbits, chunks Sugared – 5:1	6-1/2 lb. cans 33 lb. cases	A or Fancy B or Choice C or Standard Substandard	
Plums	Styles: Halved, whole pitted, crushed and broken Color Types: Purple or blue, red, yellow-green		A or Fancy B or Choice Substandard	

	Sizes, Styles or Types	Package Size	Grades (U.S.)[1]	Remarks
Raspberries	IQF, unsugared Sugar or syrup added 4:1 Red, purple or black (purple usually classed with red raspberries)	2-1/2, 10, 15, 25, 28 and 30 lb. cans	A or Fancy B or Choice Substandard	Frozen pack is almost all pink.
Rhubarb	Pink or Green Field Grown or Hothouse IQF or Sweetened	2-1/2 lb. carton, 30 lb. can Also 6 lb., 10 lb., 15 lb., 20 lb. and 24 lb. tins	A or Fancy B or Choice Substandard	
Strawberries	Whole or Sliced IQF or sweetened Sugar ratios - 3:1 or 4:1	Sliced: 6-1/2, 10, 28, 30 lb. containers Whole: 10, 20, 25, 30 lb. containers IQF: 15, 20, 25, 30 lb. containers	A or Fancy B or Choice C or Standard Substandard	
Juices:				
Orange Juice Concentrate	Styles: Without sweetener, with sweetener added	6,18,32 and 46 oz. cans	A or Fancy B or Choice Substandard	
Grapefruit Juice Concentrate	Styles: Without sweetener, with sweetener added	6,18,32 and 46 oz. cans	A or Fancy B or Choice Substandard	
Lemonade Concentrate Limeade Concentrate	Lemonade, Pink Lemonade	6,18,32 and 46 oz. cans	A or Fancy B or Choice Substandard	

Fig. 4-13. Purchasing data for frozen fruits and juices (Cont'd).

Source: United States Department of Agriculture National Frozen Food Association

	Sizes, Styles or Types	Package Size	Grades (U.S.)[1]

Asparagus	All Green
	Green and White
	-
	Spears or Stalks
	Tips
	Cuts and Tips
	Center Cuts (no tips)
	
	Stalk Sizes for Spears:
	  Small: Less than 3/8" in diameter - up to 125 stalks per carton
	  Medium: 3/8" to 5/8" in diameter - 70 to 90 stalks per carton
	  Jumbo: 5/8" to 7/8" in diameter - 40 to 60 stalks per carton
	  Colossal or Extra Large: Larger than 7/8" in diameter - 30 to 35 stalks per carton
		30 or 24 lb. cases
		2-1/2 or 2 lb. cartons
			A or Fancy
			B or Extra Standard
			Substandard

Beans, Green, Snap or Wax	Regular Cut, Shortcut French Cut, Julienne or Shoestring Whole Beans Mixed Cuts Round or Flat (Italian)	24 or 30 lb. cases 2 or 2-1/2 lb. cartons 20 lb. bulk pack cases	A or Fancy B or Extra Standard C or Standard Substandard
Beans, Lima	Thin Seeded Thick Seeded Baby Potato such as Baby Ford Hook Thick Seeded - such as Food Hook	30 lb. cases 2-1/2 lb. cartons 20 lb. bulk pack cases	A or Fancy B or Extra Standard C or Standard Substandard
Speckled Butter (Lima) Beans			A or Fancy B or Extra Standard Substandard
Corn, Whole Kernel (or Whole Grain)	Yellow or Golden White	30 lb. case 2-1/2 lb. carton 20 lb. bulk pack case	A or Fancy B or Extra Standard C or Standard Substandard
Corn, Cream Style			
Corn on the Cob	Trimmed or Natural Regular (over 3-1/2" in length), or Short Golden (yellow) or White	Carton of 4 dozen	A or Fancy B or Extra Standard Substandard
Broccoli	Spears or Stalks Short Spears or Florets Cuts Chopped Pieces	24 or 30 lb. cases 2 or 2-1/2 lb. cartons	A or Fancy B or Extra Standard Substandard

(1) Note: Grades expressed as U.S. Grade A or U.S. Fancy, except that products which fail to meet the requirements of the lowest grade classification are graded "Substandard". The Substandard classification was formerly known as U.S. Grade D.

	Sizes, Styles or Types	Package Size	Grades (U.S.)
Brussels Sprouts	Average Count per 2 lb. Carton: Small: 90-110, Medium: 60-85, Large: 40-60	24 or 30 lb. cases 2 or 2-1/2 lb. cartons	A or Fancy B or Extra Standard C or Standard Substandard
Cauliflower		24 lb. cases 2 lb. cartons	A or Fancy B or Extra Standard Substandard
Carrots	Whole, Whole Baby, Halves Quarters, Slices, Dices, Double Dices, Strips, Chips, Cuts, Crinkle Cuts	24 lb. cases 2 lb. cartons	A or Fancy B or Extra Standard Substandard
Leafy Greens (other than Spinach): Beet, Collards, Dandelion, Endive, Kale, Mustard, Swiss Chard, Turnip, Greens	Whole Leaf, Sliced Leaf, Cut or Chopped	36 lb. cases 3 lb. cartons	A or Fancy B or Extra Standard Substandard
Mixed Vegetables	Composed of: Snap Beans, Green or Wax Carrots, Whole Kernel Corn, Early or Sweet Peas, Limas. Proportions can vary widely depending on price.	30 lb. case 2-1/2 lb. cartons 20 lb. bulk pack case	
Okra	Whole, Cut		A or Fancy B or Extra Standard Substandard
Onion Rings, Breaded	French Fried (pre-cooked) or Raw Breaded		A or Fancy B or Extra Standard Substandard
Peas	Early or Sweet, Petit Pois	30 lb. cases 2-1/2 lb. cartons 20 lb. bulk pack cases	A or Fancy B or Extra Standard C or Standard Substandard
Peas and Carrots	Peas not less than 50% by weight, Carrots not less than 25% by weight	30 lb. cases 2-1/2 lb. cartons	A or Fancy B or Extra Standard C or Standard Substandard
Peas, Blackeyed or Field	Types: Black-eye, Crowder, Cream, Lady Creme, Field Peas with Snaps	36 lb. cases 3 lb. cartons	A or Fancy B or Extra Standard Substandard
Peppers, Sweet	Green, Red, Mixed Red and Green Whole Stemmed or Whole Unstemmed, Halves, Sliced and Diced	2 or 2-1/2 lb. cartons 24 or 30 lb. cases	A or Fancy B or Extra Standard Substandard

Fig. 4-14. Purchasing data for frozen vegetables.

	Sizes, Styles or Types	Package Size	Grades (U.S.)

Potatoes, French Fried	Straight Cut or Crinkle Cut
	
	Strips - Such as:
	  Shoestring - 1/4" x 1/4"
	  Thin cut - 5/16" x 9/32"
	  Regular cut - 3/8" x 3/8"
	  Steakhouse - 3/8" x 3/4"
	
	Slices - Includes Outside Pieces
	Dices
	Rissole - Whole or Nearly Whole
	Other - Any other individually
	  frozen French fried potato
	  product
	
	Length Designations (applies to
	strips only):
	  Extra Long: 80% are 2" in
	    length or longer
	    30% are 3" in length or longer
	  Long: 70% are 2" in length or
	    longer - 15% are 3" in length
	    or longer
	  Medium: 50% are 2" in length
	    or longer
	  Short: Less than 50% are 2 inches
	    in length or longer
	
	Institutional Type - to be cooked
	  in deep fat
	
	Retail Type - to be reheated in the
	  oven (completely cooked)
			A or Fancy
			B or Extra Standard
			Substandard

Spinach	Whole Leaf Chopped Cut Leaf or Sliced	30 or 36 lb. cartons 2-1/2 or 3 lb. cartons	A or Fancy B or Extra Standard Substandard
Summer Squash	Sliced, Cut Yellow or Zucchini	36 lb. cases 3 lb. cartons, 5 lb. cartons	A Fancy B
Winter Squash, Cooked	Butternut, Hubbard Puree	48 lb. cases 4 lb. cartons	A or Fancy B or Extra Standard Substandard
Succotash	Corn, White or Golden Lima Beans, Fresh - not dried Soy Beans, Vegetable Green or Wax Beans	30 lb. cases 2-1/2 lb. cartons	A Fancy B C
Turnip Greens with Turnips	Proportions vary - from 50/50% to 80/20%. Most common - 67% greens, 33% turnips. Layer Packed or Mixed		

Source: United States Department of Agriculture National Frozen Food Association

Convenience Foods

Convenience foods are usually described as food products that have gone through one or more processing steps before reaching the food service operation. They may be completely prepared and ready for service; they may require only minor finishing, such as reheating or portioning; or they may be ingredients that have had some preliminary processing and are used in combination with other ingredients in the normal preparation of the item.

Some manufacturers express this diversity of processing states as the "Raw-to-Ready Scale." The food service operator must decide at what point on the raw-to-ready scale he wants to buy his food materials. The decision may be based on the amount of equipment available, the amount and skills of the labor available, the amount of storage space available, and the desired food and payroll costs for the operation. Availability of the various types of products may also be a factor.

Convenience foods are not necessarily all frozen, although a great many of the products are. They may also be chilled, canned, fresh or dried. They may also be in the form of packaged mixes.

Purchase Specifications for Convenience Foods

Because of the wide diversity of states of processing, preserving, and packaging, it is difficult to generalize about convenience food specifications. Few quality standards exist, although the USDA has established product requirements for a number of processed meat and poultry items.

Furthermore, in many fully processed products, it is difficult for the layman to judge whether or not a complex processing formula has been followed. It may be necessary to use a testing laboratory to measure such things as fat content in ground meat or butterfat in ice cream, or to test for bacterial content.

The following are some qualifying statements that may apply to different kinds of convenience foods:

1. Portion size, when the product is preportioned. There is a wide range of preportioned raw meats available, either fresh or frozen, and branch houses can usually cut any special size portion. Prepared preportioned entrées do not have the wide range of portion sizes available.
2. Packaging material. The package must protect the product in transit and in storage. In the case of frozen prepared foods, the package is often used for reheating and serving the product. The packaging material must withstand temperatures from below 0°F to as high as 400°F without cracking or react-

ing chemically with the contents. If the package is also the serving dish, it must be aesthetically pleasing.

3. The size of the package will affect the reconstitution techniques. For reheating, the thickness of the mass being heated influences the heating time. Furthermore, the nature of the operation may require a specification for individually packaged portions, bulk package or both.

4. To maintain the safety of the product, certain maximum levels of bacterial content may be specified. If federal identity standards are available for a specific product, they may include limitations of bacterial content.

5. The proportion of ingredients in a mixture and the size and shape of pieces may be specified. These may also be defined in federal standards. The percentage of breading should be specified for breaded items.

6. Adequate instructions should be included for reconstituting the product, preferably for several different kinds of equipment.

7. Requirements may be included as to the condition of the product in transit and when delivered. This is particularly pertinent to frozen products, because their quality can deteriorate rapidly if they are exposed to temperature variations.

8. Conditions may be included to reject products broken or damaged in transit, even though frozen products may not be thawed.

Because of the complexities of specifying convenience foods, some food service operators merely specify the brand name and package size, based on tests performed by the food processing operation. This may be sufficient if the manufacturer has a good quality control program. It does not protect the operator from deterioration of the product while it is in transit.

Some food service operators contract with processing plants to manufacture custom products to their specifications. Others manufacture their own convenience products in slack time, then freeze them or operate a separate commissary operation. In the latter case, foods are specified in the raw unprocessed state, as before. When products are manufactured to custom specifications, detailed instructions and standards must be developed for each product.

Purchasing Methods

The following are the most widely used purchasing procedures.

Open Market Buying

Open market buying is used by the vast majority of all commercial operations. Quotations are requested from one or more purveyors, and after all elements of price, quality, yield, and service have been considered, orders are placed where the terms are best for the buyer.

Sealed Bid Purchasing

Sealed bid purchasing procedure is used almost exclusively by large hospitals, institutions, schools, and government agencies. Wants are advertised and sealed formal bids are returned by a stated date. This procedure is seldom used in commercial operations.

Futures and Contract Purchasing

The form of buying known as futures and contract purchasing consists of contracting for future delivery of food stocks that are now or will be available at a current or future price. This type of buying is most often done by large volume purchasing operations in a calculated attempt to ensure a supply at a favorable price. The buyer may take possession of the merchandise immediately and bear the storage costs himself, or he may take possession as the merchandise is needed, with the seller bearing the storage cost. For a very large multi-unit chain, the major advantage is in procuring a uniform product over a period of time and at a predetermined price. Contract buying is not recommended for smaller operations since they usually do not purchase sufficient quantities to obtain the lowest prices. In addition, investment charges, storage costs, losses, and balancing trends in price can quickly offset any cost saving.

Buying Routine

An established buying routine provides a framework for the mechanics of buying. Although the routine will vary to fit the needs of different establishments, it must always ensure the coordination of the purchasing, receiving, and preparation departments. The chef or kitchen manager must provide the necessary information to the food buyer in time for effective buying, and the buyer must furnish the proper merchandise.

Purchases of perishables should be scheduled to meet the requirements of the daily menus, not purchased on a par stock basis. Based on delivery schedules, raw food requirements usually should not be purchased for more than two to three delivery days hence. Refrigerators should be stocked with current menu items only. Buying to a hypothetical par stock leads to excessive inventories and is costly in the following ways:

1. It overloads the storage facilities. If storage was built to accommodate such buying practice, unwarranted expenditures have been made for oversized capacities.
2. It creates larger inventories, necessitating more attention, more handling, and higher labor costs.
3. It increases the loss from shrinkage, trim, spoilage, and pilferage.

The practice of having standing orders for any food, even for milk, cream, bread, or rolls, is generally satisfactory only when consumption is constant. In a commercial operation, the volume of business usually varies for the various days of the week, and orders should conform to the day's expected pattern of business.

Par stocks can usually be established for most grocery items to be carried in the storeroom. However, specialty items which may appear on the menu occasionally are better bought only when needed. The par stock levels selected should be sufficient to carry through from one regularly scheduled delivery to the next with a small safety margin. Orders for nonperishable merchandise should be grouped and placed for delivery on regularly scheduled days. Frequent deliveries with small orders are costly to the purveyor, who passes that cost on to the customer.

Determining the Amounts to Order

As was stated earlier, perishables and some grocery items should be purchased according to requirements. (The forecasting of sales and calculating purchase requirements is discussed in detail in Chapter 6.) The buyer must have this information well in advance of the time when the food is needed so that the purchasing function can proceed systematically. Having received the daily requirements, the purchaser must inventory his on-hand stock. The amount of inventory on hand is subtracted from what is needed to determine how much to buy.

Approved Vendor List

A list of vendors to be used should be drawn up and approved by management. Dealers who are unethical or who give poor service should be excluded from the list. Management can enforce the exclusion by notifying both the buyer and the dealer that any invoices from him presented for payment in the future will not be paid. No dealer likes an uncollectable account. This kind of restriction can help keep the food buyer from being overwhelmed with salesmen, since the policy was not made by him. If he feels a dealer should be added to the list, he can arrange an appointment with management.

The list of vendors also limits the number of purveyors to be used, thus making the purchasing, receiving, and accounts payable functions more manageable.

Getting and Comparing Bid Prices

When the buyer knows what he is going to buy and the amounts he needs, he obtains the price bids for each item from the various vendors daily or weekly. Some grocery purveyors issue price lists monthly and do not change prices without prior notification.

In the larger cities it is easy to obtain quotations from three dealers. In some smaller cities, however, this is not always possible. Sometimes there is only one dealer in town handling the requested item. Every effort should be made to get at least two quotations on each item.

Purchasing Records and Forms

Figures 4–13 and 4–14 show standard forms of purchasing records. The Daily Purchase List in Fig. 4–15 has columns for inventory on hand, the quantity wanted, and the quantity bought, as well as the previous price. The items must be written in, but forms can be printed which list the most frequently purchased items. The market quotation list in Fig. 4–16 is an example of this kind of form. With all the items printed on the form, the buyer is less likely to forget an item.

When the quotations have been entered on the purchasing form, the buyer indicates the purveyor selected by circling the lowest price. Depending on the size of the order, he may buy selected items from each purveyor at the lowest price bid, or he may give the entire order to the purveyor whose price is the lowest for the entire order.

Purchasing records are usually made out in duplicate or triplicate. The original is maintained by the buyer, and the first copy is given to the receiving clerk for checking in the deliveries. A second copy may be given to the food and beverage cost controller for checking the prices billed on the invoices against the bid prices.

When an electronic data processing system is used, the buyer is relieved of much of the manual preparation of purchasing and receiving forms. In addition, an automated system can provide management with information that would be far too costly to obtain manually. Examples are analyses of inventory turnover, product utilization and consumption, and price trends.

Price Versus Quality and Service

The basic premise behind competitive bid buying is that the merchandise will be bought from the lowest bidder. Some buyers, however, go through the whole process and then reject the lowest bidder because his quality or service is not as good as that of another purveyor. If there is a quality difference, then the purveyors are not bidding on the same merchandise, and the specifications should be reviewed. *(Text continues on page 117.)*

DAILY PURCHASE LIST

DATE_____

ARTICLE	UNIT	ON HAND	AMOUNT WANTED	AMOUNT BOUGHT	PURCHASED FROM AND PRICE						ORDER NO.	PHONED	REMARKS

Fig. 4-15. Daily purchase list.

ON HAND	ARTICLE	WANTED	QUOTATIONS				
	BEEF						
	Corned Beef						
	Corned Beef Brisket						
	Corned Beef Rump						
	Corned Beef Hash						
	Beef Chipped						
	Beef Breads						
	Butts						
	Chuck						
	Fillets						
	Hip Short						
	Hip Full						
	Kidneys						
	Livers						
	Loin, Short						
	Strip						
	Shell Strip						
	Ribs Beef						
	Shins						
	Suet, Beef						
	Tails, Ox						
	VEAL						
	Breast						
	Brains						
	Feet						
	Fore Quarters						
	Hind Quarters						
	Head						
	Kidneys						
	Legs						
	Liver						
	Loins						
	Racks						
	Saddles						
	Shoulder						
	Sweet Breads						
	MUTTON						
	Fore Quarters						
	Kidneys						
	Legs						
	Racks						
	Saddles						
	Saddles, Hind						
	Shoulder						
	Suet						
	LAMB						
	Breast						
	Fore Quarters						

Fig. 4-16. Steward's market quotation list.

ON HAND	ARTICLE	WANTED	QUOTATIONS			
	LAMB (Cont'd)					
	Feet					
	Fries					
	Kidneys					
	Loins					
	Legs					
	Lamb, Spring					
	Racks, Double					
	Racks, Spring					
	Saddles					
	Shoulder					
	PROVISIONS					
	Bacon					
	Bologna					
	Bologna					
	Crepinette					
	Salami					
	Hams, Corned					
	Hams, Fresh					
	Hams, Polish					
	Hams, Smoked					
	Hams, Virginia					
	Hams, Westphalia					
	Head Cheese					
	Lard					
	Lyon Sausage					
	Phil. Scrapple					
	Smoked Butts					
	Pig's Feet					
	Pig's Head, Corned					
	Pig's Knuckles, Fresh					
	Pig's Knuckles, Corned					
	Pig, Suckling					
	Pork, Fresh Loin					
	Pork, Larding					
	Pork, Spare Ribs					
	Pork, Salt Strip					
	Pork Tenderloin					
	Sausages, Country					
	Sausages, Frankfurter					
	Sausages, Meat					
	Shoulders, Fresh					
	Shoulders, Smoked					
	Shoulders, Corned					
	Tongues					
	Tongues, Beef Smoked					
	Tongues, Fresh					
	Tongues, Lambs					
	Tripe					

4-16. Steward's market quotation list (Cont'd).

ON HAND	ARTICLE	WANTED	QUOTATIONS			
	POULTRY					
	Chickens					
	Chickens, Roast					
	Chickens, Broilers					
	Chickens, Broilers					
	Chickens, Supreme					
	Cocks					
	Capons					
	Ducks					
	Ducklings					
	Fowl					
	Geese					
	Goslings					
	Guinea Hens					
	Guinea Squabs					
	Pigeons					
	Poussins					
	Squabs					
	Turkeys, Roasting					
	Turkeys, Boiling					
	Turkeys, Spring					
	GAME					
	Birds					
	Partridge					
	Pheasant, English					
	Rabbits					
	Quail					
	Venison, Saddles					
	SHELL FISH					
	Clams, Chowder					
	Clams, Cherrystone					
	Clams, Little Neck					
	Clams, Soft					
	Crabs, Hard					
	Crabs, Meat					
	Crabs, Oyster					
	Crabs, Soft Shell					
	Crabs, Soft Shell Prime					
	Lobsters, Meat					
	Lobsters, Tails					
	Lobsters, Chicken					
	Lobsters, Medium					
	Lobsters, Large					
	Oysters, Box					
	Oysters, Blue Points					
	Oysters					
	Scallops					
	Shrimps					
	Turtle					

Fig. 4-16. Steward's market quotation list (Cont'd.).

ON HAND	ARTICLE	WANTED	QUOTATIONS			
	FISH					
	Bass, Black					
	Bass, Sea					
	Bass, Striped					
	Blackfish					
	Bluefish					
	Bloaters					
	Butterfish					
	Carp					
	Codfish, Live					
	Codfish, Salt Boneless					
	Codfish, Salt Flake					
	Eels					
	Finnan Haddie					
	Flounders					
	Flounders					
	Flounders, Fillet					
	Fluke					
	Haddock					
	Haddock, Fillet					
	Haddock, Smoked					
	Halibut					
	Halibut, Chicken					
	Herring					
	Herring, Smoked					
	Herring, Kippered					
	Kingfish					
	Mackeral, Fresh					
	Mackeral, Salt					
	Mackeral, Spanish					
	Mackeral, Smoked					
	Perch					
	Pickerel					
	Pike					
	Porgies					
	Pompano					
	Redsnapper					
	Salmon, Fresh					
	Salmon, Smoked					
	Salmon, Nova Scotia					
	Scrod					
	Shad					
	Shad Roes					
	Smelts					
	Sole, English					
	Sole, Boston					
	Sole, Lemon					
	Sturgeon					
	Trout, Brook					
	Trout, Lake					
	Trout, Salmon					

Fig. 4-16. Steward's market quotation list (Cont'd.).

ON HAND	ARTICLE	WANTED	QUOTATIONS			
	FISH (Cont'd)					
	Weakfish					
	Whitebait					
	Whitefish					
	Whitefish, Smoked					
	VEGETABLES					
	Artichokes					
	Asparagus					
	Asparagus					
	Asparagus, Tips					
	Asparagus, Fancy					
	Beans					
	Beans, Lima					
	Beans, String					
	Beans, Wax					
	Beets					
	Beets, Tops					
	Broccoli					
	Brussels Sprouts					
	Cabbage					
	Cabbage, Red					
	Cabbage, New					
	Carrots					
	Carrots					
	Cauliflower					
	Celery					
	Celery Knobs					
	Chicory					
	Chives					
	Corn					
	Corn					
	Chervil					
	Cranberries					
	Cucumbers					
	Dandelion					
	Escarole					
	Endive					
	Estragon					
	Egg Plant					
	Garlic					
	Horseradish Roots					
	Kale					
	Kohlrabi					
	Lettuce					
	Lettuce, Ice Berg					
	Lettuce, Place					
	Leeks					
	Mint					
	Mushrooms					
	Mushrooms, Fresh					

Fig. 4-16. Steward's market quotation list (Cont'd.).

ON HAND	ARTICLE	WANTED	QUOTATIONS			
	VEGETABLES (Cont'd)					
	Okra					
	Onions					
	Onions, Yellow					
	Onions, Bermuda					
	Onions, Spanish					
	Onions, White					
	Onions, Scallions					
	Oyster Plant					
	Parsley					
	Parsnips					
	Peppermint					
	Peas, Green					
	Peas					
	Peas					
	Peppers, Green					
	Peppers, Red					
	Potatoes					
	Potatoes, Bermuda					
	Potatoes, Idaho					
	Potatoes, Idaho					
	Potatoes, Sweet					
	Potatoes, New					
	Potatoes, Yams					
	Pumpkins					
	Romaine					
	Radishes					
	Rhubarb, Fresh					
	Rhubarb, Hot House					
	Sage					
	Shallots					
	Sorrel					
	Sauerkraut					
	Spinach					
	Squash Crooked Neck					
	Squash Hubbard					
	Tarragon					
	Thyme					
	Tomatoes, New					
	Tomatoes, Hot House					
	Turnips, White					
	Turnips, Yellow					
	Turnips, New					
	Watercress					
	FRUIT					
	Apples, Cooking					
	Apples, Baking					
	Apples, Crab					
	Apples, Table					
	Apricots					

Fig. 4-16. Steward's market quotation list (Cont'd.).

ON HAND	ARTICLE	WANTED	QUOTATIONS		
	FRUIT (Cont'd)				
	Bananas				
	Blackberries				
	Blueberries				
	Blueberries				
	Blueberries				
	Cantaloupes				
	Cantaloupes				
	Honey Balls				
	Melons, Casaba				
	Melons, Honeydew				
	Melons, Persian				
	Melons, Spanish				
	Cherries				
	Cherries				
	Cherries				
	Currants				
	Chestnuts				
	Dates				
	Figs				
	Gooseberries				
	Grapes				
	Grapes				
	Grapes, Concord				
	Grapes, Malaga				
	Grapes, Tokay				
	Grapefruit				
	Grapefruit				
	Gauvas				
	Lemons				
	Lemons				
	Limes				
	Limes, Florida				
	Limes, Persian				
	Muskmelons				
	Oranges				
	Oranges				
	Oranges				
	Peaches				
	Peaches				
	Pears				
	Pears				
	Pears, Alligators				
	Pineapples				
	Plums				
	Plums				
	Pomegranates				
	Quinces				
	Raspberries				
	Strawberries				
	Strawberries				

Fig. 4-16. Steward's market quotation list (Cont'd.).

ON HAND	ARTICLE	WANTED	QUOTATIONS			
	FRUIT (Cont'd)					
	Tangerines					
	Watermelons					
	Watermelons					
	BUTTER					
	Print					
	Cooking					
	Sweet					
	EGGS					
	White					
	Brown					
	Mixed Colors					
	Pullets					
	CHEESE					
	American, Kraft					
	American, Young					
	Bel Paese					
	Camembert					
	Camembert					
	Cheddar					
	Cottage					
	Cream					
	Cream, Phila.					
	Cream, Phila.					
	Edam					
	Gorgonzola					
	Liederkranz					
	Parmesan, Grated					
	Roquefort					
	Roquefort					
	Roquefort, Broken					
	Stilton					
	Store					
	Swiss					
	Swiss, Gruyere					
	Swiss, Gruyere					
	MISCELLANEOUS					

Fig. 4-16. Steward's market quotation list (Cont'd.).

Regarding service, a purveyor that does not give satisfactory service should not be kept on the approved vendor list. There is no point in spending time obtaining and comparing bids if the sale is not awarded on the basis of price. Management should review the purchasing records from time to time to see that the lowest bid is being taken and should investigate any that were not taken.

Recent Developments in Institutional Distribution

Rising labor and operating costs have affected institutional distributors as well as food service operators. To keep their operating costs as low as possible, some institutional distributors have expanded their product lines to the point where they can offer "full-line" service to their customers. A full-line distributor will provide everything the food service needs to operate, including all food products, supplies, and small and heavy equipment. To the distributor the cost of maintaining a very large inventory is offset by increased sales volume and reduced cost of delivery. The customer buys everything he needs from one distributor, and all purchases are delivered once or twice a week on the same truck. The costly process of dispatching trucks to make numerous stops with small orders is eliminated.

The number of full-line distributors now operating in the United States has been estimated at about 24 companies, many of which have several national and regional branches. This number will probably increase since the general trend in the industry is for expansion of product lines by merging with specialized companies. Many distributors lack only a few lines to be considered full-line. Highly perishable items, such as bread and milk, work against the full-line distributor since they require almost daily delivery. Fresh meat and produce may also require more frequent deliveries than the distributor is willing to make.

The Use of Full-Line Distributors by Food Service Operators

Dealing with a full-line distributor has numerous advantages for the food service operator. Most operators using a full-line distributor mention labor saving as the most important benefit. Managers no longer need to spend time shopping the market for the best prices. Since deliveries are infrequent and on a scheduled basis, the staffing of the receiving function is greatly simplified, and the amount of manpower required is greatly reduced. Furthermore, the potential for collusion and perquisites to personnel is eliminated. Paperwork is greatly reduced, particularly in the accounts payable function. Instead of dealing with at least 25 or more accounts payable, there are at most two or three.

One-stop shopping offers further advantages to chain operators through standardization of products and services. National or multiregional distributors can extend this standardization to national food service chains. Distributors selling to a large chain will usually service a few members of the chain, which may not be profitable for them, as long as they are able to service the entire chain. Without this consolidation of business, those accounts might otherwise have difficulty getting supplies.

The full-line distributor can offer a number of services not offered by specialized distributors. Because of his customers' commitment to him, he must be able to continually supply all their needs. To do this, he has to be actively involved in the customer's business and particularly in the planning of the menu. This puts him in an excellent position to advise on total menu planning, particularly on availability, cost, and new products. Some distributors employ dietitians and menu consultants just to provide this service.

Computerized reports are another service the full-line distributor can provide for his customers. Large distributors use computers for their own inventory control, sales forecasting, and delivery scheduling, as well as for financial reports and accounting. Some also provide their customers with product movement reports, inventory extensions, portion costs, and even preparation of financial reports.

In addition to menu consulting and computer services, the full-line distributor often provides merchandising and promotional material for his customers and may even print menus. Training of the customer's employees in the use of the products is another service that is sometimes provided.

The major disadvantage to the food service operator in using a full-line distributor is that he may require more storage space, particularly refrigeration, than was needed with daily deliveries. The minimum order requirement of many of the large full-line distributors may be a disadvantage for a very small, single operator. Another disadvantage that is sometimes given is that the unit manager must plan and forecast his needs on a weekly basis, rather than from day to day. However, advance planning is obviously better management, and unit managers frequently are able to reduce their food cost simply because they are forced to plan their purchases more accurately.

Some food service executives are unable to let go of the idea that one must shop for the best price. For many years, good control procedures dictated that one did not commit oneself to buying from a single dealer and that competition was necessary in order to get the best price. Although one-stop buying does eliminate the need for daily shopping, price comparison is not eliminated; it is simply done less frequently. The selection of supplier and price is made by top management rather than by lower level personnel.

Generally, the overall prices of the full-line distributor and the specialized distributor are about the same. Studies have shown that although the full-line distributor's prices on some items may be higher than those of a specialized distributor, his prices on other items may be lower.

Whether or not the full-line distributors' prices will be above or below those paid by a specific operation will depend in part on the efficiency of the purchasing function in that operation. When the purchasing has been done on a haphazard basis, without receiving bids for specified items, a one-stop shopping policy can easily result in lower prices for that operation. On the other hand, if good buying practices have been followed, the full-line distributor may not always be able to meet the prices being paid to specialized distributors.

The full-line distributor has an advantage over the specialized distributor because he can buy by the carload lot for the most economical prices and can lower distribution costs with the more efficient delivery system. The overhead expenses are also spread over a larger volume base. Another advantage is that since the full-line distributor carries a wide range of merchandise, he can supply a wider market of different types of food services in his geographical area and does not need to travel as far as a specialized distributor (for instance, one who caters only to hotels and exclusive restaurants) in order to develop and service his accounts.

Some operators have difficulty converting to the full-line distributor. In some cases, unit employees who have been receiving perquisites from suppliers attempt to sabotage the new system. In other cases, unit managers who are not used to planning ahead to determine their needs on a weekly basis experience considerable over- or underbuying until they can develop a forecasting procedure. More often, the operators themselves do not know what their needs are, and therefore cannot communicate their requirements to the distributors. For instance, if an operator has no specifications for the items he uses, he cannot properly compare the prices bid by the distributors with the prices he is currently paying, since he does not know if the prices are for the same item.

The very rapid growth of some full-line distributors has caused problems for food service operators. Most of these distribution companies have been formed through mergers with specialist distributors, a process that can cause some temporary disorganization until new systems are developed. Other companies have had some upheaval in converting their inventory control and accounts receivable to a computerized system.

Types of Agreements with Full-Line Distributors

There are two basic types of pricing agreements that can be made with a full-line distributor: cost-plus and standard markup. With a cost-plus agreement, the customer is charged the distributor's actual cost of the item, with a percentage of the total sale added to the bill for the distributor's costs and profit. With this type of agreement, the operator can usually follow the trend of prices as quoted for the nearest distribution center and thus have a check on the distributor's prices. Determining the actual cost of an individual item requires additional arithmetic, however.

According to *Institutional Distribution Magazine,* the average institutional distributor operates at about a 16 percent gross profit level. The total range of gross profit was from below 12 percent to 26 percent and over, depending on the mix of product lines carried. Distributors specializing in canned goods and dry groceries operate on the smallest gross profit margins, usually between 9 to 10 percent, whereas those specializing in frozen foods and perishables have higher margins, in the area of 15 to 20 percent. Equipment suppliers have even higher margins, usually of 20 to 25 percent, and even as much as 30 percent, reflecting the slow turnover of inventory and the extensive design services sometimes provided. A full-line distributor may charge the same add-on cost for all purchases, or different add-on costs for different types of merchandise.

With a standard mark-up agreement, the distributor establishes a selling price for each item in the conventional way. No additional calculation is required to arrive at the unit prices.

Whatever type of agreement is used, the full-line distributor usually publishes and distributes price lists to all his customers. Prices are usually stabilized: one week or longer on perishable items, and one to three months on nonperishables. The distributors try to give sufficient advance notice of price increases so that the customers can make changes on the menus.

In shopping for a full-line distributor, price is only one consideration. Services offered is another consideration that is becoming increasingly important to the food service operator. The advantages of full-line distribution to the chain operator have been mentioned. How much service the distributor is willing to give to a chain in terms of drop shipments to remote locations may be a consideration; frequency of delivery is another. One large food service company looks for sales volume, distribution capability, depth of product line, and cleanliness of the physical facilities when shopping for a distributor. Compatibility of computerized reports is also important. If the distributor carries a private label line, the completeness of the information given on the labels should be checked. Altogether, these non-quantifiable factors may carry more weight than price alone in the selection of a full-line distributor, and the final decision must be based on the judgment of management.

5

RECEIVING AND
STOREROOM MANAGEMENT

Receiving

The receiving department is one of the most important in any food service establishment and the one most often neglected. Failure to check thoroughly all deliveries for quantity and quality can result in loss of the benefits of careful buying and in actual shortages of merchandise.

Receiving procedures are a tool of mangement for control of merchandise. It is the responsibility of management to make sure that the procedures are being properly followed and that the control system itself remains relevant to the existing conditions. For the receiving procedures to be effective, they must be thoroughly understood and consistently followed by trained personnel. There must also be adequate facilities and equipment for receiving, purchase specifications for guidance of the receiving personnel, proper receiving routine, and periodic checks of receiving methods and procedures by management or some outside, independent consultant.

A receiving clerk must have a knowledge of food since he must inspect incoming merchandise for conformity to the establishment's standards. A buyer may do the most careful specification buying, but if the receiving clerk does not check the receipts against those specifications, the establishment can lose thousands of dollars. Unfortunately, the receiver is sometimes an untrained kitchen porter or dishwasher whose only comprehension of "receiving" is to put the merchandise in the right place.

The development and use of purchasing specifications are discussed in Chapter 4. One copy of the "specs" should be posted conspicuously in the receiving area. Even though the regular receiving clerk may know the specifications for most items without referring to the manual, new or substitute employees will not.

121

In addition to checking for quality, the receiving clerk also inspects for damaged goods and for shortages in weights or in number. Deliveries are often made up hastily in vendors' establishments, and errors are bound to occur. Items may be broken in transit or stolen from an open truck, or if the delivery man is dishonest and notices that the receiving clerk does not do a conscientious job, he may make that establishment a disposal center for short orders and damaged or partially spoiled merchandise. He may exaggerate weights and counts and divert items to other destinations.

Receiving Department Layout and Equipment

For control of the flow of deliveries, the receiving department should be located between the service entrance and the storeroom or storage areas. Sufficient indoor space should be provided in the receiving area so that deliveries will not pile up and disrupt the normal receiving routine, or remain outdoors and deteriorate. The receiving entrance should be accessible to the street, with adequate driveway space to enable trucks to turn. A dock should be provided for ease of unloading trucks and movement of merchandise. If possible, the trash and garbage areas should be removed from the receiving dock to reduce the opportunities for pilferage in the guise of waste disposal.

No worker can do a thoroughly efficient job unless he has the proper equipment. Since checking weight is of prime importance in the receipt of food, an accurate scale is absolutely necessary. Faulty or inaccurate scales will discourage the most conscientious clerk and result in costly errors, arguments, and loss of payroll time. Precision weighing instruments must be serviced and maintained to keep them accurate. They must also be used properly.

Receiving department scales are equipped with various types of dials. The magnified dial visible to only one person is of dubious value. The clear-view, full-face dial (Fig. 5–1A) and the electronic dial (Fig. 5–1B) avoid disputes. Scales with face-dials are also more accurate and easier and quicker to use than balance-beam scales with weights.

Some recording scales stamp the weight of the merchandise on the invoices or receiving tickets (Fig. 5–2A and 5–2B). That is labor-saving and eliminates the possibility of clerical errors which might be made if the information were jotted down by hand.

The scale selected should have the capacity to handle the weights of merchandise most often bought. Usually, the larger the capacity, the wider the gradations. For larger operations, where a delivery can consist of hundreds of pounds of one item, a floor platform scale (Fig. 5–3) should be selected so as to eliminate the need to lift heavy weights.

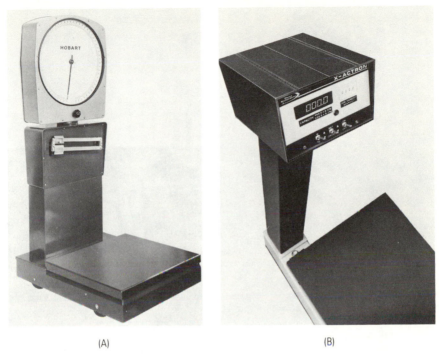

(A)   (B)

Fig. 5-1. (A) A platform receiving scale with dial. *(Courtesy of Hobart Corpora-
tion).* (B) A platform scale with an electronic indicator. *(Courtesy of Howe Richardson
Scale Company)*

In addition to the scale, the receiving clerk needs tools with
which to open crates and cartons and a table or counter on which to
work. He should have enough pallets or lugs, skids, carts, dollies, and
handtrucks to facilitate the handling of the goods between the delivery truck and the storage area or point of use. Very large operations
such as commissaries can use motorized equipment such as fork-lift
trucks to move merchandise.

Receiving Procedures

Essentially, the receiving procedure is a control function that
determines that the merchandise is received in the quantity ordered,
that its quality and condition conform to purchase specifications,
and that the invoices for the merchandise are correct as to weight,
count, and price.

As with any control procedure, the cost of the system should
be considered in relation to the amount of money being controlled. A
large hotel or a multi-outlet operation will require more manpower
and a more elaborate system than a small, single-outlet restaurant. In
either case, however, the system should provide the basic controls.

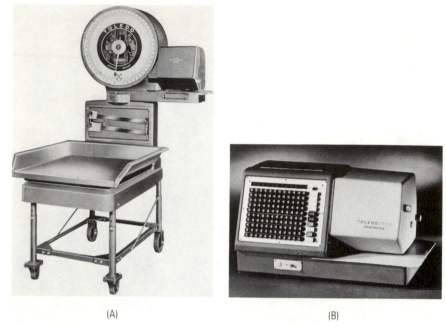

(A)   (B)

Fig. 5-2. (A) A portable bench scale with dial. This example has an attachment which prints the weight of the material on the scale, providing an accurate, legible record. *(Courtesy of Toledo Scale)*   (B) A weight printer with a keyboard that permits additional data to be printed, such as date, time of day, item identification, or code numbers. Some models can be used to print labels or tags to be attached to the product. Weight printers are also available that can accumulate data for transmission to a computer. *(Courtesy of Toledo Scale)*

Checking Quantity. All commodities purchased and billed by weight should be weighed individually and without wrappings. One questionable practice is to weigh an entire shipment of several different types of merchandise without separating them and to compare only the total weight with the total of the weights on the invoice. That practice should be prohibited. Ten pounds of top sirloin missing from the order will not be counterbalanced in value by 10 pounds more of short ribs. Each item must be weighed separately.

Very large operations such as commissaries may weigh merchandise in the containers by wheeling loaded pallets or skids onto a floor scale. To determine the weight of the merchandise for which payment is to be made, the weight of the pallet and the wrapping materials must be subtracted. Subsequent inspection and weighing can be made on a test basis. This procedure should not be used unless the purveyor agrees to accept the results of inspections made after his delivery man has left.

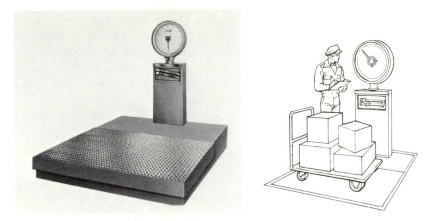

Fig. 5-3. A floor scale. The steel platform is installed level with the floor. A locking mechanism prevents the platform from moving or the weighing mechanism from being damaged by ordinary traffic. *(Courtesy of Howe Richardson Scale Company)*

A potentially costly problem is often posed in the weighing of fresh poultry and fish items that are heavily iced for delivery. The receiving clerk cannot always unpack a shipment to obtain the net weight. However, particularly in the case of a commodity of high unit value, such as shrimp, he should make an estimate of the tare (container weight) based on the gross weight. A further weight check should be made in the kitchen when the shipment is de-iced. The safest procedure is to check the actual net weight of the merchandise by test weighing periodically without the ice at least one iced shipment from each purveyor. Because short weights are found occasionally in packages of processed foods, such merchandise must be tested from time to time. Those short weights obviously are not the fault of the distributor, but he should be informed of them and an adjustment should be requested. A complaint to the manufacturer from the distributor will carry considerably more weight than one from a single restaurant, and reputable distributors are reluctant to carry lines that are the subject of too many complaints.

Items purchased by count, such as those in bags and cases, should be counted. In some operations, meats are bought by the piece instead of by weight—an incorrect purchase method that can lead to a wide variation in yield and put the receiver at the mercy of the purveyor.

Checking Specifications. Receiving clerks who conscientiously check weight and counts of items received often neglect the equally important function of checking for conformity to specifications. For example, in a large hotel, a shipment of meat received was correct in weight but was two grades below the quality specified. The overcharge amounted to more than the day's salary of the receiving clerk.

Meat cuts should be weighed individually to ensure that they are within the weight range specified, and they should be inspected at the same time for trim, condition, and grade. Heads of lettuce should be chosen at random, cut open and checked for rust. Oranges and grapefruits must be tested for taste and juice content. Fruits and vegetables in the center or bottom of crates must be checked, which can be done only by reaching in and selecting several items or by upending the crate.

Canned and processed goods should be checked for proper package size and condition. They should also be checked for brand if it is specified. Frozen foods that show signs of thawing at time of receipt should be rejected, as should damaged cartons or cans.

When any doubt arises as to the acceptability of any merchandise, the receiving clerk should call on the steward, chef, or department head for final judgment.

Checking for Adherence to the Order. The delivery should be checked against the original order to make sure that unordered merchandise is not being delivered and that no items are missing. Short orders are far more common than padded orders and if not discovered in time, can cause problems.

Most purveyors are reputable dealers and want a continuing business relationship with a good customer (especially if he pays his bills promptly). Because truck and driver's time is costly to purveyors, some dealers shorten delivery time by accepting the results of the buyer's inspection for quality and conformity to specifications after the driver has left; only the count is taken in the driver's presence. It is best that an agreement to honor the findings of a buyer's inspections taking place after the deliveryman leaves be made in writing with the purveyor.

When the volume of deliveries is very large and the merchandise is standardized, inspection for quality and conformation may be done on a sampling basis. A decision to permit sampling inspections should be made by management, not by the receiving staff, and management must determine the extent of the sampling to be made.

Returning Unsatisfactory Merchandise. The return of merchandise requires at least four steps: (1) persuading the unwilling deliveryman to take back a delivery, (2) noting the reason for the return of the merchandise on the invoice or the delivery ticket, (3) filling out a form in duplicate requesting a credit memo and sending it to the accounting department for transmittal to the vendor, and (4) notifying the department head so that plans may be changed and substitutions made in the menu if necessary. The return of merchandise is also likely to result in one or more telephone calls to the purveyor to give further explanation for the return.

Because it requires less effort to accept questionable merchandise than to return it, management must be sure that the receiving clerk understands that the acceptance of poor merchandise involves a heavy monetary loss through spoilage, waste, or dissatisfied customers. Furthermore, if unsatisfactory merchandise is accepted once, the purveyor is encouraged to send it again.

Deliverymen may try to speed up the checking of their deliveries. There may be no motive for this except their desire to be on their way. On the other hand, they may know about the shortages and hope that the incorrect weights will remain undiscovered. When receiving clerks are unduly harassed by deliverymen, it may be helpful if management posts signs stating that each incoming item must be weighed and checked.

Some drivers may offer to take their deliveries right into the proper refrigerator or storeroom, which of course would prevent proper inspection of incoming merchandise. In some operations, routemen are allowed to check the stock on hand and make up the order. Such practice may ease the work loads of the receivers, but it can be very costly to management since it leaves the operation wide open to overstocking and pilferage. Furthermore, that type of delivery is seldom checked for quantity or adherence to specification by the receiving staff.

Unauthorized personnel should not be permitted in the back-of-the-house areas. Even reputable dealers may have dishonest drivers on the payroll, or at least drivers who have little willpower to resist temptation. In one case, a very "helpful" driver not only carried the meat deliveries downstairs to the meat cooler but unwrapped the order and put it in the refrigerator. The supposedly empty wrappings that he brought out contained a number of steaks and chops. In another instance, the milkman carried out "empty" five-gallon milk cans filled with canned hams and other merchandise.

Handling Cash. Receiving clerks or stewards sometimes control a small cash fund used for making cash disbursements for truckage fees, cab fares, or similar charges. Having a bank right where receiving is handled keeps deliverymen out of the back-of-the-house area and the public areas. As with any cash fund, the bank should be large enough to cover only the amount of actual charges, and proper cash control procedures should be followed.

Storage

It is the responsibility of management to make sure that the storeroom is properly organized, that only essential supplies are kept there, and that it is being operated efficiently and competently by trustworthy personnel. It should be controlled as carefully as the cashier's safe since the goods kept there are simply another form of cash.

Location and Layout of Storage Facilities

Too often, the storeroom is a hodgepodge of supplies and a convenient dumping place for obsolete equipment, old menus, and other junk. Valuable space is taken up, and efficient operation is made impossible. In many cases, the storeroom personnel are not to blame for a lack of order. The room's location and layout may hinder efficient operation. Storerooms frequently seem to be architectural after-thoughts—too small, poorly lit, and poorly ventilated.

In a large operation with numerous outlets, the storeroom may be a major complex including bulk refrigerators and freezers, dry stores, a butcher shop and a department for the pre-preparation of vegetables. These last two areas are located in the storeroom complex so that meats, fruits, and vegetables can be partially processed before being sent to the kitchen. Some restaurants, especially those specializing in steak or roast beef, age their beef on the premises, which requires special aging rooms that are usually adjacent to the butcher shop. All food and supplies are then held and issued through a single control point.

For a small operation with a single outlet, the expense of an elaborate system of issues and requisitions is not usually warranted. A small operation usually has only one refrigeration group for both kitchen use and bulk storage. The dry stores area for such an operation should be directly accessible to the kitchen to minimize the time required by cooks to assemble their supplies.

The size of a storeroom depends, of course, on the volume and nature of the establishment's business, its location, and its food purchasing policy. There is no need for excessive storage space, which may encourage overbuying. One goal of a purchasing policy should be to operate with the smallest inventory possible without sacrificing efficiency.

There is a definite relationship between the size of the inventory and usage, which a month-to month analysis of purchase and inventories will reveal. Overcrowded conditions in a storeroom may be due partly to excessive inventories containing dead stock that has been purchased and forgotten. Another cause of excessive inventories is the use of an extensive menu that includes slow-moving items. If these items are removed from the menu and eliminated from the storeroom, more storage space will be available for storage of fast-moving items.

The ideal location for the storeroom is near and on the same level as the receiving area and the kitchen. If the storeroom is located elsewhere, the movement of merchandise will be less efficient and will result in higher labor and equipment costs.

To prevent spoilage, the storeroom must be well ventilated and not overheated. Because high temperatures play havoc with canned goods, pipes for hot water and steam are a menace and should be heavily insulated. Extreme cold should also be avoided, as should excessive dryness, dampness, and direct sunlight, all of which can have adverse effects on various food products. In some areas, health laws prohibit the storage of food under waste lines.

The storeroom floor should be of a material that will take heavy trucking without breaking up. The floor should be slanted slightly toward a drain to permit frequent hosing. Strict sanitation is the only way to keep the storeroom free of vermin. All areas should be well lighted to facilitate location of items and detection of dirt or disorder.

Storeroom Equipment

The storeroom shelving should be of heavy-gauge steel or chrome-plated wire. Wood may be used if local health codes permit. Shelving intended for canned goods should be sturdy enough to hold the heavy weight. There should be 16 inches of clear space between shelving for canned goods to permit the stacking of two No. 10 cans or three No. 2½ cans. The shelving should be 18 inches deep so that it will be able to hold two or three rows of cans. Greater depth than that makes it difficult to reach the cans in the back. If more storage space is necessary, shelves below counter level may be widened. Only canned goods items that are issued or used by the can should be removed from the cases. Those used by the case should be issued by the case.

Skids, pallets, and dollies should be available for the storage of bulk packages (such as bags of flour) and unopened cases. Good sanitation practices (and many health codes) require that all food and paper supplies be stored off the floor, both in storerooms and in refrigerators; this prevents contamination from sewage in the event of the back up of a floor drain and permits sweeping and hosing of the floor. Skids that can be taken to the receiving area loaded and wheeled into place in the storeroom or refrigerators save the time of employees and make the handling of merchandise easier. If the use of skids is not feasible, a handtruck and one or more flatbed carts should be assigned exclusively to the receiving and storeroom departments. A large-volume operation, such as a commissary, may benefit from the use of conveyors and overhead lifts or meat rails.

Another storeroom requirement is a cabinet suitable for locking up small high-value items that are easily concealed and carried away.

If the establishment is large enough to require requisitions for all merchandise issued, the storeroom employee should have an adding machine and a desk or table on which to do his paperwork. He also should have a scale if he issues small amounts of bulk products, such as sugar, rice, dried fruits, and vegetables. Adequate containers are also needed for storage of opened bulk products.

Sometimes reserve supplies of linen, china, glass, and silverware are stored in the food storeroom. These supplies should be locked up separately from the food and issued only upon properly authorized requisition. These reserve supplies should not be confused with the operating stocks, which are kept in storage spaces conveniently adjacent to the departments where they are used.

Refrigerators and Freezers

Because different types of perishable foods require different storage conditions, three separate refrigeration facilities are recommended: one for meats, fish, and poultry; one for fruits and vegetables; and one for dairy products. A very large operation with a separate fish department may have a separate fish box.

All foods in frozen storage should be properly wrapped to prevent deterioration and discoloration. Unwrapped foods quickly suffer freezer burn because of dehydration and oxidation. The loss of volatile flavors and absorption of odors cannot be reversed. The original wrappings of foods shipped frozen are designed to be vapor and moisture proof. Foods frozen by food-service operators should be wrapped in materials designed for the freezer and properly labeled with waterproof markings. Aluminum foil, a commonly used food storage wrapping, is not vapor proof and, therefore, is not suitable for wrapping food stored in the freezer. Polyethylene plastic films, such as Saran Wrap or treated paper, designed especially for freezer wrapping will provide proper protection for frozen foods.

Temperatures. Most fruits and vegetables should be stored in a high humidity atmosphere at a temperature of 32° to 36°F. A few types of fruits and vegetables, such as cucumber, eggplant, okra, hard-rind squash, and some melons and tropical fruits, require higher temperatures of 40 to 45°F. Those conditions may be maintained in a "vestibule" box adjacent to the regular box.

Meat and poultry boxes should be maintained at 32° to 36°F., but if fish and seafood are stored in a separate place, temperatures of 30° to 34°F are preferable for those items. Dairy products should be stored at 35° to 40°F.

Butcher shops are often refrigerated to maintain the quality and firmness of the meats while they are being processed. The temperature in rooms for aging meats is usually at 35° to 40°F with controlled humidity. Higher temperatures shorten the aging process, but at the cost of increased evaporation.

Freezers should be maintained at 0° to 10° F because deterioration is reduced at lower temperatures. Because fluctuation of temperatures adversely affects the quality of the food, frozen foods should be properly stored as soon as they are received, and freezer (and refrigerator) doors should not be allowed to stand open.

Some food operators manufacture their own frozen prepared food. To do so effectively, a blast-freezer with temperatures as low as -40°F is required. Food scientists have found that low temperatures must be maintained to keep the ice crystals as small as possible, thus reducing cellular breakdown in the product. Once thoroughly frozen, the product can be transferred to a 0° freezer for storage.

As ice cream is properly served at 10°F, establishments maintaining a small inventory which is quickly used might want to store all ice cream in a separate 10°F freezer. Larger operations, with large, hard frozen ice cream stocks, may need a small "tempering" box for ice cream, to bring it up to serving temperature.

Equipment and Physical Properties. Freezers and refrigerators should be constructed of materials that are cleaned easily. Special low-temperature bulbs should be used to provide adequate lighting. Doors should open easily and be hinged to provide the most convenient access. Many freezers have a tiny heating strip around the jam to prevent ice build-up. Doors may be equipped with a foot treadle to facilitate opening them, and they should be self-closing. All walk-in refrigerators and freezers should have an emergency alarm and easy means of escape for anyone accidentally locked inside.

Walk-in refrigerators and freezers can be constructed on a depressed slab, enabling their floors to be level with the outside floor. Although this adds to construction costs, it can add significantly to operating efficiency. Carts and dollies loaded with incoming merchandise can be wheeled directly into the walk-in refrigerator upon receipt. The sorting and stacking can be done later, after weighing and checking. No multiple handling is required. Issues can be assembled easily. Mobile shelving is recommended for walk-in refrigerators, because sections of it can be rolled out easily for cleaning.

Exterior or remote temperature gauges are desirable. Some refrigerators have alarm systems that sound when the interior temperature rises above a certain point. Storeroom personnel should be aware of what temperatures should be maintained in each refrigerator and should notify management of the malfunctioning of any unit.

Incorrect temperature can lead to spoilage and loss. Modern refrigeration equipment is self-defrosting, but occasionally ice will build up on the condensing unit because of a malfunction. When that happens, remedial action should be taken immediately, and the ice should be removed to avoid permanent damage to the system.

Small, high-cost items such as caviar, anchovies, imported sardines, steaks, and chops should be stored in a locked compartment within a refrigerator, if necessary, and the key should be kept by the person in charge of the food supplies.

The use of frozen and fresh perishable foods has increased so greatly in recent years that many operators have found themselves short of storage space, particularly for frozen foods. Some have solved this problem by building a walk-in box outside of the existing building or leasing a refrigerated truck that is then permanently installed. Others convert an existing refrigerator into a freezer by changing the condensing unit, which is not always satisfactory, however, because the insulation may be inadequate. Reach-in boxes may be used to supplement walk-in storage, or prefabricated walk-in boxes may be installed in the storeroom area. Large operations, chain restaurants, or multiunit institutions sometimes lease space in refrigerated warehouses or build one large, refrigerated storage box for use as a central storage point, from which issues to various outlets can be made as required.

Storage Recommendations for Various Types of Commodities

Meats, Poultry, and Fish

Fresh beef, lamb, pork, veal, poultry, and fish should be "transients" in the refrigerator because they deteriorate rapidly. The maximum holding times for these items are shown in Figs. 5–4 and 5–5.

Fresh meats and poultry should be refrigerated as soon as they are received. They should be unwrapped from the original packaging and placed on trays or in pans with the fat side up. Both fresh and cooked meats should be covered loosely with clean plastic or butcher paper to prevent drying from direct forced drafts, although there should be slight air circulation.

Fresh fish and shellfish should be covered with finely crushed ice and stored in the coldest part of the refrigerator as soon as they are received. Live shellfish should also be kept cold and moist. A temperature of about 40°F to 45°F will keep them alive for several days. If placed in tanks with water, they will live somewhat longer. Moist seaweed is effective packing for live shellfish. Cans of shucked oysters and clams should be packed in ice. Their shelf-life is about 7 to 10 days if properly stored.

	Maximum Storage Period to Maintain Quality
Fresh Meats (Beef, Lamb, Pork, Veal)	
Large roasts	3-5 days
Steaks and chops	3 days
Ground or cubed meat	1-2 days
Variety meats	1-2 days
Fresh sausage	2-3 days
Fresh or Thawed Poultry	
Whole, drawn	2 days
Cut-up	1-2 days
Fresh Fish (Well Iced)	1-2 days
Processed Meats (Bacon, Ham, Sausage, etc.) In Unopened Vacuum Package	
Cook-before-eating:	
Bacon	7-days
Corned beef	5-days
Pork sausage rolls and links	2-3 days
Tongue, cured	4 days
Tongue, cured and smoked	6-days
Fully cooked:	
Braunschweiger liver sausage, chub	2-3 weeks
slices	1 week
Dried beef	1 month
Dry and semidry sausage, uncut	1 month
slices, unopened	1 month
slices, opened	1-2 weeks
Franks	1 week
Hams, picnics, bone-in or boneless	1 week
Luncheon meats, uncut	2-3 weeks
slices	1 week
Canned hams, unopened	6 months
Cooked meats or poultry	3-4 days
Cooked fish and shellfish	2-3 days
if in broth or sauce	1-2 days

Fig. 5-4. Refrigerator storage time chart.

Frozen fish and seafood should be stored at 0°F or lower until thawed or cooked. Thawing is recommended for fish or seafood to be used in a mixture or to be breaded. Breaded and unbreaded products can be cooked without thawing. Frozen fish should be thawed in the refrigerator at 35° to 40°F. Small packages may take 24 to 36 hours, and larger packages (such as five-pound boxes) may take up to 72 hours. Frozen fish should never be thawed at room temperature or in warm water, and once thawed, it should never be refrozen.

Dairy Products

Butter exposed to the air will oxidize and turn rancid. Only the exposed surface will show discoloration, but the rancidity will permeate the entire lot. Butter should be carefully wrapped or closely

	Maximum Storage Period to Maintain Quality Months
Commercially Frozen Foods:	
Meats, fish and poultry:	
Beef:	
Hamburger or chipped (thin) steaks	4
Roasts	12
Steaks	12
Lamb:	
Patties (ground meat)	4
Roasts	9
Pork, cured	2
Pork, fresh:	
Chops	4
Roasts	8
Sausage	2
Veal:	
Cutlets, chops	9
Roasts	9
Cooked meat items	3
Chicken:	
Cut-up	9
Livers	3
Whole	12
Duck, whole	6
Goose, whole	6
Turkey:	
Cut-up and rolls	6
Whole	12
Cooked chicken and turkey items:	
Sliced meat and gravy	6
Chicken or turkey pies	6
Fried chicken	4
Fish:	
Fillets:	
Cod, flounder, haddock, halibut, pollack	6
Mullet, ocean perch, sea trout, striped bass	3
Pacific Ocean perch	2
Salmon steaks	2
Sea trout, dressed	3
Striped bass, dressed	3
Whiting, drawn	4
Shellfish:	
Clams, shucked	3
Crabmeats:	
Dungeness	3
King	10
Oysters, shucked	4
Shrimp	12
Cooked fish and shellfish items	3
Foods Frozen In-House (Wrapped Securely in Freezer Paper):	
Beef - roasts and steaks	6 to 12
Lamb - roasts and chops	6 to 9
Pork - roasts	4 to 8
Veal - roast, chops,and cutlets	6 to 9
Ground and stew meats	3 to 4
Variety meats	3 to 4
Chicken, ready-to-cook	6
Cooked meats	3 to 4
Cooked chicken and turkey	2 to 3
Fresh pork sausage, links and rolls	Up to 1*
Sliced bacon	Up to 1*
Smoked ham	Up to 1*
Fish - high fat	2 to 3
Fish - low fat	4 to 6

*Flavors deteriorate rapidly when frozen.

Fig. 5-5. Freezer storage time chart. (0°F).

covered. Protected in this way, it will last for several months at a temperature of less than 10°F. Lard, shortening, and oleomargarine may be kept safely for six or seven months at 32° to 36°F.

Cheese cannot withstand freezing. Its taste becomes flat and its texture dry and crumbly. If cheese should accidentally be subjected to abnormally low temperature, it may still be used in grated form with spaghetti or similar foods.

Dairy products, although classed under one heading, are often poor neighbors. Mild cheeses (American, Cottage, Muenster, and Edam varieties) are the only type that may be stored safely near eggs. The highly flavored cheeses (such as Parmesan, Roquefort, Bleu, Liederkranz, and Gorgonzola) should be stored at a considerable distance from eggs.

Milk and cream should be stored in a very cold refrigerator, 33° to 37°F, and away from strongly flavored foods. Ice cream can be stored at 0°F, for a maximum of one month. For proper dipping consistency, it should be tempered to 6° to 10°F before use.

Eggs and Egg Products

Eggshells are not airtight but quite porous, and they will readily take on the odors of other foods unless they are stored at a safe distance. The egg cases should be stacked in a crisscross manner, with strips of wood separating them to ensure the proper circulation of air.

Freezing spoils eggs, and they will freeze at 27° to 28° F. Close proximity to refrigerated pipes will freeze them. The cases must stand right side up, never on the sides or tops, because turning the eggs may break their air sacs and cause spoilage.

If eggs get wet or damp, they should be changed to dry cases with dry paper separators. Wet eggs will develop mold and spoil. For just such an emergency, it is well to have on hand a reserve supply of cases and separators.

Dried egg white solids may be stored at room temperature, and dried whole egg or yolk solids may be stored under refrigeration. Frozen egg products have a long shelf-life when kept at 10° to 20°F.

Fruits and Vegetables

Table 5–1 provides suggestions for the storage and handling of fresh fruits and vegetables.

Storeroom Operation

The purpose of any storeroom procedure is to ensure that food which has been received is available for processing when needed, without spoilage or deterioration, or loss through theft. A very small operation may have no storeroom at all, buying instead on a hand-to-

(Adapted from Materials of the United Fresh Fruit and Vegetable Association)

FRUITS

Apples:

Apples like cold, and they should be kept refrigerated continuously unless they are so firm when received that some ripening is desirable. Optimum storage conditions: 32°F and 90 percent relative humidity.

Apricots:

Optimum storage conditions: 32°F and 90 percent relative humidity. Use within two to three days.

Avocados:

Avocados are usually bought in a hard condition and ripened as needed. They ripen perfectly off the tree. From shipping condition to ripe and ready for eating may take a few days at room temperature. After ripening to where the flesh is soft and buttery, avocados should be kept moderately cold, or they can be stored at 50°F while firm and brought out to ripen as desired.

Bananas:

If bananas are received a little too green for immediate use, they can be ripened readily by a day at room temperature (58° to 68°F and 90 to 95 percent relative humidity). Usually a restaurant would not be justified in accepting fruit that is so green it needs more than a day for ripening. Once fully ripened, bananas need to be refrigerated until used. The peel of refrigerated bananas will brown after a time, but this is not important as long as the fruit is firm. Because of this discoloration, refrigerated bananas are not recommended for display purposes.

Blackberries:

Optimum storage conditions: 32°F and 90 percent relative humidity. Keep blackberries dry and covered and plan to use them quickly, since they have a short life.

Blueberries:

Optimum storage conditions: 32°F and 90 percent relative humidity. Keep blueberries dry and covered. Use them quickly within two to three days.

Cantaloupes:

Plan to give cantaloupes two to three days at room temperature before serving. Time and warmth will not make the melon sweeter (it should already be fully sweet if purchased properly), but they will soften the meat and make it juicier, two factors that are essential to melon appreciation. A ready-to-eat melon will have a distinct fragrance, will probably be somewhat yellowish, and will be springy when pressed lightly between the palms. Pressing the end with your thumb is not a good test, nor is shaking the melon to hear the contents slosh. If cantaloupes are to be held beyond two to three days, refrigerate them. The cantaloupe may be more flavorful if served at room temperature.

Casabas:

Optimum storage conditions: 50°F and 80 to 85 percent relative humidity. Avoid drying out.

Cherries:

Optimum storage conditions: 32°F and 90 percent relative humidity. Use in two to three days.

Coconuts:

Optimum storage conditions: 32°F and 90 percent relative humidity. Use as soon as possible.

Cranberries:

Cranberries can be frozen with no processing prior to freezing and are then available all year. While stored, they should not be allowed to thaw. When taken out of storage they should be used quickly. For shorter-term storage, the optimum conditions are 32°F and 90 percent relative humidity.

Crenshaws:

Keep at room temperature until ripe, then keep cool and use soon. Optimum storage conditions: 50°F and 80 to 85 percent relative humidity.

Figs:
Fresh figs are highly perishable and should be bought for immediate use. Optimum storage conditions: 32°F and 90 percent relative humidity.

Grapefruit:
Grapefruits are ripe and ready to use as received. They can be held at 50°F and 80 to 85 percent relative humidity.

Grapes:
Grapes are mature as received, and ready to use. Grapes do not ripen off the vine. They must be picked fully mature, fully sweet. They are highly perishable and should be refrigerated at as near 32°F and 90 percent relative humidity as practicable. Use within a week.

Honeydews:
Unless honeydews are obviously ripe when received, they should be held at room temperature a couple of days before serving. When fully ripe, they may be held satisfactorily at 50°F and 80 to 85 percent relative humidity.

Lemons:
Optimum storage conditions: 50°F and 80 to 85 percent relative humidity. If whole lemons are only kept a few days, they need not be refrigerated.

Limes:
Optimum storage conditions: 50°F and 80 to 85 percent relative humidity. Limes may be kept at room temperature for a few days.

Mangoes:
Mangoes are usually bought while quite solid and ripened at room temperature. Once fully ripened, they should be stored at 50°F and 80 to 85 percent relative humidity.

Nectarines:
When soft, keep cold and humid and use as soon as possible. Optimum storage conditions: 32°F and 90 percent relative humidity.

Oranges:
Optimum storage conditions: 32°F and 90 percent relative humidity.

Peaches:
Peaches ripen rapidly at room temperature, and in any package some will ripen sooner than others. They should be allowed to ripen well before serving. If they are to be held, the favorable temperature is 32°F and 90 percent relative humidity.

Pears:
Pears will ripen at 60° to 65°F and 85 to 95 percent relative humidity. Once ripened, or if they are to be held without ripening, they need cold as near 32°F as practicable. If winter pears from storage come in a box lined with a polyethylene sealed bag, the bag should be perforated to admit air when the pears come out of cold storage. Otherwise, as the pears warm up there may be too high a concentration of carbon dioxide, which prevents proper ripening and coloring.

Persian Melons:
Keep Persian melons at room temperature until soft and juicy. Then keep cold and humid and use as soon as possible. Optimum storage conditions: 50°F and 80 to 85 percent relative humidity.

Persimmons:
Persimmons are usually firm when received and need to be ripened by holding at room temperature. When fully ripened they are soft and their flesh jelly-like. At this point they have a delightfully rich and sweet flavor. Keep ripe persimmons cold and humid. Once ripened, they should be used quickly because they are quite perishable.

137

(Adapted from Materials of the United Fresh Fruit and Vegetable Association)

Pineapples:

If a pineapple is not fully ripe, keep it at room temperature until it is ready to eat, and then refrigerate. If ripe and to be stored for a short time, the best temperature is 40° to 45°F at relative humidity of 85 to 90 percent.

Plums:

Optimum storage conditions: 32°F and 90 percent relative humidity.

Pomegranates:

Pomegranate seeds may be placed in a large screw-top jar and frozen. When ready to use, remove the desired quantity from the jar quickly and replace the jar in the freezer so it doesn't thaw.

Raspberries:

Optimum storage conditions: 32°F and 90 percent relative humidity.

Tangelos:

Optimum storage conditions: 32°F and 90 percent relative humidity.

Tangerines:

Tangerines are highly perishable. Keep them cold and humid and use as soon as possible. Optimum storage conditions: 32°F and 90 percent relative humidity.

VEGETABLES

Asparagus:

The tenderness of fresh asparagus is quickly lost at room temperature because of formation of woody tissue. Asparagus should be kept at 32°F or as close to it as possible with a relative humidity of 85 to 90 percent. While sugar content diminishes rapidly at higher temperatures, it remains close to what it was at cutting time, if the asparagus is cooled rapidly immediately after cutting and kept cold. Use as soon as possible. Do not soak the cut ends in water.

Beans, Snap:

Snap beans can be held successfully for only short periods. Best temperature is 45° to 50°F with a relative humidity of 85 to 90 percent. They may be injured by chill when held at lower temperatures. Containers should be stacked to permit plenty of air circulation to remove generated heat.

Beets:

Best temperature in storage is 32°F at 90 to 95 percent relative humidity. Beets wilt rapidly under dry conditions, so humidity should be kept high. Bunched beets should be stored only briefly under humid conditions. Or the tops can be removed and used and the topped beets kept longer.

Broccoli:

Use broccoli as soon as possible. Store only briefly at 32°F and 90 to 95 percent relative humidity. There should be plenty of room between packages for ventilation, because broccoli generates a great deal of heat.

Brussels Sprouts:

Use Brussels sprouts as soon as possible. For brief storage, hold at 32°F and 90 to 95 percent relative humidity to keep freshness and good green color. They need adequate ventilation.

Cabbage:

Cabbage stores well at 32°F and 90 to 95 percent relative humidity if well ventilated. It wilts quickly if held in dry storage.

Carrots:

Favorable temperature 32°F, relative humidity 90 to 95 percent. Carrots keep well if topped. (Carrots with tops are rarely received now.)

Cauliflower:

Best temperature 32°F, relative humidity 85 to 90 percent. Store cauliflower with tops down to prevent accumulation of moisture on the curds.

Celery:

Favorable temperature 31° to 32°F, relative humidity 90 to 95 percent. Celery keeps well if kept cold and moist, assuming condition is good when stored.

Chinese Cabbage:

Chinese cabbage should not be stored for any long period. The most suitable temperature is 32°F and 95 percent relative humidity.

Corn:

Use corn as soon as possible, because the sooner it is used the sweeter it will be. Keep cold, 31° to 32°F, relative humidity 85 to 90 percent. The sugar of corn quickly turns to starch at higher temperatures.

Cucumbers:

Keep cucumbers moderately cold, 45° to 50°F, 85 to 95 percent relative humidity. Prolonged lower temperatures result in chilling injury. At 50°F, cucumbers ripen rapidly, so they should be used soon.

Eggplant:

Hold eggplant only briefly, at 45° to 50°F, relative humidity 85 to 90 percent. Chilling injury occurs in time at lower temperatures.

Escarole—Endive—Chicory:

Hold briefly at 32°F, relative humidity 90 to 95 percent. These salad greens keep better with cracked ice in or around the packages.

Lettuce—All Kinds:

Best temperature 32°F, relative humidity 90 to 95 percent. Use lettuce within a few days.

Mushrooms:

Store mushrooms only briefly at 32°F, relative humidity 85 to 90 percent. Deterioration is indicated by brown discoloration and opening of the veils.

Okra:

If in good condition, okra can be stored for a maximum of 2 weeks at 50°F and 85 to 95 percent relative humidity. At temperatures below 50°F, okra is subject to chilling injury manifested by discoloration, pitting, and decay.

Onions, Dry:

Cold storage is not essential, but dry storage is desirable, 70 to 75 percent relative humidity. Onions may be held at 32°F if desired. At higher humidities, onions are subject to root growth and decay in time.

Onions, Green:

Best temperature 32°F and relative humidity 90 to 95 percent. Icing helps keep green onions fresh.

Parsley:

Like other greens, parsley keeps best at low temperature, 32°F and high humidity. Use of crushed ice is desirable.

Parsnips:

Best temperature 32°F, relative humidity 90 to 95 percent. Parsnips are not injured by slight freezing in storage but should be protected from hard freezing. They wilt readily under dry conditions.

Table 5–1. Storage and Handling Recommendations
for Fresh Fruits and Vegetables (Cont'd.)

(Adapted from Materials of the United Fresh Fruit and Vegetable Association)

Peas, Green:
Temperature 32°F, relative humidity 85 to 90 percent. Green peas keep better in the pod than when shelled.

Peppers, Sweet:
Peppers are subject to chilling injury at prolonged low temperature, so they should be held at 45 to 50°F, relative humidity 85 to 90 percent. Store only briefly.

Potatoes:
Early crop, "new" potatoes are perishable and should be held only briefly. They can be held at 50°F and 85 to 90 percent relative humidity, but if intended for French frying, storage temperature of 60° to 70°F is better to avoid accumulation of sugar.
Late crop potatoes are not ordinarily refrigerated. For long storage, a temperature of 40°F is sufficient. If sweetening occurs, they will need to be kept 1 to 3 weeks at room temperature to restore natural flavor. Under most restaurant conditions, late potatoes are not kept long enough to require low temperature.

Radishes:
Best temperature 32°F, relative humidity 90 to 95 percent. If radishes are bunched, addition of ice helps keep tops fresh.

Rhubarb:
Best temperature is 32°F, relative humidity 90 to 95 percent. Bunches of rhubarb should be in crates stacked to allow ample air circulation.

Spinach:
Temperature 32°F, relative humidity 90 to 95 percent. Crushed ice in packages helps keep spinach fresh. If spinach is prepackaged in film bags, ice is useless, low temperature is essential, humidity is not important. Use as soon as possible.

Squash:
For hard-shell mature squashes and pumpkins, favorable temperature is 50° to 55°F and relative humidity 70 to 75 percent, which is on the dry side. For soft-skinned immature squashes best temperature is 32° to 40°F, relative humidity 85 to 95 percent.

Sweet Potatoes:
Sweet potatoes can be kept at room temperature for short periods. They are subject to chilling injury at temperatures below 55°F.

Tomatoes:
The tomato is a misunderstood vegetable. Too often it is held at low temperature before ripening in an attempt to retard ripening. This can result in unsatisfactory taste and texture. Before ripening, and if slow ripening is desired, tomatoes should be held at 55°F or a little higher, and relative humidity of 85 to 90 percent. For faster ripening, 60° to 70°F with high humidity (above 90 percent). After ripening, tomatoes can be held a short time at 50°F or lower.

Turnips—Rutabagas:
Favorable temperature 32°F, relative humidity 90 to 95 percent.

Watercress:
As with other leafy greens, the favorable temperature for watercress is 32°F and high humidity. Crushed ice helps keep freshness.

can be equated with usage, and there is no need for elaborate storage controls. In this case, product availability and quality must be maintained by the purveyor. (The same may be said of a commissary operation issuing to small outlets.)

Larger operations must maintain procedures for merchandise control, and very large operations with more than one outlet or cost center may require an elaborate control system to complete cost information for the different outlets.

Regardless of the complexity of the operation, storeroom or storage places and refrigerators and freezers should be kept neat and orderly, so that any item can be located quickly. There should be a space assigned for every item used. Shelves should be labeled (in more than one language if necessary), and items arranged by type of commodity in the order of the inventory book listings.

The hours that the storeroom must be kept open will depend on the size and type of the operation and the number of meals offered daily. If kitchen production is well planned and requisitions are prepared systematically, the storeroom work can be scheduled for the most productive use of the manpower.

Only authorized personnel should be permitted to enter the storeroom. Therefore, keys should be controlled and doors kept locked when a storeroom attendant is not in the area. A locked half-door at the entrance permits orders to be filled over a counter and still keeps unauthorized persons out. Such a device is particularly helpful when the entrance is not visible from all parts of the room.

One basic rule in storeroom operation is "first in, first out." Stock must be rotated to avoid being buried or forgotten. It is a little extra work to move the old stock to the front and place the new stock in the back, but the alternative can be spoilage of food, which results in loss of money, either through direct waste or through losing good customers.

Stamping the date of arrival on all incoming items is recommended. It makes it easier to follow the "first-in, first-out" rule and enables a storeroom man to keep closer watch on the flow of perishable merchandise on and off his shelves and to alert the chef or buyer if quantities ordered are excessive based on past consumption. Dairy products are usually dated by the dairy, sometimes with a code, which storeroom personnel should know. Fruits and vegetables that lack suitable surfaces for direct date stamping should be tagged with their dates of receipt. Bread, rolls, and bakery products should also be dated. Meats that are tagged already bear a date.

Food in danger of spoiling must be used quickly to avoid loss. A day's delay in using up merchandise that has begun to deteriorate may be too much. Personnel responsible for food storage should be able to detect spoilage at the very onset and immediately notify the chef, manager, or steward. If it is not possible to incorporate the items in the menu right away, immediate processing of the food for later use may be required.

Sometimes certain stock lies forgotten on shelves, usually following a change in chefs, management, or operating procedures. An alert storeroom man will bring the dead stock to the attention of the chef or manager, who can determine how to use, sell, or otherwise dispose of it. Dead stock does not improve in quality or increase in value with the passage of time.

Merchandise Control

The cost of maintaining any control system should be considered in relation to the cost or value of what is being controlled. In a small operation with low inventories, direct management supervision can effectively minimize merchandise loss so that a formal merchandise control system is not needed. In a large operation, top management cannot be directly involved with storeroom operation, and a merchandise control system is necessary.

A merchandise control system, when properly implemented, tells management the status of all merchandise received, both that in storage and that issued for use. Maintaining the system can be compared to balancing a checking account. The food in storage represents the cash balance in the account; the merchandise receipts and issues can be likened to deposits and withdrawals. The analogy can be carried further: A checking account is expected to produce a fast turnover of money, as opposed to a savings account that is used for the long-term accumulation of funds. Food in storage should be used quickly to avoid spoilage and to keep the investment in inventory and space requirements as low as possible.

In the past, control of merchandise was kept through a perpetual inventory system, and periodic physical inventories were taken in order to check the effectiveness of the perpetual system. A great deal of paperwork was required for the perpetual inventory system, and often the payroll cost of tracking down errors in the bookkeeping was greater than the actual loss of merchandise.

A control system based on cost dollars is not only easier to administer than a perpetual inventory system but also requires much less manpower and makes storeroom and kitchen personnel more aware of the value of the items they are handling. Many storerooms are equipped with a cash register on which the cost value of incoming deliveries is entered. Requisitions are then priced and rung out on the register at the same value. The running total in the machine should then be the value of all goods in storage.

Another method of merchandise control is the ingredient room, which is used mainly by institutions having standardized recipes. In an ingredient room operation, daily food issues are limited to the exact amounts of ingredients required for each recipe to be prepared that day. Assembling, weighing, and measuring of ingredients is done not by highly paid cooks but by less skilled, lower-paid employees. Partially used containers of food remain in the ingredient room, under control. When a food production system is computerized, an ingredient room operation is recommended. An ingredient room has four major advantages:

1. Food issues from storage are restricted to the items and quantities actually required, so that waste and overproduction are minimized.
2. Skilled cooks are relieved of weighing, measuring, and assembling ingredients.
3. Adherence to standardized recipes is enforced. The cook cannot put extra ingredients into a product.
4. With this adherence to recipes, inventory and production controls can be more easily automated.

The major disadvantage of an ingredient room is that it usually requires extra space.

Thawing Frozen Foods

In a large operation, the storeroom personnel should be responsible for thawing frozen foods. Frozen products should never be thawed in water or by any form of high heat because hastening the defrosting process seriously affects the quality. Once thawed, foods should not be refrozen. Each time a product is frozen, cellular breakdown is increased, hastening the deterioration process. In protein products particularly, refreezing and subsequent thawing create conditions for bacterial growth that can render the product unsafe for consumption.

Storeroom personnel should be provided with a "pull" list so that they will be able to pull or transfer items from the freezer into refrigerated storage at the proper time. If this is done, the item will be thawed when needed by the kitchen. Some items may take 24 hours to thaw, whereas others—large masses such as turkeys—may require almost a week. Some operators using frozen convenience foods like to temper them overnight in the refrigerator.

Receiving and Storeroom Recordkeeping

Receiving Records

Daily Purchase Quotation List. One copy of the purchase quotation list (described in Chapter 4) should be given to the receiving clerk so he can check each delivery against the original order. He may also

mouth basis. Since the food is usually used immediately, purchases check the invoiced price against the bid price, or the checking may be done by a cost control clerk or accounts payable clerk.

Receiving Report. The receiving report is a record of all merchandise received. It provides a record of the receiving clerk's work, an indication of what merchandise was received and accepted, a basis for authorizing payment of the invoices, documentary evidence of a discrepancy in the event of a dispute with purveyors, and a record of the distribution of expenses.

The design of the receiving report may vary. Figure 5–6 is a traditional form. Every item is listed individually, and space is provided for recording the quantity, unit price, and extension. There is also a column for entering the distribution of the merchandise— whether it was sent directly to the kitchen for immediate use (as with bread or milk) or sent to the food storeroom for subsequent issuing. The sundries column is included for nonfood items, credits for containers, or food purchased for bar use. If there are multiple outlets to which food may be sent directly upon receipt, a receiving form can be specifically designed for recording this distribution. The receiving report is usually prepared in duplicate or triplicate. The original, together with the day's invoices, is sent to the accounting office for payment, and the duplicate goes to the food cost controller for use in preparing food cost reports. When the form is prepared in triplicate, the third copy is used by the storeroom personnel for pricing merchandise. The form shown in Fig. 5–6 requires considerable writing, duplicating much of the information that is on the invoice. Because this duplication requires costly manpower, the use of this type of receiving form is diminishing.

The form shown in Fig. 5–7 lightens the writing workload by combining the daily purchase quotation record with the receiving record. Even though it consolidates purchase and receiving information, the items must still be listed by hand. This is done by the buyer when the purchase list is prepared. One disadvantage of this form is that the receiver must retain the whole sheet and corresponding invoices until all items are delivered.

The form shown in Fig. 5–8 provides for distributing purchases by commodity. The receiver enters only the date, purveyor and invoice number, and the total of the invoice. The distribution can be made subsequently by an accounting clerk or cost controller. There are also enough columns for distribution to storeroom and kitchen if that is desired. Because this form does not provide cost information for use in pricing requisitions and inventories, that information has to be taken directly from the invoices.

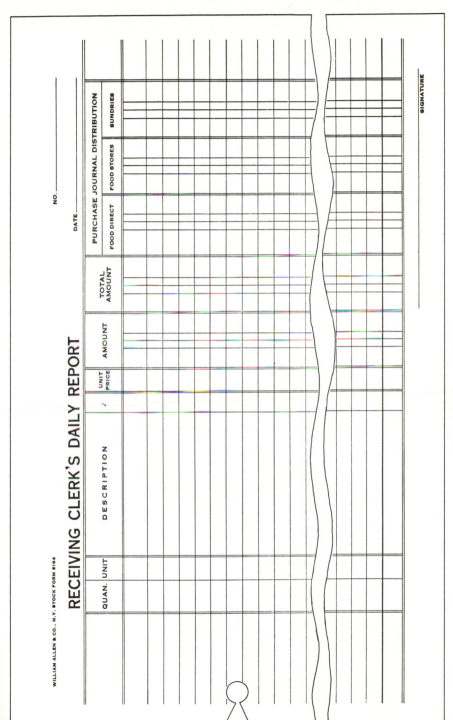

Fig. 5-6. Receiving clerk's daily report.

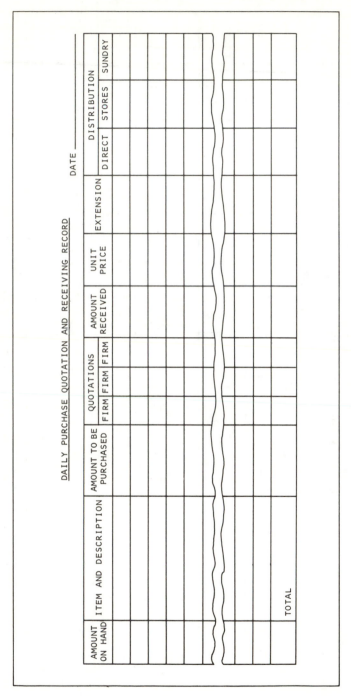

Fig. 5-7. Daily purchase quotation and receiving record.

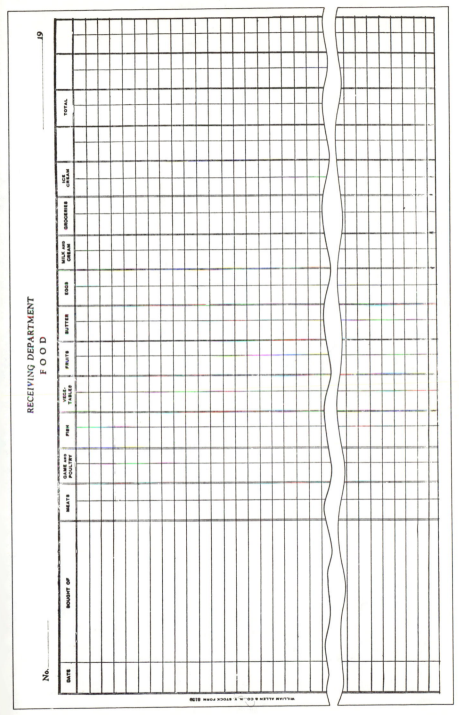

Fig. 5-8. Receiving record.

```
┌─────────────────────────────────────────────────┐
│  Date Received_____     │
│  Quality O.K._____     │
│  Quantity O.K._                                  │
│  Price O.K. _____     │
│  Extension and Footing O.K._____      │
│  O.K. for Payment_____      │
│                                                  │
└─────────────────────────────────────────────────┘
```

Fig. 5-9. Receiving stamp.

Receiving Stamp. All invoices should be stamped by the receiving clerk. A receiving stamp (see Fig. 5–9) should provide space for authorized personnel to initial their approval of the following major check points in the order listed: (1) receiving, (2) cost control, (3) purchasing, (4) management, and (5) accounts payable.

Meat Tags. In large operations using a requisition system, meat tags are helpful in determining the cost of the meats issued. Even small operations not using requisitions find the use of meat tags helpful in inventorying and in rotating stock.

A simple two-part meat tag is shown in Fig. 5–10. When delivery is made, primal cuts of meat are tagged with the date, the dealer, and the value of the cut. The stub end of the tag is removed and sent to the food cost controller. The main part of the tag remains with the piece of meat until after the cut is fabricated by the butcher and issued to the kitchen. Upon issuing, the tag is removed and attached to the requisition and sent to the food cost controller for use

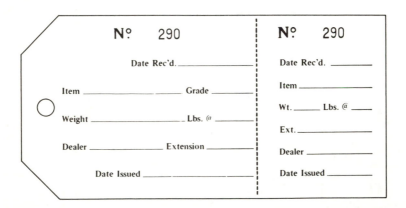

Fig. 5-10. Meat tag.

in costing the requisition. The "open" tags in the food controller's file should constitute the on-hand inventory of fresh meats.

The practice of tagging has several advantages: It facilitates checking on the receiving clerk's accuracy, it prevents disputes over the weight when the meat is issued to the kitchen, it avoids duplication of work because tagged meat need not be reweighed when issued to the kitchen, and it simplifies inventorying.

Request for Credit Memo. This form may be prepared by the receiving clerk if an invoice has been made out for the wrong amount or at a wrong price, or if the merchandise delivered fails to meet specifications and has to be returned to the vendor. The credit memo (Fig. 5–11) is made out with as many copies as are required by the accounting department. The amount of credit requested and the reason for the request are stated.

The credit form is signed by the delivery man, who retains one copy for his records. The other copy or copies are attached to the invoice for processing by the accounting department. When the prices and extensions are checked by a food and beverage controller, or bookkeeper, that person (or some other person designated by the accounting department) may initiate a request for credit memo, which is mailed to the purveyor.

WILLIAM ALLEN & CO., N.Y. STOCK FORM 7114

REQUEST FOR CREDIT MEMO. Nº 959

TO________________________________

________________________________ DATE________________

GENTLEMEN:

Please send us Credit Memo for the following:

YOUR INVOICE NO.

REASON:

BY________________________

Fig. 5-11. Request for credit memo.

The procedure just described is most suitable for a large operation such as a hotel. In a small restaurant, the information that would go on a request for credit memo in a large operation is often written directly on both the driver's and receiver's copy of the invoice. Errors found subsequently are discussed on the phone with the purveyor's bookkeepers.

Storeroom Records

Requisitions. The requisition represents the "check" drawn on the storeroom. Rather than being simply a shopping list, the requisition is a document in the internal control system of the operation. It should be written legibly and signed by the person initiating it. The names of the items and the grade and quantities desired must be clearly stated on the requisition. For example, a requisition for "four cans of peaches" is not sufficiently informative; the size of the can and the grade of peaches should be given if two or more kinds and sizes of peaches are stocked.

A list of personnel authorized to make out and approve requisitions should be made available in the storeroom. The list should note both names and titles, so that new storeroom personnel can know whether a requisition has been approved properly. It is also helpful to acquaint new storeroom personnel with the proper signatures. The storeroom person issuing the food must be specifically instructed to insist on proper approval. Methods for issuing food and the requirements for the acceptance of requisitions should be prepared by management and posted in a conspicuous place, visible both to the storeroom person and to the employee presenting the requisition. Requisitions may be initiated by a chef, kitchen manager, steward, or cook. Merchandise may be issued immediately upon receipt of the requisitions; but usually the requisitions are prepared at the close of a shift, and the merchandise is issued at the beginning of the following day's shift. The storeroom personnel can then assemble most of the orders during the off-periods and deliver them to the proper workstation when needed. Such a procedure assigns the time-consuming job of transporting goods to the low-salaried storeroom employee rather than the highly paid kitchen personnel.

The requisition form has space at the top for recording date and department, a line for the signature of the originator of the requisition, and two lines at the bottom to be signed by the person issuing and the person receiving the merchandise (see Fig. 5–12). The responsibility for the goods is plainly transferred to the person who receives them. If desired, requisitions can be made in duplicate or triplicate, thereby providing copies for the originator and the accounting department personnel or the food and beverage cost controller.

```
┌─────────────────────────────────────────────────────────┐
│                       REQUSITION                         │
│                                                          │
│   Department _____    Date _____       │
│   No. _____                                         │
│  ┌──────────┬─────────────────┬─────────┬────────────┐   │
│  │          │                 │  Unit   │            │   │
│  │ Quantity │     Items       │  Price  │   Total    │   │
│  ├──────────┼─────────────────┼─────────┼────────────┤   │
│  │          │                 │         │            │   │
│  │          │                 │         │            │   │
│  │          │                 │         │            │   │
│  │          │                 │         │            │   │
│  │          │                 │         │            │   │
│  │          │                 │         │            │   │
│  │          │                 │         │            │   │
│  ├──────────┴─────────────────┴─────────┼────────────┤   │
│                              TOTAL       │            │   │
│                                                          │
│   Approved Signature _____         │
│                                                          │
│   Issued by _____         │
│                                                          │
│   Received by_____         │
└─────────────────────────────────────────────────────────┘
```

Fig. 5-12. Requisition form.

Requisitions can also be consecutively numbered as a control against lost forms. Different series of numbers or colors of paper can be assigned to various departments to facilitate proper distribution of the cost of issues to the various preparation or cost centers.

Requisitions must be priced if a daily or departmental food cost is to be determined. If an accounting employee does this job, he will have either to guess the price or refer to numerous invoices. The best place to price requisitions quickly and accurately is in the storeroom, where the price may be entered directly from the merchandise itself. Such a system requires that the cost of every unit of merchandise be marked on the container—a procedure that facilitates both inventory taking and requisition pricing. The case price should be printed on the outside of each carton. When the carton is opened, the unit price may be stamped on each can, jar, or box, as is done in a supermarket.* Fruits, vegetables, and other bulk-packed items should

---

*The universal product codes that have been developed for the supermarket industry may someday be applicable to food service operations. Merchandise will be checked out of storerooms and refrigerators just as in the supermarket.

have the price printed or stamped on the tag used to denote the date of receipt.

Tagging meats with their weight and price when received eliminates the need to weigh the meat when it is issued. When meats are aged in-house, meat tags provide accurate information, despite discrepancies in weight caused by evaporation.

Sugar, spices, nut meats, dried fruits, and similar bulk items can be packaged, labeled, and priced ahead of time in the quantities usually requisitioned, thus minimizing the possibility of pricing errors or short weights to the kitchen. Such packaging in advance will also save time in filling and pricing the requisition. Time may also be saved in the kitchen if the packages contain the exact amounts required. Such a system has a side benefit of making employees aware of the cost of the merchandise that they handle and of the importance of avoiding waste.

Inventories. A physical inventory should be taken at the end of each accounting period. For cost control purposes, inventories should be taken at least monthly. The main storerooms and refrigerators can be inventoried after all deliveries have been received and all issues have been made for the day. The kitchen food should not be inventoried until the close of business for the day.

Inventory taking is sometimes left to the storeroom personnel, but such a policy is a lapse of managerial control. No person can properly control his own work. Inventories should always be taken by two people: usually the storeroom employee or receiver (who presumably knows what he has in stock), and a representative of management (usually one of the accounting personnel). It is good practice to have the inventory taken occasionally by the person responsible for extending inventories and preparing food cost statements, so that he becomes familiar with the items and the package sizes. The inventory takers should be able to start at a given point and proceed around the room or refrigerator in an orderly fashion. Items should be called as they are on the shelves to avoid miscounting. When the person counting has to step around to find the items, he is apt to miss a few. If the person doing the recording cannot locate the item quickly on his form, he should note it on a scratch pad and enter it on the inventory form later.

In addition to end-of-the-period inventories, weekly or semiweekly inventories may be advisable for close control of costs. Weekly inventories are not usually warranted unless the number of items to be counted is small.

The following are some common errors in inventorying: (1) counting items that were received at the very end of the period and therefore were not included in the goods purchased in the period being covered; (2) mispricing because of uncertainty about package size, grade, or quality; (3) miscounting because of carelessness. Such errors can be minimized by the maintenance of good order in the storeroom department and the use of preprinted inventory forms.

The Receiving and Storeroom Jobs

Typically in a small operation, the merchandise received by the manager or the chef is given to a porter or dishwasher to be put away. This practice is permissible so long as the employee is sufficiently aware of what he is storing and puts the merchandise in the right place, properly rotating and dating it. If the employee is illiterate, it may be helpful to label the shelves with pictures. Finally, adequate supervision must be exercised over the whole storage function. In a large operation, good management practice requires that the purchasing, receiving, and issuing be done by different people for control purposes.

Before being processed for payment, all invoices must indicate that merchandise was actually received. This reduces the possibility of "phantom" orders being placed by the purchaser or of payment being approved for goods not destined for the operation. Separation of the issuing function from the purchasing and receiving functions eliminates the possibility of charging out too much merchandise to cover up shortages in deliveries or losses in the storerooms.

In a smaller operation, it may not be practicable to separate the purchasing and receiving functions. However, in such cases it is practical to permit the same person to purchase and receive food supplies, subject to surprise receiving tests by the auditor. When the surprise tests are made at irregular but frequent intervals, there is less opportunity for shortages in weights and counts to occur. As an added safeguard, the manager or employee in the food department should make frequent receiving tests.

The accounting department or bookkeeper should be responsible for checking the numerical accuracy of invoices and for verifying that the price charged is the price bid. Request for credit memos should also be checked by this department to be sure that the credit has been received. In large operations, the food cost controller who is responsible to either the auditor or the chief executive makes the tests and checks of proper purchasing, receiving, and issuing techniques.

6

FOOD PRODUCTION MANAGEMENT

In a manufacturing plant, the production manager's job is to bring together materials, manpower, and equipment in order to produce a product. He must produce the product (1) when it is needed, (2) within the set specifications of the company, and (3) as economically as possible. To do the job properly, the production manager needs two kinds of knowledge: an understanding of production management techniques and technical knowledge of the products produced in his plant.

The commercial kitchen is a minimanufacturing plant, usually presided over by a chef or kitchen manager rather than a production manager. This person is responsible for ordering or requisitioning food, scheduling the staff, and making sure his equipment is functioning satisfactorily so that the items on the menu are produced on time and in conformance with the established standards of his operation, while the desired food and payroll costs for his department are maintained.

Unfortunately, the facilities for training chefs in this country have been limited, and most American chefs have had to learn their profession on the job where they usually were taught only the technical aspects of cookery. The managerial requirements of the job have been very much neglected. Furthermore, some chefs, having risen through the ranks, identify themselves with the employees rather than with management, of which they are an important part.

For too long, top level executives have stayed out of the kitchen because they felt that its workings were too complex and mysterious for anyone but a "food man" to understand. In years past, cooking was considered an art, shrouded in mystery, and requiring long years of apprenticeship to master. Methods of preparing food commercially have changed considerably, however, during the past

75 years, so that today only a very few restaurants employ the classical methods of cookery. In the vast majority of restaurants and in almost all noncommercial food operations, cookery is an exact science based on chemistry and on modern production planning techniques.

Food service management can no longer abdicate its responsibility in the production function. If management skills are not forthcoming from chefs, then management itself must provide them—at least until such time as this shortcoming in the training process is corrected.

There are three elements of production: materials, manpower, and machines. This chapter deals only with materials. Although some of the techniques to be described are also applicable to the management of manpower, the staffing and personnel functions are discussed in Chapters 15 and 16. The equipment found in today's commercial kitchen is relatively inflexible. Other than the procurement of small utensils and equipment, the kitchen manager's or chef's main concern with equipment is to keep it in operating order. (See *Profitable Food and Beverage Management: Planning* for a discussion of kitchen layout and design.)

Production Management Techniques

In manufacturing, the production manager uses a number of techniques that are applicable to a food service operation. Those related to materials management are:

Processing Instructions
Production Planning
Production Control
Inventory Control
Quality Control

Processing Instructions

Standardized Recipe. The standardized recipe is the blueprint for the product. "Standardized" means that a recipe has been written so that every time it is followed it will produce the desired uniformity in a product. The quantity of every ingredient is stated precisely, and every direction is written clearly. The American Dietetic Association (ADA) defines standardized recipe as a recipe that has been tested under carefully controlled conditions, for yield and quality for a specific situation.*

---

*The booklet *Standardizing Recipes for Institutional Use* can be ordered from The American Dietetic Association, 620 N. Michigan Avenue, Chicago, Ill., 60611. It is an invaluable tool in a recipe standardization program.

To be standardized a recipe must include all the detailed information necessary to prepare the item:

1. The exact amount of every ingredient should be given. Most ingredients are weighed for greatest accuracy. Fluids and very small amounts of spices and seasonings are usually measured, rather than weighed. Each ingredient should be clearly identified as defined. For ease of purchasing, as purchased (AP) weights should be specified as well as edible portion (EP) weights.

2. Ingredients should be listed in the order in which they will be combined. They may be grouped if they are combined together in one step.

3. The proper terminology should be used. "Beat," "stir" and "fold," for example, do not mean the same thing.

4. The amount of time required for any process should be indicated, as well as the baking or cooking time and temperature.

5. Equipment references, such as dial settings, speeds, and blade sizes, should refer to equipment actually in use in the operation. For example, the speeds on one mixer may be "low," "medium," and "high," while on another, speed settings may be indicated by numbers.

6. The exact pan size and the amount of product to be put in each pan should be specified.

7. The portion size and exact yield of the recipe should be given. Several yields should be given if different quantities may be required at different times. Usually three columns are sufficient if they are not merely multiples of one another.

The recipe in Fig. 6–1 is taken from the ADA's booklet. It gives two yields—for two and three pans of cake. With these two columns any combination of multiples can be produced. It might be helpful to show a one-pan yield, since many cooks find it more difficult to divide fractions than to add them.

There has been much reluctance in the restaurant business to accept standardized recipes. Some chefs feel that asking a cook to follow a recipe is to question the employee's skill, since good chefs and cooks are supposed to have the recipes "in their heads." Furthermore, they feel that making a cook follow a recipe deprives him of any opportunity for creativity or individuality, leaving the food dull and "institutional." Such reservations should be dismissed in the light of modern management know-how. Although the technique was developed in institutions, and particularly in hospitals, the standardized recipe would be "institutional" only if it were written that way. Whether the resulting product is bland and uninteresting or flavorful

Sample Recipe Format

APPLESAUCE CAKE, File No. BC-4
Cut 6x8; portion 2x2¾"

Oven temperature, 350°F.
Baking time, 30-35 min.

Ingredients	2 pans	3 pans	Method
Shortening	1# 7 oz.	2# 3 oz.	Cream well for 5 min. on medium speed with paddle.
Sugar	2# 14 oz.	4# 5 oz.	
Eggs	2 cup	3 cup	Add and beat 5 minutes on medium speed.
Applesauce	2 qt. +½ c.	3¼ qt.	Add gradually on low speed. Beat 1 minute on medium speed after last addition. Scrape down.
Cake flour	2# 14 oz.	4# 5 oz.	Sift dry ingredients together and mix with raisins. Add to above mixture gradually on low speed. Beat 2 minutes, medium speed, after last addition. Scrape down once.
Soda	1 oz.	1½ oz.	
Salt	4 tsp.	2 Tbsp.	
Cinnamon	1 Tbsp.	4½ tsp.	
Nutmeg	1½ tsp.	2¼ tsp.	
Cloves	1½ tsp.	2¼ tsp.	
Raisins	12 oz.	1# 2 oz.	
Total weight	13# 6 oz.	20# 2 oz.	Weigh into greased pans, 12 x 22 x 2". 6# 8 oz./pan.

Fig. 6-1. Sample recipe format.

and appealing is not the result of documenting a recipe. It depends on the quality of ingredients, amount of seasoning, method of preparation, and style of presentation, all of which are specified in a well-written recipe. In fact, standardized recipes are one technique that many institutions use to avoid serving dull, unappetizing food.

The idea that chefs and cooks can carry all the required recipes in their heads is naive. Individuals also take days off and vacations, get sick, and occasionally leave their jobs. Unless there is a written guide, the substitute or succeeding cook cannot duplicate the product as desired.

More serious than a lack of uniformity in the product is the total dependency of management on the employees to design and "engineer" the product. No manufacturing firm would long survive if it permitted the employees to make the products any way they saw fit each day. The ideas and suggestions of the employees should be considered when the recipe is being created, but management must make the ultimate decision concerning product design.

The standardized recipe is a tool with which a menu item having the desired characteristics can be produced consistently. The items may be unique to a particular restaurant, which is all the more reason to develop standard recipes: to protect those house specialties (on which the restaurant may have built a reputation) from loss owing to a loss of personnel or from deterioration owing to human error or omission.

The standardized recipe also provides a sound basis for determining portion cost. (The need for valid cost information as a basis for determining menu prices is discussed in *Profitable Food and Beverage Management: Planning.*) Cost information is also essential in the internal control of the operation. First, if the most economical way to produce the desired result is to be determined, there must be a starting point. Once a recipe has been documented, the item can be re-made and evaluated with various ingredients and various methods of preparation. Can frozen eggs be substituted for fresh? Can a lower grade of canned fruit be used and the desired result still be achieved? Can margarine be used for butter? This type of analysis can ulti-mately have a considerable effect on food cost and acceptability.

Once the recipes have been standardized, food cost informa-tion can be developed. The development and use of food cost data is discussed in a later section. The test shown in Table 6–1 (adapted from the ADA booklet) shows the effect of standardized recipes and production control procedures on profit:

The test in Table 6–1 effectively demonstrates the need for standardized recipes. When the baker used his own judgment, too

**Table 6–1. A Test Showing Increased Profit
from Recipe Standardization and Production Control: Cakes**

Item (from 37 lb 2 oz batter)	On the basis of baker's judgment	On the basis of standardization and production control
Number of 9" layers	10 (approx. 19¼ oz per layer)	12 (1 lb per layer)
Number of 22 x 12 x 2" sheets	3 (approx. 8 lb. 5 oz per sheet)	4 (6 lb per sheet)
Number of servings, layer	80 @ $.45 each	96 @ $.45 each
Number of servings, sheet	144 @ $.35 each	192 @ .35 each
Total income from sales	$86.40	$110.40
Cost of batter @ $.24 per lb.	8.91	8.91
Cost of frosting	8.64	8.64
Bakers' labor		
3 hrs. @ $4.00 per hr.	12.00	12.00
Labor for oven cleaning		
2 hrs. @ $2.25 per hr.	4.50	——
Total labor	16.50	12.00
Fringes and related payroll expense	3.30	2.40
Total labor and related expense	18.80	14.40
Total direct cost	36.35	31.95
Gross profit	$50.05	$ 78.45

much cake batter was put in each pan, resulting in waste as it flowed over on the oven floor. The edges of the layers also had to be trimmed before icing the cakes. Sheet cakes were so high that portions toppled over on the plates, no doubt increasing loss due to breakage. Finally, because the portion was too large, most customers ate only about three-quarters of the piece.

Standardized Procedure. The term recipe has been used in the preceding section. Some menu items, such as coffee, are not usually thought of as requiring a recipe. Clear, concise instructions for preparing every item served are essential to a well-run operation. Whether they are called recipes, formulas, standard procedures, or SOP's is a matter of semantics.

Portion Control. One aspect of product standardization that seems to give some food service operators particular trouble is uniform portion sizes. The economic effect of a lapse in portion control is shown in Table 6–1. Equally undesirable is the effect on the customer when he is served a portion that is different from·the next person's or from one he was served previously. Restaurant patrons expect to receive the same size portion for the money each time they order it, just as the food service operator expects to receive his commodities in standard sizes each time he buys.

There are many tools and implements available to assist in maintaining standard portions. Two types of portion scales are shown

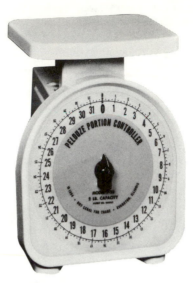

Fig. 6-2. Bounce-type portion scale. The dial is adjustable to compensate for the weight of a container. *(Courtesy of Pelouze Scale Co.)*

in Figs. 6–2 and 6–3. The balance-type scale (Fig. 6–3) is much more durable and accurate than the bounce-type scale (Fig. 6–2) but also much more expensive. Whatever type of scale is used, it should be a model designed for portioning and one that shows graduations clearly to one-quarter ounce.

Other portioning tools are scoops, ladles, and measuring cups. These implements are available in a wide variety of sizes, and custom-made measuring devices can be fabricated for unusual portion sizes if necessary. There are a few marking guides available for cutting pies and layer cakes, but markers for panned goods usually have to be fabricated.

The size of the dish or glass used also sets a limit on the size of the portion of some items, although it does not preclude underportioning. Since permanent ware is usually purchased infrequently, adequate managerial attention is usually given to ordering the proper size. With disposable ware, however, routine purchasing errors or careless receiving, if not corrected, could lead to a change in container size, ultimately affecting the size of the portion served.

Kitchen Tests

Four types of kitchen tests are mentioned briefly in Chapter 4: raw food tests for fruits and vegetables, canned food tests, butchering tests, and cooking tests. The testing of recipes might also be considered a kitchen test. The purpose of butchering, canned food, cooking, and raw food tests is to determine the amount of usable food in

Fig. 6-3. Balance-type portion scale. The desired portion size is set on the beam with the weight, and the dial indicates when the portion is over or under the desired weight. *(Courtesy of Toledo Scale)*

relation to the quantity purchased. The results may be used for the following purposes:

1. Determining portion costs. Tests for this purpose should be made both initially, when developing a new menu item, and on a continuing basis.
2. Determining a basis for calculating quantities of food to be purchased. These may be stated in terms of portions per pound (for meats) or portions per can or package (for processed items). Purchasing data are usually calculated only when the purchase specification is developed or changed.
3. Determining the best method of preparation. Cooking times and methods can have considerable effect on the resulting yield. Peeling fresh fruits and vegetables by hand may result in a different yield from peeling by machine.
4. Determining the purchase form that will give the best yield, for use in writing the specifications. This is usually done only when the specification is written or changed.
5. Testing adherence to established specifications on a continuing basis.
6. Checking on how well the employees follow established recipes and procedures. Having preparation employees per-

BUTCHER TEST CARD

ITEM #103 RIB OF BEEF   GRADE U.S. CHOICE   DATE 3/21/19—

PIECES 1   A.P. WT. 36 LBS. 4 OZ.   AVERAGE WEIGHT _____

TOTAL COST 39.88   AT $ 1.10 PER LB   SUPPLIER ABC MEATS

| A | B | C | D | E | F | G | H | I | COST FACTOR | | PURCHASE DATA | |
COMPONENTS	WEIGHT	RATIO TO TOTAL WEIGHT	MARKET VALUE PER LB.	TOTAL VALUE	COST PER LB.	PER OZ.	PORTION SIZE	PORTION COST	PER LB.	PER PORTION	NO. OBTAINED	PORTIONS PER LB A.P.
OVEN PREPARED RIB	22 13	62.9%	$1.41	$32.17								
SHORTRIBS	3 7	9.5	1.29	4.44	$1.29	$.081	10 oz	$.810	1.17	.74	5.5	.15
HAMBURGER	3 7	9.5	.95	3.27	.95	.059	4 oz	.236	.86	.21	13.75	.38
FAT AND BONE	6 9	18.1	NO VALUE	NO VALUE								
TOTALS	36 4	100.0%	$1.10	$39.88								

(See Reverse Side For Cooking Loss)

Fig. 6-4. Butcher test card.

form kitchen tests frequently and routinely as a part of their regular duties can increase their understanding of the need for following established procedures.

Butchering Tests. The butcher test card (Fig. 6–4) is used in computing the usable yields for meats, fish, and poultry. For the item in Fig. 6–4 (ribs of beef), several by-products are obtained: short ribs, hamburger, and fat and bones. In determining the portion cost of the finished ribs of beef, credit must be given for the value of those usable by-products having value.

A butcher test involves the following procedures:

1. The top of the card is filled out with the purchase information. If more than one piece is being tested, the average weight is determined and entered.
2. The cut or cuts are processed, and the weights of the component parts are recorded in column B. For computation purposes, it may be helpful to convert ounces to decimal fractions of a pound:

$$1 \text{ oz} = 0.0625 \text{ lb}$$

3. The ratio of each component weight to the total weight is calculated (column C). For example:

$$\text{Prepared rib } \frac{22 \text{ lb } 13 \text{ oz}}{36 \text{ lb } 4 \text{ oz}} \quad \text{or} \quad \frac{22.81}{36.25} = 0.629 \text{ or } 62.9\%.$$

4. The current market value of short ribs and hamburger is obtained from the local dealers, and entered in column D.
5. The total value of short ribs and hamburger is obtained by multiplying the market value times the weight of each of these two components. (If there is any market value for bones and fat, this may be entered also, but it usually is insignificant.)
6. The total value of the by-products obtained in steps 4 and 5 is subtracted from the total (AP) cost of the cut, column E, to arrive at the total value of the oven-prepared rib.
7. The total value of the oven-prepared rib, step 6, is divided by the weight of this component to arrive at the value per pound. The result in the example, $1.41, is entered in column D.
8. If there are no usable by-products, steps 4 through 7 are eliminated. Ribs of beef are portioned after roasting. Therefore, cooking tests must be made to obtain the ultimate yield from this cut. Items such as steaks and short ribs are portioned in the raw state. For this type of item, additional computations can be made on the butcher test card to obtain portion costs and yields.
9. The costs per pound of short ribs and hamburger are entered

COOKING LOSS

ITEM #103 RIB OF BEEF

COOKED 4 HOURS 15 MINUTES AT 300°F _____ DEGREES

_____ HOURS _____ MINUTES AT _____ DEGREES   INT. TEMP. 125°F

	WEIGHT (J)	RATIO TO TOTAL WEIGHT (K)	VALUE PER LB. (L)	TOTAL VALUE
ORIGINAL WEIGHT	36 4/	100.0%	$1.10	$39.88
TRIMMED WEIGHT	22 13/	62.9	1.41	32.17
LOSS IN TRIMMING	13 7/	37.1		
COOKED WEIGHT	19 0/	52.4	1.69	32.17
LOSS IN COOKING	3 13/	10.5		
BONES, TRIM AND }				
LOSS IN SLICING	4 8/	12.4		
SALABLE MEAT	14 8/	40.0	2.22	32.17

YIELD 40%   RECIPROCAL 2.5

COST PER POUND SALABLE MEAT $2.22

COST PER OUNCE SALABLE MEAT $.139

COST PER PORTION	PORTION SIZE	
	10 oz	8 oz
COST PER PORTION	$1.39	$1.11
PURCHASE DATA		
NO. PORTIONS OBTAINED	23.2	29
PORTIONS PER LB. A/P	.64	.80

COST FACTOR PER LB 2.02

Fig. 6-5. Cooking loss card.

in column F. This is the same as the market value per pound, column D.

10. The cost per ounce is obtained by dividing the cost per pound by 16. The result is entered in column G.
11. The portion size for each of the by-product items is entered in column H. The cost per portion, obtained by multiplying the portion size in ounces by the cost per ounce, is entered in column I.

Cooking Tests. To test the item in Fig. 6–4, the oven-prepared rib is roasted in the usual manner. The cooking time and the oven and internal temperatures are recorded on a cooking loss card (Fig. 6–5). It is convenient to have this form on the reverse side of the butcher test card to keep the information together. The cooking test proceeds as follows:

1. The roast is weighed after it is cooked, and the cooked weight is entered in the appropriate line of column J. Since a cooked roast will continue to shrink between the time that it is removed from the oven and the time that it is carved, this weight should be taken when the roast is ready for carving.
2. The cooking loss is obtained by subtracting the cooked weight from the raw trimmed weight.
3. The roast is sliced and portioned, and the weight of usable portions is entered in the appropriate line of column J.
4. Loss in slicing is calculated by subtracting the amount of salable meat from the cooked weight.
5. The ratio of the weight of salable meat to the original or AP weight (column K) is calculated (see step 3 of butcher test). (Other ratios may be calculated as desired for comparison to some previous results.)
6. The value or cost per pound (column L) is taken from the butcher test results: the original cost and the trimmed weight value, with credit given for the value of usable by-products.
7. The cooked roast still carries the cost of the trimmed roast, but since the weight shrank in cooking and slicing, the cost *per pound* is now higher. The cost per pound of the cooked, salable meat is obtained by dividing the weight of the salable meat by the total value (cost) of the trimmed roast.
8. The cost per ounce and cost per portion are calculated as for raw meat (steps 9–11).

Purchasing Data. Purchasing data can now be calculated for roast ribs of beef. Salable cooked ribs amounted to 40 percent of the AP weight. The reciprocal of this number may be more useful in calculating purchasing requirements. A reciprocal of a number is that number divided into one: 1/0.40. The reciprocal of 0.40 is 2.5, which means that in order to get 1 pound of salable cooked ribs of beef, 2.5 pounds must be purchased.

If only one portion size is used for a menu item, it may be more helpful to calculate a purchase factor based on portion size. This is done by dividing the number of portions obtained in the test by the AP weight. In this case, about 23 portions were obtained from a piece weighing 36 lbs., 4 oz., or 0.64 servings per pound as purchased.

To use this factor, divide it into the number of portions desired. For 100 portions:

$$\frac{100}{0.64} = 156 \text{ lb required}$$

Purchasing data can also be calculated for short ribs of beef. The salable yield of short ribs from the #103 primal rib in Fig. 6–4 was 9.5 percent. In other words, on the basis of this test, 9.5 pounds of short ribs could be expected from every 100 pounds of primal rib. Using the reciprocal, 10.5 pounds of primal ribs must be purchased to get one pound of usable short ribs. Since short ribs are a by-product, purchases are usually made on the basis of the requirements for the main product, the rib roast. Using the salable yield, the amount of usable short ribs that will result from a given quantity of primal ribs can be calculated. The same is true of hamburger.

Cost Factors. The cost factor is simply the relationship of the cost per portion or per ounce of the salable product to the original price. The use of these factors permits cost information to be updated easily when the purchase prices change. For example, to obtain the cost factor for ribs of beef, divide the cost per pound of salable meat by the AP cost per pound.

$$\frac{\text{Cost per pound, salable meat:}}{\text{Cost per pound, AP:}} \quad \frac{\$2.22}{1.10} = 2.02, \text{ cost factor}$$

If the price per pound rose to $1.20, all that would be necessary to update the cost data would be to multiply the new price by the cost factor:

$1.20 \times 2.02 = \$2.42$, new cost per pound of salable meat

Cutting and cooking yield tests must be made on a large enough sample to provide an average yield for the kind of merchandise being bought. When these average yields have been determined, it should not be expected that each piece will meet the yield exactly, although it should be close, depending on the tolerance of the purchase specification. On the average, the yield figures being used should be quite accurate.

Yield tests must be made in each operation and must fit the menus, recipes, and purchase specifications being used. There are no standard tables that can be applied because the purchase specification (amount of trim, type of cut, and weight range, the method of cutting and cooking, and the portion size) will affect the resulting yields. If there is any change in purchase forms or preparation method, new yield tests must be made. It is a good idea to have yield tests made on a periodic basis, not only to test the figures but also to test the employees, and to be sure that the expected number of portions are actually being obtained from the raw product.

In addition to meats, yields can also be calculated for all other items on the menu. When there is little or no processing involved, standard yield figures are available, such as for canned or frozen goods. Yields can also be calculated for fresh fruits and vegetables, although most operations today use too little fresh produce to warrant the effort. Such items as lettuce and salad greens may be yielded occasionally for cost purposes.

Production Planning—Forecasting

Production planning begins with a sales forecast made in production units or portions rather than in dollars. If no forecast is made, the employees are forced to use their own judgment about how much food to prepare, often with undesirable results. In most cases, a cook will produce the quantity he prepared previously, giving no consideration to what was left over; or he will produce too much to avoid running out of food. If he does not have enough raw food to produce the quantity he thinks he needs, he may affect the quality of the product by extending or "stretching" it with other ingredients. If unaware of a particular event that may affect the day's sales, a cook may not prepare enough food.

Sales forecasting must be a function of management. Initial forecasts should be made one to two weeks ahead, and should begin with an estimate of the number of covers to be served daily at each meal, in each outlet. Forecasts developed for use in planning the budget do not provide the detailed current information required for production planning. Initial production forecasts should take the following into consideration:

1. The number of covers served on a corresponding day of the previous year and the circumstances pertaining to that business, such as weather or special events. Special function covers should be distinguished from regular public dining room or "walk-in" business.
2. Recent trends in business, such as the past week's or past month's cover counts in relation to those for the corresponding periods a year ago. Cover-count statistics are more valid than

dollar sales because the effect of any price increases is eliminated.

3. Special events, such as local conventions, programs, athletic events, or other functions that will attract guests.
4. For a hotel, the projected house counts or reservations, and for a hospital, the census forecast.
5. Special advertising or promotional efforts being planned.
6. The occurrence of holidays or other special events that may alter the normal meal pattern.

Since special parties or banquets are usually booked ahead, their requirements can easily be forecast. For this reason, forecasts should separate party business from walk-in business. Figure 6–6 shows a weekly forecast of covers. Banquet forecasts are taken from

THE EXAMPLE RESTAURANT

FORECAST OF DINNER COVERS

WEEK OF MARCH 22-28

		BANQUETS	DINING ROOM	TOTAL
MONDAY	3/22	–	500	500
TUESDAY	3/23	100	750	850
WEDNESDAY	3/24	–	825	825
THURSDAY	3/25	–	450	450
FRIDAY	3/26	–	550	550
SATURDAY	3/27	90	1260	1350
SUNDAY	3/28	–	1600	1600
TOTAL		190	5935	6125
Actual Same Period Last Year			5896	

(BANKERS' CONVENTION noted between Tuesday and Wednesday dining room entries)

Fig. 6-6. The Example Restaurant forecast of dinner covers.

actual bookings, whereas walk-in covers are forecast on the basis of historical information and current trends. In this instance, dinner forecasts take into consideration a convention that will be in town.

Popularity Ratio. Once the total number of covers is forecast for each meal, it is necessary to determine the sales mix that will make up the total. Using cover sales records, a popularity ratio can be developed. A popularity ratio is the number of portions sold of each entrée in relation to the total number of entrées sold, expressed as a percentage. For example:

Portions of prime ribs sold: $\dfrac{160}{1000}$ = .16 (or 16%) Popularity of prime ribs
Total number of covers sold:

If a set menu is used, the ratio can be a cumulative figure, or it can be the result of periodic sales analysis. If a cycle menu is used, a separate ratio must be calculated for each menu. One advantage of using a cycle menu instead of writing a new menu every day is obvious: The cycle provides more accurate data for forecasting. The salability of any given item will be influenced by the other choices on the menu. Without a history of the relative popularity of one item in combination with others, the sales mix must be forecast by guesswork, but a record should be kept to accumulate this information for future use.

An analysis of the sales history may reveal that the relative popularity of the various items on a set menu changes according to the day of the week. Families dining out on Sunday may order differently from couples on Saturday night. Lower-priced items may sell better earlier in the week. Thus, it may be necessary to develop a different ratio for different days of the week.

At the Example Restaurant (Fig. 6–7), popularity ratios are calculated for each item on the menu on the basis of past sales experience. Different sets of ratios are used for weekdays, Saturdays, and Sundays. The number of servings to be made of each menu item is determined by multiplying the total number of covers forecast for each meal by the popularity ratio for each item. Thus, for Monday dinner, prime ribs of beef has a popularity ratio of 16 percent. Therefore, 16 percent of the total covers forecast (500) should be roast prime ribs.

Some operators add a cushion of 10 percent to their total cover forecast to reduce the possibility of run-outs. Others prefer to work closer to the base forecasts and are less concerned about running out of one or two items. The proportion of the menu items prepared to order and thus controllable is a major factor in determining this policy.

After the number of portions of each item has been forecast, the information must be converted into preparation units (such as number of pans, gallons, pounds, or pieces) that must be prepared.

THE EXAMPLE RESTAURANT

MENU ITEM FORECAST

DINNER   Week of __MARCH 22-28__

Dining Room Covers Forecasted	MONDAY 3/22 Pop. Rat. .500		TUE. 3/23 750	WED. 3/24 825	THU. 3/25 450	FRI. 3/26 550	SATURDAY 3/27 Pop. Rat. .1260		SUN. 3/28 1600
PRIME RIBS OF BEEF	16%	80	120	132	72	88	20%	252 ⑨⓪	288
FILET OF SOLE	6	30	45	50	27	33	15	189	160
LOBSTER	5	25	37	40	22	27	12	151	112
SIRLOIN STEAK	9	45	68	74	41	50	18	227	192
YANKEE POT ROAST	20	100	150	165	90	110	10	126	288
ROAST TURKEY	20	100	150 ⑩⓪	165	90	110	14	177	320
CORNED BEEF & CABB	10	50	75	83	45	55	7	88	80
CHICKEN FRICASSEE	14	70	105	116	63	77	4	50	160
TOTAL COVERS	100%	500	850	825	450	550	100%	1350	1600

Fig. 6-7. The Example Restaurant menu item forecast. Pop. Rat. means Popularity Ratio. In this example, the same ratio is applied Monday through Friday, and a different ratio is applied for Saturday and Sunday. Circled numbers represent party or banquet requirements.

Yield factors are applied and recipes consulted. The forecast units may not coincide with recipe units, and an adjustment may be required. For example, in Fig. 6–7, 70 portions of chicken fricassee were forecast for Monday dinner. The Example Restaurant's recipe for chicken fricassee was written in multiples of one gallon, with one gallon yielding 21 six-ounce portions. In this case, the production manager would have to decide whether to order three gallons (63 portions) or four gallons (84 portions) of fricassee for Monday. Portions of roast meat should be rounded to multiples of the yield of a piece of meat, sized according to the purchase specifications.

These initial forecasts should be reviewed just prior to production for any last-minute changes. Weather is a major last-minute consideration, since unusual weather conditions may drastically affect the sales volume or mix. Availability of the items planned for the menu may also affect production requirements. An item may not be available on the market when needed, and a substitution may have to be made. On the other hand, there may be items available that represent a particularly good value and that can be offered as a "special." The addition to the menu may require a reduction in the production requirements of the other items.

Banquet production requirements may also have changed since the time the party was originally booked. Usually, the guaranteed number is required 24 to 48 hours in advance of the party, so that production schedules can be adjusted.

Production Sheets. The actual recording of the food production forecasts is done on a production work sheet (Fig. 6–8). This may be a preprinted form with the set menu shown, or a blank sheet, with the items written in by hand. There should be enough space for six columns: the forecast, the amount to make, "need to buy," the amount actually made, the amount sold, and the amount of leftovers. A separate sheet may be used for each meal. Operations with a limited set menu sometimes use a form with space for seven days. If an item sold out, the leftover column can be used to show the time when it ran out. When completed, this sheet becomes a record for forecasting future sales. For control purposes, unit sales of each item can also be compared with sales counts tallied by the cashier (or some other nonproduction employee). This and other control uses of the production sheet are discussed in greater detail in the section on food cost control. Appetizers, soups, desserts, vegetables, and cold items should be recorded in the same way.

Purchasing Requirements. When the number of portions forecast has been entered on the production sheet, the items and quantities required can be determined. The number of portions required must be translated into purchasing units and preparation units. (The use of purchasing factors to calculate the amounts of solid meat items is discussed in the section on Purchasing Data, p. 165). The poundage calculated must be possible within the weight range of the purchase specification, and if it is not, the amount must be rounded up or down.

Forecasts for items made from recipes must also be adjusted to conform to the recipe units, such as pans or gallons. The purchasing requirements for the desired quantity can be taken directly from the recipe card. When the AP requirements are shown on the card, in addition to the trimmed or usable raw weights, the purchase requirement does not have to be recalculated each time.

For efficient purchasing procedures to be followed, the buyer should receive purchase requirements in advance of the time they are

THE EXAMPLE RESTAURANT

FOOD PRODUCTION WORKSHEET

DINNER MON. MAR. 22   Weather COOL, CLEAR

	FORECAST	AMOUNT TO MAKE	NEED TO BUY	AMOUNT MADE	AMOUNT SOLD	NUMBER LEFT
PRIME RIBS OF BEEF	80	4 pc / .64	125 lbs NO. 103, 34-38 lb	4 pc	77	1/4 pc
FILET OF SOLE	30	30 ∦ / 1.3	25 lbs SOLE	30 ∦	25	5 ∦ raw
LOBSTER	25	25 pc	25 pc	18	18	7
SIRLOIN STEAK	45	45 pc / 1.0	45 lbs NO. 175	3 pc + 1/2 pc	53	USED 8 MORE REORDER FOR TUES.
YANKEE POT ROAST	100	45 lb / 2.2	45 lbs NO. 164	50 lb	113	-0-
ROAST TURKEY	100	2 TURKEYS / 2.2	45 lbs TURKEYS (24-26 lbs) 6 lb BREAD, 3 lb ONIONS	120 ∦ (49 lb)	107	13 ∦
CORNED BEEF & CABB	50	20 lbs / 2.5	20 lb BRISKET 25 lb CABBAGE 15 lb CARROTS 20 lb ME. POTS.	19 lb	51	OUT 8:30
CHICKEN FRICASSEE	70	4 gals 84 ∦	42 lbs FOWL 3 lb MUSHROOMS 2 CN MED WHOLE ONION 6 lb EGG NOODLES	3 gal + 1/2 gal	75	-0-
TOTALS	500				519	

Fig. 6-8. The Example Restaurant food production worksheet.

needed. These requirements or needs do not constitute the purchase order. The on-hand inventory must be considered, and the order amounts adjusted for any merchandise on hand. (Purchasing procedures are described in Chapter 4.)

Requisitions and Cooks' Worksheets. If a requisitioning procedure is used, requisitions can be prepared from the "need to buy" column of the food production worksheet, with adjustments for quantities already on hand in the kitchen. Only amounts required for current production should be requisitioned. Requisitions should be prepared by the chef, production manager, or some other authorized person, and properly signed.

Cook's worksheets are used to assign the items to be prepared. These worksheets are often the printer's galley proofs of the menu, but they may be handwritten lists of the items to be prepared, the amounts to be produced, and any special instructions. One worksheet may be made up for each person or for each work station. During the preparation and service of the meal, the cooks keep track of how much they make of each item and how much is left over, and return the worksheet to the chef at the end of the meal. This information is then consolidated on the production sheet.

Scheduling the Work. The worksheets and recipes required are usually distributed a day ahead of time. This enables the cooks to begin any advance preparation required and ensures removal of only the necessary merchandise from the control of the storeroom.

Advance preparation is a factor of production scheduling that can seriously affect not only the timing of the completed product but also its quality. Some products (such as gelatin, marinated items, or doughs that must set) must be made a day or more before use. In other cases, the meal and staff schedules do not permit the product to be prepared completely on the day of service. One example of this is a pot roast requiring long hours of slow cooking that must be done one day ahead for luncheon service. Advance preparation may be scheduled to equalize the work load but only if the advance work will not affect the quality of the product. For example, lettuce cleaned the day before use and properly stored will become crisp and dry, whereas if tomatoes are sliced too long before service, they will become limp and soft.

Some menu items lend themselves to the preparation of small batches, which is another technique in production management. Preparation can be "staggered" to meet the sales demand. Components of a dish can be prepared and combined as needed. Any components left over can be utilized in other ways, or they can be freshly combined for use at a subsequent meal. In addition to the control advantages of small-batch preparation, it also provides the guest with the most freshly prepared food, short of cooking to order. The difficulties involved with small-batch preparation are related to the timing of the batches and the communication of the status to the service personel when there is a short wait.

Fast-food operators have borrowed from the manufacturing industry the principle of producing for inventory rather than producing to order. Their limited menu, speed of service, and volume of sales make cooking for inventory a very useful technique. Production must be closely coordinated with sales, however, to prevent finished food in inventory from standing too long and deteriorating. In a sense, cafeteria operators have always produced for inventory, but they limited their menus to products that could be held on the steam table. It is the fast-food industry that has applied the technique to the foods now preferred by the public: hamburgers, French fried potatoes, and the like.

Forecasting is an attempt to relate production to sales. It is also possible to relate sales to production, which is particularly important with fully prepared items that cannot be reused, such as stews or baked goods. A well-trained sales staff can promote the sales of slow-moving items with selling suggestions and also can "slow" the sales of an item that is running low. The order and manner with which food is displayed on a cafeteria or buffet will also affect the sales mix. By moving a slow-moving item into the first, or most visible, position, it may be possible to influence its sales. The addition or removal of one or more items from the menu during the meal period will alter the sales mix of the remaining items in such a way that leftovers can be minimized.

Production and Inventory Control

Several aspects of production and inventory control have already been introduced, namely, forecasting of sales, standardized recipes and procedures, purchasing based on forecast needs, kitchen tests, requisitions based on forecasts, and the assignment and scheduling of the work. The following are other important techniques.

Adequate Supervision. There is no substitute for on-the-spot observation by someone who can recognize a problem when he sees it and can correct it before it is too late. Some chefs of necessity are "working chefs." Because they work in a very small operation, they must do some of the preparation themselves. They are often the only ones on the staff with the necessary skills. Nevertheless, they are still responsible for the operation of the entire kitchen and must be aware of what the rest of the staff are doing.

Disposition of Leftovers. Some leftovers are inevitable, but if there is an accurate system for forecasting and if production is controlled, the amount of food left over should be minimal. The amount of food left over and the way it is handled can have a serious effect on the food cost. The first thing to be considered is the safety of the food. If it has stood on a steam table or at room temperature for any length of time, it may be unsafe. Temperatures between 40° and 140°F are highly conducive to bacterial growth, and only a few hours may be required for a product to become unfit for consumption. The rule "When in doubt, throw it out," should apply. If safety is not in doubt, the quality of the product should be considered. Will it stand chilling and reheating in its present state, or will it stand saving until tomorrow? If the leftovers consist of partially prepared or raw food, there is a good possibility that most of the quality of the original product is retained. Some leftovers may be usable in another product. Bread and rolls may be dried for crumbs. Cooked meat trimmings may be made into hash or other extended dishes. Baked potatoes can go into potato salad or fried potatoes.

Small-Batch Cooking. Cooking small batches minimizes the amount of fully prepared food that is left over. When food is cooked to order, there will be no fully cooked leftovers, and any food remaining will be in the raw or unassembled state. Small-batch cooking, combined with to-order cooking at the end of the meal period, usually provides the freshest food and best service for the guest, and the closest control of the leftovers.

Planning Staff Meals. In some operations, leftovers constitute the staff meals for the following day. There are several disadvantages to this policy, the major objection being that it encourages overproduction across the menu, without cost consideration. Occasionally, one even finds the staff eating better than the guests! High-cost items such as steaks, lobster, shrimp, or ribs of beef may be purposely prepared in excess so that the employees will *have* to eat them. Another objection to the use of leftovers for staff meals is the understandable negative effect on employee morale (assuming the employees are not getting the high-cost items). Where there is a sizable staff, employee meals should be scheduled and forecast on the same basis as guest meals. The planned use of low-cost items from the guest menu on the same day can be a morale booster.

Quality Control

In the past, food service management placed a great deal of emphasis on food cost control but paid relatively little attention to quality control. The word "quality" is sometimes equated with "expensive." As used here, "quality" refers to any characteristic or attribute of an object. The purpose of a quality control program is to make sure that products have the characteristics or attributes desired for the particular situation. Therefore, a quality control program is just as valid and necessary in a low-budget institutional food service as it is in an expensive restaurant.

There are two aspects of quality control: the consistent production of products that meet certain specified requirements and the minimization of waste. For a commercial food service, a quality control system is based on the standardized recipes and procedures (including portion sizes) and the related purchase specifications. If there is adherence to these requirements, products of the desired quality should be produced with a minimum of waste. The difficulty in maintaining quality arises from the fact that people must operate the system. Automated equipment may remove some of the possibility of human error, but at present there is very little fully automated equipment suited to the small food service operation. One example of equipment that is available is French fryers with temperature-sensing devices, coupled with other automatic devices to lift the cooked food out of the fat at the proper time. Conveyor-type broilers and automatic coffee urns are other examples. Most of the devices available to the small operator for quality control are timers which shut off an appliance or remove the product from it at a preset time. Larger operations, such as commissaries, have more elaborate equipment available to them and are more likely to work with large enough quantities to warrant an investment in specialized equipment, but there is still a need for improved quality control devices for both large and small food services.

How, then, can management be sure that purchasing and production standards are being followed? First, by visual observation and personally tasting the food. The appearance of a dish can tell quite a bit about the quality. By regularly observing what is being served in the dining room, a manager can detect many of the potential lapses in quality. He should taste food on a regular schedule, either by taste-testing in the kitchen or by ordering a variety of dishes when he dines in the dining room. The latter is not as desirable as taste-testing sessions prior to the service of the meal, because errors should be corrected before the meal is served. Furthermore, observations of the guests' plates will show what is not being eaten. Some people are hesitant to complain and will simply say nothing if a dish is not to their liking (and not every person will like every dish, no matter how well it is prepared), but if there is something wrong with a dish, a pattern will develop. Customer comment cards are sometimes helpful in measuring guest satisfaction.

The use of outside "shoppers" can also be helpful. These services send shoppers to eat in a restaurant on a regular basis. Reports on their visits are then made by the shopper, covering not only the quality of the food, but also the service, sanitation, and any other aspects of the operation requested by the management. These shoppers are trained to look for certain things and are presumably more objective than most guests.

Dining room supervisors can be required to keep a detailed log book of guest complaints. These reports, plus shoppers' reports and any complaint letters received by the manager, should be reviewed immediately with the staff to determine the cause of the complaint. Management should then be sure that the cause is corrected.

Clubs may have a house committee to receive complaints from members about quality, and the same function is performed by the food committee in an institution. These committees then refer all valid complaints to the proper department head for action.

Raw materials should be inspected periodically to be sure that they conform to specification. Some products may require testing by a laboratory (to determine factors such as the fat content of ground beef or the butterfat content of ice cream), but an astute manager should be able to detect many deviations from standard quality simply by personal examination.

Improper temperature often causes a product to be substandard. Improper cooking, inadequate holding equipment, or a breakdown in the timing of the cooking and service can cause a hot item to be served cold. Conversely, inadequate holding equipment and hot dishes can contribute to cold or frozen items being served lukewarm or melted. Food temperatures can be tested quickly with a pocket thermometer. The best time for checking temperatures is during taste testing before the beginning of the meal service.

The following are recommended serving temperatures:

Soups	180°–195°F
Hot dishes except rare meats, fish	160°–180°F
Salads, sandwiches, and other chilled foods	40°F
Ice cream	8°–12°F

Roast meats and poached, sautéed, or broiled fish must be served at the optimum temperature for the degree of cooking or "doneness" desired.

Poor sanitation practices can cause food products to be of undesirable quality—unappetizing or actually contaminated. Visual inspection should reveal any unsanitary conditions, but some operators prefer to hire an outside service to provide comprehensive sanitation reports including bacterial swab counts.

Techniques of Cookery

It is not the intent of this chapter to provide a complete discussion of the principles of cookery; whole books are devoted to that complex subject. However, several topics are pertinent to a discussion of food production management: meat cookery, as it affects yields, food costs, and resulting quality; deep-fat frying; and the use of convenience foods.

Cookery of Meat, Fish, and Poultry

Meat, fish and shellfish, and poultry may be cooked by either dry- or moist-heat methods, or a combination of the two. Dry-heat methods include baking or roasting, broiling, and frying. Moist-heat methods are steaming, stewing, and simmering. Braising or pot roasting is a combination of dry- and moist-heat methods (searing, then stewing). The American Home Economics Association has defined these cooking processes* as follows:

Bake. To cook in an oven or oven-type appliance. Covered or uncovered containers may be used. When applied to meats in uncovered containers, it is generally called roasting.

Boil. To cook in water or a liquid mostly water in which bubbles rise continually and break on the surface. The boiling temperature of water at sea level is 212°F.

Braise. To cook slowly in a covered utensil in a small amount of liquid or in steam. (The meat may or may not be browned in a small amount of fat before braising.)

Broil. To cook by direct heat.

Fry. To cook in fat; applied especially (1) to cooking in a small amount of fat, also called sauté or pan-fry; (2) to cooking in a deep layer of fat, also called deep-fat frying.

Grill. See *Broil.*

Pan-broil. To cook uncovered on a hot surface, usually a fry pan. The fat is poured off as it accumulates.

Poach. To cook in a hot liquid using precautions to retain shape. The temperature used varies with the food.

Pot roast. A term applied to cooking large cuts of meat by braising. See *Braise.*

Roast. To cook, uncovered, by dry heat. Usually done in an oven, but occasionally in ashes, under coals, or on heated stones or metals. The term is usually applied to meats but may refer to other food as potatoes, corn, chestnuts.

Sear. To brown the surface of meat by a short application of intense heat.

Simmer. To cook in a liquid just below the boiling point, at temperatures of 185° to 210°F. Bubbles form slowly and collapse below the surface.

Steam. To cook in steam with or without pressure. The steam may be applied directly to the food, as in a steamer or pressure cooker.

Stew. To simmer in a small quantity of liquid.

Handbook of Food Preparation, American Home Economics Association, 2010 Massachusetts Avenue, N.W., Washington, D.C. 20036.

Some variations of these processes are:

Barbecue. To roast slowly on a gridiron, spit, over coals, or under a free flame or oven electric unit, usually basting with a highly seasoned sauce. The term is popularly applied to foods cooked in or served with barbecue sauce.

Blanch (precook). To preheat in boiling water or steam. (1) Used to inactivate enzymes and shrink food for canning, freezing, and drying. Vegetables are blanched in boiling water or steam, and fruits in boiling fruit juice, syrup, water, or steam. (2) Used to aid in removal of skins from nuts, fruits, and some vegetables.

Fricassee. To cook by braising; usually applied to fowl, rabbit, or veal cut into pieces.

Scallop. To bake food, usually cut in pieces, with a sauce or other liquid. The top may be covered with crumbs. The food and sauce may be mixed together or arranged in alternate layers in a baking dish, with or without crumbs.

Scald. (1) To heat milk to just below the boiling point. (2) To dip certain foods in boiling water. See *Blanch.*

The cooking method used depends on the type of cut of meat. The tender cuts of meat with a minimum of connective tissue are cooked by dry-heat methods, whereas moist heat is required to break down the connective tissues in less tender cuts. Tender cuts of beef include the rib and short loin of beef (strip loin and tenderloin), and portions of the sirloin. The top beef round may be roased if of high grade, cooked slowly at low temperatures, and sliced thinly. Tenderizers may make other cuts suitable for dry-heat cookery, but they are effective only on thin cuts, since they do not penetrate much below the surface. Ground meat may also be cooked by dry-heat methods since the connective tissues have been broken down mechanically in the grinding process. Almost any cut of veal, pork, or lamb (except the shanks) is tender enough to be cooked by dry-heat methods. The same is true of young poultry, although some dry-heat methods can produce a dry product since young birds have a low fat content. Fish and shellfish have no connective tissue and therefore need very little cooking to coagulate the protein. In fact, fish and shellfish are frequently overcooked, resulting in a tough, stringy, dry product. Fish is classified as fatty and non-fatty, the latter requiring basting with fat (usually butter) during dry-heat cookery to prevent the flesh from becoming dry.

There are several variations on the dry-roasting technique. The most recent development in meat cookery is the "cooking bag" that seals the cut in its own juices. Technically, this is not dry heat because the product is actually steamed by its own juice. The resulting product is more moist, with less shrinkage, but it lacks the characteristic flavor of a dry-roasted cut.

The heavy use of salt in roasting is an ancient technique from times when oven temperatures could not be regulated. The salt acted as an insulator, slowing down the cooking process in the hot ovens. It is no longer necessary to coat the surface of roasts heavily with salt, and some authorities hold that it is detrimental to the flavor. Certainly, the juices produced are very salty and may be unsuitable for service. If salt is desired for flavoring, adding it in small amounts throughout the cooking period increases its absorption into the meat.

Searing, once thought to seal in the juices, has been found to do just the opposite. If the rich crust flavor of caramelized fat is desired, the temperature can be raised during the final minutes of cooking, with a minimum loss of juices.

The meat thermometer is an important aid in meat cookery. Many persons still believe that controlling the cooking temperature makes a meat thermometer unnecessary, but both the oven temperature and the internal temperature, as indicated on a thermometer, must be controlled to produce the desired product.

Controlling Meat Shrinkage. Shrinkage is the difference between the weight of meat before cooking and its weight after cooking. Shrinkage is the weight lost in cooking, either owing to evaporation of moisture or in the form of drippings in the pan. Two factors have been shown to influence the amount of cooking loss: the temperature of the oven and the internal temperature reached (degree of "doneness"). Both of these factors can and should be controlled to minimize the loss through shrinkage. Low cooking temperatures not only reduce the amount of cooking loss but also improve appearance, palatability, and nutritional content of the meat. Roasts cooked at high temperatures are more difficult to slice and therefore increase the loss through increased cutting waste. Tests have shown that normal cooking losses due to shrinkage are approximately 10 to 15 percent when an oven temperature of 250°F to 325°F is used, compared with losses of as much as 25 percent or more at higher temperatures.

Deep-Fat Frying. Deep-fat frying is one of the most popular methods of cookery not only for meat, seafood, and poultry but also for vegetables such as potatoes and onion rings and specialty items such as hot hors d'oeuvres. The hot fat is the medium that transfers heat to the product to be cooked. In a fast-food operation with heavy emphasis on fried foods, fat for the fryer can be an important element of food cost. Also, the type of fat used and the care of the fat and the fryer can have an important effect on the quality of the fried products. The fat selected should be designed for heavy-duty frying. It should have a high smoke point and resist oxidation or breakdown. It should not contribute any undesirable flavor to the product.

All fats have a certain life span, after which they begin to break down and cause off flavors in the foods fried. Oxidized fat can be detected by tasting a piece of food fried in the fat. Broken-down fat can usually also be detected by odor or visually by its smoke, foaming, or dark color.

With proper care, the usable life of frying fat can be prolonged. Fats should be filtered frequently, even daily, if used heavily. Filtering removes the particles and sediment left from batches of food and also removes some of the gummy residues of deteriorated fat. If permitted to remain in the fryer, this gummy substance speeds the breakdown of the rest of the fat, affects heat transfer by coating the heating elements, and produces a poor quality product.

Particles on the surface of the fat should be skimmed off after each batch of food is cooked. This prevents these particles from clinging to successive batches and helps to prolong the life of the fat. The addition of small amounts of fresh fat can prolong the life of the frying fat. Enough should be added to make up for the amount lost through evaporation.

Frying baskets should not be overloaded. Overloading depresses the temperature to a point where the product is not properly cooked and the fat takes longer to recover the desired temperature. Overloading also introduces excess moisture into the fat, which speeds up its deterioration. Salting food over the fat can also have a serious effect on the fat's useful life. Fried foods should be moved away from the fryer before salting.

High heat can also speed the breakdown of fat. The temperatures of fat should be checked occasionally with a pocket thermometer to test the accuracy of the thermostat. Since there are few foods which require frying temperatures of 375°F, or above, fryers should not be set at higher temperatures. When the fryer is not required for immediate use, the temperature should be lowered to 200°F.

When filling the fryer or when turning it on for the day, the temperature should be set at 200°F until all fat is melted and heated. It should then be raised to the desired temperature just before it is to be used. Setting the temperature too high will not speed the heating and will break down the particles of fat closest to the heating elements.

Convenience Foods

Convenience foods are now a fact of life in food service operations, although the degree to which they are used depends on the type of operation and the type of product. Institutions and noncommercial operations are more likely to use convenience foods than are hotels, motels, and specialty restaurants. Very few food service operations, commercial or noncommercial, prepare French fries from the raw product any more, and few prepare vegetables from the raw fresh state. Desserts (such as pies, cakes, and puddings) are more likely to be purchased in convenience form than are main course entrées. Among the entrées, poultry (particularly breaded chicken) is most frequently used. Breaded frozen fish and seafood are also very popular. Hotels and restaurants are frequent users of raw processed meats such as portioned steaks and hamburger patties.

Objectives of a Convenience Food Program

Menu Expansion. One objective of a convenience food program may be to expand the menu. Being able to offer greater variety without materially increasing the existing workload may be an important part of a marketing strategy. Space or equipment limitations that prevent an operator from offering certain items can sometimes be overcome with convenience foods.

Overcoming a Shortage of Skilled Labor. Convenience food manufacturers sometimes advertise "no highly skilled chefs are necessary in order to serve these elaborate dishes." In areas where a shortage of trained cooks exists, this a very valid reason for using convenience foods.

Food Cost Control. In some situations, the use of fully prepared, preportioned products can reduce food costs. This is especially true in situations where sales patterns are very erratic and difficult to forecast accurately. One example is in highway feeding, where traffic is affected hourly by conditions which the operator may not even know about. For close control over food preparation, items may be made in the traditional way for service during the busy periods, supplemented by convenience items that are reconstituted to order in the slower periods at the close of the meal period. In a highway food operation, the same menu may be offered 24 hours a day, with convenience items used during the "off" hours. This not only eliminates the waste of keeping all items available on the steam table, but it also provides the patron with a fresher product.

Expansion of Service. Convenience foods can be served in places where food service is not possible using traditional production methods—for example, in snack bars in remote locations, restaurants in spaces too small for traditional kitchens, and places without adequate utilities for regular cooking equipment.

Reduction of Construction, Equipment, and Occupancy Costs. A full convenience food operation requires considerably less space than a traditional kitchen. For this reason, the planners of a food service operation may decide to use only convenience foods if there is limited building space. The investment in construction and equipment costs will be lower. During the life of the project, the cost of occupying the smaller space will also be lower, either in actual rents or in applicable interest and depreciation. Maintenance and utility costs will also be lower on the smaller space.

Reduction of Labor Costs. Reduction of labor costs is a common reason for using convenience foods. Management, however, must have a program for reducing the staff, whether it be by a policy of attrition, reassignment of employees to other jobs, or by layoffs. If management adds convenience foods to the menu without eliminating any labor-heavy items, food costs will be increased while the payroll remains the same.

More Productive Use of Labor. Some operators use convenience foods to free their employees for more important tasks such as preparing a few specialty items, garnishing, and other details. Management is able to spend more time in the dining room with the guests and in supervision of service. No reduction of labor costs is usually anticipated when convenience foods are used for this purpose.

Implementing a Convenience Food Program

In the past, planning a convenience food program often began with a survey of the products on the market. This was probably a necessary starting point at a time when availability and variety were limited. Now, however, a wide variety of products in almost all menu categories is available, and the restaurant operator can even select the quality and price range for many widely used items.

Perhaps a better starting point for convenience food study is the operation itself—the market it caters to and the equipment, skills, and cost required to produce the items offered in the menu. Whether to buy fully prepared, partially prepared, or only certain processed ingredients will depend in part on product quality, resulting portion cost, and labor requirements. Another alternative is to prepare one's own menu items from the raw state during slack time and freeze them. To do this satisfactorily, an investment in a blast freezer is usually required.

Once the products have been selected, reconstitution methods must be established. Often, this is done in connection with product testing. The method of reconstitution can greatly affect the resulting quality of the item, and sometimes it is necessary to test different reconstitution methods. It is important that the personnel be trained to follow the desired method.

Garnishing and merchandising of the food becomes important in a convenience food operation, particularly in a commercial food service such as a hotel or restaurant. Giving an item an individualized touch should not be limited to these operations, however. Merchandising is equally important in an institutional food service.

Most operators are able to use convenience food products in their conventional kitchens, although some require more refrigerator and freezer space. Of course, having a new kitchen especially designed for convenience foods is more efficient, in terms of both space and labor.

Kitchen Organization

In a traditional French kitchen organization, the kitchen brigade is organized under a *chef de cuisine.* Second in command is the *sous* chef, who is in charge when the chef is not present and is usually the leader of the cooks working at the range. Under the *chef de cuisine* and the *sous* chef are the *chefs de partie,* or the section chiefs. In a very large French kitchen, the following *chef de partie* positions may be found:

French Titles	*English Titles*
Saucier	Sauce chef* (most important station)
Garde Manger	Cold meat chef (all cold items)
Rotisseur or grillardier	Roast or grill chef
Entremetier or legumier	Vegetable chef
Patissier	Pastry chef
Poissonier or friteur	Fish chef
Potager	Soup chef
Glacier	Ice cream chef
Hors d'oeuvrier	Hors d'oeuvre chef

Each *chef de partie* supervises a crew of assistants, called *commis,* and apprentices.

In smaller kitchens, the roast cook may prepare the fish, the vegetable cook may prepare the soups, and the pastry cook may prepare the ice cream and frozen desserts. The *garde manger* prepares the hors d'oeuvres in a smaller kitchen. Either the *garde manger* or the *sous* chef may be responsible for the butcher shop.

The following are other positions that may be found in a French kitchen: *chef tournant,* or relief man; *chef communard,* or staff dining room chef; *chef trancheur,* or carver (in the dining room);

---

*Or cook if he has no assistants.

and *chef travaillant seul* (working alone chef), the equivalent of a general cook, found in very small kitchens.

In an American kitchen, the term *chef* is used differently from the way the French use it. A large hotel with several kitchens may have an executive chef in charge of all kitchen operations. An executive chef is a member of the management staff and performs all the traditional duties of the chef. An individual kitchen will have a chef. He may or may not be responsible for the supervision of others. Often, where a kitchen supervisor is employed (or where the owner directs the kitchen operations himself), the leading cook is called "chef" although he does not manage or supervise.

In a hotel or large restaurant, the station organization is similar to the French organization. A *sous* chef is the leader of the range crew. The *saucier* is second under him. Sometimes the terms second cook and third cook are used for these positions. Also working at the range are the roast cook, broilermen or fry cooks, and vegetable cooks. The assistants are usually classed as "cooks' helpers." Because of high labor costs, many managements prefer to class every cook as "general cook" rather than designate specific assignments. This permits greater flexibility in staffing the range.

The *garde manger* position is retained in most hotels and many restaurants. This station is responsible for all salads, sandwiches, cold plates, and cold appetizers. It may also be responsible for dishing desserts, although that job is usually done by a lower-paid employee. Sometimes the *garde manger* is also responsible for butchering, although this may be a separate station, with the head butcher reporting to the chef.

The pastry chef is in charge of the bake shop. Of all the station chefs, probably only the pastry chef functions as a real supervisor of his department, in the manner of the French organization. In some cases, the pastry chef even plans his menus and orders his own supplies from purveyors.

In an institution the kitchen may be run by a chef, kitchen or production supervisor, or dietitian. Cooks are more likely classed as general cooks, or designated according to the shift they work (breakfast cook, dinner cook). Those working with cold food are called pantry workers, and those on the serving lines of cafeterias are counter workers or servers. Large institutions may have butchers but are not likely to have pastry cooks because fancy pastries are not required. They may have bakers, however, who prepare desserts as well as breads and rolls.

7

FOOD COST CONTROL

In the preceding chapters, the basic procedures of purchasing, storage, and production management were discussed: forecasting, the use of standardized recipes, purchase specifications, and yields, requisitions, and portion control. These represent one aspect of control, that is, techniques to get the job done, to have the right materials and manpower available at the right time in order to fill the orders satisfactorily. This type of control is called concurrent or preventive control. Its objective is to prevent undesired events from taking place.

The other type of control is called reactive or corrective control. It reacts to events that have happened by comparing the actual results to the desired results. Action must then be taken to prevent any undesired results from happening again. Obviously, prevention is preferable to correction. Financial statements, particularly those that measure actual operating results against a budget or a standard, or against previous performance, are a form of reactive control.

A Hierarchy of Control

Control procedures should be designed to fit the needs of the particular operation. In a one-man operation, such as an individual who sells hot dogs from his cart, an elaborate control procedure is not required. He handles his own merchandise and collects the cash.

In an extremely small operation, most of the control is visual observation by the owner or manager—for instance, a partnership or mom-pop operation when one person runs the back of the house and the other runs the front. If there is a reasonable amount of trust between the partners, relatively few controls are necessary. One partner controls the cash, while the other controls the merchandise, and each has a check on the other.

In a large operation, and when the ownership is farther from the actual operation, there is a greater need for controls. The simplest control system is nonquantifiable: It is visual observation by those with direct personal interest in the business. The next type of control involves counts of units of production—in this case, portions of food. On a day-to-day basis, food production employees and first line supervisors usually concern themselves with numbers of portions, or quantities to be produced, rather than dollars. Food cost goals may be transmitted to these employees in terms of ratios based on dollars, but the number of portions left over are more meaningful.

The objective of all cost control is money control. The question is always: How much will it cost and how much (how many dollars) could we save?

Qualities of a Good Control System

In designing a cost control system, one consideration is cost effectiveness. To use an old expression, one should not chase a dime of savings with a dollar of cost. For example, a restaurant with sales of $300,000 and a food cost of 33 percent would be purchasing $100,000 worth of food. The cost of a food and beverage cost controller with no other functions would probably not be justifiable by the savings made. Control must be assured by other management techniques.

A cost control system should not interfere with the operation of the business and particularly should not be apparent to or inconvenient for the guest. The system should be designed to fit the business, not vice versa.

The cost control system must provide accurate, detailed data so that the need for corrective measures can be identified and the proper steps taken. The system should not generate unnecessary data that could confuse or distract from the basic problem. A good cost control system provides information quickly, so that if corrective action is required, it can be taken at once.

A good cost control system should be simple to operate. It should consist of a regular routine incorporated in the day-to-day activities. All forms used should be easy to read and should provide all necessary information. Duplication of work should be avoided.

There should be a separation of duties so that no one person has control over a transaction from start to finish. Line operating functions should be separated from staff control functions. It should be noted that cost control is an operating function, not an accounting function. The function of the accountant is to provide information for management so that corrective action can be taken if necessary. In doing this, the accountant may analyze and recommend (a staff function), but it is the line operating personnel who must ultimately take action.

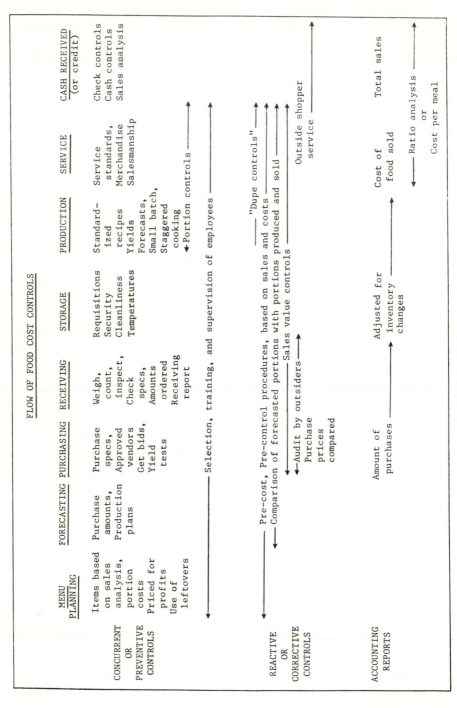

Fig. 7-1. Flow of food cost controls.

Cost control and cost reduction are not the same. Cost control involves making costs conform to standard or expected costs. Cost reduction questions whether or not and by what means those standard or expected costs could be reduced without altering the end product. Altering the end product goes beyond cost reduction to market analysis.

Food Service Control Systems

Figure 7–1 shows various types of food cost controls as merchandise moves through the operation. The various controls are listed in the left-hand column. Concurrent with these controls are various functions, shown in the following column. These functions are discussed in connection with the various controls. (See *Profitable Food and Beverage Management: Planning* for cash and check controls.) Reactive controls are charted in the third column. Many of these corrective procedures are also preventive since their existence may deter undesirable actions by the employees. (For example, if a waiter knows that he must submit a "dupe" in order to get a steak for a customer, and he also knows that these dupes will be matched with the guest checks, he will be less likely to try to get a steak for himself.) The income statement shows the effectiveness of the concurrent and reactive control measures.

A Summary of Concurrent Food Cost Controls

Concurrent control of food cost begins with menu planning (see Chapter 2). Menus should be written and priced so that the sales mix will ultimately produce an expected food cost. Sales forecasts determine how much will be produced and the purchase requirements, based on standardized recipes and yields (see Chapter 6). These purchase requirements are adjusted for on-hand merchandise, and orders are placed on the basis of competitive bids (see Chapter 4). Purchase specifications ensure that the bids are for comparable merchandise, and that the merchandise ordered and delivered meets the requirements of the operation (see Chapters 4 and 5). Proper receiving procedures (Chapter 5) require that all merchandise be weighed (or counted) and correctly invoiced, and that all merchandise meets the specifications. Invoice prices (Chapter 5) should be checked to ascertain that they are the prices quoted.

Merchandise not required for immediate use is sent to a storeroom, where it is kept under proper conditions in order to maintain quality (see Chapter 5). Proper security is maintained to prevent loss.

Standardized recipes are tools for producing food of the desired quality and characteristics on a continuing basis, and for reducing waste (see Chapter 6). Portion sizes are established and maintained to ensure that patrons receive the value intended and that the cost of the portions is not excessive.

Production sheets are maintained, showing the amounts of food to be produced, the amounts actually produced, the amounts left over, and the amounts consumed (see Chapter 6). The amounts consumed are then compared with tabulations of portions sold, and any discrepancies are investigated. The production sheet then becomes the basis for future forecasting.

Precost, Precontrol Food Accounting System

"Precontrol" is a familiar name in the food service industry for a technique that is both a preventive and reactive form of control. Precontrol is a system by which the food cost of any given menu can be determined in advance and evaluated. Menus can then be restructured if the cost is not within the desired range. Actual food costs can also be compared with potential costs, and sources of high costs can be pinpointed on a daily basis.

Precontrol Procedures

Evaluating the cost balance of a menu:

1. Determine the portion cost of each item on the menu, based on standardized recipes and procedures, purchase specifications and prices paid, and standard portion sizes.
2. Estimate the number of portions of each item that will be sold.
3. Extend these estimates by the cost and the selling price to determine the total sales and total cost of that menu. Divide the total cost by the total sales to obtain a food cost ratio.
4. If this cost ratio is not within the budget of the operation, the menu must be changed until a desirable cost ratio is achieved.

Evaluating the actual food cost:

5. Calculate portion costs as in step 1 above.
6. Tabulate the actual number of portions sold of each menu item.
7. Extend these portion counts by the portion costs and selling prices to determine the total sales and potential cost. Divide the potential cost by the sales to obtain a potential cost ratio.
8. Compare this potential cost ratio with the actual cost ratio obtained by dividing the actual cost by sales. Actual cost is de-

termined from the sum of direct purchases on the receiving sheets, plus the total of food requisitioned from the storeroom.

Precontrol was developed in the late 1940s, primarily for use in hotels. At that time, labor was relatively cheap, and hotel menus were written daily and offered a wide selection of items. Hotel owners and managers had become more sophisticated in their management techniques and sought to maintain the profitability their properties had achieved in the "full house" days of World War II. In later years, however, labor costs rose, and the system was thought to be too expensive to maintain. More recently, several developments have brought some elements of the precontrol system back into prominence.

Electronic data processing now permits the speedy accumulation of data on sales and costs without costly labor. Menus are more likely to be set on a limited cycle and with fewer items offered, thus reducing the number of calculations required. A set menu can be precosted on a test period basis and kept up to date with minor adjustments. Finally, the entry of publicly owned corporations into the hotel and food service business has demanded a more systematic approach to food production and cost control. The previously discussed elements of production management have become standard operating procedures, and once these procedures are in effect, a precontrol system is easy to operate. Precontrol is particularly suited to operations using portion-controlled items, such as steak houses and fast-food operations.

Elements of a Precontrol System

Determining Portion Costs. The first step in a precontrol program is to determine the exact cost of every item listed on the menu. For these portion costs to be calculated accurately, the following information is required:

1. Standardized recipes that show the amounts of all ingredients in the menu items, the portion sizes, the yield of the recipe, and all items that accompany the menu item.
2. Portion sizes for all items that do not require a recipe for preparation.
3. Purchasing specifications and usable yield statistics for all commodities purchased.
4. Purchase prices paid. If the price paid for a commodity varies widely during the year, an average price should be established for the period in which the item will be served. Information on the monthly range of wholesale commodity prices is published by the U.S. Department of Commerce in its *Sur-*

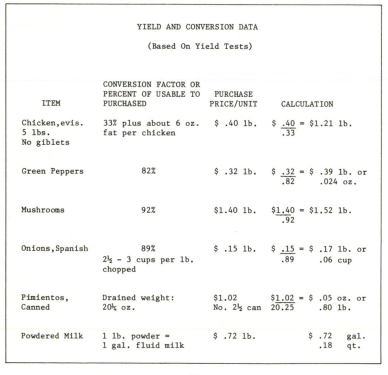

RECIPE NO. _P-37_   RECIPE COST CARD   DATE _2/28/19–_

ITEM _CHICKEN À LA KING IN PATTY SHELL_   QUANTITY COSTED _2-1/4 GAL._

NUMBER OF PORTIONS _48_ PORTION SIZE _6 oz_ PORTION COST _$.37_

QUAN-TITY	INGREDIENTS	PUR-CHASE PRICE	UNIT PRICE	TOTAL COST	QUAN-TITY	INGREDIENTS	PUR-CHASE PRICE	UNIT PRICE	TOTAL COST
12 oz	CHICKEN FAT	–	–	–	TO TASTE	SALT	–	–	–
14 oz	FLOUR	$.11/lb	$.11	$.10	5 lbs	CHICKEN, COOKED	FOWL $.40/lb	$1.21/lb	$6.05
1 gal	CHICKEN STOCK	–	–	–	9 oz	GREEN PEPPERS	.32/lb	.024 oz	.22
1 qt	DRY MILK	.72/lb	.18 qt	.18	1 lb	PIMIENTO	NO.2½ CN 1.02	.80/lb	.80
1 lb	FRESH MUSHR.	1.40/lb	1.52	1.52	48 ea	PATTY SHELLS	20.00 CS OF 144	.14 ea	6.72
2 tbsp.	CH. ONIONS	.15/lb	.06 cp	.01	48 ea	CRAB APPLES 40-50 CT.	1.67 NO.10 CN	.04 ea	1.92
8 oz	SHORTENING	.25/lb	.016 oz	.13		TOTAL COST OF RECIPE			$17.87
5-1/4 oz	EGG YOLK-FZ.	.65/lb	.041 oz	.22		COST PER PORTION			$.37

ITEM _CHICKEN À LA KING, PATTY SH._   PORTION COST _$ .37_   PORTION COST FACTOR _$ .34_

(A)

YIELD AND CONVERSION DATA

(Based On Yield Tests)

ITEM	CONVERSION FACTOR OR PERCENT OF USABLE TO PURCHASED	PURCHASE PRICE/UNIT	CALCULATION
Chicken, evis. 5 lbs. No giblets	33% plus about 6 oz. fat per chicken	$ .40 lb.	$ .40 / .33 = $1.21 lb.
Green Peppers	82%	$ .32 lb.	$ .32 / .82 = $ .39 lb. or .024 oz.
Mushrooms	92%	$1.40 lb.	$1.40 / .92 = $1.52 lb.
Onions, Spanish	89% 2½ – 3 cups per lb. chopped	$ .15 lb.	$ .15 / .89 = $ .17 lb. or .06 cup
Pimientos, Canned	Drained weight: 20¼ oz.	$1.02 No. 2½ can	$1.02 / 20.25 = $ .05 oz. or .80 lb.
Powdered Milk	1 lb. powder = 1 gal. fluid milk	$ .72 lb.	$ .72 gal. .18 qt.

(B)

Fig. 7-2. (A) A recipe cost card. (B) Yield and Conversion Data.

vey of Current Business. The Department of Agriculture also publishes market price information.

All required information can be organized on cost cards (see Fig. 7–2). The necessary yields and conversion information are included. Sometimes volume measures must be converted to weights (or vice versa) in order to cost certain ingredients. Once determined, these conversion factors will remain the same unless an ingredient is subsequently purchased in a different form.

The portion cost factor shown in the lower right-hand corner of the recipe cost card in Fig. 7–2 can be used to update the cost calculation quickly. It represents that portion of the total cost that is contributed by the main ingredient, in this case, the cooked chicken meat: $6.05/17.87 = 0.34$. This is the same as saying that the chicken represents 34 percent of the total cost of the recipe.

If the purchase price cost of fowl rose from $0.40 per pound to $0.50 (a $0.10 or 25 percent increase) the portion cost could be updated simply by multiplying the percentage increase by the portion cost factor to find the percentage increase in the total recipe. This percentage increase is then applied to the original portion cost to get the amount of increase.

$25\% \times 0.34 = 0.085$ (percentage increase in total cost of the recipe)
Original portion cost $0.37 \times 0.085 = \$0.031$ (increase in portion cost)
$\quad\quad\quad\quad\quad\quad\quad\quad \$0.37 + 0.03 \quad = \$0.40$ (new portion cost rounded)

These cost factors are used in the same way as the cost factors that were calculated on the butcher and cooking test cards described in Chapter 6. The only difference is that in recipes for "made" dishes, the main ingredient cost is only a portion of the total cost of the recipe. As a rule, however, the cost of any other single ingredient is usually a small part of the total cost, and changes in purchase prices of those ingredients will have little impact on the total cost. In Fig. 7–2, however, the pastry shells actually contribute more than the cost of the main ingredient. These particular shells are purchased in prepared form, and any increase in the purchase price can be readily translated into an increase in the portion cost.

One major source of costing errors is omission of some components of an item, such as the garnish or the accompaniment. Nonedible components may be included for the purpose of menu pricing, but are usually excluded for the purposes of food cost control. Paper goods may be an important part of the cost. Many large fast-food and take-out operations include packaging in their food cost calculations. Salad bars and buffets and some institutional feeding situations where the patron serves himself are particularly difficult to cost because there are no standard portions and the diner may take multiple entrées.

Cost data are determined as an average based on experience. All food offered on the buffet should be recorded, and the total cost calculated. Food left over and returned to the kitchen should be credited only if it is in usable condition and can be served again. The average per-person cost of the meal is determined by dividing the net cost of food used by the number of patrons served.

In addition to the cost of the main dish, the cost of the other courses (appetizer or soup, vegetable, potato, salad, dessert, beverage, rolls, and butter) must be computed. Since most of the precosting concerns the table d'hôte meal or forms of it, it is necessary to have the cost of the "surrounding" courses for each restaurant. It is best to compute the average cost of the "surrounding" courses and add the total to the entrée cost.

Forecasting Using the Sales Analysis. The collection of data and the development of a sales history with respect to menu writing and its importance in forecasting for production planning are discussed in Chapter 6. The same information is used in the precontrol system to forecast the cost of the planned menu. On a day-to-day or week-to-week basis, the forecasts made for purchasing and production planning can and should be used in calculating the potential costs.

Frequently, the production forecasts are calculated in numbers of portions for the entrées only whereas the rest of the menu is forecast in production units such as gallons of soup or numbers of pies. The cost and sales value of any such unit can be calculated.

Figure 7–3 is a precost form showing the calculated potential cost for the meal in the "forecast" columns. At this point, the projected cost ratio can be evaluated and any desired menu changes made. Any last-minute changes in forecasts and menu items should also be made in the precontrol calculation.

Comparison of Potential Cost with Actual Cost. The "actual" section of the precontrol form shown in Fig. 7–3 is completed with data from the daily sales analysis. The cost and selling prices are extended, and a potential cost ratio is calculated. This ratio is then compared with the actual cost ratio. These calculations can be summarized in a report to management, as shown in Figs. 7–4 and 7–5.

Determining Actual Cost. In Chapter 5, several different types of inventory controls were discussed. The one most commonly used in operations of any size requires the separation of the cost of merchandise sent directly to the kitchen from that sent to the storeroom. Merchandise issued from the storeroom is then costed on requisitions. The total of the daily requisitions plus direct charges is the cost of food used for the day. This assumes that the inventory in the kitchen remains constant, when actually it does not, because of varying

HOTEL ___Metropolitan___

MENU PRECOST AND ABSTRACT

DAY & DATE ___Sat. 6/10___

HOUSE COUNT ___275___

WEATHER ___Clear – Hot___

Entree	Cost Per Ptn.	Forecast					Actual Sales				Ratio to Total
		No.	Total Cost	Sales Price	Total Sales	Cost %	No. Sold	Total Sales	Total Cost	Cost %	
Dinner – À La Carte											
Prime Ribs of Beef	$2.06	16	$ 32.96	$7.75	$124.00		18	$139.50	$ 37.08		12.0
Sirloin Steak	2.68	7	18.76	8.00	56.00		10	80.00	26.80		6.7
Filet Mignon	2.53	6	15.18	8.00	48.00		4	32.00	10.12		2.7
Chopped Sirloin Steak	1.03	7	7.21	4.25	29.75		10	42.50	10.30		6.6
Broiled Chicken	1.10	7	7.70	5.25	36.75		6	31.50	6.60		4.0
Pork Chops	1.51	9	13.59	5.50	49.50		8	44.00	12.08		5.3
Filet of Sole	1.20	6	7.20	5.25	31.50		9	47.25	10.80		6.0
Fried Shrimp	1.97	9	17.73	6.00	54.00		6	36.00	11.82		4.0
Lobster Tail	3.80	4	15.20	9.75	39.00		3	29.25	11.40		2.0
Total		71	$135.53		$468.50	28.9	74	$482.00	$137.00	28.4	49.3
Complete Dinners											
Short Ribs of Beef	$1.66	16	$ 26.56	$6.00	$ 96.00		12	$ 72.00	$ 19.92		8.0
Roast Leg of Lamb	1.55	17	26.35	6.00	102.00		20	120.00	31.00		13.3
Roast Duck	2.43	6	14.58	7.50	45.00		9	67.50	21.87		6.0
Chicken Pot Pie	1.55	11	17.05	5.75	63.25		11	63.25	17.05		7.4
Crabmeat Supreme	2.41	13	31.33	6.75	87.75		10	67.50	24.10		6.7
Stuffed Flounder	2.05	10	20.50	6.50	65.00		14	91.00	28.70		9.3
Total		73	$136.37		$459.00	29.7	76	$481.25	$142.64	29.6	50.7
Grand Total		144	$271.90		$927.50	29.3	150	$963.25	$279.64	29.0	100.0

Fig. 7-3. Menu precost and abstract.

DATE April 22
DAY Saturday
WEATHER Fair

	Today Number Sold	Today Actual Sales	Today Calculated Cost	Today Cost Per Dollar Sale	This Month to Date Number Sold	This Month to Date Actual Sales	This Month to Date Calculated Cost	This Month to Date Cost Per Dollar Sale
Coffee Shop:								
Breakfast	183	$ 176.45	$ 56.46	32.0%	4,804	$ 4,566.40	$ 1,461.27	32.0%
Luncheon	49	86.45	28.18	32.6	1,502	2,710.05	907.80	33.5
Dinner	43	121.25	39.43	32.5	1,391	3,745.80	1,235.74	33.0
Buffet	-	-	-	-	669	1,671.75	977.75	58.5
A La Carte Entrées	42	89.95	36.68	40.8	625	1,352.15	449.58	33.2
A La Carte Others	137	170.10	53.75	31.6	3,026	3,751.93	1,203.14	32.1
Total	454	644.20	214.50	33.3	12,017	17,798.08	6,235.28	35.0
Cafe:								
Luncheon	46	81.25	22.16	27.3	1,082	1,919.80	552.24	28.8
Dinner	38	147.60	49.18	33.3	848	3,447.80	1,185.82	34.4
A La Carte Entrées	62	207.63	79.31	38.2	1,590	5,222.89	2,004.52	38.4
A La Carte Others	64	126.52	43.78	34.6	1,136	2,204.82	776.83	35.2
Total	210	563.00	194.43	34.5	4,656	12,795.31	4,519.41	35.3
Dining Room:								
Dinner	97	589.90	186.87	31.7	1,168	6,702.35	2,313.71	34.5
Supper	26	103.75	35.90	34.6	219	880.60	302.24	34.3
A La Carte Entrées	48	212.75	102.42	48.1	524	2,252.70	1,045.45	46.4
A La Carte Others	17	348.05	127.04	36.5	169	3,371.40	1,226.71	36.4
Total	188	1,254.45	452.23	36.1	2,080	13,207.05	4,888.11	37.0
Room Service:								
Breakfast	60	124.10	37.47	30.2	1,087	2,174.30	658.99	30.3
Luncheon	2	2.70	.66	24.4	52	174.35	44.56	25.6
Dinner	8	54.00	17.50	32.4	118	707.90	239.91	33.9
A La Carte Entrées	32	132.93	52.51	39.5	681	2,802.93	1,083.30	38.6
A La Carte Others	23	71.52	24.75	34.6	456	1,388.72	476.38	34.3
Total	125	385.25	132.89	34.5	2,394	7,248.20	2,503.14	34.5
Total Dining Room Potential Cost	977	2,846.90	994.05	34.9	21,147	51,048.64	18,145.94	35.5
Banquets	657	4,527.50	1,121.76	24.8	5,537	37,099.60	10,336.18	27.9
Total Potential Net Cost	1,634	7,374.40	2,115.81	28.7	26,684	88,148.24	28,482.12	32.3
Summary								
Total Gross Cost - Actual	1,634	7,374.40	2,500.38	33.9	26,684	88,148.24	36,206.32	41.1
Less: Employees' Meals	-	-	265.00	3.6	-	-	5,736.58	6.5
Total Net Cost - Actual	1,634	7,374.40	2,235.38	30.3	26,684	88,148.24	30,469.74	34.6
Total Net Cost - Potential	1,634	7,374.40	2,115.81	28.7	26,684	88,148.24	28,482.12	32.3
Total Potential Savings	-	-	119.57	-1.6	-	-	1,987.62	2.3
Net Dining Room Cost - Actual	977	2,846.90	1,113.62	39.1	21,147	51,048.64	20,133.56	39.4
Net Banquet Cost - Actual	657	$4,527.50	$1,121.76	24.8%	5,537	$37,099.60	$10,336.18	27.9%

J. J. Jones
Food Cost Accountant

Fig. 7-4. Daily food cost report.

RECAPITULATION OF PRECOST PRECONTROL

RESULTS IN THE FOOD DEPARTMENT

FOR THE MONTH OF FEBRUARY 19 _ _

	Number Sold	Actual Sales	Calculated Cost	Cost Per Dollar Sale	Ratio to Total Net Sales
Lounge					
Items PreControlled					
Luncheon	2,085	$ 5,172.45	$ 1,898.66	36.7%	7.59%
Dining Room					
Items PreControlled					
Breakfast	2,415	4,466.85	1,320.52	29.5	6.55
Luncheon	1,742	5,937.65	1,853.48	31.2	8.71
Dinner	1,449	7,276.29	2,962.85	40.7	10.67
Other items	2,396	5,414.91	1,732.72	32.0	7.94
Total	8,002	23,095.70	7,869.57	34.1	33.87
Room Service	2,128	6,833.40	2,114.86	30.9	10.02
Banquets	4,792	33,500.44	10,130.58	30.2	49.14
Total Potential Cost			22,013.67	32.2	
Allowances		[423.85]			[.62]
Adjustment to Cost					
Expenditures over					
potential cost			1,006.37	1.5	
Grand Total	17,007	$68,178.14	$23,020.04	33.7%	100.00%

Fig. 7-5. Recapitulation of precost precontrol results in the food department.

amounts of advance preparation that may be required. In determining the actual cost of food used, a month-to-date figure is usually more meaningful than a "today" figure.

An operation that purchases on a hand-to-mouth basis and uses no system of issuing from the storeroom can use actual purchases as a cost basis, but this figure will have to be adjusted at the end of the period for changes in inventory. Again, the use of a purchases-to-date figure is more meaningful.

Some Thoughts on Precontrol. (1) The calculation of cost potential does not measure the efficiency of the purchase price. In other words, it does not say if the price paid was the lowest that could have been obtained. (2) If portion costs are not kept current, the potential cost ratio will be inaccurate. (3) The potential cost will not reflect any shortages in receiving or the storeroom if cost is calculated on the basis of requisitions. Shortages in merchandise charged directly to preparation areas will be reflected. (4) The potential cost will show waste or loss in production and service. Losses in receiving and storage will show up only if actual costs are based on purchases and physical inventories.

How Precost, Precontrol Is Used Today

Since the development of the precost, control system, the food industry has changed drastically. When precontrols were first used, the cost of food generally took the largest portion of the sales dollar. Today, although the ratio of food cost to sales remains at approximately the same level, the cost of labor takes a larger portion of the sales dollar. Because of this, labor cost now receives more management attention than food cost.

The higher cost of labor has adversely affected not only the cost of producing and serving food but also the cost of operating a system of cost controls. In some operations, the difference now between a noncontrolled food cost and a controlled food cost is less than the labor cost of operating the control system. A simplified approach to food cost control was not only desirable but necessary. Accordingly, some of the time-consuming procedures (such as the daily abstract of checks and the daily computation of potential and actual cost of sales by meal periods for each dining room) were eliminated.

The Use of Test Periods for Determining Sales Mix

In lieu of the daily abstract of checks, a test period is used to determine the sales mix of the menu items. The length of the test period varies with each operation. A sales pattern usually develops after the items have appeared on the menu several times. When the pattern begins to repeat, the test period is long enough. In an operation using cycle menus, the length of one complete cycle is generally sufficient for a test period. For a set menu, a one- or two-week test period is usually used.

During the test period, a tabulation is made of the number of portions sold of every item on the menu. The cost of each item is then multiplied by the number of portions sold of that item, and the total of these costs is obtained. The selling price of each item is also multiplied by the number of portions sold of each item. The total of these selling prices represents the total sales value. The total cost of food sold divided by the total sales value results in a *potential food cost ratio* or standard by which the future actual food cost ratios will be evaluated by management.

With the use of a test period, precontrol still operates as before, except that when used in evaluating actual food cost (see "Precontrol Procedures"), steps 5, 6, and 7 are not performed daily. The potential food cost ratio is developed during the test period and should be applicable until such time as something happens to affect the sales mix or the item costs.

The sales mix can be affected by the following changes:

A change in menu listings
A change in selling prices
A change in season
A change in the market

It must be emphasized that the potential cost ratio, developed from the sales in a test period, represents an average for that period. When comparing it to actual performance, it should be applied to the costs for a similar period rather than one day's costs.

Using a Purchase Price Index to Update Potential Food Cost Ratio

Because purchase prices change daily, the cost of the menu items must be kept current if the potential food cost is to be of value. Instead of constantly updating the cost on the cost cards, a monthly purchase cost index is prepared. The information provided is then used to adjust the potential cost ratio. The purchase price index is prepared as follows:

1. Select the major items purchased during the month in which the sales mix test was made and compute the total purchase cost of each item. The items selected should represent between 65 and 70 percent of the total food purchases for the test period. (Do not include unusual purchases such as items purchased for special banquets.) For purposes of identity, this test period will be referred to as the base month.
2. To arrive at the average unit price paid for the items purchased, divide the purchased quantities of each item into the total purchase cost of the related item. These average unit costs are necessary for potential cost ratio adjustments in subsequent months.
3. For any month subsequent to the base month, list the quantities purchased and the total purchase cost of the same item as selected for the base month. Also, using the unit price developed in step 2, extend the quantities purchased during the subsequent month to arrive at what the total cost of these

items would have been if purchased at the base month's average unit prices.

4. The difference between the total purchase cost of the items in the subsequent month and what the cost would have been during the base period, when reduced to a percentage relationship, indicates the extent of adjustment required to the potential cost ratio developed during the base month.

5. Multiply the potential cost ratio developed in the base month by the percentage of change in the cost of purchases as computed in step 4 in order to update the potential food cost ratio.

See Fig. 7–6 for an example of a completed purchase cost index. The simplified food cost control method is not as precise as the precontrol system. However, the general indications are that the lower cost of operating the simplified system offsets any losses caused by its diminished preciseness.

There are two other important aspects of the simplified system of control:

1. The sales mix must be tested periodically. The change of seasons is a good time for tests.

2. The base period for the purchase cost index should be recalculated at least once a year.

Production Sheet Controls—by Portions

Comparing Forecasts with Actual Production

The production sheet described in Chapter 6 is an important tool for food cost control, and it is used in several ways. First, the quantities produced should be compared with the quantities forecast (updated for last minute changes) and any discrepancies investigated. Underproduction may be the result of poor purchasing or receiving practices. The proper amounts of merchandise may not have been received, or the merchandise may not have conformed to the purchase specification. Other reasons for underproduction are waste in cutting or trimming, improper preparation methods (such as overcooking, underbeating, or omitting an ingredient), pilferage, or overportioning. Overproduction can also result from improper preparation methods, improper portioning, or overbuying. Errors can also result from a lapse in communication between the cooks and the production manager.

Comparing Consumption with Sales

After the meal is served, a comparison made of the portions sold as tabulated by a representative of the accounting department

COST OF FOOD PURCHASE INDEX

	Base Period			Current Period	
	Quantity Purchased	Unit Price	Total Cost of Purchase	Current Price	Cost of Base Period Purchases At Current Prices
Beef Ribs	4,198 lbs.	$ .87	$ 3,652.26	$ 1.05	$ 4,407.90
Beef Tenderloins	562 lbs.	1.89	1,062.18	2.48	1,393.76
Beef Chuck	353 lbs.	.72	254.16	1.15	405.95
Beef Round	185 lbs.	1.22	225.70	1.38	255.30
Beef Strip Loins	392 lbs.	1.99	780.08	2.45	960.40
Pork Loins	800 lbs.	.63	504.00	1.00	800.00
Canned Hams	228 lbs.	1.14	259.92	1.59	362.52
Leg of Lamb	290 lbs.	.89	258.10	1.10	319.00
Turkeys	1,357 lbs.	.54	732.78	.69	936.33
Chickens - 5 Lb.	1,181 lbs.	.38	448.78	.56	661.36
Chickens - 3 Lb.	1,051 lbs.	.34	357.34	.59	620.09
Chicken Legs and Thighs	420 lbs.	.47	197.40	.66	277.20
Ducks	1,047 lbs.	.59	617.73	.83	869.01
Flounder Fillet	150 lbs.	1.15	172.50	1.24	186.00
Small Flounders	546 lbs.	.60	327.60	.65	354.90
Lemon Sole	375 lbs.	.53	198.75	.57	213.75
Shrimp - U' 15's	500 lbs.	2.85	1,425.00	2.75	1,375.00
Shrimp - 15 - 20's	150 lbs.	2.75	412.50	2.63	394.50
Shrimp, Broken	120 lbs.	1.95	234.00	1.92	230.40
Scallops	60 lbs.	2.45	147.00	3.23	193.80
Crabmeat, Backfin	500 lbs.	3.81	1,905.00	4.19	2,095.00
Lobster Tails	160 lbs.	4.80	768.00	5.42	867.20
Lobsters	90 lbs.	1.80	162.00	2.01	180.90
Oysters	11 bu.	13.00/bu.	143.00	14.30	157.30
Clams, Cherrystone	4,000 ea.	.0375	150.00	.042	168.00
Baking Potatoes 80's	80 cs.	4.25 cs.	340.00	7.90	632.00
Whole Green Beans Fz.	27 cs.	10.32 cs.	278.64	9.36	252.72
Lettuce	34 cs.	4.75	161.50	8.50	289.00
Tomatoes, Fresh	17 cs.	10.45 cs.	177.65	8.00	136.00
Orange Sections	52 gal.	3.25 g.	169.00	4.06	211.12
Grapefruit Sections	72 gal.	3.25 g.	234.00	3.45	248.40
Milk	24 disp.	6.40	153.60	7.00 e	168.00
Ice Cream	35 cns.	5.20/cn.	182.00	6.80 e	238.00
Chip Butter	486 lbs.	.92 lb.	447.12	.97	471.42
Whole Eggs, Frozen	360 lbs.	.42	151.20	.51	183.60
Bakers Best Flour	15 cwt	8.70	130.50	11.38 e	170.70
Coffee	400 lbs.	.88	352.00	1.24	496.00
Corn Relish	14 cs.	12.75	178.50	14.02	196.28
Total			$18,351.49		$22,378.81
Total Percentage for Period			$25,216.00		
Percentage of sample			73%		

Fig. 7-6. Cost of food purchase index.

(cashier, food controller) with the amounts consumed as indicated by the production sheet may be even more revealing. The sales tabulation will only show those portions that were paid for by the customer. Any portions for which no revenue was collected, such as those consumed by a customer who "walked out" or those served by a dishonest waiter and not recorded, would not be tabulated. If employee meals are permitted, some means of identifying that consumption should be devised, or this too can distort the comparison.

Overportioning can also affect the comparison. The portions sold and the recorded consumption should be very close, and for high-cost preportioned items (such as steaks or lobsters), it should be exact, with credit given for any returns or misorders (the frequency of "wrong orders" should be investigated, however). Many restaurants prepare a separate Steak Report or Special Merchandise Report in addition to the other control procedures.

Duplicate Check Control

A duplicate check control system requires the waiter to present some evidence in the kitchen that an item has been recorded on a guest check before he can get the food for his guest. These "dupes" may be carbons of the actual checks and bear the same serial numbers; they may be separate chits obtained from a cashier or automatically from a cash register; or they may be captains' orders in dining rooms where captains are employed. In the latter case, the order is transcribed by the waiter on a guest check obtained in the kitchen from a food checker, upon presentation of the captain's dupe.

The dupes can be used in several ways. They may be matched with the guest checks to see if any checks are missing, and they may be used by the chef or production manager to compare the food dispensed with the records of consumption. Although the system is primarily a responsive form of control (if food or checks are missing, an investigation is needed), the use of dupes can prevent the sales staff from "swinging" checks or giving food gratis in return for a larger tip.

The duplicate check system is a very effective method of control, provided the matching of dupes to checks is done at least on a test basis. Because this matching is a time consuming and monotonous task, it is often discontinued. Once it becomes known that the matching function is no longer performed, the control will be ineffective.

Sales Value Control

When merchandise is obtained in salable form, such as in a coffee cart or snack bar that receives its food from a central commissary, the issues can be made at sales value rather than at cost. This technique is also used for the control of liquor in a bar. Sales values are assigned to items coming into the operation, and stock on hand is inventoried at sales value. The amount sold must equal the amount of money in the cash register. When the same item may be used in different ways with different sales prices, a weighted average price must be calculated. Only the main component of an item is priced, such as hamburgers but not the buns. Thus, in a limited menu, fast-food operation, sales value control becomes easy and effective. Sales value control is much less effective when merchandise must be processed in the unit, or when there is a large menu with numerous variations using the same ingredients.

Accounting Reports

Accounting reports are stated in dollars and sometimes in ratios, and they are one form of reactive control. The figures by themselves are more meaningful when compared with something such as a budget, a standard, or with past performance, since a comparison can help to isolate areas where management should direct attention.

These reports can be used for food cost control by a comparison of ratios of food cost to sales. These ratios can then be compared to past ratios, to budgeted ratios, or to calculated potential cost ratios. In a situation where there are no sales, such as in an institution, food cost is stated as "cost per meal," or "cost per day." Hospitals and nursing homes use the term "cost per patient day."

Accounting reports (or income statements) are important in evaluating the overall performance of the operation and the effectiveness of actual food cost control procedures. Accounting statements are not timely enough for food cost control purposes. They generally cover a month or four-week period (although some operators do prepare weekly statements) and may take a week or more to prepare after the end of the period. Also, these reports rarely provide sufficient data to determine where corrective action is necessary. Sales are stated and may be broken down by outlet or by meal period. Total food cost is also stated and may be based solely on purchases. Preferably, food cost is based on purchases adjusted for changes in inventory and the cost of employee meals, calculated as follows:

> Beginning inventory
> + Purchases
> _____
> = Food available for sale
> − Ending inventory
> _____
> = Cost of food consumed
> − Employee meals
> _____
> = Cost of food sold

PART TWO

Bar Management

8

BEVERAGE

MERCHANDISING

The Economic Significance
of Changing Attitudes toward Alcoholic Beverages

The attitude of the American public toward alcoholic beverages has changed greatly since the days of Prohibition. Alcoholic beverages are now served in coffee shops, fast-food operations, cafeterias, and in such semiinstitutional operations as museum restaurants and department store tearooms. They are also an important merchandising tool of airlines both in lounges on the ground and as part of the in-flight service. Wine service has been introduced into nursing homes and hospitals for therapeutic purposes. Although the service of wines in such institutions is not yet a common practice, it is predicted that it will grow.

The growing public acceptance of the use of alcoholic beverages in moderation has had a significant impact on the overall national economy as well as on the economy of the distillers, vintners, brewers, and ancillary industries. The public's change in attitude has also been of significant economic importance to the restaurant business. The repeal of Prohibition saved some restaurant operators from bankruptcy during the severe economic depression of the 1930s, and there are many today that could not survive without the profit derived from the sale of alcoholic beverages. In some parts of the country, sales of alcoholic beverages average 34 percent of food sales in public restaurants, approximately 40 percent of food sales in hotels, and from 40 to 60 percent of food sales in private clubs.

An efficiently operated "free-standing" beverage operation will often produce an operating profit equal to 38 to 48 percent of sales after direct expenses but before occupation costs, whereas an efficiently operated restaurant that does not serve alcoholic beverages often will have an operating profit less than 25 percent of sales.

Federal, State, and Municipal Regulations

Although all states now permit the sale of alcoholic beverages, there is no uniformity of practice among them. Some states permit local options, which allow the county residents to decide whether the sale of beer, wines, or liquors should be legalized.

At the state-wide level, alcoholic beverage sales usually are regulated by a state authority or board. There is a wide range in the degree of control enforcement. In some instances, the size of the containers used in the sale of alcoholic beverages at the bar is controlled, which can have a bearing on the type of automated dispensing unit that can be used. In addition, there are the overall federal laws on the taxation of alcoholic beverages and the granting of licenses for their manufacture, distribution, and sale.

Because of the lack of uniformity in the regulatory provisions, the purveyor of alcoholic beverages should acquaint himself with the beverage laws and regulations in his own state and city. Many states and localities require special bookkeeping procedures. Some specify dates on which liquor bills must be paid. Others limit the number and locations of bars in a restaurant. Still others set eligibility requirements for holders of liquor licenses and their employees, and regulate the number and type of advertising signs. Failure to comply with all governmental requirements may mean revocation of a restaurant's license, penalties, and the loss of a substantial investment in bar and restaurant equipment.

Organization of a Beverage Operation

Beverage operations can range in size from a one-man, open-bar operation to a multisales outlet such as a large convention hotel where at any given time, alcoholic beverage service may be offered in many dining rooms, several function rooms or ballrooms, cocktail lounges, hospitality suites, and in room service. In such hotels, sales in one day can amount to tens of thousands of dollars.

In a typical commercial hotel operation, the responsibility for the beverage operation is delegated to a food and beverage director (or manager). If the banquet operation is large, a banquet manager may assist the food and beverage director. In a smaller operation, a head waiter supervises the service of beverages in dining rooms and the cocktail lounge, while a head bartender is in charge of all bar operations.

Sales Outlets in Food Operations

Although in some restaurants alcoholic beverages are sold only in the dining rooms, many restaurants and, indeed, most large hotels have several outlets. Hotels can have any or all the following types of outlets:

> Front bars
> Cocktail lounges
> Dining rooms
> Function rooms
> Guest rooms
> Hospitality suites

Front Bars

The facilities for front bars are arranged in such a way as to enable patrons to have a full view of the preparation of drinks. Because the drinks are prepared in full view of the patron and then served by the bartender, a front bar must be staffed with experienced bartenders who are well groomed and pleasant and who maintain cleanliness and orderliness in all aspects of the bar operation. The bartenders also should know how to handle the patrons and understand the legal aspects of serving alcoholic beverages.

Bartenders in front bars usually also act as cashiers. The services of a cashier are required only in extremely busy operations where the bartenders are kept so busy preparing and serving drinks that they do not have the time to be cashiers.

Cocktail Lounges

Cocktail lounges are designed for leisurely drinking. They may be furnished with cocktail tables and chairs, with larger tables if food is served in addition to alcoholic beverages, and with sofas and easy chairs. In some cocktail lounges there are open bars; in others, drinks are prepared in a service bar. In some lounges, carts bearing the more popular alcoholic beverages are wheeled from patron to patron, and each drink is prepared in full view of its recipient. This type of service has a certain amount of ego appeal because the drink is custom-made under the direction of the patron.

Entertainment is frequently provided in cocktail lounges. The entertainment may range from a solo pianist or guitarist, to a singer with an accompanist, to an orchestral combination with singers and specialty acts.

Pricing policies in cocktail lounges vary depending primarily on the type of entertainment. If the entertainment consists of only a soloist, no extra charge will be made in most cases. When more expensive entertainment is provided, as in a night club, the price of the drink may be increased during the period of entertainment, or a minimum check (minimum amount per person) or a cover charge is accepted by the public.

In an operation using a cover charge policy, each patron pays a fixed amount in addition to the charges for drinks ordered. The cover charge is in force during the period of entertainment, and all patrons present in the room at that time are subject to this charge. Some operations with a cover charge policy make exceptions for patrons at the bar, especially if the bar is separated from the entertainment area.

Policy should be decided by management after considering their objectives. Normally, the objective will be to maximize the profit of the lounge as a center, but it may also be to create image and promote other related profit centers.

Dining Rooms

If alcoholic beverages are sold in a coffee shop or a dining room with informal table service, drinks are obtained by the server from a service bar not visible to the public. If the service bar is located too far from the dining room, a bus boy or a runner may bring the drink. Where the demand is heavy, a cocktail waitress is employed.

In a formal dining room—either an American or a European plan operation—a wine steward or *sommelier* is employed in addition to a cocktail waiter or waitress. In dining rooms where the demand for wines is small, cocktail as well as wine orders are taken and served by a wine steward. The prices for beverage service may be listed on the food menu, but usually it is preferable to have a separate menu for alcoholic beverages and wines.

The service of beverages in a night club dining room is similar to that in a formal dining room except that wine stewards are almost always used and the pricing policies are different. Night club operations use cocktail lounge pricing methods and variations of the minimum check method. In some night clubs, a beverage minimum is required regardless of the amount of the food check. In others, a minimum is placed on foods as well as on beverages. Still others have a minimum check for food and beverages and give the patron the option of ordering either food or beverages in the amount of the minimum.

Banquet or Function Rooms

Beverage service in a function room may mean a cocktail party, a social get together at any hour, or it can be a reception held for a variety of reasons, such as honoring a dignitary, introducing a newcomer to a group, or a new product to a market, serving as a prelude to a banquet or as a part of a social festivity. In addition to alcoholic beverages, some food snacks such as canapés or hors d'oeuvres are served. A banquet is an occasion when a meal is served, usually with wine and other alcoholic beverages. Full bottles of liquor and set-ups are sometimes put on each table. A cordial or liqueur may be offered after the meal, and if dancing or entertainment is to follow, the bar may be reopened.

Banquets that include beverage service are usually arranged at an all-inclusive price per person. Another arrangement is to have a "cash bar" where banquet guests pay separately for their drinks when served. Under this arrangement, the host usually pays a separate charge for labor.

Cocktail parties are usually charged in one of the following ways:

- By the bottle—payment is made at an agreed-on price for all opened bottles.
- By the drink—payment is made at an agreed-on price for the number of drinks served. Agreement is also reached in advance on the sizes of the drinks to be served.
- By the hour—a flat rate is charged per person present on the basis of the length of time that beverages were served.

A separate charge may or may not be made for bartenders and use of the room where the party is held, depending on the size of the party and the amount of money involved.

Room Service

Room service is a source of minimal beverage revenue in most hotel operations. The guest calls in the order for a bottle or individual drink to a room service order station. The order is transmitted to a waiter who brings the bottle or individual drink to the guest's room. In-room vending machines are popular when permitted under state liquor authority rules.

Hospitality Suites

Hospitality suites are found mostly in convention hotels. Receptions in these suites are sponsored by vendors or manufacturers who provide goods or services to the convention attendees and invited guests. Receptions in hospitality suites are in effect smaller versions of cocktail parties, and a number of them may be in operation at the same time.

The charges for beverage service in hospitality suites are usually on a per-bottle basis. Whether a charge is made for a bartender or for the use of the suite depends on the amount of sales revenue derived from the service of the beverages and is usually agreed on in advance.

Merchandising of Beverages

Because of the comparatively high profit ratio of an alcoholic beverage operation, management should exert every effort to increase sales. A good program of merchandising is important. The comments that follow are restricted to merchandising and promoting beverage sales internally. (External promotion is discussed in *Profitable Food and Beverage Management: Planning.)* In recent years, there has been greater recognition of the value of decor and atmosphere in merchandising both alcoholic beverages and food. Internal media such as display and test cards, wine and beverage lists, wine and liquor displays, and entertainment are also effective in increasing sales.

In some university clubs and business men's clubs, carts bearing the ingredients for the more popular drinks are wheeled to the members in the cocktail lounge or reading room. Upon request, specific drinks are custom mixed in the presence of the member. In other clubs, members mix or pour their own drinks. With some modifications, this idea may be used in certain cocktail lounges.

In some cocktail lounge operations, as well as in night club operations, when waiters may not serve beverages during the entertainment, full bottles of liquor with the requested mixer are set on the table on a pour-it-yourself basis. The patrons are charged on the basis of consumption, the amount of which is determined by the waiter and agreed on by the patron before the liquor is removed from the table.

Creation of a new drink, with proper image-building exploitation of the originality of the creation, has been extremely profitable to some operators. The Roosevelt Hotel in New Orleans, which is credited with originating the Sazarac cocktail, has drawn many a tourist to its bar to taste the famous Sazarac as it is mixed by the people who first made it. Operators of Polynesian restaurants find that their original drinks, which are not only different but also have a great deal of eye appeal, contribute handsomely to the volume of beverage sales in those restaurants.

Package pricing is another method frequently used in the merchandising of beverages. Examples are the offering of second drinks at half price (usually for table service in the dining rooms), including a cocktail, wine, or beer in the price of a meal, charging half price for all drinks during a certain period of the day, and offering free canapes and hors d'oeuvres at cocktail time.

Proper training of the service staff to be alert and responsive to the wants of the customer can be important for sales promotion. All too frequently it is difficult for a patron to order the first drink and next to impossible to reorder a drink. Many patrons who have to make a train, get to a theater by the start of a performance, or meet some other deadline leave after one drink when they might have ordered two or more rounds that could have been served if the service staff had been alert enough to provide quick service. The cause of such loss of business can be a lack of training, discipline, and supervision more than a lack of a sufficient number of employees. In an operation with a properly trained staff, the waiter unobtrusively inquires if the patron desires to reorder as soon as the glasses are empty. If the patron does not desire to reorder at that time, he is told that the waiter will be nearby when he desires to do so. This approach is prevalent in European operations and is quite effective.

The claim is often made that patrons resent the "hustling" of drinks, but looking after the patrons' needs is one of the fundamental requirements of being a good waiter. Objections are justified if after inquiring whether the patron wishes to reorder, the waiter immediately removes all the glasses, thus indicating that he wishes the patron to leave. The practice of quick removal of the glasses and other utensils associated with serving of the beverage is defended by some operators on the ground of the unfavorable appearance of a table bearing empty, soiled glassware. One food and beverage merchandiser prefers that the empty glasses remain on the table (unless they are badly soiled) as a reminder to the patron that it is time to reorder.

The sale of wines has increased dramatically in recent years, perhaps as a result of the promotional efforts of the wineries and distributors and also because of the merchandising efforts of some restaurant operators. A knowledgeable, well-trained service staff is the first requirement for increasing a restaurant's wine sales. The servers should know the taste and quality characteristics of the types of wine being offered—whether they are dry, medium dry, or sweet, light or heavy bodied. They are then in a position to assist a guest who may be hesitant about ordering, perhaps because of a lack of knowledge, by determining his preferences and then making appropriate suggestions.

Bulk wine service by the glass or carafe is usually well received and is now found in many luxury restaurants as well as in more moderately priced operations. Perhaps this is because the patron is not overwhelmed by a large selection and unfamiliar names and because carafe service is generally lower priced than wines sold by the bottle.

9

BEVERAGE SELECTION

Many patrons have distinct likes and dislikes when it comes to brands of their favorite beverages. They may be quite naive about brand names generally, but they are "wedded" to certain brands for their own consumption. Substitutes will only annoy them, particularly inferior substitutes. Serving beverages of poor quality will lose the patronage of brand-minded guests.

There are distinct regional preferences in types of liquor. The beverage buyer should learn the extent of the local trade in relation to transient business. In a hotel, a geographical breakdown of house guests will show what percentage of them come from a radius of less than 200 to 250 miles. These guests are likely to have tastes similar to those of local guests. If a substantial percentage of the patrons come from greater distances, regional preferences will carry less weight, and the sales patterns will probably conform to national patterns. The trade press is a good source of information about national patterns and trends.

The beverage buyer should talk with the bartenders and service personnel in his operation to find out what the customers are requesting. Although it may be possible to determine from beverage records what is selling, it is extremely important to know whether customers are making requests that cannot be filled. Some operators have their bartenders and service supervisors record in a log book any requests that cannot be filled.

All alcoholic beverages are fermented, and certain of them are also distilled to concentrate the alcohol created by the fermentation process. Alcoholic beverages have three classifications: distilled spirits, which include whiskey, rum, brandy, gin, and so on; fermented malt liquors, such as beer and ale; and wines, which are the product of natural grape and fruit fermentation.

Distilled Spirits

Distilled spirits are classified as whiskies, rums, brandies, gins, vodkas, liqueurs, and "other spirits." The last category includes a large group of products, such as akvavit and tequila, that are not in great demand.

The beverage purchaser should know the terms used in the distillation process because they decidedly affect the quality of the product. The term *proof* indicates the alcohol content. Each degree of proof is equal to one-half of 1 percent of alcohol. A distilled spirit that is 90 proof contains 45 percent of alcohol by volume; a distilled spirit that is 100 proof contains 50 percent of alcohol by volume. Any distilled spirit over 100 proof is considered "overproofed." A rectified spirit is one that has been altered in some way from the original state after distillation. Blended whiskies are rectified spirits.

Whiskies

The United States federal government has established standards of identity for distilled spirits and other alcoholic beverages. Whiskey is defined as follows:

> . . . an alcoholic distillate from a fermented mash of grain produced at less than 190 proof in such a manner that the distillate possesses the taste, aroma and characteristics generally attributed to whiskey, stored in oak containers . . . and bottled at not less then 80 proof. . . .

The regulations* identify nine types of whiskies and are quoted herewith:

1. (a) "Bourbon whiskey," "rye whiskey," "wheat whiskey," "malt whiskey," or "rye malt whiskey" is whiskey produced at not exceeding 160 proof from a fermented mash of not not less than 51 percent corn, rye, wheat, malted barley, or malted rye grain, respectively, and stored at not more than 125 proof in charred new oak containers; and also includes mixtures of such whiskies of the same type.

   (b) "Corn whiskey" is whiskey produced at not exceeding 160 proof from a fermented mash of not less than 80 percent corn grain, and if stored in oak containers stored at not more than 125 proof in used or uncharred new oak containers and not subjected in any manner to treatment with charred wood; and also includes mixtures of such whiskey.

   (c) Whiskies conforming to the standards prescribed in subdi-

---

Regulations under the Federal Alcohol Administration Act: Title 27, Code of Federal Regulations. Department of the Treasury, Bureau of Alcohol, Tobacco and Firearms. ATF Publication 1, Revised July 1973.

visions (a) and (b) of this subparagraph, which have been stored in the type of oak containers prescribed, for a period of 2 years or more shall be further designated as "straight"; for example, "straight bourbon whiskey," "straight corn whiskey," and whiskey conforming to the standards prescribed in subdivision (a) to this subparagraph, except that it was produced from a fermented mash of less than 51 percent of any one type of grain, and stored for a period of 2 years or more in charred new oak containers shall be designated merely as "straight whiskey."

2. "Whiskey distilled from bourbon (rye, wheat, malt, or rye malt) mash" is whiskey produced in the United States at not exceeding 160 proof from a fermented mash of not less than 51 percent corn, rye, wheat, malted barley, or malted rye grain, respectively, and stored in used oak containers; and also includes mixtures of such whiskies of the same type. Whiskey conforming to the standard of identity for corn whiskey must be designated corn whiskey.

3. "Light whiskey" is whiskey produced in the United States at more than 160 proof, on or after January 26, 1968, and stored in used or uncharred new oak containers; and also includes mixtures of such whiskies. If "light whiskey" is mixed with less than 20 percent of straight whiskey on a proof gallon basis, the mixture shall be designated "blended light whiskey" (light whiskey —a blend).

4. "Blended whiskey" (whiskey—a blend) is a mixture which contains at least 20 percent of straight whiskey on a proof gallon basis and, separately or in combination, whiskey or neutral spirits. A blended whiskey containing not less than 51 percent on a proof gallon basis of one of the types of straight whiskey shall be further designated by that specific type of straight whiskey; for example, "blended rye whiskey" (rye whiskey—a blend).

5. "A blend of straight whiskies" (blended straight whiskies) is a mixture of straight whiskies. A blend of straight whiskies consisting entirely of one of the types of straight whiskey, and not conforming to the standard for "straight whiskey," shall be further designated by that specific type of straight whiskey; for example, "a blend of straight rye whiskies" (blended straight rye whiskies).

6. "Spirit whiskey" is a mixture of neutral spirits* and not less

---

*"Neutral spirits" is defined by the federal government as ". . . distilled spirits produced from any material at or above 190 proof, and, if bottled, bottled at not less than 80 proof." For blending with whiskey, neutral spirits distilled from grain mash are used. Neutral spirits may also be distilled from materials such as sugar cane and grape.

than 5 percent on a proof gallon basis of whiskey, or straight whiskey, or straight whiskey and whiskey, if the straight whiskey component is less than 20 percent on a proof gallon basis.

7. "Scotch whiskey" is whiskey which is a distinctive product of Scotland, manufactured in Scotland in compliance with the laws of the United Kingdom regulating the manufacture of Scotch whiskey for consumption in the United Kingdom: *Provided* That if such product is a mixture of whiskies, such mixture is "blended Scotch whiskey" (Scotch whiskey—a blend).

8. "Irish whiskey" is whiskey which is a distinctive product of Ireland, manufactured either in the Republic of Ireland or in Northern Ireland, in compliance with their laws regulating the manufacture of Irish whiskey for home consumption: *Provided,* That if such product is a mixture of whiskies, such mixture is "blended Irish whiskey" (Irish whiskey—a blend).

9. "Canadian whiskey" is whiskey which is a distinctive product of Canada, manufactured in Canada in compliance with the laws of Canada regulating the manufacture of Canadian whiskey for consumption in Canada: *Provided,* That if such product is a mixture of whiskies, such mixture is "blended Canadian whiskey" (Canadian whiskey—a blend).

The term *bottled in bond* means that a straight whiskey of 100 proof has been stored in a charred oak barrel in a warehouse under the supervision of the United States government for a period of four years or more. Such specification does not in any way guarantee the quality of the whiskey. In fact, the Treasury Department, which controls the bonded warehouses, states that the bottled in bond stamp in no way guarantees the purity or quality of the spirits. It is merely proof of four years' storage in a government-controlled warehouse.

In the yeasting process of making whiskey, sweet mash whiskies are yeasted by using a freshly developed batch of yeast for each mash. Sour mash whiskies are yeasted by using a small amount of mash plus an additional amount of new yeast. The yield per bushel of grain is likely to be greater for sour mash than for sweet mash whiskey. The quality of both types depends on the other processes of whiskey making.

Foreign and Other Distillations

Scotch Whiskey. Scotch whiskey is light bodied and smoky flavored. The grain is dried over open peat fires, and the whiskey keeps its smoky quality during the entire making and bottling process.

Almost all Scotch whiskey is blended rather than straight. The blend includes whiskies from all of the four Scotch-producing regions: the Highlands, the Lowlands, Campbelltown, and Islay. It is usually aged in sherry barrels or uncharred oak barrels, and its age is indicated on the bottle. One should not make the mistake of believing that age is an absolute guarantee of quality. A poor Scotch whiskey retains its poor quality regardless of age.

Liqueur Scotch whiskey, very fine to begin with, has a mellow and distinctive flavor. Usually such Scotch is at least 12 years old. However, caution must be used in assessing the value of this designation on a bottle. It is sometimes used indiscriminately.

Irish Whiskey. Irish whiskey is made in the same manner and with the same ingredients as Scotch whiskey. The only difference is that the grain of Irish whiskey is dried over a closed fire instead of an open fire; hence, the smoky flavor of Scotch is absent. Irish whiskey is the only whiskey distilled three times.

Irish whiskies are sometimes blended whiskies but are usually straight, pot-still whiskies. All Irish whiskies shipped to this country are at least seven years old and are usually of very fine quality.

Vodka. Vodka has enjoyed a striking growth in popularity in recent years, owing in part to a trend toward lighter tastes. Its popularity may also be due to heavy promotional campaigns by some distillers. Vodka is distilled from fermented grain mash at high proof, then further processed to make it colorless, odorless, and tasteless. It requires no aging and therefore can be produced and sold at a lower cost than most other alcoholic beverages. Because of its neutral quality, vodka mixes well with many other beverages, especially fruit juices. Popular vodka drinks include the bloody Mary, screwdriver, vodka martini, and vodka sour. Most vodka marketed in the United States is produced domestically, although some vodka is imported from England, Poland, and Russia.

Rum. Rum is distilled from the fermented juice of sugar cane products. It is not rum if it is mixed with any other spirits. The two principal types of rum in greatest use at present are the light-bodied and the full-bodied rums.

Light-bodied rums sold in the United States are mostly from Puerto Rico, marketed under two labels: the white and the gold. The designation corresponds roughly to the general coloring of each type. Gold label rums have a darker color than white label rums because of differences in the amount of caramel coloring. These light-bodied rums are distilled at proof ranging from 160 to 180. They are stored and matured in oak casks.

Most of the full-bodied rums imported into the United States come from the island of Jamaica in the West Indies. Other Caribbean areas produce full-bodied rums, but they are not as well known as those from Jamaica. The full-bodied rums are distilled at between 140 and 160 proof to produce a heavy flavor. Caution should be exercised when purchasing little-known full-bodied rums because quite a number of these are "monkey rums," so called because of their explosive or fiery taste caused by improper aging and inferior ingredients.

Brandy. Brandy is a distilled spirit derived from a fermented mash of fruit and aged in the wood. Unless otherwise specified, brandy is generally taken to mean grape brandy, although excellent brandies are also made from apples, cherries, apricots, and plums.

Cognac is a type of grape brandy that obtains its name from the Cognac region of France and is generally regarded as brandy at its best. Its high standing is due not only to the special process of distillation used in the Cognac district but also the grape, which acquires its quality characteristics from an ideal combination of soil, climate, and growing conditions. Brandy produced in other areas may have some of these qualities, but none of them have ever approached the acclaimed quality of brandy from the Cognac district.

Although brandy from any other part of the world cannot be classified as cognac, misleading merchandising "angles" are sometimes used. One subterfuge is to make the label look like a cognac label and to use a similar name. The following significant abbreviations appear on a cognac label:

E —Especial	S —Superior
F —Fine	P —Pale
V —Very	X —Extra
O —Old	C —Cognac

Thus, the letters VSOP mean Very Superior Old Pale.

Stars on a brandy bottle have no special significance. Each firm sets its own standards. Three stars used by one company may mean something quite different on another company's product.

Cognac will improve while aging in the wood for about 5 to 55 years. Because this extremely long period of storage ties up capital and increases the price considerably, relatively little cognac is aged for longer than a generation. Once it is bottled, cognac will not improve with age. Bottles that have been made to look as though they were a century old are just an attempt to fool the credulous purchaser. A good quality cognac, aged in the wood properly for 6 to 10 years, will be quite suitable for consumption. The best age for cognac is between 20 to 40 years, aged in the wood. A method of testing the quality of cognac is to pour it into a glass, empty it out, and observe the glass 24 hours later. If the glass still bears noticeable traces of the bouquet, the cognac may be considered of high quality.

Of the French brandies other than cognac, armagnac enjoys a favorable reputation in this country, and one or two brands will be found on high-grade drink lists. Spanish brandy, generally sweeter than French brandy, is highly regarded by some patrons. Another popular sweet brandy is Metaxa, a product of Greece. It is often found on the drink lists of fashionable establishments.

Although California produces a large quantity of excellent brandy, the demand for it, like the demand for any brandy, has been increasing only very slowly. California's production, almost exclusively from grapes, represents a major portion of the total brandy production of this country. Outside California, the brandy made in the United States is mostly from fruit other than grapes.

Apple brandy, more commonly known in this country as apple jack, is quite popular in some regions. Calvados is a French cousin of our American apple jack, and following the invasion of Normandy, near the end of World War II, it became a favorite of many American soldiers. It is normally aged for a longer period than apple jack.

Fruit brandy is not defined as precisely in Europe as it is in the United States. In this country, federal regulations have established rigid standards for the use of the term *brandy* on a fruit brandy label. The brandy must be made from the fermented juice or mash of the fruit specified.

Fruit liqueurs are made by infusing a fruit flavor into a brandy through a process of immersing the fruit in brandy for several months. Strictly speaking, such liqueurs are not true brandies and cannot be bottled as such in the United States. In European countries, fruit liqueurs are indiscriminately bottled as fruit brandies without any legal restrictions.

Gin. Gin is a simple spirit to make. That fact makes gin generally less expensive than most. It consists of neutral spirits distilled or redistilled with juniper berries and other aromatics. The higher the quality of the neutral spirits, the better the quality of the gin. Aging does not improve gin, and for that reason it is not stored in wooden casks but in earthenware or glass-lined vats.

Flavoring is accomplished through two different methods: distillation or compounding. Distilled gin is distilled all the way either by direct distillation or redistillation. In direct distillation, heat is applied to fermented mash. The spirit vapors rise through a container of juniper berries and other herbs to extract the flavoring. Compounding consists of mixing neutral spirits with juniper.

The English make a dry gin, a sweet gin (called "Old Tom"), and a sloe gin, which is actually a liqueur. American gins are made from neutral spirits distilled at a very high proof (190 proof or more) and reduced to the desired level. American fruit-flavored gins are compounded and generally artificially flavored. English and American gins are used almost entirely for mixed drinks. Holland's gin is generally consumed as a straight drink because it is too heavy for mixing.

Liqueur. Some liqueurs are processed by secret formulas that have never been made public, but most liqueurs (or cordials, as they are frequently called) are made by either the infusion or the compounding method. A spirit of some kind, usually a brandy, is infused with flavoring in excess of 2½ percent of the volume.

Outstanding and world-famous liqueurs have been copied to the point where the market is often flooded with cheap and undesirable substitutes. The beverage purchaser should be alert for misleading labeling.

A fine assortment of high-quality liqueurs lends distinction to the wine list and helps to attract a discriminating clientele. The following are long standing favorites:

Anisette	Cointreau	Drambuie
Apricot Liqueur	Cordial Medoc	Grand Marnier
Benedictine	Crème de Cacao	Kummel
Blackberry Liqueur	Crème de Menthe	Maraschino
Chartreuse (Yellow	(White or Green)	Peach Liqueur
or Green)	Crème de Cassis	Sloe Gin
Cherry Heering	Curaçao	

Occasionally, Southern Comfort is included in this grouping, although it is much higher in proof than the others on the list. In fact, it is equal in proof to some whiskies. Among the high-quality liqueurs, there are no bargains. Some of the so-called bargains are such cheap substitutes that they are likely to produce undesirable aftereffects that will reflect against the establishment serving them. It is advisable to indicate clearly on the drink list the brand names of liqueurs when more than one brand may be available.

Miscellaneous Spirits. Certain drinks that are practically national drinks in some countries have developed considerable popularity in various parts of the United States. The most prominent of these include akvavit from the Scandinavian countries, tequila from Mexico, and okolehao from Hawaii.

Akvavit (or aquavit) is made from grain or potatoes and flavored with caraway seeds and other flavoring agents. It is always served ice cold.

Tequila is made from the hardy century plant. Because of its extremely fiery quality, half of a lemon or lime and a small pinch of salt are usually taken to clear the way for this potent drink.

Okolehao is derived from sugar cane molasses. It is most commonly used as an ingredient for mixed drinks, some of which are served in coconut shells.

Other Mixed Drink Ingredients

To be successful, a bar must always sell first-class products. Some beverage buyers erroneously believe that the average person does not recognize quality, especially in mixed drinks. Risking the patrons' displeasure and the loss of their business to make a few pennies more on each drink served is foolish. The good margin of profit provided by beverage sales makes any compromise with quality unnecessary.

Mixes. Good quality is necessary for the basic ingredients, especially for mixes. An inferior mix can make a quality liquor taste and look decidedly substandard. This is particularly true of ginger ale, which must have excellent ginger flavoring and a high concentration of carbonation to make it taste right as a mix. The greater effervescence of high-quality carbonated drinks enables the contents of opened bottles to remain alive hours longer than inferior carbonated mixes, which usually are flat within 15 minutes after the bottles are opened.

The use of splits (6½ oz bottles) is highly advantageous in many operations and is required in high-price operations. Splits assure individuality of service, in addition to perfect carbonation for each drink. It is extremely unwise to use inert or dissipated mixes with high-quality liquor

Carbonated mixes are also available in pressurized containers that can be connected to dispensers built into, or as an adjunct to, the bar. Such containers allow these beverages to be at a peak of effervescence when dispensed. The dispensing systems are often provided free of charge by the companies supplying the mixes.

Fruit Mixes. In busy bars, bartenders often request the purchase of prepared fruit mixes, since they save the time it would take to squeeze lemons or cut up fresh fruit. Use of prepared fruit mixes is quite common today even in the better bars, but the quality of a drink can easily be lowered by the use of inferior fruit mixes.

Customers with sensitive palates are likely to insist that there is no satisfactory substitute for fresh fruit. If the clientele of a particular establishment is composed largely of connoisseurs, the management might consider adjusting the bar procedures to conform to their tastes.

Fermented Malt Liquors

From available records, it appears that beer was the second alcoholic beverage made after wine. It was produced first by the Egyptians. Beer, ale, porter, and stout are made from fermented cereals and malts, or malt alone, flavored with hops.

Beer

Beer is an all-embracing term usually signifying all malt beverages. Used in the commercial sense it refers to light-colored brews, generally lagers, that are bright, clear, and effervescent, with an alcoholic content of about 4 percent by volume. Imported beers are usually labeled "lager" or "pilsner." The latter is a very light-colored brew.

Ale

Ale is dark, heavy, and slightly bitter, containing about 6 percent alcohol.

Porter and Stout

Porter and stout are English brews. They are very dark and have a sweet taste. Stout has a pronounced hop taste not present in porter. They are both rich and heavy, have a decided malt flavor, and contain about 6 percent alcohol by volume.

Bock Beer

Bock beer is heavier, darker, and sweeter than regular beer. It is made during the winter and is generally offered for sale in the early spring for a period of about six weeks.

Preparation and Packaging

Domestic beer is usually prepared in two different types: the full brew and the check brew. Full-brew beer permits the malt and cereals to develop to their full alcoholic content, which may run up to 14 percent by volume. The alcoholic content is then reduced to the desired strength before aging. Check brew beer is drawn off and processed when the desired alcoholic content is reached, thus eliminating one step in the brewing process. Check brews are usually cheaper beers.

Brands of beer vary from region to region, since many of them are sold practically on a local basis. As a result of intensive advertising and promotion over a period of years, a few nationally known domestic as well as some imported brands of beer and ale are popular everywhere.

Water Content. Since water constitutes approximately seven-eighths of the total volume of beer, the quality of the water (usually determined by its source) is of the greatest importance. Mountain water is very advantageous for brewing beer. However, water suitable for beer tends not to make good ale.

Packaging. Beer is packaged in three forms: kegs or barrels, bottles, and cans. Bottled and canned beer is pasteurized. Pasteurization puts an end to yeast action, but this does not mean that these products may be mishandled or improperly stored. Beer cannot be stored in wooden containers because it will take on the flavor of the wood. Wooden barrels used for beer are lined with pitch, which will not dissolve in beer. Aluminum is one type of metal that, if used in a container, will not affect the flavor of beer. Containers made of other metals are lined with pitch. Beer in kegs is not pasteurized, and therefore the yeast is still active. Strong odors, warm temperatures, bacteria, and light can all ruin beer. Therefore, beer must be stored in a place where it is protected from potentially harmful conditions.

Wine

Classifications

Wine is the fermented juice of grapes. In addition, juices of certain fruits and other berries are fermented to make wine. Wine has a cycle of life. It begins with infancy and grows to maturity; after it reaches a year of quality, it will stay there for a while and then decline slowly or rapidly, depending on circumstances. The rates and causes of change vary. Some changes are brought about by temperature, others by light.

In recent years, wine authorities have come to place all wines in five main classifications on the basis of principal uses and characteristics: appetizer wines, white table wines, red table wines, sweet dessert wines, and sparkling wines. The wines most generally found on sale in the United States are described below.

Appetizer Wines. Aperitifs are favored for before-meal use and are served with appetizers. Sherry, the most popular, is characterized by its "nutty" flavor. Most sherries have an alcoholic content of 17 to 20 percent by volume. Vermouth is another favorite, as is Dubonnet. They are aromatic wines flavored by the steeping in them of herbs and other aromatic substances, or by the addition of an infusion of herbs. Aromatic wines are frequently used as mixers. Dry and pale vermouth (French type) is used extensively for martini cocktails, sweet and dark amber vermouth (Italian type) for Manhattans, and Dubonnet for Dubonnet cocktails. These wines range from 15 to 20 percent in alcoholic content.

White Table Wines. White table wines vary from extremely dry and tart to sweet and mellow, with delicate flavors, and by tradition are consumed with white meats, fowl, and seafoods. They range in color from pale straw to deep gold and in alcohol content from 10 to 14 percent. The still white wines consumed in this country come principally from France, Germany, and Italy or are native to the United States. The following are the better-known regions that produce the still white wines most popular in America:

France:

> Bordeaux (Graves, Sauternes, and Barsac)
> Burgundy (Chablis, Côte d'Or, Côte de Beaune)
> Alsace (Haut-Rhin and Bas-Rhin)
> Rhone Valley

Germany:

> Rhine Valley (Rheingau, Rheinhesse, Palatinate)
> Moselle Region (Bernkastel, Piesport)

Italy:

> Tuscany
> Piedmont (Turin, Monferrato, Langhe)
> Umbria (Orvieto)
> Marche
> Veneto (Verona, Lake Garda region, Lessini Mountains)
> Campanis (Naples and Mt. Vesuvius regions)
> Latium (Rome region, Frascati)

United States:

> California (Sonoma, Mendocino, Napa Valley, Livermore, Contra Costa)
> New York (Finger Lakes, Niagara, Harbor Valley)
> Ohio (Lake Erie, Cincinnati)

Red Table Wines. Red table wines are usually dry. Rich, sometimes tart, and even astringent in flavor, they are by tradition consumed with red meats, pastas, and highly seasoned foods. Their alcohol content ordinarily runs from 10 to 14 percent by volume. (Pink or rosé wines are normally produced by leaving grape skins in the juice for only a fraction of the fermentation time.) Red table wines come principally from France and Italy or are native to the United States. The following are the better-known regions that produce the more popular still red wines consumed in the United States:

France:

> Bordeaux (Medoc, Saint-Emilion, Pomerol, Graves)
> Burgundy (Côte de Nuits, Côte d'Or, Côte Chalonnais, Côte de Beaune, and Beaujolais)

Italy:

> Tuscany
> Piedmont (Monferrato, Langhe)
> Lombardy (Valtellina)
> Veneto (Verona, Lake Garda region, Lessini Mountains)
> Compania (Mt. Vesuvius regions)

United States:

> California (Sonoma, Mendocino-Napa Valley, Solano County, Livermore, Mission, San José, Santa Clara, San Benito, and Santa Cruz)
> New York State (Finger Lakes, Hudson Valley)
> Ohio (Cincinnati)

Dessert Wines. Dessert wines used chiefly after meals are still wines, containing generally over 14 percent and less than 21 percent alcohol. The name has legal significance: In many countries all wines of more than 14 percent alcohol are grouped together for taxation purposes, usually as "dessert wines." "Table wines," or wines with alcoholic content not over 14 percent, are taxed at lower rates. For legal purposes, and to some extent in use as well, appetizer wines, such as sherries and vermouth, come under the dessert wine heading, as do some of the sweeter table wines, such as those from Sauternes and Barsac, France. More typical of dessert wines are ports (both red and white), Madeira, Marsala, Malaga, muscatel, and Tokay, which generally contain around 20 percent alcohol.

Sparkling Wines. Sparkling wines are table wines that have been made naturally effervescent by a second fermentation in closed containers. They are white, pink, or red, with a wide range of flavor characteristics and varying degrees of dryness or sweetness. Their usual alcohol content is 10 to 14 percent by volume, like that of still table wines. Champagne is the most widely known, followed by sparkling Burgundy, Moselle, rosé, and Asti Spumante.

The Wines of France

Bordeaux. The greatest wine-producing region of France is the area surrounding the ancient seaport of Bordeaux, comprised of the districts of Saint Emilion and Pomerol, the Medoc, Graves, Sauternes, and Barsac. The Medoc, Saint Emilion, and Pomerol produce red wines; Graves produces both red and white; Sauternes and Barsac produce sweet white wines. The most famous châteaux of the area are Château Lafite, Château Latour, and Château Margaux in the Medoc, Haut-Brion in Graves, Cheval-Blanc and Ausone in Saint Emilion, and Yquem in Sauternes.

The châteaux and vineyards are all small holdings with limited production. Because of the small supply, the prices of wines of the great châteaux are always high, particularly in a good vintage year. Even lesser vintages can bring top prices, depending on the state of the world economy. For a luxury restaurant, a selection of these *premiers crus* Bordeaux wines is a requirement for a respectable wine list. For a more modest list, many good values can be found among the lesser châteaux of the region.

Fig. 9-1. Label of a château-bottled Bordeaux wine.

There are four methods of labeling Bordeaux wines:

1. *Château-bottled wine* is produced, bottled, and labeled at the vineyard and distributed to the shipper. The word "château" and the name of the vineyard appear on the label, as well as *Mis en Bouteilles au Château* (see Fig. 9–1). *Mis en Bouteilles Par* on a label means that the wine is not château-bottled but has been bottled by the establishment whose name appears below the legend. Château-bottled Bordeaux wines are, as a rule, the finest obtainable.
2. *Château wine* is produced in a quantity too great to be bottled by the vineyard. It is sold to a merchant who is permitted to bottle it under the name of the château, provided that the bottler's name appears on the label as in "Bottled by Blank & Co."
3. *Trademark Bordeaux wine* is bought by a shipper, labeled, and shipped under his name. The word "château" does not appear on the label. Each shipper establishes his own standard, which will vary only slightly from year to year.
4. *Parish or district Bordeaux wine* is the collective product of the parish or district named on the label, similar to farm cooperatives in the United States. All wines from a particular district are labeled under the parish label. Quality and price on these wines may vary considerably.

Burgundy. The wines of Burgundy are as famous as those of Bordeaux, and there is great rivalry between the regions. The total output of Burgundy is much smaller, however.

Fig. 9-2. A French white burgundy label.

The regions of Burgundy are Chablis in the north, famous for its white wines; Côte de Nuits, which produces the great, heavy reds; Côte de Beaune, which produces both red and white wines; and the Côtes of southern Burgundy—Maconnais, Chalonnaise, and Beaujolais. The red wines of southern Burgundy are lighter than those of the north and are best drunk young. Great red burgundies bear the names of Clos Vougeot, Nuits Saint Georges, and Chambertin; among the whites are Montrachet and Meursault.

Burgundy does not follow the same labeling practices as Bordeaux (see Fig. 9–2). Estate-bottled burgundy may be labeled *Mis en bouteilles par le propriétaire*, or *Mis au domaine*, with the name of the proprietor. Wines that are not estate bottled may bear the label of the shipper of *Negociante*, or of a commune or district that has established its own standards and requirements. The latter may bear the designation *Appellation Contrôlée* of that district or commune.

Champagne. Champagne is a naturally fermented, sparkling, white wine from the province of Champagne, near Paris. It is a blended wine, produced from the growths of several vineyards. For that reason, no vineyard name ever appears on a champagne label (see Fig. 9–3). The firm name of the bottler is the criterion of quality. Champagne is labeled as to flavor: *Brut* or *Nature*, *Extra Sec* or Extra Dry, *Sec* or Dry, *Demi-Sec Doux*. *Brut* or *Nature* is extremely tart, and the

Fig. 9-3. A champagne label.

flavor range goes through diminishing degrees of dryness (or tartness) to *Demi-Sec*, which is the sweet, and *Doux*, which is very sweet.

Champagne is shipped in bottles of various sizes to avoid waste because it should be consumed at one sitting. Champagne cannot be recapped successfully because the carbonic gas escapes rapidly and the wine becomes flat. The most commonly used sizes of bottles in this country are the following:

Split	6.4 ounces
Half-bottle	12.8 ounces
Bottle	25.6 ounces (fifth)
Magnum	51.2 ounces (two-fifths)

Occasionally a jeroboam of 104 ounces (four-fifths) is used, but this is quite rare. The rehoboam of 156 ounces (one gallon and a fifth) is practically unknown in this country. Larger sizes than this are usually not shipped here. The new federal standards will apply to these bottles. Effective January 1979 all wines, both imported and domestic, will be sold in the following metric sizes:

Metric size	*Fluid ounces*
3 liters	101.4
1.5 liters	50.7
1 liter	33.8
750 milliliters	25.4
375 milliliters	12.7
187 milliliters	6.3
100 milliliters	3.4

Other Wine-Producing Regions of France. The Rhone Valley, south of the Burgundy region, has a number of small wine-producing districts, but few export their product to the United States in any sizable amounts. Among those available in the United States are the rosé wines of Tavel and the reds of Châteauneuf, Côte Rotie, and Hermitage.

From the Loire Valley, in the northwest of France, come the white wines of Muscadet and Pouilly Fumé, and the rosé of Anjou.

Alsatian wines are known as French Rhine wines and are labeled according to the type of grape used. They are all white wines and are seldom listed in smaller establishments. The best known Alsatian wine in this country is Riesling. Some of the larger hotels and restaurants also list Traminer.

German Wine and Its Labeling

German wines are classified under three major types: (1) Rhine wines (Rheingau, Rheinhesse, and Rheinpfalz), (2) Moselle wines, and (3) steinwein. In English-speaking countries, Rhine wines are quite commonly called hocks and sparkling hocks.

The three major types of German wines are easily distinguished by their bottles as well as by their labels. Rhine wines are always bottled in tall, flute-shaped, dark brown bottles. Moselle wine bottles are the same shape, but the color is dark green. Steinwein has a squat bottle known as *bocksbeutel.*

German wines have essentially the same labeling as the French Bordeaux wines. The classifications are: (1) estate bottled, (2) estate wine, bottled by a shipper, (3) trademark brand, and (4) district or township. The bottle labels of all wines produced and bottled in Germany are required by law to list the vintage year, the township or district where the grapes were grown, and the name of the shipper (see Fig. 9–4).

The best known of the Rheingau Rhine wines are Rudesheimer Schlossberg and Schloss Johannisberg. The best known of the Rheinhesse wines is the Niersteiner. Trockenbeeren wine is the most highly prized among the Rheinpfalz. Of the Moselle wines, the most famous is the legendary Bernkasteler Doktor.

Liebfraumïlch, one of the most popular German wines sold in the United States, is not a term applied to one specific wine. Rather, it is a term used to denote any Rhine wine of good quality and delightful character. Since the definition allows for a subjective determination on the part of the bottler, the wine buyer should beware of any bargains in regard to this wine.

Auslese and *Spatlese* are terms that find their way into some wine lists. The former means selected picking of the grapes; the latter

Fig. 9-4. A German wine label.

specifies late picking. *Trockenbeerenauslese* means selected, over-ripe, semidried grapes that yield a relatively small quantity of wine. This accounts for the high cost of this type of sweet, white wine.

Labels on German wine bottles are likely to appear confusing, because they carry a great deal of information. In addition to the required vintage date, township or district designation, and shipper's name, quite frequently the type of grape and manner of picking will be specified. The terms *Original Abzug* or *Original Abfullung*, indicating original bottling at the estate, are usually found in abbreviated form as *Orig. Abz.* or *Orig. Abf.*

Hungarian Wines

The most notable Hungarian wine is Tokay, a very sweet wine usually served with dessert or immediately after it. Wine fanciers consider it to be one of the truly great white wines. Because it takes several years to develop, it is more costly than some others. For that reason, in purchasing Tokay, the age of the wine should be a factor. It is always shipped in long-necked bottles that add distinction to any beverage display. Virtually no other Hungarian wine is sold in the United States.

Spanish and Portuguese Wines

There are many wines produced in Spain, but the most familiar is sherry, an Anglicized version of the Spanish name, *Jerez*. Sherry was extremely popular in England before the days of the Pilgrims, and it is one of the best known and most widely used imported wines in all English-speaking countries.

In addition to being an excellent straight wine drink, sherry is a splendid mix, and sherry flips and cobblers are very popular. The tart or dry sherries should be slightly chilled for serving, but the rich, sweet sherries should be served at room temperature. A dry sherry is most generally served as an aperitif, whereas sweet sherries are after-dinner favorites.

Sherries are classified according to varying degrees of tartness or sweetness. The very tart or dry sherry is Manzanilla. Next is Fino, still very dry, followed by Vino de Pasto and Amontillado. Amoroso is a medium dry sherry. Oloroso is a rich, sweet sherry, and Brown, the richest and sweetest, is dark brown in color. Of these types, Amontillado is the best known and the most frequently ordered in America.

The most famous Portuguese wines are the port wines, which are medium sweet and full-bodied, with a very fine bouquet. There are both red and white port wines, but in this country we know best the ruby and tawny ports. Ruby port is ruddy in color, as the name implies, and is generally a younger wine than tawny port, which is lighter in color and tarter in taste.

Madeira wines, produced on the island of Madeira, more than 600 miles from the Spanish peninsula, are generally very sweet wines developed mostly from a mixture of several grape varieties, using a heating process. Some, however, are the product of a single type of grape. The best known of the latter type is Malmsey. These wines are popular as aperitifs or as dessert wines.

Italian Wines

The most frequently used Italian wines in the United States are Chianti, Asti Spumante, Moscato, Marsala, vermouth, Soave, Orvieto, and Valpolicella.

Chianti is extremely tart, red, and usually drunk with spaghetti, macaroni, and highly seasoned foods.

Asti Spumante is a sparkling wine, sweet in taste. It is produced in much the same manner as champagne.

Moscato wines are made from the famous Muscat grape. They are usually dark brown, sweet, and rather mellow in taste.

Marsala wines are fortified wines, also dark brown. They bear a general resemblance to sherry. They are used quite extensively in cooking.

Soave and Orvieto are two of the finer Italian white wines. Soave has a smooth, light taste, and Orvieto has a refreshing fruity taste with a touch of bitterness.

Valpolicella is a soft, ruby red wine with a delicate bouquet.

Italian vermouths are used throughout the world as aperitifs, mixers, and after-dinner beverages. They are actually white wines to which some brandy has been added to bring the alcohol to between 17 and 20 percent, after which they are mixed and blended with a number of herbs and other flavoring agents. It takes several years to make a good vermouth.

Vermouths are made wherever wines are produced, but those most extensively used come from France, Italy, South America, eastern United States, and California. All these countries produce both sweet and dry vermouths, but France is better known for its dry vermouth and Italy for its sweet vermouth. California produces most of the wine used in making both dry and sweet American vermouth.

Vintages

Most European wines, except for those of Spain, will include on the label the year when the contents of that bottle were produced. The year (known as the vintage year of that wine) is shown because the quality of many wines varies from year to year as the result of climatic variations in the wine-growing regions. Although vintage should be considered when buying wine, it should not be the sole criterion because the exceptional vintage wines may be priced at a level that will make them unmarketable to restaurant patrons. It may be more prudent to look for wines from the good but less publicized vintages.

American winemakers, instead of putting a vintage year on the label, blend the products of several different harvests to produce wines of a consistent quality from year to year.

Wines of the United States

Since World War II, wine has become increasingly popular in the United States because of educational programs established by the wine industry. As a result, the restaurant sales of both imported and domestic wines have been rising.

Wines of the United States can be divided into two relatively distinct classifications: California wines and "American" wines. California is the source of all but a small percentage of the nation's wines. The European grape varieties *(Vitis vinifera)* flourish in California, and the state has such a range of climate, soil, and topography that it possesses eight distinct viticultural districts, each capable of yielding good wines.

East of the Rockies, the European grapes usually do not thrive, but numerous native varieties, principally of the *labrusca* family, have been domesticated and crossbred to provide wines with a distinct, "foxy" or sour taste. To modify this taste, which some people find unpleasant, some producers blend wines made from *labrusca* family grapes with wines from grapes of the *vinifera* family (such as California wines).

Outside California, the most important wine-growing regions are the Finger Lakes and Niagara districts of New York State (noted especially for excellent champagne, as well as for table and dessert wines), and the Sandusky-Lake Erie islands region of northern Ohio (also a champagne and table wine area). A great many wines are also produced in New Jersey, Michigan, Missouri, Iowa, and in restricted areas in Virginia, North Carolina, South Carolina, Georgia, Washington, and Oregon. Eastern wine producers market their still wines under such names as claret, sauterne, burgundy, rhine, sherry, and port, qualified by the word "American" or the name of the state where produced if at least 75 percent of the volume is derived from fruit grown and juice fermented in that state, and if the wine has been fully produced and finished within that state. The eastern white wines are generally better than the red wines, and the eastern champagnes are especially well known and appreciated. Although the eastern grape, different from the French grape, has a distinctive flavor, eastern champagne is produced by the traditional French method of bottle fermentation. In many cases the American champagnes compare favorably with the finest vintages shipped from France. The best American champagnes are from the Finger Lakes district of New York State and from certain sections of the Lake Erie district.

American champagne cannot be called "champagne" without qualifying the term with the place of origin—for example, California champagne, New York State champagne. If the secondary fermentation has taken place in bulk containers instead of in the bottle, the wine must be labeled "sparkling wine" and may also be designated "champagne style" or "champagne type" or "American (or New York State, California, etc.) champagne bulk process."

There is also carbonated wine. Such wine is made effervescent by the addition of carbon dioxide rather than through secondary fermentation of the wine within a closed container, tank, or bottle. Compared with sales of naturally fermented sparkling wine, sales of carbonated wine are negligible, and the wine is seldom on wine lists.

In the United States, American champagne and American vermouths are outselling their imported counterparts. Before World War II, the United States produced less than half the sparkling wines consumed here and comparatively little vermouth. During the war years, because of greatly restricted imports, American sparkling wine and vermouth production increased greatly.

Labeling Wine Types

In California (as well as in many other wine-growing regions in the United States and abroad), most wine types are named according to geographic regions where they originated. Many type names are varietal, representing the principal grape varieties used. Some names are proprietary, being the names of the producers of the wines or fanciful titles adopted by individual vintners. Such universally familiar type names as claret, burgundy, sauterne, rhine wine, port, and sherry (all having a geographic basis) are now used in many countries to designate wines with characteristics similar to those of the original products.

At various times in the last two centuries, France and other great wine-producing countries of Europe have tried to restrain producers in other countries from using the names of the European regions where the wines originated when establishing generic names for their native wines. International agreements and many national wine laws and regulations have resulted from those efforts. In most countries, including the United States, generic names based on geographic origin may be used only when the actual place of production is stated in direct conjunction with the type names, that is, Australian burgundy, Argentine champagne, California sherry, or American claret.

California sells many of its table and dessert wines under such generic names. Among red table wines will be found California claret, burgundy, and chianti; among white table wines will be found California rhine, sauterne, and haut sauterne; and among dessert wines, California port, sherry, and Marsala, all of which bear a general resemblance to their namesakes.

In the United States today, greater attention is being given to production of high-class varietal table wines named for the principal grape variety used. In California, among the whites will be found the Riesling, a rhine type of wine produced from one or more of the Riesling grape varieties. Other outstanding whites are Semillon and Sauvignon Blanc (the two traditional grapes of the Sauterne district), White Pinot and Traminer. Among the red varietals are Zinfandel (exclusively a California grape) and particularly Cabernets and Pinots (being respectively the traditional grapes of the Bordeaux and Burgundy districts of France). Other well-known red varietals are Gamay and Barbera.

Among the white table wines of the eastern states, we find Elivira, Delaware, and Catawba, all made from the *Labrusca* variety of grapes.

Varietals have been produced in California for many decades by small growers of premium wines. All buyers of wines should be aware that some of the larger California producers now have worthy premium wines of varietally designated wines.

A barely passable job has been done by the restaurant industry in the merchandising of United States wines. In the first place, it is poor merchandising policy to use the term *domestic wines*. Because of the quality associated with imported wines over the years, the use of the word domestic relegates American wines, in the mind of the consumer, to an inferior level of quality. Place names such as New York State Wines or California Wines should be used instead of the term *domestic wines*, and the term *native wines* is sometimes acceptable. Customer education may be necessary to convey the fact that many of our champagnes are on a par with the finest shipped from other countries.

The Treasury Department in Washington, D.C., has a publicly available list of regulations governing the labeling of wines in this country. Familiarity with these regulations will prevent the wine buyer from making a dubious purchase.

The Wine List

The wine list is to beverage service what the menu is to food service, and the same rules apply. It should have variety, an attractive and easily read format, and, to a certain extent, a limited choice. The beverage purchaser must keep these factors in mind.

The variety offered should be enough to please only those customers who constitute a profitable market, because overloaded wine lists and wine cellars are costly. As an aid to operating with low inventories, a record should be kept of requests that cannot be filled from the available stocks. A study of that record will indicate the extent and direction any expansion or reduction of the wine inventory should take. A well-trained wine steward or captain with knowledge of wines can suggest a suitable substitute for a brand not in stock. The guest will often be satisfied and pleased that his wants and knowledge of wines are so well understood.

When a new brand of wine is being considered for purchase, it should be sampled not only by the purchaser but also by various members of the staff who have an appreciation of wine. If the wine passes this impartial test, it is reasonable to suppose it will appeal to the patrons.

10

BEVERAGE COST CONTROLS

The fact that alcoholic beverages sell at $100 and more per gallon should convince restaurant operators of the importance of controlling their beverage merchandise. There are four basic points of control in a beverage operation: purchasing, receiving, the storeroom, and the bar.

Purchasing

The purchases of all wines and liquors should be made by a person with sufficient technical knowledge of these products to perform this function competently. A basic requirement of a good internal control system is the separation of operating and control functions. Therefore, the beverage buyer should not receive incoming merchandise or be responsible for other beverage control functions.

Quantities to Be Purchased

Amounts to be purchased should be determined on the basis of stock on hand, par stocks that have been established for the storeroom, and the needs for any special functions or banquets that have been booked.

Every beverage storeroom should have a definite par stock based on the actual needs of the business and approved by management. This par stock can be tested periodically against the issues to see if any items are being overstocked. An accumulation of slow-moving stock or an oversupply of an item means that cash is being tied up in inventory. In some states, it is possible to obtain discounts on quantity purchases of liquor. To determine whether an investment in liquor inventory is really the best use for available cash, the amount of the discount should be considered in relation to the prevailing interest rates the business may be paying.

Brands to Be Stocked

Many beverage purchasers fear that sales may be lost because a certain brand or type of liquor is out of stock. Some may feel it practically a matter of honor that no customer should ask for a particular brand and be told it is not available. To be sure, one should endeavor to meet the demands of customers, but this should not be carried to such extremes as to overload inventories with unusual brands or types of liquor that move slowly. There is actually a monetary loss on a supply of liquor that moves slowly when the value of the interest that could be earned on tied-up money is considered in addition to the loss from evaporation of the distilled spirits. Adequate inventories are certainly necessary, but liquor stocks must move if maximum profits are to be realized.

Ratio of Inventory Sales to Monthly Sales

Unless an establishment has an exceptional clientele that demands wine and liquor stocks so fine that they are difficult to replenish, it is sound policy not to allow the total beverage inventory to exceed one month's sales in value. On that basis, if the beverage cost is 33⅓ percent of sales, the beverage inventory should be turned over about once every three months in an average first-class restaurant. In areas where the supply of liquors and wines is good and if large stocks of foreign wines are not needed, operators can maintain a turnover rate of once every 45 days or less. Achieving a turnover of that frequency requires study of the sales movement of items. The inventory and sales figures should be reviewed monthly to see that they are in line. Scanning items in the inventory and comparing the quantity of each at the end of the past two or three months will disclose the presence of any slow-moving or "dead" stock. If slow-moving items are found, the banquet manager or convention sales manager may be able to move them out by offering them at lower prices. Purchases of slow-moving items should be curtailed until further notice.

Purchase Orders

For reliability, liquor purchase orders should be written rather than verbal. Purchase orders requiring management authorization are a means of avoiding excessive inventories. Furthermore, a copy of the purchase order tells the receiving clerk what and how much he is authorized to receive.

Verification of Invoices

The beverage buyer should be responsible for personally approving every invoice before payment is made. Since he negotiated the purchase, he knows the terms of purchase and the brands and

BEVERAGES   RECEIVED

DISTRIBUTOR	ITEMS	CASE GOODS				DEPOSIT CHARGE	INVOICE AMOUNT	DEPOSIT CREDIT	NET PURCHASE	DISTRIBUTION			
		No. of Cases	Size of Units	Units Per Case	Cost Per Case					Ale and Beer	Wines	Spirits	Mineral Waters
C.B. Jones & Co	Budweiser Beer	15	12oz	24	4 80		72 00		72 00	72 00			
Smith & Brown	Schenley Reserve	6	5ths	12	63 49		380 94		380 94			380 94	
Int'l Bev. Co	Grant's - 12 year old	3	5ths	12	94 48		283 44		283 44			283 44	
Main Street Co	Old Taylor	4	5ths	12	58 72		250 88		250 88			250 88	
Miller Liq. Dist.	House of Lords - Gin	5	5ths	12	57 70		288 50		288 50			288 50	
Wine Importing Co.	B & G - Sauterne	2	24oz	12	37 28		74 56		74 56		74 56		
" "	B & G - Medoc	2	24oz	12	30 52		61 04		61 04		61 04		
	Total						1,411 36		1,411 36	72 00	135 60	1,203 76	

WINE STEWARD

RECEIVING CLERK

DATE

Fig. 10-1. Beverage receiving report.

quantities ordered. His approval can also serve as a check on the performance of the receiving clerk.

When invoices are examined by accounting department personnel or the beverage controller, four points should be checked: (1) proper purchase authorization, (2) comparison of prices with quoted prices, as well as prices of prior purchases, (3) arithmetical accuracy, and (4) periodic check for possible overstocking.

Comparison of prices of current purchases with those of prior purchases is advisable to assure proper investigation of any serious price variations and to uncover errors. Checking the arithmetical accuracy of every invoice is an absolute necessity. A recheck of present and past inventory positions on items arriving in substantial quantities will prevent overstocking.

Receiving

In all but the largest operations, beverage receiving and storage are handled by the same employees who receive food. Although the design of the beverage receiving report differs from the food receiving report, the basic objectives and procedures are the same (see Fig. 10–1).

Standard Weights

Liquor has an amazing propensity for "evaporating" even when it is tightly bottled. To prevent theft, every reasonable receiving safeguard must be established and observed.

A list should be compiled of every standard case weight and be kept by the receiving clerk for handy reference. Every major brand should be weighed in case form and recorded. Weighing each case and checking its weight against the list will identify any cases with missing bottles.

Beverage Storeroom Operation

The beverage storeroom is comparable to a vault where coins or currency are kept because each of the bottles on the shelves represents a sizable sum of money. If the storekeeper is not also the receiving clerk, then he must be sure that he receives all the incoming merchandise that is charged to his storeroom because he is held accountable for the inventory. This means that he must check all merchandise that the receiving clerk delivers to him.

Physical Requirements

A beverage storeroom should have three separate units:

1. The major unit, maintained at a temperature of 50° to 60°F.

2. A smaller unit, maintained at a temperature of 40°F to be used for the storage of sparkling wines for short periods. This chamber will also serve for prechilling other wines prior to serving.

3. A storage room for beer, mineral waters, and empty bottles on which deposits have been paid. Refrigeration is not necessary, but this unit should not be near boilers, furnaces, or hot water pipes.

Since delicate white wines and sparkling wines should not be chilled for a period exceeding a week, the unit used for prechilling should be checked carefully and restocked frequently.

The lock on the door of the chill room should have a handle on the inside to prevent anyone from being locked in the chill room accidentally. It also is a protection against raising the temperature of the room when the wine cellar attendant is working inside. Wide fluctuations in temperature can be very detrimental to the quality of wine and beer.

Ventilation and Cleanliness

Clean air must circulate in beverage storerooms if the quality of the merchandise, especially wines, is not to be impaired. Dry, clean conditions in a storeroom prevent the growth of fungi which, in time, would permeate the cork of the wine bottle and contaminate the wine.

Methods of Storing Wines

Table wines with an alcoholic content of less than 14 percent should be stored on their sides to keep the cork wet and tight in the bottle. This is to prevent acetification or oxidation, caused by air entering through a dry, porous cork.

Fortified wines (such as dessert wines) and spirits may be stored safely in an upright position. Their high alcoholic content prevents them from being noticeably affected by air entering through the cork.

Sparkling wines, white wines, and beers should be stored near the floor where the cooler temperatures prevail. Red wines should be placed on the middle shelves, with dessert wines and spirits above. All wines should be delivered several days prior to use so that any sediment in the bottles will have an opportunity to settle before serving. Some vintage wines require several weeks to settle after moving.

Size of Shelves and Bins

The upright partitions of the storage bins should be spaced so that the base of each section will contain a specified number of bottles to facilitate counting while taking inventory. Bottle sizes vary considerably. The bin size that seems to accommodate the most frequently used bottles with the least waste space is 22 inches wide by 14 inches high by 18 inches deep. The lowest shelf should be four inches or more above the floor. Small, wooden, triangular wedges should be used to position bottles kept on their sides.

The most satisfactory height for shelves in the storeroom is 7½ feet. If shelves are higher, it means too much climbing up and down ladders to put away stock and fill requisitions.

Handling Wines

Wines, particularly sensitive red wines, should be handled as little as possible while being issued and after removal from the storeroom. Employees must be instructed in the necessary care. Careless handling will disturb any sediment present in these wines, and their clarity will be lost.

Fine burgundies or other choice wines should be stored horizontally in wooden or metal racks that are inserted or built into the bins. When withdrawn, they should be set carefully in wicker wine baskets and carried directly to the patrons' tables.

Care of Beer

Beer kegs should also be handled as little as possible. They must not be moved or jostled for at least 24 hours before being tapped or excessive foaming is certain to result. "Wild," that is, excessively foamy, beer also occurs when the temperature is too high. If it is kept between 40° and 50°F, beer will maintain its sparkle and vitality. If the temperature drops much below 40°F, the beer becomes flat.

After draught beer is brought to the bar, the pressure should be watched closely. Too little pressure will cause "flat" beer whereas too much makes the beer "wild."

Locks and Keys

The keys to the beverage storerooms should be entrusted to only one person so that responsibility for shortages may be easily traced. The person responsible for the bar should not have the key to the wine cellar. This is an insurance against the temptation to charge off to spillage and evaporation any shortages he may incur. The locks of the wine cellar should be changed periodically and whenever there is a change in storeroom personnel.

Schedule of Hours

A regular schedule of hours should be established for the beverage storeroom. There is no reason for this storage room to be open at all hours of the day. The variety of items is small, and it is easy for the barman to maintain a complete stock at the bar. Only rarely will items be ordered unexpectedly to necessitate a visit to the wine room. The beverage storeroom hours will depend upon the routine of the individual establishment and the hours the bar is open for business.

Inspection

Once a beverage storeroom has been established and satisfactory controls set up, management should make periodic inspections to see that the rules are being followed and order is being maintained. A review of the methods used for storing bottles, controlling empties, and maintaining proper temperatures will indicate to the storeroom personnel the importance of strict adherence to the rules.

Storeroom Controls

Requisitions

Access to liquor stock, whether it is in the beverage storeroom or at a bar, should be controlled rigidly. Besides the fact that many enjoy the consumption of alcoholic beverages, such merchandise is easily convertible into cash. It is a target of pilferage not only by employees of the establishment but also by employees of vendors.

For the storekeeper to maintain control over his inventory all merchandise must be issued on a properly approved requisition, no matter what its final destination. This includes issues to the kitchen for cooking wines, cooks' beer allotments, complimentary liquors to guests, and so on. The requisitions should be made out in triplicate, the original and duplicate to be signed by the employees issuing and receiving the stock. The requisitions should be signed when they are filled.

WILLIAM ALLEN & CO., N. Y. STOCK FORM 7040

No. 24988

BAR INVENTORY AND REQUISITION

BAR NO.________ DATE________

LIST NO.	SIZE	DESCRIPTION	PAR STOCK	ON HAND	REQUISITION					INVENTORY	
					QUANT.	UNIT COST	TOTAL COST	UNIT SALE VALUE	TOTAL SALE VALUE	UNIT COST	TOTAL COST

INVENTORY TAKEN BY: ________ ISSUED BY: ________ RECEIVED BY: ________

Fig. 10-2A. Bar inventory and requisition form.

The original requisition should be forwarded to the accounting department, and the duplicate retained in the wine cellar where it can be used for inventory record purposes. The triplicate should be kept for record purposes by the person in charge of the bar receiving the merchandise. A bar requisition form is shown in Fig. 10–2A. (The purpose of the Unit Sale Value and Total Sale Value columns is explained in the section on selling price controls.)

Separate requisitions can be used for mineral waters. Requisitions for food items will necessarily be separate forms, since they will be sent to the food storeroom instead of the beverage storeroom.

Banquet Procedures

For banquet service, the banquet manager should prepare all requisitions and use separate sets of requisitions for each banquet (Fig. 10.2B). They should indicate, aside from the date and time of day, the room where the banquet is to be served and the name of the person or organization to be charged. This will greatly facilitate the

William Allen & Co., Stock Form 7038

WINE CELLAR

REQUISITION FOR BANQUET **Nº 1766**

Banquet.. No. of Persons..................

Room.. Hour.................. Date..................

Bin No.	Description	Size	Number of Bottles			Unit Cost	Total Cost	✓
			Issued	Ret'd	Used			
	Total							

ISSUE	RETURNS	
Issued by:	Returned by:	Authorized by:
		Maitre d'Hotel
Received by:	Received by:	
	THIS COPY TO AUDITOR'S OFFICE	Wine Steward

Fig. 10-2B. Banquet requisition form.

all-important matter of sales reconciliation and collection of the banquet accounts.

Close control is particularly necessary for banquets because there are so many opportunities for abuse. Patrons may be charged for champagnes and other expensive liquors that are never served, or they may be charged for more than the amount actually consumed.

The return of unused wines and liquors from the banquet department to the wine cellar requires close attention. Returns must be handled properly to guard against accidental or deliberate errors. After each banquet, a credit memo should be prepared for the return of all full bottles. The memo should list the name of the banquet, the date, the total amount issued, and the number of bottles returned. Partially used bottles or those on which the seal has been broken should not be returned to the beverage storeroom but transferred to another bar. The credit memo for full bottles returned and transfers of bottles with broken seals should be made out in duplicate. The original should be sent to the accounting department, and the duplicate should be retained by the wine steward.

Another way to handle the return of partial bottles is to use a special banquet requisition form (Fig. 10–2B), which provides space for entering bottles returned.

Cooks' Beer and Cooking Wines

A strict accounting should be made of the cooks' beer and cooking wines. If these items are issued without regular requisitions, accurate control is difficult if not impossible. The manager should authorize the number of bottles of beer to be issued daily from the wine cellar for the cooks, and this issue should be made only on the receipt of a properly authorized and executed requisition signed by the chef. Cooking wines should be handled in the same way. Filling these requisitions soon becomes a matter of routine, but they allow the accounting department to have a full set of records at its disposal.

Container Control

When deposits are made on containers, the accounting department must control the payments and refunds. A form of perpetual inventory is the best method of calculating the value of quantities on hand. In many establishments, the large number of containers in comparison to the relatively small sum of money representing deposits paid on containers encourages carelessness in handling or control. A restaurant should maintain container control as sound as that kept by purveyors.

Storeroom Procedures Related to Bar Controls

Several procedures necessary for controlling the bar operations must originate in the storeroom. First, all bottles issued to the bars or to banquets must be marked in some way to identify them as "house" bottles. Bartenders are thus prevented from bringing their own stock in and pocketing the sales. It also identifies any outside stock that room service or banquet guests may try to return in order to get a credit on their bill at the marked-up sale prices.

A second bar control requirement is that all requisitions presented to the storeroom must be accompanied by the empty bottles, making it a bottle-for-bottle transaction. This enforces the par stock on the bar and also is a double check for outside bottles. As soon as the issue is made, all empty bottles should be broken to prevent them from being refilled and resold. These procedures are explained more fully in the bar control section later in this chapter.

Storeroom Records and Accounting Procedures

Monthly Inventory Count

A periodic physical count of the liquor stock in the beverage storeroom should be made by a representative of the accounting department or some other employee not connected with the beverage operations. To facilitate the count of the stock, the brands of liquor listed in the inventory count record should be arranged to correspond with the order of their storage.

To save time and labor, some managers accept the liquor quantities stated on bin cards when inventories are being recorded. That is unwise because if an actual physical count is not made, there is no cross check of the accuracy of the data on the bin cards. Moreover, the effectiveness of the beverage controls is lessened because a dishonest storeroom keeper can "doctor" the records to suit his purposes and thus cover up shortages. The storekeeper's accountability can be determined either by the beverage controller or some other representative of the accounting department. Two methods may be used: (1) Compare the units of each brand in stock (indicated by the physical count) with those that should be on hand (indicated by perpetual inventory records maintained by the beverage controller or the accounting department); or (2) Determine the dollar value at cost of the inventory that should be in the storeroom at any time and then compare that value with the aggregate cost value of the inventory (determined by a physical count of the units). The second method is much simpler than the first.

Bin Cards and Perpetual Inventories

Bin cards (Fig. 10–3A) are used primarily for determining stock status and reordering points for large beverage operations. The beverage purchaser can determine quickly whether his inventory is sufficient to meet his needs, and when it is time to reorder. It also provides a complete history on stock movement.

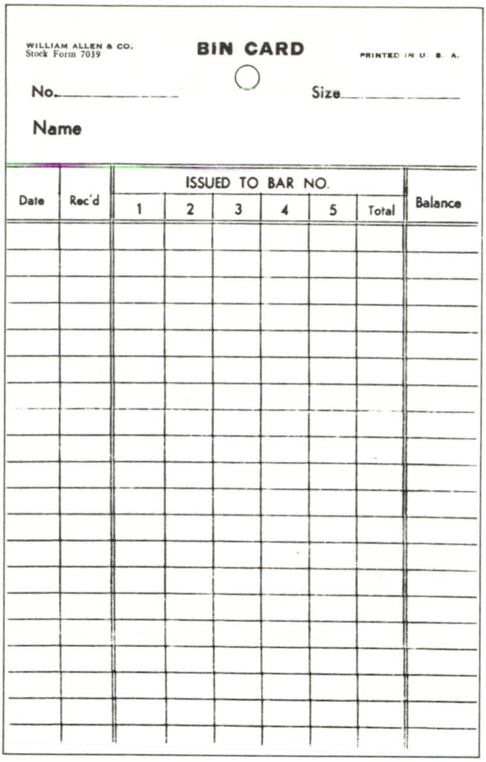
WILLIAM ALLEN & CO.
Stock Form 7039

BIN CARD

PRINTED IN U. S. A.

No.________ Size________

Name

Date	Rec'd	ISSUED TO BAR NO.						Balance
		1	2	3	4	5	Total	

Fig. 10-3A. Bin Card.

Perpetual inventories (Fig. 10–3B) are another form of bin card system, although they are more likely to be maintained by a food and beverage controller, especially if his office is not convenient to the beverage storeroom and records. The perpetual inventory cards provide a means for maintaining price information for costing requisitions. However, when bin cards are used, this information can easily be obtained from the card.

Both the bin card system and the perpetual inventory card system require the manual or automated posting of all bottles received and issued each day. A periodic physical count must be made to check the accuracy of the recorded inventory. Any differences should be investigated.

Dollar Value Controls

A simpler, less expensive means of control is based on a record of the dollar value of the merchandise in the storeroom. Under this system, the amount of inventory at the beginning of the period plus the amount of beverages purchased during the period, less the amount

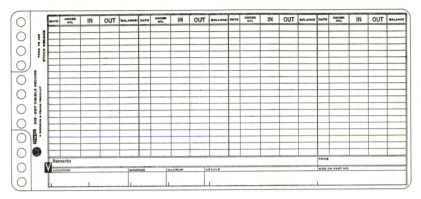

Fig. 10-3B. Perpetual inventory form.

issued during the period, is the value of the beverages that should be in the storeroom at the end of the accounting period. This computed ending inventory is then compared with the value as determined by a physical count. If the shrinkage is less than 1 or 2 percent of the total inventory, it is usually acceptable; larger discrepancies should be investigated. This actual value determined by physical count becomes the opening inventory for the following period.

The cost value of the inventory that should be in the storeroom at any given date is determined as follows:

Inventory at beginning of period—at cost $_____

Add: Purchases actually delivered to
the storeroom—at cost $_____
Returns from banquets or bars
(unopened bottles only)—at cost   _____   _____
Total   _____

Less: Issued to bars—at cost $_____
Issued to kitchen—at cost   _____
Approved storeroom, spoilage and
breakage loss—at cost   _____   _____

Cost value of beverages to be accounted
for at the close of business on (date) $_____

Cost value of beverages as determined by
physical count at the close of business
on the same date $_____

Difference $_____

It is true that use of the dollar value control does not disclose what brands may be the cause of a difference between a computed inventory value and a physical or counted value. However, managers who advocate the dollar value control system believe that which brands are missing is immaterial; what is important is the dollars that are missing. Furthermore, the amount of manpower needed to maintain a perpetual system is often substantially greater than any actual losses, provided that good operational controls are in effect, such as physical security of the merchandise, careful selection of the employees involved, and a good requisitioning system. Many times, a great deal of labor is expended in tracking down simple errors in arithmetic.

Perpetual inventory maintenance is an excellent application for electronic data processing with other benefits as well, such as preparation of purchase orders automatically at prearranged reordering levels. These systems are usually costly to install and maintain and may not be cost justifiable.

Except for the perpetual or bin card records, the dollar value control system requires the same record keeping as the perpetual system—requisitions costed and extended, receiving records showing the total beverages received, and periodic physical inventories. A weekly inventory status report, accompanied by test checking of physical counts, may provide a good control while minimizing the cost of the control system.

Controls in the Bar

Bar control is an absolute necessity in any operation. In a small establishment, it may seem to be a luxury, but it is definitely desirable. In one small establishment enjoying a fine reputation in the community, the bartender decided to become an "unofficial partner." He brought a bottle or two to work and sold the contents to the customers, keeping the entire return. He had no overhead and no salaries to pay, and his profit was very high, eating into the establishment's legitimate revenue. Unless management has a clear-cut picture of what the beverage revenue and cost should be, sooner or later someone may be tempted to share the profits or pour substandard drinks to cover shortages.

Control Methods

There are two methods of bar control: manual and automated. The basis for these controls is the accountability for the retail value of the beverages sold or for the quantity or ounces sold. Ounce control is very seldom used in manually operated systems because it is both complex and laborious. Therefore, comments on manually operated systems will be restricted to those based on sale value (selling price) control. In an automated system, ounce control is relatively simple and easy. Certain set procedures are required or advisable for the operation of both systems.

Standardization of Drink Sizes and Glasses

It is not possible to have meaningful controls unless the size of all drinks offered to the public is established for each beverage sales outlet. Furthermore, the size of the glasses prescribed for service must be compatible with the drink sizes established. Use of a four-ounce martini glass when the size of a martini cocktail has been established at 2½ ounces invites both control problems and adverse customer reaction.

It is very important that all shipments of purchased beverage glassware be checked carefully. Vendors sometimes make mistakes and send glasses that are the wrong size. It is difficult visually to detect a difference of one-eighth or one-fourth of an ounce in the size of a whiskey glass. This may not appear to be a significant difference from the correct size, yet a discrepancy of one-eighth of an ounce on a one-ounce drink is equal to a cost difference of 12½ percent; and a discrepancy of one-fourth of an ounce is equal to a difference of 25 percent.

Par Stock for Bars

A daily par bottle stock must be established for each brand of alcoholic beverages. The amount of the par stock should be based on the number of bottles of each brand of liquor sold on the busiest day of a period plus provide a margin of safety. The pars can be changed seasonally or for periods in which special events are scheduled. A daily inventory is taken, and the employee in charge requisitions what he needs to bring the bar stock back to par. The incoming bartender should make certain that he starts the day with a par stock.

If this procedure is used, a combination inventory and requisition form can be used (Fig. 10–2A). This form provides for a listing of the stock items and the par established for each item. In addition, this form provides space for recording the inventory count and the quantity of each item to be requisitioned to restore the par stock. Also a space may be provided for pricing the quantities requisitioned to facilitate selling price control. The form should be printed in triplicate. One copy is retained at the bar, one copy is used by the beverage storekeeper as the requisition form for the issuance of replacement stock, and the third copy is directed to the accounting department for selling price control. The form requires the signature of the head barman, the storekeeper issuing the stock, and the bartender receiving the goods.

Instead of taking a daily inventory of the bars to determine the quantity required to bring the bar stock up to par, some operators use the much simpler procedure of replacing the empty bottles at the end of the day. Care must be taken to prevent outside bottles from being brought in and exchanged for full ones, or empty "house" bottles from being reused. To prevent this, bottles issued from the storeroom should be marked in some unusual way, and empties should be broken immediately upon receipt by the storeroom keeper, as mentioned previously.

If a sale was made by the bottle instead of by the drink, the bartender probably will not get an empty bottle back to exchange. This usually occurs with table wines, in hotel room service, and in some night clubs. When this type of beverage sale occurs, a full bottle slip (Fig. 10–4) is used. This slip is presented to the bartender by the waiter. The bartender then turns it in to the storeroom in place of the empty bottle, to support his requisition for a replacement bottle.

Manual System of Selling Price Control

Daily selling price control consists of comparing the actual sales in each of the various sales outlets with the sales potential of the merchandise issued to each outlet from the beverage storeroom. When a par stock system is used, the comparative figures for a single day's sales do not take into account the differences in partly sold bottles. The figures are based solely on the sale value of the bottles issued on the basis of requisitions. The cumulative activity of seven to ten days usually provides a more accurate picture.

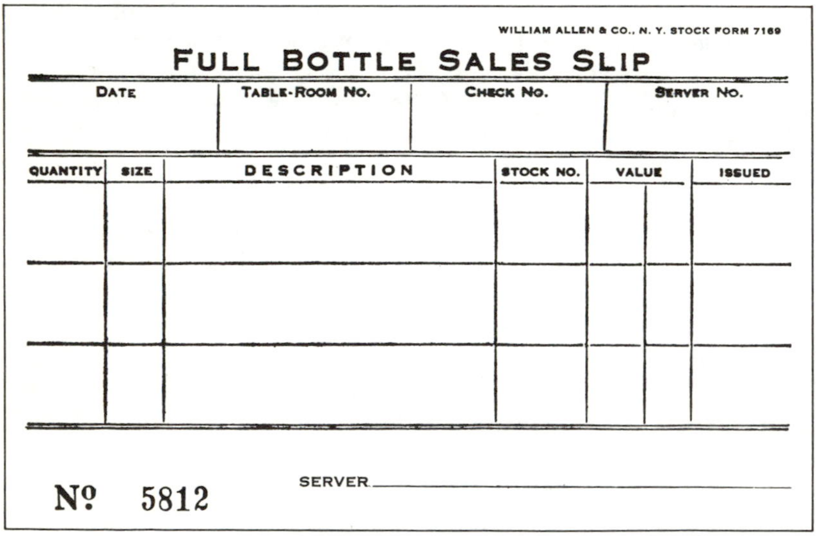

Fig. 10-4. Full bottle sales slip.

Sales Value Potentials

The number of drinks that may be poured from a bottle of liquor may be computed, given the size of the bottle and the established drink size. Under the sales value system of control, liquor issues from the storeroom to a bar are valued both at cost and at the potential sales value of each bottle. The bar inventories are also extended at cost and sales value. The total actual sales for the period are then compared to the computed or *potential* sales of the beverages sold.

Not all beverages are sold as straight drinks or highballs, however, and adjustments are necessary for mixed drinks and for full bottle sales. Since the mark-up on full bottles is much smaller than on straight drinks, the difference between the sales value by the bottle and the sales value by the drink must be subtracted from the total calculation. A simple worksheet can be used for this purpose (see Fig. 10–5).

The adjustment for mixed drinks is also deducted from the total value of all drinks sold. The only time an adjustment is required is when the ounce size of the basic liquor (gin, bourbon, scotch, etc.) in cocktail service differs from the ounce size of the liquor when it is served as a straight drink, or when the price of cocktails differs from the price of straight drinks. Computation of this adjustment requires the number of each kind of cocktail served. This information can be

SALES REVENUE ADJUSTMENT
FOR BOTTLE SALES

FOR THE PERIOD FROM 4/1 TO 4/15
BAR NO._____

Date	Description	Sales Slip#	Unit Size	No.of Units	Unit Drink Sales Value	Bottle Sales Sales Value	Difference
4/2	Four Roses	27	F	1	$ 20 50	$ 11 00	$ 9 50
4/7	J&B	28	F	2	55 30	31 00	24 30
	Totals				$ 75 80	$ 42 00	$ 33 80

Fig. 10-5. A worksheet for figuring sales revenue adjustment for bottle sales.

obtained in several ways. One way is to abstract from the bar checks the number and type of cocktails served. This is a time-consuming and costly method, especially if the accountability periods are frequent. A less costly method is to reduce the adjustment to a percentage of total sales revenue after a number of check abstracts have been made. A much simpler, though perhaps less accurate, method is to compute the number of the more popular cocktails served on the basis of the consumption of the additive or complementary ingredients (such as vermouths) used in the cocktail mix. The rationale for this method is that these liquors are rarely sold as straight drinks. There are, of course, exceptions. Green crème de menthe, which is used as an additive in some cocktails (such as a Green Devil), is more in demand as a straight drink (as a cordial or crème de menthe frappe) than as an ingredient in a mixed drink. On the other hand, white crème de menthe is very seldom sold as a straight drink but is used as an ingredient, along with brandy, in a Stinger cocktail, a popular cocktail. Therefore, the consumption of white crème de menthe could be used in making an adjustment for brandy consumption in Stingers while green crème de menthe would be assumed to be sold in a straight drink, the sale of Green Devil cocktails being too infrequent to be significant.

Obviously adjustment computation based on the consumption of complementary ingredients requires knowledge of the sales popularity of the various cocktails. It would be prudent first to make an abstract of mixed-drink sales for a test period in order to select those that are to be the basis for this computation.

The following illustrates the computation for adjustment on the sale of dry martinis, based on a one-ounce shot of gin in a gin and tonic and 1½ ounces of gin in a martini.

1. A gin and tonic takes 1 oz of gin and sells for $1.00. Therefore, the sales value of a fifth of gin (25.6 oz) is $25.60.
2. The martini recipe calls for 1½ oz of gin and ¾ oz of French vermouth.
3. The consumption of this vermouth during the period of accountability was 90 oz.
4. At the rate of ¾ oz of vermouth per cocktail, 120 dry martinis were served during this period. At 1½ oz of gin per cocktail, 180 oz were consumed from seven fifths of gin (180 ÷ 25.6).
5. These seven fifth-size bottles of gin were issued to this bar on a straight gin drink basis at $25.60 per fifth, or a total of $179.20.
6. At 1½ oz per cocktail, the bottle yield was 17 cocktails. At

$1.25 per cocktail, the revenue derived was $21.25, or a total for seven fifth-size bottles of $148.75.

7. Therefore, the sales potential of the bar must be reduced $30.45.

Notice that all the foregoing computations have been rounded to the nearest multiple of five.

It is too costly to make these computations exact. Furthermore, it has been demonstrated in practice that only rarely is the difference between the adjustments computed according to complementary ingredient consumption and those computed on a check-abstract basis large enough to distort the results.

When the potential sale value has been established for the beverages consumed, it must be compared with the actual revenue received for the period under consideration. The primary importance of selling price control is the margin of difference between potential and actual sales. Minor variations are to be expected; major ones should be investigated. The sales potential indicates what money should have been received. The revenue figures indicate what was actually received. A comparison indicates how close to normal the operation is. Actual revenue in excess of the sales potential should also be investigated. It may mean that the customers have been served substandard drinks.

Periodic Summary of Sales Price Control

At the end of each month, the accounting department or the beverage controller should prepare a summary of the sales price control results for each bar. The summary should be based on the actual requisitions from the beverage storeroom for the various bars, extended at the sales values for each bar respectively and at cost. After proper credit has been given for any returns to the beverage storeroom, the net issues from the storeroom should be added to the inventories on hand at the beginning of the month at sales value and cost. The total of the net issues plus the opening inventory represents the total amount available for the particular period. From the total amount available, the physical inventory at the end of the month at sales value must be subtracted in order to arrive at the monthly potential sales. Before a valid comparison with actual sales can be made, due allowance must be made for any bottle sales or special sales at lower-than-customary selling prices per drink and for promotions. All such sales must be supported by appropriately approved memoranda. After all the special sales are applied, the net result will yield the overage or shortage of the retail selling price control for the period. The following formula presents the information just described:

> Requisitions
> − Returns
> + Inventory on hand at beginning of month
> _____
> = Amount available

> Amount available
> − Inventory at end of month
> _____
> = Monthly potential sales revenue before adjustments

> Unadjusted monthly potential sales revenue
> − Bottle sales
> _____
> = Potential sales revenue

A worksheet that can be used in determining the revenue accountability of a bar is shown in Fig. 10–6.

If reports are rendered on a fifteen-day basis, one interim report will be rendered each month. If reports are rendered on a ten-day basis, two interim reports will be given every month, in addition to the month-end report.

The preparation of interim reports does not require pricing the entire inventories at the beginning and end of the period. Only the inventory difference need be priced and extended. If the closing inventory is less than the opening inventory, the operation has "lived off," or used up, a portion of the opening inventory, and the inventory difference must be added to the issues for the period. If the closing inventory is greater than the opening inventory, the inventory position has been increased or "built up," and the difference is deducted from the issues for the period to determine the exact consumption.

Automated System of Selling Price Control

The procedures in an automated system of selling price control of bar operations are, with some minor variations, the same as those in a manual system. To what extent the manual procedures are automated depends on the kind of equipment installed. Automated equipment ranges from a bottle-top metered dispenser (Fig. 10–7) to a highly sophisticated equipment system (Fig. 10–8). The latter automatically connects the dispensing of each drink with its registration in a cash or sales register. In all automated systems, the registers that record the dispensing of drinks are built so that the mechanism for

```
         DETERMINATION OF SALES REVENUE ACCOUNTABILITY

                      FOR BAR # 1

            FOR THE PERIOD FROM 4/1 TO 4/15
```

Explanation	Total Cost	Total Sales Value
Storeroom Requisitions for the Period	$1837.60	$7250.19
+ or – Transfers To or From Other Bars	–	–
Subtotal	1837.60	7250.19
Add: Inventory at Beginning of Period	764.54	2927.61
Total Merchandise Available	2584.14	10177.80
Less: Inventory at End of Period	624.87	2395.07
Adjustments for:		
Bottle sales		33.80
Mixed drink sales		198.31
Total		2627.18
Total Cost and Potential Sales Value	$1959.27	7550.62
Sales Revenue Reported for the Period		$7506.80
Difference		$ 43.82
Ratio of Cost To:		
Potential Sales Revenue		25.9%
Actual Sales Revenue		26.1%

Fig. 10-6. A worksheet for determination of sales revenue accountability of a bar.

resetting them is locked. Bottle-top dispenser registers are arranged so that they cannot be removed from the bottles.

In a manual system of selling price control, the potential unit yield from each bottle is difficult to obtain even if measuring devices are used. Furthermore, because many bartenders "free pour" when they are busy, it is not possible for them to be accurate. In an automated system, the liquor container is attached to or locked into a device that will pour only the exact amount at which it is set, so that the overpouring or underpouring of liquor is not possible. The automated dispensing units are available for dispensing not only

Fig. 10-7. A bottle-top metered dispenser. *(Courtesy of Quantico Manufacturing, Inc.)*

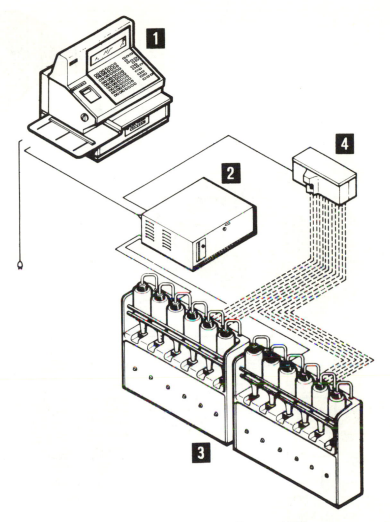

Fig. 10-8. An automated liquor dispensing system. *(Courtesy of NCR)*
1. Control register with preset keys. These keys trigger the automated dispensing mechanism. 2. Logic unit which controls the system. It is a mini computer which times the pouring and counts the ounces while maintaining a perpetual liquor inventory control. 3. Bottle racks. Large systems permit linking a series of bottles to avoid running out in the middle of service. 4. Dispensing head, which is mounted under the bar near the control register.

straight drinks but also cocktails. The cocktail dispensing unit has the various liquor ingredients of the cocktail so arranged as to dispense only the measured amounts of each liquor.

In a manual system of selling price control, the sales revenue to be accounted for at any bar is determined by an inventory of the

REGISTER	ADD CHECK	STD LIQR	9	90	$9	$90	BRANDY	VODKA	BOURBON	GIN
CASH BAR	X & Z INVEN (+)	PREM LIQR	8	80	$8	$80	BRANDY MANHATTAN	VODKA MARTINI	BOURBON MANHATTAN	MARTINI
READ	INVENTORY (−)	SPEC LIQR	7	70	$7	$70	DRY BRANDY MANHATTAN	EXTRA DRY VODKA MARTINI	DRY BOURBON MANHATTAN	EXTRA DRY MARTINI
SET PRICE	TIPS	STD CKTL	6	60	$6	$60	BRANDY SOUR	VODKA SOUR	BOURBON SOUR	TOM COLLINS
RESET	CHECKS CHARGED	PREM CKTL	5	50	$5	$50	BRANDY OLD FASHIONED	COCKTAIL VODKA	OLD FASHIONED	COCKTAIL GIN
INVENTORY (+)	TAX	SPEC CKTL	4	40	$4	$40	SCOTCH	WHISKEY	PREMIUM WHISKEY	PREMIUM GIN
CLOSE CHECK	CASH TOTAL	BEER	3	30	$3	$30	ROB ROY	MANHATTAN	PREMIUM MANHATTAN	PREMIUM MARTINI
RESET PRICES	SUB TOTAL	WINE	2	20	$2	$20	DRY ROB ROY	DRY MANHATTAN	PREMIUM DRY MANHATTAN	PREMIUM EXTRA DRY MARTINI
T O T READ RESET INV	TOTAL	MISC	1	10	$1	$10	SCOTCH SOUR	WHISKEY SOUR	DAIQUIRI BACARDI	RUM

Fig. 10-9. Keyboard of a drink-dispensing sales register.

unconsumed liquor (usually measured in tenths of a bottle). Since the measure is based on a visual inspection of the bottle contents, the accuracy of an inventory taken by this method is questionable. The value of the method might be questioned, because a difference of only one-tenth of a fifth-sized bottle containing a total of 25.6 ounces represents a little more than 2½ ounces. Actually the extent of inaccuracies resulting from estimates based on visual inspection of bottles is not likely to be very great, because the overestimates and the underestimates tend to offset each other.

The determination of the sales accountability in an automated system is more accurate then in a manual system because the drink-dispensing registers indicate the number of unit drinks of a controlled size that have been dispensed from any bar during a given period. The number of unit drinks sold, as shown by the drink dispensing registers, is multiplied by the sale price of the drinks to arrive at the potential sales revenue of the bar. That revenue is then compared with the actual revenue reported (cash register readings of total sales) for the same period. When drink dispensing registers mounted on the tops of bottles are used, the compilation of the number of drinks sold during the period must include not only the readings from dispensers on the partially filled bottles at the bar but also the readings taken from all the empty bottles at or removed from the bar during the period.

In the more sophisticated systems, where a sales register activates the dispensing unit, a sale is automatically recorded at the set sale price on the sales register whenever a drink is dispensed. The sales register is provided with special keys for the more popular drinks, as well as keys for cash collected and charge sales (see Fig. 10–9). There are also ounce (plus and minus) inventory keys that are used to record requisitioned liquor (+ key) and any adjustments requiring reduction of inventory (− key). This automated drink-dispensing system controls the liquor from the point of its delivery, to the bar, to its sale. It also controls the settlement of the sales, either cash or charge.

Also available now is automated equipment for control of beer service. The amount of beer to be served is set on the equipment. The dispenser will also put a "head" on the beer, according to the patrons preference. Some of the automated drink-dispensing systems include equipment for the automatic mixing and dispensing of mineral waters for highballs.

The entry of the larger manufacturing companies into the field of automated dispensing equipment in recent years accounts for the better design and added sophistication of the equipment now available. This field, however, is still relatively young, and anyone interested in this equipment should request up-to-date information from the various manufacturing companies.

Summary of Control Procedures

The following lists summarize the procedures necessary for proper control of wines and liquors. These procedures may be adapted to meet existing conditions, but the basic requirements should not be relaxed.

Purchasing, Receiving, Storing and Issuing:

1. Prepare purchase order showing quantity, brand, size of container, and unit price of items purchased.
2. Check items delivered against purchase order.
3. Prepare receiving sheet.
4. Prepare and maintain bin cards.
5. Issue beverages from storeroom on approved requisition only.
6. Control access to storeroom.

Bar Operations:

1. Replenish bar stock only upon written and signed requisitions.
2. Check bars to ascertain that sizes of drinks being served are in compliance with those prescribed.
3. Check to see that drinks are recorded on guest checks and processed via sales register.
4. Test open bar stock for possible water dilution.

Accounting—Beverage Control:

1. Check each invoice against the receiving sheet.
2. Check extensions and additions of invoices.
3. Call attention to discount bills.
4. Compare footings of total purchases on receiving sheet to distribution totals of types of purchases.
5. Maintain daily summary of container charges and credits to match month-end inventory.
6. Post receipts of merchandise and requisitions in perpetual inventory book. If a dollar control is used instead for storeroom control, accumulate the cost value of all merchandise purchased and of all issues from the storeroom.
7. At regular intervals of not more than a month, determine what should be in the storeroom and compare that total with what is in the storeroom.
8. Enter on all requisitions the unit cost and total cost, and also the unit sale value and total sale value if selling price control is used.

9. Compile bottle sales summary. Deduct bottle sales differential and also mixed-drink adjustments from total of requisitions.
10. Add reductions in inventory to, or deduct additions in inventory from, total of requisitions for 7-, 10-, or 15-day period to determine net consumption.
11. At end of month and every 7, 10, or 15 days, take physical inventory to verify consumption.
12. Make adjustments for issues to food department (such as cooking wines) and requisitions from food department (such as lemons, oranges, cream, and olives).
13. Compare actual and potential sales.
14. Develop cost percentages for each outlet.

PART THREE

Service Management

11

TABLE SERVICE AND DINING ROOM MANAGEMENT

The quality of service can determine the ultimate success or failure of a restaurant. The guest's impression of the food he is served is influenced by his mood and by the service he is given. Although good service cannot make poor food seem appetizing, it is too often true that an excellent meal is ruined by poor service.

Regardless of the type of service, certain elements are always necessary for good service, the most important being efficiency and courtesy. Efficiency does not necessarily mean speed. Rather, efficiency is achieved by serving each course at the right time and at its proper temperature. Whereas efficient service in a coffee shop is fast service, in a luxury restaurant, it is service that allows the guest to enjoy a leisurely meal, with each course served when he is ready for it.

Courtesy can make the customer feel kindly toward the establishment and even overlook small flaws in the service. When courtesy is missing, nothing can make the customer enjoy his meal. The primary prerequisites for good service, therefore, are warmth and graciousness in extending the hospitality of the establishment to the guest. Anyone who does not have or cannot learn this "service attitude" does not belong in a food service operation.

Types of Dining Room Service

There are three major types of dining room service: French, Russian, and American. For special occasions or for large parties and banquets, two additional services are sometimes used: English and buffet.

French Service

French service is found in restaurants offering classic French cuisine and in other types of operations that cater to a sophisticated clientele. It is expensive to maintain, and the expense is reflected in high check averages. The food is brought from the kitchen on silver platters, carefully arranged and suitably garnished, and presented to the guest for his inspection before the service starts (Fig. 11–1). Chafing dishes are used to maintain the temperature of hot foods. Each detail of true French service is done in consideration of the guest and is not a pointless ritual.

Fig. 11-1. French service. The waiter prepares medallions of beef on the gueridon at the guests' tableside. *(Courtesy of The Four Seasons, New York City)*

French service is distinguished by the fact that all or part of the preparation of the dish, or at least the finishing, is done in the dining room. Usually this is done by the captain on a cart or gueridon next to the guest's table. Hot dishes are kept warm on a small heater or rechaud. Occasionally, because of space limitations, one finds the finishing being done at a side table out of the guest's view. This should be avoided because the purpose of French service is to finish the dish exactly to the guest's preference and in his presence.

A skilled staff is required to give good French service. A captain must know how to carve meats, bone fish and poultry, dress salads, and prepare flaming and chafing dish items. Waiters must be familiar with the ingredients and methods of preparation of numerous classic dishes, and bus boys must be trained in the proper service techniques.

Unfortunately, many operators attempt to offer French service without having a properly trained staff. This results in service that at best is a poor imitation, lacking one of the prime ingredients that gives French service its dignity: professionalism.

When planning a restaurant's style of service, the cost should be carefully considered before French service is adopted. A large staff of waiters, captains, and bus help is needed, and tableware washing and the maintenance of the table appointments can be very costly. A large inventory of hollowware must be bought and maintained. Because of the numerous pieces of tableware required for the service to each guest, dishwashing can become a major expense. Furthermore, because of the side tables needed for French service, fewer guest tables can be placed in a given area. French service cannot be rushed, and usually only one seating can be obtained for each meal. This type of service should not even be attempted unless there is a large enough market that is willing to pay for it.

Russian Service

Service à la Russe (Russian service), is a variation of French service. The major difference is that in Russian service all carving and finishing are done in the kitchen. The individual portions are then arranged on trays or platters and garnished attractively. The waiter carries the tray directly to the table and, after presenting it for inspection, serves the food onto the empty plate before the guest (see Fig. 11–2). This service is most often used for banquets where all the guests are served the same item.

American Service

In American service, all food is plated and garnished in the kitchen. The filled plates are then carried to the dining room and placed before the guest (see Fig. 11–3). There are many advantages to

Fig. 11-2. Russian service. The veal cutlet has been arranged on the platter and garnished in the kitchen. *(Courtesy of The Four Seasons, New York City)*

this type of service, all of which are cause for its widespread use. The highly skilled waiter and captain are not required for American service. Plating and garnishing can be done under the supervision of the chef, and a more attractive arrangement of the items and garnitures can be devised. The food is also more likely to be the proper temperature when it is set before the guest.

Buffet Service

Buffet service involves the arrangement of food on platters that are displayed on large tables. Usually a separate table is used for each course. Plates, silverware, and sometimes linen are conveniently arranged, and the guests serve themselves or are assisted by servers. Buffets can involve a large menu with many elaborately decorated dishes, or a simple reception with tea and cakes. (See Chapter 13 for a detailed discussion of buffet service.)

Fig. 11-3. American service. The food has been plated in the kitchen. American service is from the left. *(Courtesy of The Oyster Bar & Restaurant, New York City)*

English Service

Sometimes known as "host" or "holiday" service, this type is usually requested at special functions or on holidays. The carving and service are the responsibility of the host. Sometimes, he serves the vegetables or they may be passed in serving dishes by the waiter and each guest serves himself. A waiter always stands at the left of the host and takes the plate, as it is filled, to each guest in turn. He is usually instructed in advance which person is the hostess (if one is present) and which the guest of honor so that they may be served in their proper order. Birthday cakes or elaborate desserts are often served in this manner even though the service of the meal, up to that time, has been of a different type.

Other Types of Service

Several other types of table service are occasionally found in public restaurants and in some institutional food services.

Family Style Service. Family style service is the presentation of food in bowls or platters that are passed from hand to hand by the guests, who serve themselves. This kind of service is unusual in an urban food operation but is suited to a country-style operation which offers a limited menu with unlimited portions for a set price. Such service is in keeping with an informal, rustic theme.

Family service is also found in some institutions, such as the military service academies. In these cases, the residents usually have no choice of entrées. Food is brought to the tables by a hired staff or by specified residents at each table.

Tray Service. Tray service was once thought suitable only for feeding the sick, but with the increasingly sophisticated food services offered on airplanes, it has become known as "airline service." Tray service is usually used in a fast-service operation with a very limited menu. The server takes the order, goes to a serving pantry and places everything required for the order on a tray and makes only one trip back to the guest. Clearing the table is also fast, requiring only the removal of the tray.

Counter Service. Counter service must be mentioned because of its popularity in certain sections of this country and also because it is often a part of a dining room operation. Counter service is particularly suited to people eating alone. It is found in department stores, railway stations, office buildings, airline terminals, and wherever else it is important to save time.

Counter service must be geared for rapid turnover. The time of the average patron is generally limited. Proper counter service has the capacity to handle comparatively large volumes of business because of the rapid turnover.

Combination Styles of Service

Very often, the type of service is a mixture of several of the styles mentioned. Some entrées may be plated in the kitchen, while others are served in the French or Russian style. For example, a casserole or potpie may be dished out on the plate before the guest in the Russian style, while a steak is plated in the kitchen and a flaming dish prepared on the gueridon. The guest may serve himself the first course from an hors d'oeuvre buffet table, with the rest of the meal being served to him.

What is important is not that the service is of several styles but that the details of the service be planned to suit the menu, the physical facilities, the kind of clientele, and the seat turnover desired. The staff should then be trained to follow these details.

Classification of Service by Means of Delivery

Service is sometimes classified by the means used to deliver the food to the guest: tray service, arm service, or cart service. In a classical French service, the food may be brought to the gueridon by cart. This eliminates the problem of the weight of a number of heavy silver service pieces and the problem of where to set a loaded tray. It is also more elegant in appearance.

Tray service may be of several types. Large trays, called hotel ovals, may be used in American service to transport plated food to a side stand (Fig. 11–4). The plates are then carried by hand to the table. Because of the size of these trays, they are usually heavily loaded and carried over the shoulder. A large size may be both an advantage and a disadvantage. A waiter who is not particularly service-oriented may be tempted to delay his service until he has a full tray in order to cut down on the number of trips he has to make to and from the kitchen.

Small trays, either round, oval, or rectangular, are carried on one arm at waist level and are used for American service and cocktail service (see Fig. 11–5). If properly used, these small trays are not set down. Plates are carried from the kitchen and placed directly on the table from the tray held by the server. This type of tray service is suited to low- and medium-priced table service operations with a rapid turnover.

Arm service is usually found in low-priced surroundings such as diners and coffee shops. Plated food is carried by hand directly to the table. If plate covers are used a number of plates can be handled at the same time.

Dining Room Organization

Staffing for French Service

In the European system of staffing, the maître d'hôtel is in charge of not only the dining rooms but also all areas of the food and beverage operations except those specifically supervised by the *chef de cuisine*. Depending on the size of the operation, there may be one or more assistant maîtres d'hôtel assigned to different dining rooms and to the banquet or catering function. Other subordinate management positions are:

Chef de service	Director of service
Chef d'etage	Director of service on a floor
Maître d'hôtel de carré	Supervisor of a section of a dining room

Fig. 11-4. Hotel tray used for American service. *(Courtesy of The Oyster Bar & Restaurant, New York City)*

In the dining room, the *chef de rang* (chief of the station or row of tables) is an experienced waiter who takes orders, does the difficult carving and finishing of the dishes, and is responsible for the service at his station. He has one or more assistants, called *commis de rang*. The *commis* is a less experienced waiter who brings the food from the kitchen and assists the *chef de rang* by passing plated food to the guests and clearing used dishes from the table. An apprentice is an employee who spends three years learning the trade before he can become a *commis*.

Fig. 11-5. Cocktail service. Small trays are carried at waist height. This service may also be used for fast turnover table service operations such as coffee shops. *(Courtesy of The Oyster Bar & Restaurant, New York City)*

Each position in the traditional hierarchy of the French dining room is a training ground for the next highest level. This assures a supply of labor that is well trained in this complex service, and it also develops a pride and professionalism in restaurant service.

Staffing for American Service

In American restaurants, the French-style training and profes-sionalism are generally lacking. The usual hierarchy is stratified and rigid, with less opportunity for those in lower positions to rise to better jobs. The stratification is as follows:

Maître d'hôtel
Captain
Waiter
Bus boy

The staffing for American service can follow that of French service, using captains, waiters, and bus boys. Often, however, since the highly skilled captain is not required, that position is eliminated. In a very large dining room, captains take the orders, or they may supervise the service and seating in different sections of the room. In such a situation, a *maître d'* is stationed at the door, and ushers are used to direct guests to the tables or stations he specifies.

Waiters or waitresses may work stations individually or in teams. Depending on the menu and the merchandising plan of the restaurant, restricted service positions such as roll or salad server or coffee pourer may exist.

Very often the *maître d'hôtel* is "master" in name only and is responsible only for the reservation desk in a dining room and for greeting the guests. Because this type of position does not warrant a very high salary, the *maître d'* may supplement his income by "selling" tables—i.e., reserving the best tables in the dining room for those guests who will tip him well. This preferential treatment is not usually condoned by management because it often alienates patrons and gives the establishment a bad reputation.

Captains, waiters, and bus boys usually work in teams, with one captain and one bus boy to two or four waiters. The captain takes the orders and may supervise the service on his station. He also does the complicated carving or finishing. The waiters work in pairs, with one serving as the runner to and from the kitchen and the other remaining at the station. A bus boy may assist one or two teams of waiters.

The *sommelier* is the wine steward in the European service. He is in complete charge of the wine cellar and may supervise a staff of assistants who sometimes serve liquor and cocktails as well as wine. The position of *sommelier* is sometimes retained in American restaurants, but more likely, the job is strictly a matter of fetching and serving, with the selection of the wines that are purchased being made by a representative of management.

Headwaiter or Hostess. The headwaiter is responsible for all phases of service, including the appearance of the room and the staff and the seating of patrons. The duties of the hostess are the same, although in a room employing a headwaiter the type of service is likely to be more elaborate, the beverage service more extensive, and advance reservations more numerous.

In some restaurants, the headwaiter or hostess is little more than an usher and does not function as the floor supervisor. This means that someone else must assume the responsibility, or supervision is neglected. In some organizations, the position "supervisor of service" is created. The supervisor is free to move about the dining room to oversee service and is not preoccupied with greeting and seating the guests. This is a management position with full authority and responsibility for operating the food and beverage service department.

Captains. When captains are used, the dining room is divided into sections, each section being assigned to a captain. A section is made up of several stations, and each captain remains in or near his section. Depending on the size and type of operation, the captains may assist in seating the guests.

At the table, the captain makes sure that the menus are presented and that water and other table appointments are placed on the table. Either the captain or the waiter may take the order, but the captain remains responsible for all service in his section. In many operations, it is the captain's duty to prepare and present the checks.

Waiters and Waitresses. In some operations, the patron never sees the manager, the chef, or any employee except the waiter or waitress, who therefore represents the operation. This is one reason the manner and appearance of the waiter or waitress are important. Also, food will not be appetizing if it is served by a person who is in any way objectionable in attitude, personal appearance, or cleanliness. Uniforms must be clean and well pressed. Lightweight uniforms should be changed daily. If food is spilled on uniforms, some provision should be made for quick changes. Hands and fingernails should always be clean and well groomed. Hair should be clean and neatly styled. Long, loose hair arrangements have no place in a food service operation. Many health departments require caps or hairnets for food service workers. Daily baths are necessary, and the use of a deodorant for both waiters and waitresses cannot be stressed too firmly. The headwaiter and hostess must insist that all employees under their jurisdiction meet these standards.

Bus Help. The bus help assist in setting up the tables. They fill and refill water glasses and pitchers, remove all the tableware after a meal, keep side stands supplied with linen and silverware, replenish supplies for a coffee station (if there is one in the dining room), and reset the tables after each patron or group has left. In some establishments, they may perform any of the tasks assigned to waiters except some order taking and serving. They may also act as runners, bringing food in from the kitchen.

The bus help also assist the waiters and waitresses. Occasionally their work will overlap that of the dining room porters, for instance when a cleaning-up job is necessary during meal service. In hiring bus help, the manager should consider their possible promotion to the serving staff in order to promote a longer tenure of employment. Bus help may need a little closer supervision than the service staff. When service is slow or inefficient, it is reflected in tips. If the bus help participates in the tips, they may be motivated to be more helpful.

When captains are used in a dining room, they can best supervise the activities of the bus help. If a hostess supervises the dining room, the seating of patrons is likely to keep her occupied, and control of the bus help is difficult. In such cases, a floor or service supervisor may be able to assume supervision. It is not wise to permit waiters or waitresses to supervise the bus help directly. Too many bosses may only be confusing.

Dining Room Management

Scheduling the Service Staff

The mechanics of staffing are discussed in depth in Chapter 16. It is sufficient to say here that the service staff is one department in which staffing can be varied directly according to the levels of anticipated business. In fact, it is not worthwhile for too many waiters and waitresses to work when business is slow, since most of their income comes from tips.

The service staff schedule should be based on the forecast of sales that may vary according to days of the week and by seasons. These fluctuations can be managed with the use of part-time or temporary employees, although having a regular, trained staff is, of course, more desirable.

In a five-day operation, days off are no problem, but they may become a problem in a seven-day operation. Employees usually prefer to have their days off each week consecutively, but not always. The staffing needs of the operation should be considered first, and then, if possible, the requests of the employees. Schedules should be prepared far enough in advance and posted conspicuously so that employees can know their schedules and make their personal plans accordingly.

Dining Room Inspection

The appearance of the dining room and the staff should be checked by actual inspection before each meal. The supervisor or host

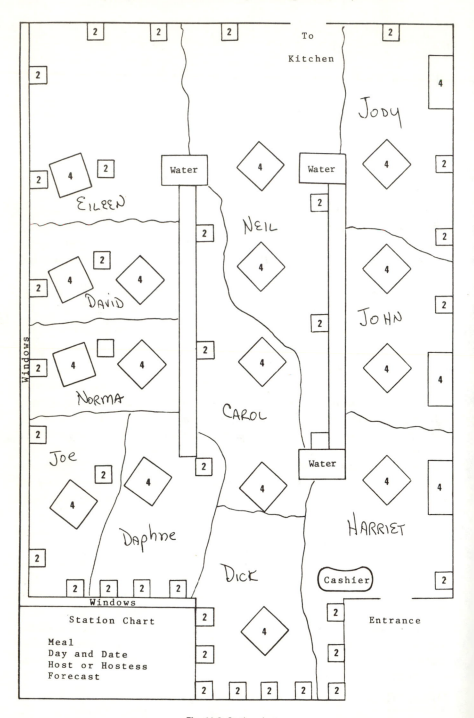

Fig. 11-6. Station chart.

should allow enough time to make his inspection and have any unacceptable conditions corrected before the dining room opens. If a standard check list is used for this purpose, then anyone substituting in the job may have a precise blueprint of the inspection routine. Check lists will vary, depending on the type of place, its equipment, and certain architectural details. The major items to be checked in most food service operations are as follows:

Doors	Table settings
Cashier's station	Ash trays
Floors	Menus
Walls	Lamps and lamp shades
Windows	Condiment containers
Curtains, shades, and draperies	Table legs (for steadiness)
Mirrors and pictures	Table cloths (for even hanging)
Table linen	
Chairs, including reserve high chairs	Both table legs and chair legs (for splinters)

The room's light, heat, and ventilation should also be checked.

Assigning Stations

The seats and tables assigned to each server or team of servers is a station (Fig. 11–6). The number of tables assigned will depend on the number of seats, the frequency of their turnover, the competence of the particular server, distance to the kitchen, and the number of servers scheduled for the particular meal. At a fast turnover counter operation, a server may be able to handle only six or seven seats, even though the distance to the pickup areas may be only a few feet. On the other hand, in a dining room with only a moderate turnover and an even flow of patrons, a server may be able to serve as many as 16 to 20 seats.

In some dining rooms, stations are fixed and permanently assigned to each server. A relief server, usually one with little seniority, relieves each station on the permanent server's day off. The fixed station system is usually unfair to younger members of the staff because the older members are assigned to the busier stations. Once this system is in practice, however, it is very difficult to change.

A more flexible and equitable arrangement is to rotate stations and to vary them according to the volume of business expected and the number of servers scheduled. Every dining room has some seats and stations that are more desirable to the guests than others, and it is quite impractical to try to force the guests to the less desirable stations when more attractive seats are available. Seating should be in consideration of the guests and not of the staff. Although stations can be planned to balance some of the workload, the rotation of stations among the staff is a more equitable way of balancing the work.

When a low volume of business is forecast and the dining room is not staffed to capacity, station assignments can be enlarged, so that the entire room is assigned, or sections of the room can be closed off. This will depend on the architectural plan of the room and the expected flow of business.

Line-ups

Every waiter or waitress should report for line-up before each meal. Line-ups are short staff meetings at which the staff is inspected for neatness of dress and cleanliness. Station assignments are also made at that time. The service staff should be briefed on the menu before the meals. This briefing should include the following:

1. The prices of all menu items, their contents, and the method of preparation.
2. Which items are made to order.
3. The location in the kitchen where an item is to be found.
4. The approximate time required to wait for items prepared to order.
5. The items that should be promoted and any planned substitutes in the event of run-outs.
6. New dishes may be tasted and instruction given for their service.
7. Review of the correct service of other menu items.
8. Discussion of any guest complaints pertaining to service.

Sidework

Sidework is the name given to the housekeeping jobs usually assigned to the service staff. Since time spent in this work does not produce tips directly, some servers object to doing it. Unfortunately, some of them do not realize that poor housekeeping affects the appearance of the room and the future sales potential. Typical sidework jobs include cleaning the salt and pepper shakers and the sugar bowls, care of condiments and containers, polishing silver, dusting, straightening, and replenishing side stands, care of flowers or plants, polishing table tops and care of decorative items in the room. These jobs may be scheduled daily or weekly and should be specifically assigned on a rotation basis. Written instructions and assignments help to eliminate any misunderstanding.

Training

When training new employees for the dining room staff, many operators simply assign the new person to follow one of the more experienced servers. The burden of training is then placed on the experienced employee rather than on management. Some of the staff may consider it a compliment, but to many others, having a trainee assigned to them is a burden.

There is another disadvantage to this system of training. Waiters and waitresses as a group are quite mobile, moving frequently from job to job and place to place. From their different work experiences, they develop a set of work habits and ways of serving that may or may not be acceptable to their current employer. Any bad habits are then passed on to any new employees they may train.

Many companies with well-defined standards of service prefer to hire completely inexperienced people for waiters and waitresses and train them in their own style of service. Classes are conducted by supervisors, and training materials are provided that may include audiovisual presentations or employee handbooks. New servers practice carrying trays and setting tables and then serving meals to one another or to the supervisor. Only when the desired standards of service have been impressed on them are they permitted to observe the actual operation of the dining room. They may then be assigned to another server, or they may be given a table to serve under the guidance of the training supervisor.

Training should not be limited to new employees but should be a continuing process. Line-ups, review classes, posters and printed materials, plus constant supervision are required to maintain the desired standards.

Standards of Service

In a well-run dining room, the standards of service which management wishes to attain are well defined. These standards are usually of four types: the merchandising and sales procedures to be used; the procedures for taking the orders, delivering the food, and clearing the tables; the proper table setting; and the details of the service—that is, the tableware and accompaniments to be used in the service of each menu item.

Merchandising and Sales Procedures

The service staff should be not only order takers but also active salesmen. Suggestions to the guest indicate the server's personal interest in the guest's enjoyment of his meal, which not only increases the operation's income but also increases the server's tips. Salesmanship can be applied in snack bars and coffee shops ("Would you like some French fries with your hamburger?") as well as in the finest table service restaurants ("May I bring you a cognac with your coffee, Mr. Brown?"). The presentation of desserts on carts and displays of cheeses and fruit brought to the table by the service person are ways of increasing both sales and the guest's satisfaction with his meal.

How the food and beverages are presented also adds to the image of the overall operation. A special side dish or other accompanying item may be presented to every guest "with the special compliments of Owner Smith." Servers can be alert to parties celebrating a special event, such as a birthday or anniversary, and present some special complimentary item in accordance with the management's policy on such gifts.

Procedures for Taking and Delivering Orders and Clearing the Table

The following are the basic steps necessary in serving a guest:

1. Seating and presenting the menu.
2. Cocktail service, if requested.
3. Taking the orders.
4. Placing on the table the water, rolls, relishes, or whatever is required by the style of service.
5. Placing and obtaining the orders from the kitchen.
6. Preparing and presenting the check, and collecting the money.
7. Clearing the table and resetting it for the next customer.

Seating the Guests and Presenting the Menu. Seating the guests is usually done by a headwaiter or hostess. The work load of each server should be considered, because it will affect the service of the arriving guests and the guests already seated. Unless another table is clearly preferable to the one indicated by the headwaiter or hostess, most guests will accept the table assigned to them. If the arriving guests are seated in each station in rotation, each server should ultimately receive about the same number of guests and therefore have a fairly equal share of the work load and the tips.

When guests seat themselves, a more flexible station assignment is needed in order to spread the workload and the tips and to give the best service to all guests. A way to do this is to assign fewer seats to the server on the most popular station.

The menu is usually presented by the person seating the guests. If guests seat themselves, the menu must be presented by the server. Posting the menu on the wall or on a placemat eliminates this step.

Cocktail Service. When cocktail service is offered, either the host or the server may ask if a cocktail is desired. After the order is taken, the server goes to the bar, places the order, obtains and serves the drink. Very often, the glassware for the drinks is stored outside the bartender's reach, because of limited space behind the bar, and in order to keep bar porters and bus men who replenish the supply of clean glassware from having to enter the bartender's work area. The serving person is responsible for giving the bartender the proper glassware. The server must know which glass to use for each kind of drink and should also recognize the finished drinks by sight. In some high-volume bars, the servers also garnish the drinks, adding the olives, fruit, swizzlers, and so on as required. An identification system should be devised so that the bartender and the servers can identify drinks made with premium or specially ordered brands. Failure to serve the brand ordered can cause guest dissatisfaction, particularly when there is a price premium involved.

When serving drinks, the server should not have to ask the guests to identify their drinks. If he took the orders in proper sequence around the table, he should be able to serve them in the same sequence without interrupting the guests. After the cocktail order has been served, the server should be alert for some indication from the guests that another round of drinks is desired or that they are ready to order the meal.

Taking the Orders. In some types of restaurants, the menu is posted outside or at the door, and the guest may be ready to give his order as soon as he is seated. Usually, however, the guests like to look over the menu and make their selection at their leisure. While they are doing this, the server or bus person can fill the water glasses and serve the butter, breads, or crackers, relishes, or any other items required by the style of service. When the guest turns his attention from the menu, he is ready to give his order.

Orders may be written directly on a guest check or on special preprinted forms or captain's order pads. Orders are usually taken from the ladies first, although some women may prefer to have their escorts order for them. To keep track of who ordered what, some sort of system should be devised. The simplest system is to establish one point in the room, such as the door, as a starting base. All seats facing that point are designated as No. 1, with the other seats numbered consecutively, clockwise around the table. If the guests at seats No. 2 and No. 4 are ladies, their orders can be taken first but designated according to their seats. In this way, the party can be served their orders properly, without the server having to keep a number of orders in his head or to interrupt the guests' conversation with questions. As an added advantage, any other server can also serve the orders efficiently, if the whole staff uses the same system of notation.

A common set of abbreviations can facilitate order taking and minimize errors. Sometimes items are numbered on the menu for fast ordering. If numbers and abbreviations are used on the guest check, they should give sufficient indication of what the item is so that the guest can identify the items he is being charged for.

Placing and Obtaining the Orders from the Kitchen. Orders must be transmitted clearly to the kitchen to avoid errors or misunderstandings. If some items must be prepared to order, the servers should know how long the orders will take and coordinate them, so that the whole party's order will be ready at the same time. An expediter may act as coordinator. When the entrées are prepared to order, the server puts in his order, then assembles the first course. If no soup or appetizer was ordered, the salad is sometimes served in its place, especially if the entrée is being prepared to order.

The server may dish up or garnish some items himself. The amount of such items to be served should be established and followed. Some servers mistake generous portions for good service and think that serving an overly large helping of rolls, butter, cream, jelly, and so on will increase their tips. The dining room supervisor should be alert to waste of this nature. Management should establish a policy on the service of extra large helpings—how much is to be served when requested, and what, if anything, is to be charged for such requests.

When picking up orders in the kitchen, the server should pick up all cold items first and hot foods last. The tray should be loaded so that the weight is balanced and, whenever possible, with the items arranged in order of the service. In American service, the entrées may be covered and stacked in the same order in which they will be served to provide quick, efficient service in the dining room with a minimum time lapse in which the hot food may get cold. All accompanying items should be collected and taken on the same trip. It is helpful if all the requirements for an item are kept together in the same place. This organization is easier for the servers and keeps a guest from having to wait for the server to bring some forgotten piece of tableware or condiment from the kitchen. If the servers can be trained to think "iced tea—lemon—underliner—iced tea spoon," instead of merely "iced tea," service is greatly enhanced.

Organization of the server's tray and station should be stressed when training new servers. Before leaving the station to go to the kitchen, the server should check the progress of each party and anticipate their needs. If one party is almost finished with their appetizers, they may be ready for the main course before the server returns from the kitchen. If the orders are ready, they can be brought immediately.

Preparing and Presenting the Check; Collecting the Money. In many operations, the check must be made out and properly priced before the server can pick up his orders from the range. This is known as "prechecking." There are various other methods of controlling guest checks and cash. Since this is an important aspect of internal control, it is discussed in *Profitable Food and Beverage Management: Planning.* The use of duplicate checks is also discussed in Chapter 7 of this book.

Clearing the Table and Resetting for the Next Guests. The faster the table is cleared and reset after the guest has left, the sooner the next party can be seated. In some establishments, clearing is left solely to the bus help. A server can be made aware that the faster his tables are reset, the more guests he can serve and the more tips he will make. Where union regulations permit, servers should be encouraged to bus their own tables. Taking soiled ware when going to the kitchen does not take any more time than going with an empty tray. Furthermore, uncleared tables are unsightly if allowed to stand and can detract from the appearance of the dining room.

In some types of operations, guests may be seated at uncleared tables. This should be done only when it cannot be avoided, as in fast turnover, high-volume operations such as coffee shops.

The proper way to clear or bus a table should be established. If silverware is separated and plates scraped and stacked as the table is cleared, the dishwashing function becomes much more efficient and breakage costs are reduced.

When the tablecloth is changed during service, it should be done discreetly, without a flourish that could be distracting to nearby diners. The correct way to change a tablecloth is to fold back one edge of the soiled cloth and to position the clean cloth on the uncovered edge of the table. The soiled cloth is then folded back as the clean cloth is unfolded in position on the table. Any crumbs are wrapped in the soiled cloth, rather than shaken out on the floor or on guests.

Table Settings

For many years, etiquette has dictated the "correct" way of setting a table. Although standards of etiquette may change over time, people look for certain table implements in certain places. Minor variations can be devised to suit the merchandising plan of a certain restaurant, but they should not be too different from the accepted pattern.

If tablecloths are used, a silencer pad is put on the table first. A silencer pad is a cloth of felt or other thick material that cushions the surface and muffles the sound of china and silver on the table top. In many restaurants, an undercloth is also used to hide the less presentable silencer pad when the cloth is changed during the meal period. Also, by using a larger undercloth, the top cloth can be smaller. Use of the smaller cloth will save on laundry costs.

The dining room supervisor is responsible for seeing that there is an adequate supply of table linen of the proper size. He may deal directly with the laundry in placing orders, or he may transmit his needs to a steward, housekeeper, or some other office.

Paper placemats and napkins may be used in place of linen. Some fast-service operations even eliminate the placemats and put all the silverware on the napkin. Putting silverware directly on the bare table is not an acceptable sanitary practice.

Placemats are usually set about two inches from the edge of the table, and any art work or reading matter should face the guest. Napkins, either paper or linen, should be placed so that one corner is facing the guest. In this way, he can pick up the top corner, open the napkin, and place it on his lap with one hand.

In years past, napkin folding was an art. In keeping with the ostentatious food and table appointments of past periods, napkins were folded into all sorts of intricate shapes, including fans, flowers, swans, and hats. An intricately folded napkin can add to an attractive and distinctive table, but folding can be a time-consuming and very costly operation.

The space and utensils for each guest is called a "cover." (The term is also used in the sense of "a meal served," as in "the number of covers served today.") Sufficient space should be allowed for each cover, so that the guest is not crowded and can be served properly. At least 24 inches of space should be allowed per cover. The arrangement of the items required for the cover should be balanced and attractive.

Silverware is arranged about two inches from the edge of the table. The accepted placement of the knives, forks, and spoons is based on the European style of eating. The utensils used with the left hand (fork) are placed on the left, and those used with the right hand (knife and spoon) are placed on the right. Americans eat in a less efficient manner than Europeans, with the fork held in the left hand while cutting food and switched to the right hand for transporting the food to the mouth; but the placement of the silverware on the table remains unchanged. The pieces are arranged in the order of use, starting from the outside.

The pieces of china and silver used should depend on the requirements of the meal. At a banquet, only the pieces actually required are set, but in dining rooms, a standard setting must be established. (A knife is always set, whether the menu requires it or not, because the European style of eating requires it.) Different standard settings may be used for different meals. Figures 11–7 and 11–8 show settings for informal and formal meals.

A center set-up consists of sugar bowl, ash tray and matches, salt and pepper shakers, and sometimes a bud vase or condiment

Fig. 11-7. An informal place setting used at The Oyster Bar & Restaurant, Grand Central Station, New York City. This seafood restaurant includes sea salt and oyster crackers in its center set-up. *(Courtesy of The Oyster Bar & Restaurant, New York City)*

bottles. It may also contain a napkin dispenser, but such dispensers are more often found in self-service or fast-food operations. Sugar bowls and salt and pepper shakers are placed in the center of a table that seats four, and along one side of a table for two. If the table for two is a wall table, the side toward the wall is the one to use; if it is not a wall table, the side away from the main traffic aisle should be used, for safety.

The ash tray and matches belong beside the sugar bowls. When the table is cleared, the ash tray should be cleaned, and matches restocked whenever necessary. During the meal, if the ash tray is used, it must be emptied as often as necessary or replaced with a clean tray.

Details of Service

The details of service for each item on the menu should be spelled out. If special orders (nonlisted items) are frequently served, instructions should be included for these items. For example:

Fig. 11-8. A formal place setting used at The Four Seasons, New York City. The place setting includes (left to right): a butter knife and the bread and butter plate, fish fork, salad fork, and place fork. To the right of the service plate are the place knife, fish knife, and place spoon. Above the knife are a red or white wine glass, a sherry or port glass, and a tall champagne glass. *(Courtesy of The Four Seasons, New York City)*

Soup, cup. Serve one ladle of soup, *dipped from the bottom of the pot,* in a soup cup. Follow the instructions given in line-up for garnishing. Serve on a saucer or an underliner. Serve with a bouillon spoon. Be sure there are crackers in the roll basket, and offer another basket if there are none.

Soup, plate. Serve 1½ ladles *dipped from the bottom of the pot.* Use an eight-inch underliner, and serve with a soup spoon. Follow other directions given for a cup of soup.

Shrimp Cocktail. Fill supreme dish with crushed ice, cover with ring, and place insert dish in the ring. Be sure the cocktail has five shrimp. Use a seven-inch underliner with paper doily. Serve one lemon wedge on the underliner. Be sure there are crackers in the roll basket; offer another basket if there are none.

Salad, tossed green. Serve in a wooden bowl. Place salad dressing rack on the table when salad is served.

Entrées. Eight-inch plates used at lunch, nine-inch at dinner. Garnishes will be specified at line-up for the various daily entrées. Standard items:

Lamb chops:	Mint sauce in a relish boat, steak knife. Mint jelly available on request.
Steaks:	Steak knife. Steak sauce available on request.
Chopped Steak:	Catsup in a relish boat on request.

All hot plates are to be covered when taken to the dining room.

Pies. Serve on seven-inch liner. Set the pie so the point faces the guest. Serve with a place fork.

Ice cream. Serve in an ice cream dish. Use a seven-inch liner with paper doily. One cookie on the underliner. Serve with a place spoon.

Coffee. Serve individual pots of coffee for each order. Offer to pour the first cup. Serve a small pitcher of cream for one or two guests, a large pitcher for three or four.

These details of service should be compiled and given to each trainee, and they should also be posted at the appropriate points in the kitchen and pantry. Dining room supervisors should review the details of service at line-ups from time to time and should be alert to any incorrect service during meal periods. Improper service should be corrected in the kitchen, and not in the presence of the guests.

Service Staff Behavior

Although a long list of rules can be a source of poor morale, certain standards of behavior are essential to good service. Smoking, eating and drinking, and gum chewing while on duty should not be allowed. When they are not busy with service, servers should be at their stations and alert to the needs of their guests. They should not be permitted to congregate in the kitchen, or in a corner of the dining room, or where loud conversation can be distracting to nearby guests.

Work rules should not be made for their own sake but rather for the purpose of providing good service to the guest. They should be uniformly and fairly enforced by the dining room supervisor.

Breakdowns of Service

When the standards of service are not met, a breakdown in service occurs. There are a number of causes of service breakdowns, many of which are not the fault of the server.

Poor Seating

When a server's station is all seated at once, he may get stuck through no fault of his own. If seating is staggered, the server can devote attention to each table in turn. There are times, however, when it is impossible to avoid fully seating a station or even a whole dining room in a very short period. Most guests are willing to wait if their presence is acknowledged by the server, who may say "Good evening, I'll be with you in just a moment." No one likes to be ignored. Dining room supervisors should be alert to potential breakdowns caused by the seating pattern and get help for any server who may get stuck.

Physical Layout

Bottlenecks in the kitchen or the distance to be traveled may be a cause for service breakdowns. If the kitchen is far removed from the dining room, team service may be required. In this way, at least one server is available on the station at all times to attend to the guests.

Sometimes only minor changes in the kitchen or layout procedures will eliminate a serious bottleneck. If this is not possible, it may be desirable to study the possible relocation of some of the functions performed. For example, carts can be used instead of carrying used dishes to remote or congested dishwashing areas; or instead of one large coffee station, single-pot brewing equipment can be set up at each station.

Shortage of Ware

Some operators feel they save money by continually operating with a shortage of silver, china, and glassware. This is a rather dubious practice since it can be a major source of poor morale to the staff and poor service to the guest. Servers may resort to the unsightly and unsanitary practice of carrying silverware and other equipment in their pockets, taking it from each other's stations, bribing bus boys and dishwashers, or washing their own tableware. This last practice is the most undesirable because it takes time away from serving the guests and also because the server cannot achieve the sanitation level of machine washing.

Poor Communication with the Kitchen

When orders are transmitted verbally to the kitchen, there is considerable chance for error. Items can be misordered, misunderstood, not heard at all, or forgotten completely. When cooks take orders directly from the servers, there is also the possibility of willful loss of orders if a personality conflict exists.

In many of the busier kitchens, the chef or some other person of authority acts as an expediter. (In the French kitchen this position is the *abboyeur* or barker.) The expediter receives the written orders from the waiter and transmits them to the proper stations. He also coordinates the timing of the various orders, approves the dishes going out, and provides some control by seeing that no food is dispensed without being recorded on a guest check.

Some operations have found the use of mechanical communication devices such as the tel-autograph or pneumatic tubes very helpful in transporting written orders to a distant kitchen, or various telephone arrangements useful for communicating verbal orders.

Waits or Run-Outs of Food

Delays in preparation or run-outs of food are beyond the control of the dining room supervisor. He can only insist that the kitchen communicate this information to the servers as quickly as possible and that the servers report to the guests for a possible change of orders. Most kitchens use a blackboard for posting the status of items during the meal period. Frequent problems of run-outs or delays should be referred to management for correction.

Accidents

Accidents are inevitable, but they can be kept to a minimum by a staff that is trained to be safety conscious. Spills should be wiped up immediately and floors kept clean. Nonskid surfaces can be installed on particularly hazardous floors, such as those in dishrooms or on ramps. Personnel should be trained to announce their presence when passing others loaded with trays. When an accident has occurred that will delay service to the guest, the supervisor should inform the guest and offer apologies in advance to avoid subsequent dissatisfaction.

12

BANQUETS

In the last decade, banquet business has grown impressively. To meet the demands of this growth, food service operations that cater exclusively to groups have come into being. Some of the large urban convention hotels find that their sales to groups are as great as their sales in their public restaurants and bars. Aside from the overall size of this market, banquet business, if handled properly, can be more profitable than the traditional food service operations catering to individuals.

One feature of banquet operations that contributes to its profitability is that the volume of business is known for each operating day. Because many operators require a guaranteed attendance, they eliminate any losses from overpreparation of food and, even more important, they are able to schedule labor for preparation and service more efficiently and more economically. These types of operations, however, are not without problems. The most difficult problem encountered by those who cater exclusively to group business is to have a steady flow of patronage to keep intact numerically its key personnel. The problem of finding extra help in some localities often forces operators to carry a larger staff than is necessary in order to have the staff available when needed.

Banquet Sales Office

The successful operators have learned that although good food is still the prime requisite for building banquet business, other attributes are needed to promote and develop this market. These attributes include well-designed and pleasantly decorated function rooms, appealing presentation of food, orderly, fast, and courteous service, parking facilities, and, of course, competitive prices.

The operators have also learned that although these factors contribute to growth, a hard-hitting sales force will accelerate this growth. Accordingly, they have established banquet sales offices staffed with a capable sales force and provided with the proper tools to enable them to sell.

In establishing a banquet sales office, it is advisable to separate it from the business office. The decor of the sales office should be impressive but not ostentatious. The meeting with the representatives of the group should be conducted in a quiet atmosphere undisturbed by noise or interruptions. Some operators create a feeling of attention and relaxation by serving coffee or cocktails.

Several display tables are set up with different color combinations of linens as well as china and silver hollowware and flatware to visually demonstrate the table set-ups that can be used to service the prospective guest. In addition, the sales force is provided with colored photographs of group functions served in the past, showing not only the table set-ups but the food arrangements on the plate or platters. Pictures of weddings, wedding cakes, ice carvings, beautifully arranged buffet displays are all impressive and demonstrate the capabilities of the operation to provide satisfaction to all clients.

A well-organized sales office maintains a group file folder containing all the information pertaining to the parties serviced in the past, including the names of the representative or committee to be contacted for the next affair. In addition, to provide its sales force with additional leads, there will be notices from clipping services of social affairs, fund raising drives, weddings, and other such events that will be held in the future.

Review of all the possible arrangements listed on a preprinted form, such as those shown in Tables 12–1 and 12–2 and Fig. 12–1, will give the prospective guest a feeling of thoroughness and of the custom tailoring of the arrangement to suit his own specifications rather than a prepackaged banquet formula.

When the banquet manager discusses arrangements with a prospective customer, he should have at his finger tips a complete list of all functions booked for the date under discussion. When the same group has patronized the hotel on previous occasions, the menus served at those times should be reviewed to prevent repetitions. The purchasing agent, steward, or food cost accountant can provide the banquet manager with a list of seasonal price fluctuations of various items that will serve as a guide to proper pricing of menus. The chef should make a list of certain dishes that will require extra kitchen personnel, and if these dishes are chosen, a surcharge may be required. Preparation problems of all kinds of dishes should be indexed on cards for easy reference. It is helpful for the banquet manager to keep a list of banquet problems and their history. This history should contain all the difficulties encountered in every banquet function and how they were met.

BANQUET CHARGE SHEET

HOURS OPENED _____ SET UP FOR _____ TIME FINISHED _____ PARTY LEFT _____
GUARANTEED _____ SERVICE _____ SERVED _____ CHARGED _____

Room Rental _____				BROUGHT FORWARD _____		
Breakfasts _____						
Luncheons _____				SPECIAL GRATUITIES _____		
Reception & Teas _____						
Dinners _____				GRATUITIES _____		
Suppers _____						
Musicians' Meals _____				OTHER GRATUITIES _____		
Entertainers' Meals _____						
Special Cake _____				COAT ROOM FEES _____		
Hot Appetizers _____						
Cold Appetizers _____				TOTAL CHARGES _____		
Food Check # _____				SALES TAX _____		
_____				GRAND TOTAL _____		
Beverage Check # _____						

REMARKS

Corkage _____			
Bar & Bartender _____			
Cigars _____			
Cigarettes _____			
Flowers _____			
Corsages _____			
Boutonnieres _____			
Tags _____			
Menu Place Cards _____			
Escort Cards _____			
Candles _____			
Check Room _____			
Engineer _____			
Spotlight _____			
Amplification _____			
Photographer _____			
Motion Picture _____			
Security _____			
Cocktail Napkins _____			
Book Matches _____			
Miscellaneous _____			
TOTAL FORWARD			

ITEMIZE BEVERAGES & CORKAGE

Waiter to make all charges after function, complete all information
and return this account immediately to Banquet Office

HEAD WAITER _____ CAPTAIN IN CHARGE _____
DIRECTOR OF CATERING _____ BANQUET REVENUE AUDITOR _____

Fig. 12-1. Banquet charge sheet.

Banquet Menus

The banquet menu differs from the dining room menu in that it is "custom tailored," whereas that for the dining room is "ready made." For a banquet, the menu is adjusted to the customer; in a dining room, the customer adjusts himself to the menu. The banquet menu is usually made up weeks and sometimes months ahead of time. This creates problems because some convention banquets are booked a year or two in advance. It is not possible to predict so far in advance the market and labor conditions and the prices. When bookings are made far in advance, the contractual agreements should provide for the right of the food service operator to increase his menu price on the basis of the formula spelled out in the agreement. The formula may be based on such indices as the Consumer Price Index or the Cost of Living Index, both of which are prepared by governmental agencies and private financial institutions.

Ready-Reference Banquet-Pricing Data

To expedite the pricing of a menu tailored to the needs of a banquet prospect, the banquet manager should have available ready-reference banquet-pricing data established by the food cost accountant and revised every 30 to 60 days to reflect serious changes in the market prices of the foods purchased. These data can be presented in many different forms. Tables of main entrées and accompanying courses are shown in Table 12–1 and Table 12–2.

These tables are set up in two sections for most convenient reference. One section should indicate the various entrées in different price ranges, these prices being dependent on the accompanying dishes. The other section is the make-up menus of these accompanying dishes offered at various price levels. With key letters in the first section indicating the various make-up menus in the second section, the banquet manager or his sales staff can quote prices without the need for time-consuming calculations. As an example, if the sponsor has decided on a broiled filet mignon as a main course for the banquet dinner, Table 12–1 shows that this main course item can be served at nine different prices per cover (person) depending on the number of courses served and the cost of the items desired within each course. For instance, at the lowest price, make-up menu "A" would be served, which consists of three courses (not counting the main course or coffee). The items in each of the courses are the lower cost items. In the $12 price range, the items in make-up menu I would be served, consisting of five courses (not counting the main course or beverage service). Furthermore, the variety of items offered for selection in each course is greater and of higher cost.

Table 12–1. Ready-Reference Banquet Pricing Chart

ENTRÉE SELECTIONS	Portion Size	PRICE RANGE								
		$3.00	$3.25	$3.50	$3.75	$4.00	$4.25	$4.50	$4.75	$5.00
Chicken a la King	2½ oz.	A	B	C	D	E	F	G	H	I
Chicken Patty	5 oz.	A	B	C	D	E	F	G	H	I
Half Broiled Chicken	½ each				A	B	C	D	E	F
Breast of Chicken or Capon	½ each						A	B	C	D
Half Roast Stuffed Chicken	½ each				A	B	C	D	E	F
Roast Stuffed Turkey	6 oz.							A	B	C
Filet of Sole	5 oz.			A	B	C	D	E	F	G
Broiled Scrod	6 oz.	A	B	C	D	E	F	G	H	I
Baked Halibut	6 oz.				A	B	C	D	E	F
Poached Salmon	6 oz.				A	B	C	D	E	F
Sea Scallops Saute	4 oz.		A	B	C	D	E	F	G	H
Broiled Cape Scallops	4 oz.			A	B	C	D	E	F	G
Baked Lobster Thermidor	4 oz.								A	B
Broiled Chopped Sirloin Steak	8 oz.		A	B	C	D	E	F	G	H
Broiled Salisbury Steak	8 oz.		A	B	C	D	E	F	G	H
Yankee Pot Roast	6 oz.						A	B	C	D
Roast Top Sirloin of Beef	5 oz.				A	B	C	D	E	F
Broiled Hip Steak	8 oz.								A	B
London Broil on Toast	5 oz.				A	B	C	D	E	F
Roast Leg of Lamb	6 oz.							A	B	C
Lamb Chop Mix Grill	6 oz.							A	B	C
Roast Stuffed Shoulder of Lamb	6 oz.			A	B	C	D	E	F	G
Grilled Pork Chop	6 oz.		A	B	C	D	E	F	G	H
Roast Loin of Pork	7 oz.						A	B	C	D	E
Baked Sugar Cured Ham	6 oz.						A	B	C	D
Broiled Ham Steak	8 oz.						A	B	C	D
Roast Leg of Veal	6 oz.							A	B	C
Scalopine of Veal	4 oz.				A	B	C	D	E	F
Breaded Veal Cutlet	5 oz.						A	B	C	D	E
Roast Stuffed Shoulder of Veal	5 oz.				A	B	C	D	E	F

ENTRÉE SELECTIONS	Portion Size	PRICE RANGE								
		$5.25	$5.50	$5.75	$6.00	$6.25	$6.50	$6.75	$7.00	$7.25
Half Broiled Chicken	½ each	G	H	I						
Breast of Chicken or Capon	½ each	E	F	G	H	I				
Half Roast Stuffed Chicken	½ each	G	H	I						
Roast Stuffed Turkey	6 oz.	D	E	F	G	H	I			
Filet of Sole	5 oz.	H	I							
Baked Halibut	6 oz.	G	H	I						
Poached Salmon	6 oz.	G	H	I						
Baked Lobster Thermidor	4 oz.	C	D	E	F	G	H	I		
Yankee Pot Roast	6 oz.	E	F	G	H	I				
Roast Prime Ribs of Beef	10 oz.						A	B	C	D
Roast Sirloin of Beef—U.S. Good	8 oz.					A	B	C	D	E
Broiled Hip Steak	8 oz.	C	D	E	F	G	H	I		
London Broil on Toast	5 oz.	G	H	I						
Roast Leg of Lamb	6 oz.	D	E	F	G	H	I			
Lamb Chop Mix Grill	6 oz.	D	E	F	G	H	I			
Roast Stuffed Shoulder of Lamb	6 oz.	H	I							

Table 12-1. Ready-Reference Banquet Pricing Chart (Cont'd.)

ENTRÉE SELECTIONS	Portion Size	\$5.25	\$5.50	\$5.75	\$6.00	\$6.25	\$6.50	\$6.75	\$7.00	\$7.25
					PRICE RANGE					
Roast Loin of Pork	7 oz.		F	G	H	I				
Baked Sugar Cured Ham	6 oz.	E	F	G	H	I				
Broiled Ham Steak	8 oz.	E	F	G	H	I				
Roast Leg of Veal	6 oz.	D	E	F	G	H	I			
Scalopine of Veal	4 oz.	G	H	I						
Breaded Veal Cutlet	5 oz.	F	G	H	I					
Roast Stuffed Shoulder of Veal	5 oz.	G	H	I						

ENTRÉE SELECTIONS	Portion Size	\$7.50	\$7.75	\$7.50	\$7.75	\$8.00	\$8.25	\$8.50	\$8.25	\$9.00
					PRICE RANGE					
Roast Prime Ribs of Beef	10 oz.		E	F	G	H	I			
Broiled Filet Mignon	8 oz.								A	B
Roast Sirloin of Beef—U.S. Good	8 oz.			F	G	H	I			
Roast Sirloin of Beef—U.S. Choice	8 oz.					A	B	C	D	E
Broiled Sirloin Steak—U.S. Good	8 oz.	A	B	C	D	E	F	G	H	I

ENTRÉE SELECTIONS	Portion Size	\$9.25	\$9.50	\$10.00	\$10.50	\$11.00	\$11.50	\$12.00	\$12.50	\$13.00
					PRICE RANGE					
Broiled Filet Mignon	8 oz.	C	D	E	F	G	H	I		
Broiled Sirloin Steak—U.S. Choice	8 oz.		A	B	C	D	E	F	G	H

Minimum Guarantee

Years ago, in some sections of the country, food service operators were reluctant to ask for guaranteed attendance. Those who did obtain guaranteed attendance did not always enforce their contractual rights for fear of losing repeat business. However, with the current high food and labor costs, the operators find that when the attendance drops appreciably below the number expected, it cuts deeply into the profits of a banquet. In the last decade, booking banquets on the basis of a guaranteed attendance has become a normal business procedure.

When the arrangements for a banquet are confirmed, the sponsor provides the operator with an estimated guest count, with the understanding that a guaranteed amount must be submitted in writing not later than a stipulated number of hours or days before the date of the banquet. Forty-eight hours advance notice regarding the guaranteed attendance is the time most frequently used.

Operators may prepare for about 5 percent above the guaranteed amount and will permit the sponsor to increase the guaranteed amount. However, should the attendance fall below the guaranteed amount, the billing is prepared on the basis of the minimum guaranteed attendance.

Table 12–2. Make-up Menus.

MAKE-UP MENU (A)

Grapefruit Juice   Tomato Juice   Vegetable Juice
Potatoes du Jour   Vegetables du Jour
Cole Slaw   Mixed Greens
                                    French Dressing
Pudding du Jour
Fruit Jello with Whipped Cream   Ice Cream Slice
                                  (Brick Ice Cream)
Rolls and Butter   Coffee

MAKE-UP MENU (B)

Tomato Juice   Half Grapefruit   Grapefruit Juice
Fruit Cup   Vegetable Juice
Potatoes du Jour   Vegetables du Jour
Cole Slaw   Lettuce and Tomato
Mixed greens   Salad Dressing   Chef's Salad
Fruit Jello, Whipped Cream   Pudding du Jour
Ice Cream Slice (Brick)   Layer Cake
           Apple Pie (9 Cut)
Rolls and Butter   Coffee or Demi-Tasse

MAKE-UP MENU (C)

Orange Juice   Pineapple Juice
Grapefruit Juice   Vegetable Juice
Fruit Cup   Half Grapefruit
Antipasto   Seafood Cocktail Copley
Tomato Juice   (No Shrimp or Crabmeat)
    Parsley, French Fried, or Whipped Potatoes
Carrots and Peas   Corn Saute   String Beans
Carrots Vichy   Green Peas
Hearts of Lettuce   Tossed Green Salad
Lettuce and Tomatoes   Combination Salad
    Mexican Slaw, French or Russian Dressing
Fruit Jello with Whipped Cream   Pudding du Jour
Ice Cream Slice (Brick Ice Cream)   Layer Cake
Apple Pie (9 Cut)   Fruit Compote
Rolls and Butter   Coffee, Demi-Tasse, Tea, or Milk

MAKE-UP MENU (D)

Tomato Juice   Grapefruit Juice
Orange Juice   Pineapple Juice
Antipasto   Vegetable Juice
Orange and Grapefruit Cup   Half Grapefruit
Fruit Cup   Seafood Cocktail Copley
           Chilled Celery and Olives
Potatoes: Parsley   French Fried   Whipped
        O'Brien   Hashed Brown   Rissole
Carrots and Peas   Garden Spinach   Green Beans
Green Peas   Corn Saute   Carrots Vichy
        Macedoine Vegetables
Hearts of Lettuce   Lettuce and Tomato

Menu D *(Cont.)*

Tossed Green Salad   Fruit in Aspic
Chiffonade Salad   Combination
    French, Russian, or 1000 Island Dressing
Fruit Jello with Whipped cream   Pudding du Jour
Ice Cream Slice   Layer Cake
Apple Pie   Fruit Compote
Bisquit Tortoni   Cherry Sundae
Rolls and Butter   Coffee, Demi-Tasse, Tea, or Milk

MAKE-UP MENU (E)

Fresh Fruit Cup   Half Grapefruit
Antipasto   Orange and Grapefruit Cup
Small Shrimp Cocktail   Seafood Cocktail Copley
    Avocado and Diced Celery Dressing
    Celery   Radishes   Olives
Consomme   Chicken Broth with Rice
Potatoes: Whipped   Delmonico   French Fried
        Hashed Brown   O'Brien   Rissole
Buttered Green Peas   String Beans Orientale
Buttered Macedoine of Vegetables   Carrots Vichy
Buttered Lima Beans   Garden Spinach
Whole Kernel Corn   Buttered Brussel Sprouts
Chef's Salad   Combination Salad
Chiffonade Salad   Lettuce and Tomato Salad
Fruit in Aspic   Floridian Salad
    French, Russian, or 1000 Island Dressing
Ice Cream Slice (Brick)   Apple Pie
Layer Cake   Cherry Sundae
Biscuit Tortoni   Parfait
            Ice Cream Pie
Rolls and Butter   Coffee, Demi-Tasse, Tea, or Milk

MAKE-UP MENU (F)

Fresh Fruit Cup   Orange and Grapefruit Cup
Avocado with Diced Celery Dressing   Antipasto
Half Grapefruit Maraschino Seafood Cocktail Copley
        Celery   Radishes   Olives
Consomme Pastina   Chicken Broth with Rice
Chicken Gumbo Creole   Fresh Vegetable Soup
            Tomato Bouillon en Tasse
Potatoes: French Fried Julienne   Hashed Brown
Whipped   Delmonico   Au Gratin   O'Brien
Buttered Green Peas   String Beans Orientale
Buttered Mixed Vegetables   Buttered String Beans
Buttered Lima Beans   Carrots Vichy
Whole Kernel Corn Braised Celery Garden Spinach
Chef's Salad   Tossed Garden Greens
Chiffonade Salad   Lettuce and Tomato
Fruit in Aspic   Combination Salad
Cottage Cheese and Pear   Floridian Salad

Table 12.2 Make-up Menus (Continued)

Menu F *(Cont.)*

French, Russian, or 1000 Island Dressing

Ice Cream Slice	Fruit or Cream Pie
Layer Cake	Ice Cream Sundae
Biscuit Tortoni	Parfait
Sultana Roll	Ice Cream Pie

Ice Cream Eclair with Chocolate Sauce

Rolls and Butter　　Coffee, Demi-Tasse, Tea, or Milk

MAKE-UP MENU (G)

Fresh Fruit Cup	Half Grapefruit Maraschino
Antipasto	Orange and Grapefruit Cup
Seafood Cocktail Copley	Shrimp Cocktail (4) (20 size)

Avocado with Diced Celery Dressing

Celery　　Radishes　　Olives

Consomme Pastina	Chicken Broth with Rice
Chicken Gumbo Creole	Tomato Bouillon en Tasse

Cream of Tomato

Potatoes:　Hashed Brown　　Rissole　　Julienne
　　　　　　Delmonico　　Long Branch　　Oven Brown
　　　　　　O'Brien　　French Fried　　Au Gratin

Buttered Green Peas	String Beans Orientale
Buttered Mixed Vegetables	Buttered Green Beans
Buttered Lima Beans	Carrots Vichy
Whole Kernel Corn Mexican	Garden Spinach
Buttered Brussel Sprouts	Braised Celery
Chef's Salad	Salad Bowl
Chiffonade	Combination Salad
Fruit in Aspic	Lettuce and Tomato Salad
Cottage Cheese and Pear	Floridian Salad

Waldorf Salad—Mayonnaise　Tossed Green Garden
French, Russian, or 1000 Island Dressing

Cream or Fruit Pie	Ice Cream Slice
Layer Cake	Ice Cream Pie
Biscuit Tortoni	Nesselrode Pudding
Ice Cream Sundae	Parfait
Sultana Roll	Ice Cream Eclair with Chocolate Sauce

Rolls and Butter　　Coffee, Demi-Tasse, Tea, or Milk

MAKE-UP MENU (H)

Fresh Fruit Cup	Half Grapefruit Maraschino
Avocado with Diced Celery Dressing	Shrimp Cocktail
Seafood Cocktail Copley	Orange and Grapefruit Cup
Antipasto	Assorted Canapes

Celery　　Radishes　　Olives

Consomme Pastina	Chicken Broth with Rice
Chicken Gumbo Creole	Tomato Bouillon en Tasse

Cream of Tomato

Potatoes:　Delmonico　　Hashed Brown　Au Gratin
　　　　　　O'Brien　　Lyonnaise　　Oven Brown
Baked:　　Long Branch French Fried　　Julienne

Menu H *(Cont.)*

Buttered Green Peas	String Beans Orientale
Buttered Mixed Vegetables	Buttered Green Beans
Buttered Lima Beans	Carrots Vichy
Whole Kernel Corn Mexicaine	Garden Spinach
Buttered Brussel Sprouts	Braised Celery

Buttered Asparagus

Chef's Salad	Tossed Green Garden
Chiffonade Salad　Floridian Salad	Salad Bowl

Fruit in Aspic　Waldorf Salad　Combination Salad
Cottage Cheese and Pear Lettuce and Tomato Salad
French, Russian or 1000 Island Dressing

Fruit or Cream Pie Sultana Roll Nesselrode Pudding

Layer Cake	Frozen Pie	Parfait
Biscuit Tortoni	Sundae	Ice Cream Slice (Brick)

Ice Cream Eclair with Chocolate Sauce

　　　　　　　　　　　　　　　Ice Cream Cake

Rolls and Butter　　Coffee, Demi-Tasse, Tea, or Milk

MAKE-UP MENU (I)

Fresh Fruit Cup	Half Grapefruit Maraschino
Avocado with Diced Celery Dressing	Shrimp Cocktail
Seafood Cocktail Copley	Assorted Canapes
Antipasto	Orange and Grapefruit Cup

Celery　　Radishes　　Olives

Consomme Pastina	Chicken Broth with Rice
Chicken Gumbo Creole	Tomato Bouillon en Tasse

Cream of Tomato

Potatoes:　Hashed Brown Julienne　　French Fried
　　　　　　Delmonico　　Lyonnaise　Oven Brown
Baked　　O'Brien　　Long Branch　Au Gratin

Petit Pois au Beurre	String Beans Orientale
Buttered Mixed Vegetables	Buttered Green Peas
Buttered Lima Beans	Carrots Vichy
Whole Kernel Corn Mexicaine	Garden Spinach
Buttered Brussel Sprouts	Braised Celery

Buttered Asparagus

Chef's Salad	Salad Bowl
Chiffonade Salad　Floridian Salad	Combination Salad

Fruit in Aspic Waldorf Salad Lettuce and Tomato Salad
Cottage Cheese and Pear　Tossed Green Garden Salad
Choice of Salad Dressing

Fruit or Cream Pie	Ice Cream Slice (Brick)
Layer Cake	Ice Cream Pie
Biscuit Tortoni　Sultana Roll	Ice Cream Cake
Ice Cream Sundae　Baked Alaska	Parfait
Glace Meringue	Bombe Glace

Ice Cream Eclair with Chocolate Sauce

Rolls and Butter　　Coffee, Demi-Tasse, Tea, or Milk

Banquet Room Layouts

Excessive crowding in a banquet is a frequent cause for complaint by patrons. This is one phase of banquet operation where fairly specific formulas can be set forth as a guide.

If circular tables approximately 72 inches in diameter are used to seat 10 to 12 patrons each, a minimum of 10 square feet of floor space per patron is a safe guide to avoid overcrowding.

If long tables, 30 by 72 inches or 30 by 96 inches are used, seating eight to 10 patrons, the absolute minimum should be eight square feet per patron. Knowlege of the square footage of any room will indicate the reasonable seating capacity.

Banquet Personnel

Banquet Manager

The position of a banquet manager is an important one. He is responsible for the selling, booking, arranging, and serving of all banquet functions. These functions include dinners, luncheons, suppers, special breakfasts, dances, teas, weddings, anniversary parties, meetings, fashion shows, commercial displays, pageants, and various civic functions. He is responsible for arranging local publicity stories after he has the permission of the people planning the banquet. This should be done at the time the preparations are made. Frequently, the patrons will prefer to send out their own publicity.

Unless every detail of the agreement made between the hotel or catering establishment and the chairman of the banquet committee is in writing, misunderstandings are bound to arise. The person who sells the banquet should see to it that there is a contract or letter containing all details, signed by the chairman of arrangements or some equally responsible person. Copies of the menu selected should be distributed to the manager, chef, pastry chef, banquet headwaiter, beverage and accounting departments, head checker, and steward. To minimize the possibility of error or omission, these menus should include all special arrangements that have been made.

Arrangements may have been made for floral displays, wedding canopies, ice cream service parades, multicolored spotlights, patriotic motifs, public address or photographic equipment, radio or television hook-ups, or other special requirements. All these details should be listed on a function sheet and sent to the various department or subdepartment heads concerned with making the necessary arrangements.

Weekly lists of functions should be prepared and dispatched to all appropriate department heads. Signatures should be required to ensure the actual receipt of these lists. Daily function lists should be delivered to all department heads concerned, to remind them and to permit them to make last minute arrangements. These schedules for advance notification should be spelled out carefully to avoid difficulties resulting from last minute details.

The final arrangements for every function should be checked by the banquet manager or an assistant responsible to him. For future reference, approval of arrangements should be initialed by the banquet manager or a delegated representative.

Banquet Headwaiter

The duties of the banquet headwaiter are considerably more complex than those of the headwaiter in a public dining room. Each function has different arrangements and personnel requirements. The banquet headwaiter must draw up the floor plan and notify the housekeeper of the room and equipment requirements. He must also check linen supplies, floral decorations, special menu cards, programs, place cards, and ticket collecting arrangements, if tickets are used. His major responsibility is, of course, the service. Engaging extra waiters, captains, and bus help is his responsibility, as well as maintenance of their time records and the authorization of payment vouchers for wages due.

The banquet headwaiter must obtain a verification of his count of the number of persons served from the head checker or the chef, and prepare the check for payment or signature. He must determine in advance, on information received from the credit manager, whether cash payment is required. He must collect for all checks not approved in advance for credit.

Serving the food is the difficult part of the banquet headwaiter's job. Timing the courses so that all guests are served and finished at approximately the same time is no simple trick and requires complete cooperation from everyone concerned.

Chef

The chef must estimate the required amount of food sufficiently in advance to permit proper purchasing. He must arrange a time schedule for food deliveries to his department and prepare his requisitions accordingly. Supervision of all preparation details and the service to the waiters is his responsibility. If he needs extra help in his department for the banquet, he must engage them after appropriate approval has been given, maintain time records, and authorize wage vouchers.

Steward

The steward must supervise the supplying of all special banquet equipment and check refrigerators for storage of items prepared in advance of service. Control over warewashing, storage of leftovers, and proper restorage of all equipment used for the banquet are also his responsibility.

Supervision of Extra Employees

Banquets of any size require extra help in the kitchen for preparation and dishwashing, and in the dining room for service. Since these extras are not regularly employed, their work may be deficient and require more supervision, which means that there should be an adequate staff to supervise banquet service. The crew of captains is too often reduced to a minimum since the more there are, the less each waiter's share of gratuities. Unless there are specific union requirements, the person in charge of food operation should be the only one to decide the ratio of the number of captains to the number of covers. Failure to observe this point can result in poor service and loss of repeat business.

In the absence of definite union requirements, decisions regarding the proper number of captains will depend largely on the menu, the type of service expected, and the architectural features of the dining room. To achieve outstanding service, it is advisable to have one captain for every five or six waiters. For less elaborate service, one captain may be able to adequately supervise eight or 10 waiters, but certainly no more.

Extra employees engaged for banquets are usually paid on a per-meal basis, which is usually something under four hours. They should report early enough to be thoroughly briefed before the meal so that they will know the menu and where to find everything that they will need.

Interdepartmental Functions

The supervision of the checkroom must be delegated to a responsible employee unless it is handled by a concessionaire. If the use of the checkroom facilities has not been included in the cost of the function and gratuities are permitted, the accounting department must be consulted on engaging checkroom attendants who must be issued proper working instructions. The supply of checks and hangers must be checked in advance.

In a hotel, the housekeeping department must schedule a sufficient number of housemen to prepare the dining room for the banquet and to clean up afterward.

Many hotels have a number of banquet rooms, and patrons must be directed to the proper area. The superintendent of service is held responsible for instructing all uniformed employees who may direct guests to the location of a function. The assistant manager in charge of the front office must similarly be charged with the responsibility of giving these same instructions to all front office employees. A schedule of daily events posted near each street entrance will minimize the number of guests' questions. The bulletin board should provide complete information, such as the room location, which elevator to use, or the location of a convenient stairway.

The chief engineer must be notified of all the requirements that are under his jurisdiction. Any special electrical, carpentry, or painting work should be specified in writing. The expected schedule of each function should be included in the notification to the chief engineer so that a responsible employee in his department can be assigned to the operation of lighting and ventilation equipment.

The head house officer must be notified in advance of the type of function and the need for special protection by the local police department if it is warranted.

The beverage department must be informed of the beverage requirements so that extra help may be engaged in advance. Supervision of banquet beverage service is extremely important to prevent errors or faulty handling. Quantity mixing of standard cocktails in advance is allowed only under certain conditions. Local, state, and federal regulations must be complied with in all respects. The accounting department must provide beverage checkers to control the service of individual beverage orders.

Supervision of interdepartmental functions in medium-sized or large hotels will generally be handled best by a banquet manager or his assistant. Since this work must take in several departments that have other tasks to perform, the specific authority of this employee must be carefully charted.

13

Public Cafeterias

Cafeteria Management

The traditional cafeteria with its long counter laden with a huge assortment of foods had its greatest growth during the 1920s and 1930s, when it provided inexpensive hot meals to a large market: working people. These cafeterias were located in central city business districts. They were huge places, noisy and crowded, with no frills, no decor, and minimum service. The only service provided was aimed at keeping the long lines moving and the seats turning over. Menus were gigantic, with some operations offering as many as 300 items, including 20 or more hot entrées, large selections of soups, salads, fresh vegetables, and potatoes, and freshly baked breads, rolls, and pastries. Many offered ethnic dishes for their foreign-born customers. These operations were profitable because of low wage scales and large sales volume.

Few full-line public (for profit) cafeteria operations have survived. Significantly, the cafeteria business is the healthiest today in the South, where wage scales are still the lowest in the country. Cafeteria operators who have survived are those who have adjusted their businesses to changing market, social, and economic conditions. Specifically, they have done the following:

1. They have recognized that eating habits have changed, and they have altered their menus accordingly.

2. They have looked for new, more promising locations in the suburbs when their center-city operations have begun to decline. In many cases, this decline has been due not only to the general decline in downtown areas but also to the trend toward subsidized employee cafeterias and other types of in-plant feeding by large employers

3. Today's full-line cafeteria operators have developed new markets to replace the demand lost to employee cafeterias. They now identify their markets as young families and older, retired persons— both groups with limited income for discretionary activities such as dining out.

4. In catering to this new market's increased level of education, sophistication, and standard of living, modern cafeteria operators place great emphasis on elegant decor and extra services. Dining rooms have thick carpets, upholstered chairs, comfortable booths, chandeliers, and paneled walls hung with paintings. Dining room attendants pour free refills of coffee, and in some places, they carry trays for the patrons. For families with small children, high chairs equipped with wheels and tray rests permit the child to be wheeled safely through the serving line while the mother selects the meal. Some cafeterias have cocktail service or offer beer and wine on the serving line.

5. Today's successful cafeteria operators have adapted their operating methods to meet the economics of the labor markets. Although a large selection of items is still offered, the menu is greatly reduced from the huge selection once offered. Many chain companies are turning from complete on-premises production to central commissary operations or are supplementing their menus with partially prepared or convenience items.

6. They are designing their new operations for improved use of space and labor productivity. Smaller menus and centralized production mean smaller serving areas and kitchens, with a greater proportion of space used for seating. Smaller dining rooms are built containing 200 to 300 seats, compared to a large operation of 400 to 500 seats in an old-style cafeteria.

Cafeteria service has been adapted to other types of merchandising programs. Some fast-food operators use a modified cafeteria style of service. Other applications are the low priced steak house and prix fixe soup operations.

Operating Aspects of Cafeteria Management

Food Merchandising and Display. Nowhere is the appearance and display of food more important to sales than in cafeteria operations. People eat with their eyes, and many extra, impulse sales can be made if items look too good to pass up. Clean, neat counters, well arranged for the customers' view, are essential. Hot foodpans should be changed frequently to prevent dried-on crusts of food from building up around the sides. Spills should be wiped up immediately. Some hot mixtures such as stews or goulashes can be merchandised by dishing them into casserole dishes in the kitchen and garnishing them with a rosette of whipped potatoes or a hot biscuit. Not only is the appearance on the steam table improved, but portioning is more accurate and service is speeded on the line. Small pans with a few attractive portions also appear much fresher than one large pan half full of food, swimming in sauce, and steam-table-tired. If moist heat is used, pans should fit tightly into the steam table inserts to prevent steam from escaping and reducing the visibility of the food.

Cold food items must also be attractively garnished and arranged so that the display is highly visible to the patrons. Cold pans and ice beds must be kept clean and fresh. It is on the cold food counters—salads, appetizers and desserts—that the extra, impulse sales are made.

Effective lighting of the food displays can improve sales volume. Since fluorescent lighting can change color values, incandescent display lighting is usually preferable. Elongated incandescent bulbs are available for installation under the pick-up shelves, at the steam table, and over cold food displays. Spotlights can highlight special displays such as carving stands.

The more leisurely pace of the modern cafeteria operation permits merchandising opportunities not possible in the old high-speed, fast turnover cafeteria. Many cafeterias now feature steaks and chops cooked to order, roasts carved on the line, and sandwiches made to order. The customer can place his steak order on a special telephone in the lobby and have it served in the dining room or as he approaches the end of the serving line. Some cafeterias even encourage the patrons to dish their own ice cream and concoct their own sundaes (which incidentally saves on payroll costs.)

The most difficult aspect of cafeteria merchandising is keeping food fresh and appetizing during slow periods. Many suburban cafeterias do not attempt to operate in off hours, closing down between lunch and dinner and in the later part of the evening. Other operators remove all hot food from the steam table and convert to a limited to-order menu, with all cooking and plating done in the kitchen. Attractive color photographs of the menu items are displayed at the hot food section of the serving line.

Supplying the Line. Having attractive, well-merchandised displays implies that the counters are kept well supplied. This frequently requires that one or more employees be assigned to the job of "runner" or "supply." This person must anticipate what items will be needed on the line and how soon, so that he can coordinate his supply function with the kitchen production, especially for items prepared in small batches. Supplies of china, trays, silverware, and glassware must also be maintained.

Menus. The menus offered in most public cafeterias include a combination of standard items and daily specials, which usually appear on some cyclical basis. Within this cycle, however, some menu flexibility is available to the cafeteria operator that is not available to the table service restaurant operator who uses a printed menu. Within the limitations of his serving-counter space, the cafeteria operator can vary the number and type of items offered each day. Leftovers can be added to the menu and "run out." If inclement weather threatens to reduce sales on a given day, an item cam be eliminated from the menu, forcing sales to other, more perishable items. The same principles can be used to alter the sales mix during the meal period. If a production item such as a stew or mixture is not selling, its position on the steam table can be shifted, or a more popular (but perhaps less profitable) item can be removed from the menu to force a shift in the sales mix and reduce the amount of prepared food left over.

New mobile serving equipment also permits flexibility in menu planning that was not previously possible. Specialized carts and serving counters are available that can be used for specified meal periods or seasons of the year. For example, in hot weather, greater emphasis can be placed on merchandising cold plates and salads by placing an extra cold pan or a salad counter on the line; in cold weather, the same space can be used for a hot cart offering hot carved sandwiches. Different configurations can also be arranged for lunch and dinner menus or for weekday and Sunday menus.

Keeping the Line Moving. Slow-moving lines can be exasperating to customers who are in a hurry, or to families with small children, and can ultimately lead to lost sales volume. To prevent waits, the serving counters must be kept fully supplied with food items and ware. Counter personnel can also encourage customers to select their entrées before they reach the hot counter. Menu boards with prices should be prominently located in the lobby or at the beginning of the serving line so that customers can be considering their choices in advance. It may also help to have prices displayed prominently on the serving counters, since price is a major consideration for the cafeteria's primary market.

Physical layout can also be a factor in the speed of the line. For a straight line cafeteria, sufficient space should be provided in the line for one customer to pass another with a tray. Since customers are often reluctant to pass others on line, serving counter attendants should be trained to direct them to pass a person who must wait for an item. (Physical layout and traffic flows are discussed in *Profitable Food and Beverage Management: Planning.*)

Dining Room Operations. Some cafeteria operations, especially those in the South, employ servers to carry trays, serve water and extra coffee, and to clear the tables. Generally, however, the function of carrying trays is eliminated except when it is necessary to speed service or to increase seat turnover, or when a large number of patrons are unable to carry their own trays (as with elderly persons or small children). When seating capacity is limited, tray carriers can direct seating and force patrons to share tables in peak periods, thus improving the seat turnover and increasing capacity.

The primary function of dining room personnel is to bus tables. A breakdown in busing quickly produces an unsightly dining room full of dirty tables. It can also be a major source of customer dissatisfaction, as customers must wander about the dining room with their trays, looking for a clean place to sit, or else be forced to clear a place themselves. If the operation must wash and reuse china and silverware during a meal, slow busing can result in a shortage of tableware.

Industrial and Institutional Cafeterias

Cafeteria service is now found much more often in institutional and industrial feeding situations than in public (for profit) operations. Cafeterias are found in manufacturing plants and offices, in schools, colleges, camps, military posts, penal institutions, and homes or hospitals with ambulatory populations. The major distinction between this type of operation and the public cafeteria is the captive nature of the market. In an industrial feeding operation, the employees may be "captives" because of a lack of acceptable commercial dining alternatives nearby, because of a low cafeteria price structure, or because of limited time allowances for meals and breaks. Employee feeding operators still must compete with the "brown bag" lunch packed at home and brought to work. The percentage of employees using a company cafeteria can vary considerably, depending on the price structure and acceptability of the food and service and the availability of alternatives. The brown bag lunch is always one possible alternative for them.

Residents in institutions do not usually have even the brown bag alternative. In such situations, food service management has not only a financial responsibility but also a moral responsibility to provide nourishing, acceptable meals to the institutionalized population. The marketing techniques described in *Profitable Food and Beverage Management: Planning* can be used to measure acceptability and to determine needs and preferences of the institutionalized market group.

Employee Cafeterias

The first employee cafeterias were established to provide low cost, nutritious meals on the premise that an improved diet would lead to healthier, more productive workers. Later it was found that subsidized employee cafeterias kept workers from taking too much time for lunch and, in some cases, kept them out of nearby taverns and bars.

Modern employers are greatly concerned about worker productivity. The emphasis on providing nutritious meals has been enlarged to include consideration of the workers' total environment. The employee cafeteria has expanded into an entertainment and recreational complex, providing not only dining facilities (often with several types of service available), but also lounges, games, arts and crafts, movies, and sports facilities. It is felt that by providing recreational facilities for the workers on their lunch breaks, productivity is improved, especially when the workers are engaged in monotonous, repetitive types of work.

Even when increased productivity is not an objective of the food service, many employers consider the cafeteria an important fringe benefit and are willing to provide sizable subsidies for its operation. On a per-employee basis, cafeteria subsidies are usually much less costly and more visible to the employees than other types of fringe benefits. In some unionized companies, cafeteria prices are a bargaining point.

Institutional Cafeterias

Cafeteria service is used extensively in school and college food operations. In the school lunch program, children may pick up assembled trays from a window or hatch-type serving line. These meals may be fully prepared in the school or they may be delivered preprepared and assembled from a central kitchen or by a private contractor. Frequently, the school's dining room is a multipurpose room that also serves as the gymnasium and assembly room. The kitchen may contain only a reconstituting oven, a sink, a refrigerator, and a compactor for the waste.

College and university food services include several types of cafeteria operations. Cash operations may be run as public cafeterias for students who live off campus. For those living in residence halls, contract cafeterias or "commons" offer food services on a contractual basis. In addition, faculty facilities may include a cafeteria operation.

Military posts, nursing homes, hospitals with ambulatory populations, and other types of institutions use cafeteria-style service as the fastest, most efficient way to feed large numbers of people.

Operational Aspects of Industrial and Institutional Cafeterias

Menus. Menus are much more limited in industrial and institutional cafeterias than they are in public operations. In many institutions and school lunch programs, no selection is offered at all, although the trend is away from the nonselective type of menu. When there are no cash sales, as in college commons, the choices are usually limited to two to four entrees, with limited selections of other items. Cash operations usually offer a greater choice, with the number of entrées augmented with short-order items and sandwiches.

Busing. Most industrial and institutional cafeteria operators have adopted self-busing in order to reduce payroll costs. Patrons remove their own soiled dishes and waste to a conveyor belt or dish carts located near the dining area exits. Some institutions using compartment trays and disposable tableware have carried the self-busing principle even further by having the residents deposit their garbage in a container and then place their trays directly onto the circular belt of the tray-washing machine. This eliminates the need for an employee to scrape and stack the trays and to feed them into the machine.

Self-busing not only reduces payroll costs, it also provides a means for clearing tables quickly, an important factor when high seat turnovers must be achieved. Since the patron takes his soiled dishes with him when he leaves, the table is cleared immediately and is ready for the next person.

Monotony Breakers. For a captive clientele, even the best food service eventually becomes monotonous. To relieve the sameness of meal service, special events are scheduled. These may include nationality meals with special menus, decorations, entertainment, and favors. Other themes may be used, such as holidays (real or imaginary), or special types of menus. Steak and lobster dinners with table cloths and candlelight may be served to college residents.

An employee cafeteria may offer a roast beef dinner, with a steamship round of beef carved on the serving line. Management may wish to celebrate a company achievement with a special menu or giveaway item. If facilities are available, picnics, clambakes, or wiener roasts can be a pleasant diversion for institutionalized persons.

Public Relations. In operations such as school or employee food service, the market is composed of the same individuals every day. Communication with these individuals is an important part of the food service manager's job, since his staff and he must keep these individuals satisfied. Calling customers by name and remembering their personal preferences are good for public relations. Employees who deal directly with the customers should be pleasant and courteous in their service. Special requests should be honored whenever possible, as long as they are within the limits of budget and policy considerations and do not disrupt service to other customers.

In any group, there are always a few complainers, and it is important to be able to determine when a complaint is justified and when it is not. College food service managers expect complaints to increase during examination periods as the students give vent to their tensions. Whether or not a complaint is justified, the way in which it is handled can influence the attitudes of the individual and his friends toward the food service just as much as the resolution of the complaint itself.

Many organizations have a food committee that acts as a communications link between the cafeteria users and cafeteria management. The committee receives all complaints and suggestions and screens out those it considers invalid or unjustified. The rest are then discussed with the cafeteria management at regularly scheduled meetings. Alert management can often use the food committee as more than a complaint pipeline. By being responsive to customer dissatisfactions and receptive to new ideas and suggestions, management can achieve a good rapport with the customers. Food committee members can also provide a customer's viewpoint on proposed changes in the operation, on new products or recipes, or any other ideas offered by cafeteria management.

Coffee Cart Service

Coffee cart service is an important part of many large, industrial food service operations. Commercial restaurant operators may also operate coffee cart services in nearby office buildings to supplement their luncheon sales. In downtown areas where there is a high density of multitenant office buildings, commercial operators may specialize in cart service alone, operating in a number of buildings under agreements with the building owners.

For employers, taking refreshments to the workers means less time spent on breaks and increased productivity following the breaks. Employees benefit from the convenience of having their refreshments delivered to their work areas and not having to go to the cafeteria or to a public take-out store. For the food service operator, coffee carts provide a source of additional revenue and utilize some of the excess cafeteria workers' time in the off hours.

The products vended from coffee carts are determined by the market on each cart route and the carrying capability of the carts. In the morning, hot beverages, juices, and baked goods (such as doughnuts, danish, muffins, and rolls) are usually the best sellers. On afternoon runs, cold drinks, juices, desserts, fruit, and snacks (such as cookies and potato chips) may be preferred. Some carts are equipped to carry ice cream. When carts are operated at lunch, they may also carry soup and prewrapped sandwiches in addition to desserts, beverages, and snacks. Lunch-time operation is undertaken only when there is a full-time cart staff available, as in the case of the specialized commercial operator.

The carts used may be ordinary utility carts equipped with trays of pastries, insulated containers of coffee and hot water. Or they may be of the latest design, with a premix carbonation dispensing system for soft drinks and specially designed storage sections for ice cream, milk, cream, additional varieties of canned soft drinks, and dispensers for cups, napkins, and so on. Major operators of coffee carts often have custom-designed carts to meet their specific needs.

Cart operators have found that sales are maximized if the carts operate on specific routes, stopping at specified locations at pre-determined times. In this way, the employees know when and where to expect their cart and are prepared to make their purchases. Therefore, cart routes must be planned not only to maximize sales with minimum travel between stops but also to coincide with the work schedules of each shift in each department. In some cases, union work rules specify break times, and the cart operator must be prepared to sell at those times.

Coffee Service

The most recent development in self-service is the Office Coffee Service (OCS). The OCS operator provides coffee brewing equipment for an office location and sells kits containing ground coffee, sugar, stirrers, cups, and powdered cream or lightener. The kits may also contain tea bags, cocoa mix, or dried soups. The OCS operator keeps the machines repaired, but making the coffee and cleaning the area is done by the user. Most machines are very simple to operate, and brew 8- to 12-cup batches.

Most OCS locations are small offices, plants, or stores that are too small to warrant a manual food service or an expensive, full-size vending machine. In many cases, the coffee is available free to the employees; in other cases, a small vending machine is used, and a small charge is made to recover the cost of the service.

Buffets and Smorgasbords

Buffets are becoming increasingly popular, both with food service operators and with the public. For the operator, buffet service provides considerable opportunity for reducing labor costs and flexibility in the selection of items to be offered and in the use of leftovers. Because of the lower menu prices, reduced tipping requirements, and the unlimited portions, the buffet seems to offer the public a better value than table service.

Buffets may be of many types. Brunch buffets are very popular in some areas on weekends. A commercial restaurant may offer a special buffet lunch or dinner to boost sales on low-volume days, or it may operate a buffet all the time. One very popular type of service offers appetizers, salad, and breads buffet style, with the rest of the meal served at the table. Occasionally, a luxury restaurant may display menu items—usually appetizers and hors d'oeuvres—on a buffet table. The guest makes his choice, but then the items selected are plated by the waiter and served to the guest at his table. This style of service applies the merchandising aspects of the buffet to fine table service.

Smorgasbord restaurants are very popular in many areas. A true smorgasbord offers a strictly Scandinavian menu with heavy emphasis on fish and seafood items. Many smorgasbords actually offer a combination of Scandinavian items and other local or national dishes that have appeal for their particular markets.

Buffet service is also very popular for function and group business. It may be used for receptions and cocktail hours before a regular table service banquet. Buffet service lends itself to every type of meal from breakfast to steak roasts. Breakfast buffets are a quick, efficient way to serve breakfast to a group.

Classical and Modern Buffets

The classical buffet offers the elaborately decorated *pieces montees* of the classic French cuisine. These may include ice carvings, tallow or butter sculptures, or sugar-work architectural pieces. Several *grosses pieces* may be displayed, such as whole decorated hams or turkeys.

Materials used for food decoration in the classical manner include raw and cooked vegetables, fresh, canned and candied fruits, herbs, hard-cooked eggs, fish roes, tiny pastries such as tartelettes and barquettes, and cheese spreads or butter piped through a pastry tube. Fruits and vegetables may be carved or arranged to form flowers, birds, decorative borders, or designs in geometric shapes. Coatings such as aspics, *gelées* and *chaud-froid* sauce are often used to preserve the flavor and appearance of the items, to form a background for the presentation, or to provide an adhesive medium for the decorations.

This type of work is the responsibility of the *garde manger* in the French kitchen organization. In a hotel with a large banquet department, the *garde manger* station is usually one of the largest and most important in the kitchen, and the *chef garde manger* is one of the most highly paid chefs. In smaller operations, the executive or head chef may be the only person in the kitchen with the necessary skills for *garde manger* work. A good *garde manger* must have not only excellent cooking skills but also artistic and architectural talents.

Because of the high labor costs involved and the costly food items usually offered on a classical buffet, this type of service commands a very high selling price and is usually limited to banquets or group functions, or occasionally to a special display in an expensive restaurant.

Most buffets offered today are modeled after the classic buffet, but the elaborate decorations are usually limited to a few specialty items such as a ham or turkey. The decorations used frequently carry out some theme. Other dishes on the table are attractively but simply garnished to provide an appealing display. The rigid rules of garnishing and decoration that applied to classic cuisine have been abandoned, but certain guidelines should still be observed in food decoration for buffets:

1. Garnishes used should complement the main ingredients in color, flavor, texture, shape, and size. Overdecoration should be avoided.
2. The proper containers should be used to frame and enhance the items. Silver bowls and platters are used on the most elegant displays, although other materials may be used, such as mirrors, glass or wooden bowls for salads, or bowls carved out of ice. For less elegant displays, stainless steel bowls and trays and serving bowls of china, earthenware, or plastic may be used if they are suited to the menu items.
3. Containers should be of the proper size: large enough so that the food does not hang over the edges of the platters but is contained within any decorative borders on the container. Enough food should be put out so that the bowls and platters do not constantly require refilling, but not so much that the food sits for hours, deteriorating in quality and becoming subject to spoilage. Highly perishable items should be displayed on ice.
4. Inedible decorations should not be mixed with edible food, since some guests may not be able to distinguish the difference when serving themselves. The food should be sliced or cut in manageable pieces so that guests can serve themselves easily.

Table Arrangement

There are many types and shapes of buffet table arrangements. The shape selected should provide enough space for all the items on the menu and put each dish within reach of the guests. For large groups, two or more duplicate arrangements are frequently required to serve the entire group in a reasonable amount of time.

The buffet tables should be located where they become the focal point of the room, yet are easily replenished from the kitchen. Since guests are carrying their own plates, the lines of traffic should be studied and cross traffic minimized.

Food is arranged on the buffet table in the order of the menu. Desserts and appetizers are often displayed on separate tables, and the guests go to each table separately. This speeds service and reduces traffic congestion. In the case of a banquet, the appetizer course may be set up in a separate room for the reception and cocktails.

The arrangement of the food on the table is often enhanced by the use of bases or pedestals to vary the heights of the dishes. Each dish should be presented so that its appeal is maximized. Crowding too many bowls and platters on a table detracts from the overall appearance, and reduces the appeal of individual dishes. A bit of tablecloth should show around each dish to set it apart. Sauces, dressings, and other accompaniments should be placed next to the dishes they accompany, and all items should have the proper serving utensils.

A focal point or centerpiece should be placed on the buffet table where it is visible to guests entering the room and to those already seated. This centerpiece is usually a floral piece, but it may be an ice carving or some other decoration that carries out a theme for the meal.

Serving Buffet Style

Some buffets are planned so that the guest helps himself to all dishes offered, taking as much as he wishes. With others, hot entrées are served by attendants, while the guest serves himself the other menu items. Whether servers are used depends on the speed of service desired, the amount of control needed over multiple choices, and the amount of food to be given.

For true buffet style, the guest carries his plate in his hand. Some permanent buffet operations offer lavish buffet-type displays, but provide the guests with trays and a tray rail. This type of service is easier for the guests and reduces the possibility of accidents, but it is not as elegant as the decorated linen-draped buffet table. The use of trays and the permanent counter installation is closer to a cafeteria operation than to a buffet.

Whether the guests serve themselves or are served, personnel are needed to keep the table supplied with plates and freshly filled bowls and platters. Since the buffet's major attraction is its eye appeal, maintaining the table is a very important function. Dishes should be refilled before they are half empty. Generally, when the items are set up, at least two dishes are prepared of every item, and the second dish is reserved for replenishing. This way, the second, full dish is set in the place of the partially empty dish, and the table never has an empty space or a shortage of food. The partially empty dish is then refilled and held in the kitchen until needed. Toward the close of the meal period, the food on display should be as attractive for the latecomers as it was for the first guests served.

The amount of service rendered to the guests at their seats can also vary. Guests may be served only drinks and beverages at their tables, or they may be served everything except salads and relishes. Waiters may carry the guests' plates to the tables and bring refills from the buffet, or they may only clear the dishes from each course as the guests return to their tables for the next course.

Other Types of Self-Service Operations

Fast-Food Operations

Fast-food restaurants are characterized by convenience, speed of service, and low prices. To provide speedy service and minimize customer waiting time, all menu items must be ready for service on demand. Food is therefore prepared for inventory rather than to order. This is the crux of fast-food service and the difference between today's fast-food services and the traditional short-order method of preparation. The difficulty that arises with fast food is that the items that constitute the basis of most fast-food menus—hamburgers, french fried potatoes, and soft drinks—suffer considerable deterioration in quality if not eaten very quickly after they are prepared. Therefore, the operator using the inventory system must become very skilled in forecasting sales, item by item and minute by minute, in order to have an adequate inventory to service the business but not so large that quality deteriorates before the items are sold. In fact, to ensure that the patron is served a product of acceptable quality, some fast-food companies set limits on how many minutes a product can be held. Any products not sold within the time limit must be discarded.

Self-service, fast-food operations are generally based on one of five basic systems:

Counter Operations. This is the traditional snack bar plan. Patrons approach a counter where they give their order to an attendant. The attendant then fills the order, often preparing some of the items himself, and usually collects the payment. The patron either eats at the counter or carries the food away. There are no specific service stations or queues, and each attendant is assigned to service a certain section of the counter.

The Window or Service Station. Customers queue up at windows or service stations where an attendant takes the order, assembles and bags the items, and collects the money. This is the system most commonly used today. Service capacity can be altered directly by varying the number of service stations in operation.

One variation of the window approach has been developed by McDonald's for use in high-volume operations. In this system, the order is taken and the money collected by a counter attendant. As the order is entered for pricing on a computer terminal, it is simultaneously relayed to an order assembler who gathers the items and bags them. With this system, the order assembly and the cash transaction are done simultaneously by two different individuals, thus reducing the time required to service an order.

The Double Window. In this system, the customers queue up at a single window where the orders are placed. They then move in a line to a second window where they receive their bagged order and make payment. This system is applicable where orders are processed along an assembly line. Although it is more difficult to increase capacity with this type of layout, it does provide a more orderly flow of traffic than with multiple service stations and queues, and service is provided on a first-come, first-served basis. It is not applicable to high-volume operations.

Cafeteria Style. Prepackaged items are displayed, and the patrons assemble their own orders. Hot items are prepared and packaged for inventory as in the window operations, except that instead of being arrayed for pick-up by counter attendants, they are displayed for customer pick-up. Other aspects of the operation are similar to the straight-line cafeteria operation.

Clusters. A recent development has been the clustering of several different fast-food operations into a single operation. The first clusters were groups of various types of individually owned operations, with common seating and service areas. Each operator contributed to the maintenance of these areas. In the newest cluster operations, a group of stalls, all under common management, is arranged much like a scramble cafeteria with separate beverage stations. Payment to cashiers is made upon leaving the serving area.

Vending

For today's consumers, self-service by means of coin-operated machines has become an accepted way of life. One can purchase everything from ice cubes to hosiery, from photographs to insurance policies, from dry cleaning to I.Q. tests from a coin-operated machine. In this text the discussion of vending is limited to food products vended for on-premises consumption and to cigarette and tobacco vending.

Vending is probably the ultimate in self-service. It also permits service in remote places and at off hours when manual service would not be feasible. The field is sometimes referred to as "automatic retailing," or "automatic vending," but operators in the field know that a successful vending business is far from "automatic." Even though the products are mechanically dispensed to the customer, the vending business is essentially one of providing service. Routemen must keep their machines well stocked with products that will sell in each location, and they must keep machines and vending areas clean. Machines must be properly serviced and maintained to minimize mechanical failures, which annoy customers. Because machines are often the only source of food or refreshment available to a certain market, empty or out-of-order machines can cause considerable customer dissatisfaction.

Vending management must also be service-minded in seeking out locations for new machines and in determining what product mix to vend in these locations. An understanding of the market is essential.

Vending Locations. According to *Vending Times* magazine, there were almost 1.1 million vending locations in the United States in 1975. Table 13–1 shows the types and numbers of these locations.

Public locations can include such spots as transportation terminals, stores, entertainment places (such as theaters), arenas, parks, tourist attractions, community centers, or any other public place where there is a potential market for food or refreshments.

Locations in offices, plants, and schools may include a fully automatic cafeteria offering vended cold sandwiches and platters, canned or refrigerated entrées that the customer heats himself in a microwave oven, hot and cold beverages, ice cream, desserts and pastries, milk, snacks and candies, and cigarettes. This type of operation is usually found in small companies or locations that do not provide a large enough market for a manual cafeteria operation, but where the market requires a more extensive selection than only beverages and snacks. An automatic cafeteria operation usually still requires an employee on the premises to service the machines and keep the vending area clean and stocked with accessory supplies.

Table 13–1. Vending Locations, 1975

	Total Locations
Plants, factories	195,000
Primary and secondary schools	19,000
Colleges, universities	7,000
Public	590,000
Government and military	9,000
Offices	125,000
Hospitals and nursing homes	15,000
Other	120,000
Total	1,080,000

Source: *Vending Times,* Vol. 16, No. 6–A, June 1976.

Schools or employee feeding operations may also provide some vended items in conjunction with a manual cafeteria operation. Cigarettes, hot and cold beverages, candy and snacks may be vended to ease pressure on the serving lines. Employees who bring their lunches from home can purchase a beverage from the machines without going through the serving line. Vending machines may also provide improved control over small items such as cigarettes and candy. In locations such as in hospitals or plants where the employees work on evening or night shifts vending machines provide service for workers when the manual cafeteria is closed.

Products Vended. The basic and most profitable products in most vending operations are the "Four C's": coffee, cold drinks, candy, and cigarettes. Machines vending highly perishable items such as sandwiches, milk, and refrigerated entrées are usually the least profitable because they require daily servicing, and unsold merchandise must be discarded. These less profitable machines are usually offered only in an automatic cafeteria location where the wider selection of items is required by the market, and daily servicing of a group of machines is feasible. Table 13–2 shows the composition of vending sales in 1974, as reported by the National Automatic Merchandising Association.

Types of Machines. Candy and cigarette machines are the least costly to operate and the least expensive to purchase. Mechanical machines are available that do not even require an electrical outlet. These

Table 13–2. Vending Sales in 1974

Items Vended	Composition of Sales at Retail	Average Sales Per Machine
Cigarettes	25.35%	$2319
Candy nuts, gum and biscuits		
(5¢ or more)	10.57	1298
Cold cup beverages	10.10	2537
Hot cup beverages	17.05	3151
Ice cream	.61	978
Milk	5.31	2613
Sandwiches, salads, pastry, etc.	14.04	2563
Hot food (all types)	2.66	1962
Bottled and canned drinks	2.55	2720
Misc. vending machine prods.	2.77	830
Total or Averages for Above	91.01	$2186
Sales other than through machines	8.99	
Total sales	100.00%	

Source: *Vending Times*, Vol. 15, No. 6-A, June 1975.

machines have rather small capacities, however, that limit their use to low-traffic locations. Electrically operated machines have considerably larger capacities and also provide for illuminated display panels and other merchandising devices.

Cold-drink machines may be can vendors or post-mix machines. Because of the bulk of the cans, can vendors have a limited capacity and are not as profitable as post-mix machines, which have a much greater capacity. "Post-mix" means that the drink syrup and carbonated water are mixed after the coin is inserted in the machine. These machines require water and electrical connections and more maintenance and servicing than a can vendor.

Coffee machines usually dispense more than coffee. Practically all coffee vendors also dispense hot cocoa, and many also dispense tea and hot soups. Some of the modern machines are "fresh-brew," brewing each cup of coffee individually from ground coffee; others reconstitute a freeze-dried powder or concentrated coffee syrup.

Vending machine manufacturers usually offer a complete line of machine types, all of uniform sizes and with coordinated exteriors, so that an installation of a group of machines will present an attractive appearance. A number of extra features may be offered on the machines, such as slug detectors, coin changers, a wide range of pricing alternatives, self-cleaning features, and product alternatives such as no ice, extra ice for cold drinks, extra lightener, extra sugar for hot beverages, and interchangeable parts for ease of maintenance.

The number and type of machines to be installed in a location will depend on the number and type of clientele expected to patronize that location and the amount and type of items they will buy. The space available for a vending alcove, the machine capacities required, and the amount of servicing needed will also affect the number and type of machines selected. Vending managers try to achieve a balance of machines to minimize the number of servicing trips required for a particular location. Other than product perishability, the factors determining servicing requirements are the sales volume and cleaning requirements.

14

Other Types of Sales and Delivery Systems

Food Service in Hospitals and Nursing Homes

Food service for patients in hospitals and nursing homes fills an extremely important role that has no counterpart in other food service establishments. Diet is an important factor in the healing process. Not only must each patient's meals be planned in consideration of his particular condition, but the food must also be appealing and acceptable to the patient. Food which the patient finds unacceptable and does not eat contributes nothing to his convalescence.

Types of Service

Hospitals must feed patients, visitors, unskilled employees, nurses, and the professional staff, and to do this, several different types of service are required. In many instances, several partially or totally different menus are used. The following types of food service may be found in a hospital:

1. Tray service for patients. Trays are assembled in a central kitchen or in pantries on the patient floors.
2. Dining room service for ambulatory patients.
3. Cafeteria service for employees.
4. Table service dining room for physicians and executive staff.
5. Snack bars, canteens, or coffee shops for staff and visitors. These are frequently operated by the hospital's volunteer organization as a fund-raising activity.
6. Some form of vending service may be used to supplement other types of service or to provide service at off hours in place of manual service.

Patient Tray Service. Of the various types of service listed above, patient tray service comprises the largest portion of hospital food service. In most hospitals, trays are assembled in a central kitchen and sent to the patient floors on vertical tray conveyors or dumbwaiters, or in food carts via elevators. This is in contrast to the older method of decentralized service in which food is sent in bulk to serving pantries on the floors where trays are then assembled. Decentralized service is now used only where logistics prohibit the use of tray carts.

Centralized tray assembly offers numerous advantages: more efficient use of labor, improved control over food and reduced waste, better supervision and checking of the finished trays, use of less space and less equipment, and reduction of maintenance.

The disadvantage of centralized tray assembly is that the time lapse between plating the food and delivery to the patient can be quite detrimental to the quality of the meal. Breakfast eggs and toast are especially difficult items to serve in this manner. When the old serving pantries were located close to the patient rooms, breakfast trays were assembled as the patients were readied by the nursing staff. In the central kitchen, trays are assembled in order of the room numbers, without knowing which patient is ready for his breakfast tray. The result is that some meals may stand for quite a while before being served. Some hospitals have reached a compromise by having breakfast eggs and toast prepared in small floor pantries, while the rest of the tray is assembled in the central assembly area.

The scheduling of tray delivery can be a complicated procedure. In a central assembly process in a large hospital, tray assembly may continue for more than an hour, with finished trays arriving on each floor successively at regularly scheduled times. These times must be established in conjunction with the nursing service schedules, and every effort must be made to deliver trays on time. A delay by food service can seriously upset nursing care schedules for the rest of the shift. Delays can also upset the patients, especially elderly or custodial care patients for whom meal time is the highlight of the day.

One new approach to meal scheduling is the five-meal plan. Patients are served a continental breakfast early in the morning. Brunch is served at 10:00 or 11:00 A.M., an afternoon snack about 2:00 P.M., and dinner is served between 4:00 and 5:00 P.M., followed by a bedtime snack. There are several advantages to the five-meal plan. First, in essence, it is much more like today's normal eating pattern, with numerous coffee breaks and snacks. In addition, consumption of a number of small meals rather than three large meals is more beneficial to the digestion of elderly and convalescent patients. From an operating standpoint, preparation and delivery of the two main meals falls generally within the range of one work shift, permitting a reduction in payroll costs. Brunch and snack trays are not usually set up on an assembly line but instead are served directly to the patient from a specifically equipped beverage or snack cart. Disposable tableware is usually used. With the early meal limited to juice, coffee, and rolls, there is less interference with early morning nursing care routines and fewer problems with held or late trays for patients undergoing tests.

Patient Menus

The trend toward centralized tray assembly has been hastened by the implementation of selective menus. The old institutional no-choice menu is no longer acceptable to most hospital patients. The difficulty with offering a selective menu is in forecasting the consumption of the various items. With numerous serving pantries, this problem was multiplied. Either too much food was sent to each pantry, causing waste, or too little was sent, causing patient dissatisfaction and operating problems. With a central assembly system, these problems are greatly reduced.

Selective menus, therapeutic diets, and remote tray assembly require some type of preselection on printed menus by the patient (if he is able) or by the dietitian. A common practice is to distribute menus at breakfast so that the patient can select his lunch and dinner for the same day and breakfast for the following morning.

Since all menus are theoretically selected in advance, the exact number of portions required for each item can be prepared. In practice, however, this would require manually tallying or counting every item on every patient's menu. This is a time-consuming task, and the results are apt to be inaccurate. Many hospitals have dispensed with tallying and instead forecast production requirements based on patient census, the number of special diets ordered, and past consumption records.

Methods of Delivery

In high-rise buildings, completely assembled trays may be transported to patient floors by means of tray conveyors. Food is kept hot by means of insulated plate covers and containers or by hot metal pellets placed under the plates. Trays are taken off the conveyor on the proper floors and loaded onto small carts that hold four to six trays each for delivery to the patients' rooms. When properly managed, this method takes very little time between the plating of the food and delivery to the patient.

When tray conveyors are not feasible, trays are loaded into carts for delivery to patient floors. Several types of carts are used. One type contains separate sections for hot and cold items. Trays are assembled with all cold items, utensils, and condiments and are placed in the cold section. Hot foods are dished up and put into the hot section. On the patient floors, the proper hot items are then placed on the corresponding tray.

The disadvantage of this cart system is that the completely assembled trays are not inspected by the dietitians. A more modern type of cart contains hot and cold zones separated by flexible bumpers. The trays are separated into "hot side" and "cold side" by a ridge which is aligned with the insulating bumper. Trays are completely assembled and inspected before being loaded into the carts. A third type of cart contains no heating elements or refrigeration. Food is plated and placed in insulated containers or on hot pellets. An alternative method is to plate and transport all food in a chilled state and reheat it in a microwave oven just before serving.

A recent development in tray service equipment is a completely insulated tray and cover. The tray has compartments that separate hot and cold foods and maintain the proper temperatures. These trays require no special carts and can be stacked so that an entire wing or group of rooms can be served without the servers retracing their steps.

Serving Trays

In many hospitals, trays are distributed to the patients' rooms by members of the dietary staff. In other hospitals, the dietary department is responsible only for delivering the trays to the patient floors where the nursing staff delivers the trays to the rooms and then returns them to the cart or conveyor. Whatever method is used, it is essential that the dietary management and nursing service supervisors work together to coordinate their schedules and the supervision of the tray delivery process.

Hotel Room Service

Hotel room service is probably the least labor-productive way to serve food and beverages, but room service is a requirement in a high quality hotel.

Low productivity in room service is caused by several factors. First is the logistical aspect. Much of the room service waiter's time is spent in nonproductive walking from the kitchen to the guest rooms and back, and he may spend additional time waiting for service elevators. In addition, the bulk of room service orders are for breakfast, the meal with the lowest average check, or for unprofitable setups—ice, glasses, and mixers for serving drinks (the guest supplying his own liquor). Another frequent contributor to low productivity is a requirement that the department be staffed and prepared to serve on demand from early morning to late at night to a market limited solely to guests registered in the hotel.

There are two basic approaches to the problem of room service profitability:

1. Discouraging room service orders by charging higher prices, adding special room service charges, and providing limited menus or even no menus at all in the guest rooms.
2. Promoting room service heavily, on the assumption that high sales volume will overcome low profitability.

Minimizing room service is an approach taken by many motels and moderately priced hotels. When a room service order is received, it is assembled by a bus person or kitchen worker and delivered by a bellman. Disposable tableware is often used to eliminate the need to retrieve the used dishes.

Promotion of room service business requires a well-staffed and well-equipped room service department. Complete menus and liquor and wine lists are placed in guest rooms. In resorts and convention hotels, special items such as hors d'oeuvres, cheese trays, and fruit baskets may be promoted for parties. Drink lists include liquor by the bottle and may promote special host combination packages for martinis or other mixed drinks.

Speed of service is an important factor in room service, especially at breakfast. In high-rise buildings, one or more service elevators are usually assigned exclusively to room service. A service elevator may be equipped with the supplies required for a continental breakfast, including coffee. Orders are phoned to the waiter in the elevator who assembles the trays as the car travels to the desired floor. Trips are made to the kitchen only when a hot order must be picked up.

To provide guests with at least some level of service without incurring added costs, many motel and hotel operators provide a limited selection of snack and beverage items (soft drinks and mixes) in vending machines on the guest floors or even in the guest rooms. For drink setups, ice machines are located on each floor, and each guest room is equipped with an ice bucket and extra glassware. A vending machine called a "Bell Captain"* is available for use in guest rooms. It is controlled by a special key which is given to the guest when he registers. When he wishes to select a snack or beverage from the machine, he inserts his key and presses a button that releases the merchandise and also registers the amount of the sale at the front desk for posting to the guest's account. Another type of "Bell Captain" machine dispenses a continental breakfast (see Fig. 14–1).

Some hotels provide small refrigerators in each room for storage of snacks and soda and for supplying ice cubes. Others provide free instant coffee, tea, and chocolate, with a small pot for heating water.

---

*Manufactured by Captain International Industries, Inc.

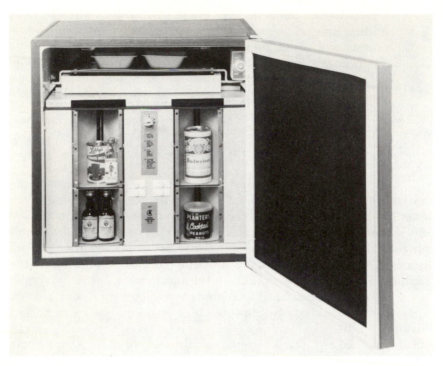

Fig. 14-1. Bell Captain in-room service bar. The unit provides 24 selections. Master controls at the front desk switch the unit off when the guest checks out. *(Courtesy of Captain International Industries, Inc., Montgomeryville, Pa.)*

Room Service Department Operations

The hotel room service department is usually headed by a room service head waiter who supervises the work of the room service waiters and telephone order clerks. A large department may also have one or more captains in charge in the head waiter's absence, and busmen who retrieve the soiled dishes and keep the room service area stocked with supplies.

Because the room service waiter must enter the guest's room and carry out his duties in a situation where he may be alone with the guest, employees selected for this position must be carefully screened. They must be able to work well without supervision and must be of good character and capable of dealing with unusual situations.

Order Taking. Correct order taking is vital to good room service because correcting an error can cause considerable delay. The telephone order clerks should be located in an area away from the noise of the kitchen so that they can hear the guests' orders correctly. The clerks should have a pleasant telephone manner and be familiar with the menu and with food and beverage terms.

Some hotels with a large volume of room service breakfast business place a breakfast order form in each room to encourage guests to order in advance. (See Fig. 2–7 in Chapter 2.) The guest marks his selections, indicates the time he wishes to be served, and puts the order outside his door before retiring for the night. The orders are collected during the night and sorted according to time of delivery. Advance ordering permits orders to be grouped to save steps during delivery; it also provides prompt service to the guest and eases the load on the telephone order clerks during busy periods.

Order Placement and Assembly. For busy periods, room service tables may be set up in advance with linen, china, glassware, and condiments. When the orders are received, the hot items are ordered from the range, and the cold items are assembled either by the waiter or by a helper. The waiter then picks up the hot items and completes the order.

Delivery. The elaborateness of the service will affect the amount of time the waiter spends delivering each order. He may be required only to deliver a tray to the room, obtain the guest's signature on the check, and then return to the kitchen. If a complete meal has been ordered for several people, he may have to arrange the table (opening the dropleaves that are folded in transit), obtain extra chairs, open wine, remove hot food from the warming oven, and perform other finishing touches, all of which can take considerable time.

Dish Removal. Unless the room service department is very large, the waiter who delivered an order is responsible for collecting the soiled tableware. A very busy operation may require a separate bus person for this task, particularly when the equipment must be reused several times during the morning. Soiled room service equipment is frequently put in the corridors, either by the guests themselves or by the housekeeping personnel when they make up the rooms. If this equipment is not removed promptly, the corridors can become very unsightly.

Mobile Catering

Mobile caterers provide meals and snacks in places where manual food service or vending machines are not feasible. Most of the mobile caterer's customers are workers on the job, but others may be travelers, commuters, or those attending a sporting event or recreational facility.

Typical locations for mobile catering sales are construction sites, small industrial plants with no food service facility, large plants which are spread out over a wide area, office buildings, commuter bus and train stations, trucking depots, military posts, colleges, parks, and recreation areas. Special one-time or short-term events such as fairs and expositions may also provide sales opportunities for mobile caterers.

As a rule, the mobile caterer obtains agreements with employers or property owners to provide food service at specified times and days in specified locations. He then puts these scheduled stops together into a route, trying to group the optimum number of stops with a minimum amount of driving time in between. This route is then the property of the contractor, who may sell or lease it to an independent driver.

On the average, a driver route man makes about 20 stops a day with his specially designed catering truck, and he may make four or more stops a day at a good location to provide service to the employees before their shift, for meals, and for coffee breaks.

Many route men are independent operators who own their own trucks and routes and buy their merchandise from a commissary operator. Others may operate trucks on routes leased from a mobile catering company, and some may be employees of that company. Independent drivers set their own selling prices, based on competition and on the prices they pay for the merchandise; company-employed drivers usually work on a commission, with selling prices set by the company.

Sandwiches, hot and cold beverages, pastries, snacks, and dairy products constitute the largest proportion of mobile catering sales. Many trucks also sell cigarettes and candy, canned entrées, and commissary prepared entrées and salads. In some areas, health and sanitation laws may limit the type of items that can be sold from a truck. Time lapses and weather conditions can also limit the type of products offered. Except for coffee, which many drivers make right on their trucks, no food preparation is done by the driver. All food is obtained from a commissary, completely prepared and packaged. The route man usually selects the items and quantities he thinks he can sell on his route.

The route man's job is largely one of selling and public relations. The products he brings to the location and the service he gives can greatly influence the sales volume. The customers at each location are virtually captive, which is the reason for the mobile caterer's business: Only such a caterer can service this remote or temporary market. The competition is often very keen for good locations, and drivers or companies who give poor service or take advantage of the captive aspect of the market by overpricing will often find their locations taken over by a competitor.

Airline Food Service

Airline food service appears to be similar to hospital food service: Service to the ultimate consumer takes place far from the preparation area and out of range of food service supervision. The time lapse between preparation and service is even greater in in-flight feeding than in hospital feeding, with a corresponding increase in the difficulty of maintaining quality. The airline food service, like the hospital, must please a wide range of tastes with a nonselective or very limited menu. Operationally, airline tray assembly employs an assembly-line technique, but there the similarity to hospital food service ends.

Airline food service is primarily a merchandising technique in the highly competitive air travel business. Menus are planned, snacks offered, drinks are merchandised, all in consideration of what the competition is offering on the same route. Special lounges with beverage service and entertainment, choices of wines with meals, delicatessen sandwiches, specialty dishes from internationally known restaurants, chateaubriand carved on special carts, international menus, fruit and cheese trays, espresso coffee, pastry carts, and make-your-own-sandwich promotions are all part of the merchandising program.

To carry out these merchandising programs, flight kitchens on the ground must be prepared to board a wide range of menus, depending on the class of service, destination, and length of flight. Since flight schedules tend to be clustered around the early morning and dinner hours, airline food service must be able to meet peak volumes in very short periods. Furthermore, accuracy is imperative. At 30,000 feet in the air, one cannot run back to the kitchen for a forgotten item. The aircraft must be provisioned not only with enough food and supplies to serve the planned menu but also with a stock of items to meet special requests and unexpected situations. Special meals may also be required for religious or dietary reasons, but these are usually ordered in advance by the passenger.

Operating Systems

Flight kitchen managers spend a considerable portion of their time dealing with materials handling and logistics. They are concerned with types of aircraft and their particular equipment requirements, with coordinating truck movements between the flight kitchen and the boarding areas, and with arrival and departure schedules, as well as the normal requirements of kitchen operations.

Three basic systems are used in serving airline meals: Main items are boarded on the aircraft either in a frozen, chilled, or heated state. Frozen or chilled entrées are reheated on the aircraft in microwave or convection ovens. The entrée and accompaniments are usually preportioned and heated in the casserole dishes in which they are served. For certain first-class service, entrées may be boarded in multiple portion packages and dished up in the plane's galley, or served from a cart at the passenger's seat.

Most meals are served on trays that are preassembled in the flight kitchen with utensils, condiments, and cold items. Hot items are then added at the time of service. For longer flights, such as on transcontinental routes, the longer flying time permits more leisurely service, and the meal may be served in several courses. In first class, particularly, a more elegant service may be offered, with table linen, china, and crystal ware. The use of permanent tableware requires careful planning of logistics to maintain an adequate supply of equipment in each location.

The introduction of the wide-bodied aircraft with greatly increased passenger capacities required the airlines to develop new ways to provide in-flight service. For short- and intermediate-haul flights, some airlines have dispensed with serving full meals on preassembled trays. Snacks are offered, usually consisting of one or more small sandwiches with garnishes, preassembled and wrapped in plastic. A selection of beverages is also offered. This type of meal can be served quickly to a large number of people with less equipment and storage space than full-meal service requires.

Sports Arenas, Race Tracks, Convention Centers, Public Beaches, and the Like. Food and beverage service at sports events, trade shows, and amusement parks is almost an integral part of the action for the patron. The players and staff must also be provisioned. This type of food service has become highly specialized and largely concentrated in a few companies that have the capital and skills required.

Contracts for sports event catering are frequently opened to competitive bidding, and this procedure may be mandated at publicly owned facilities. Since the concession rents paid by operators are an important revenue item for owners, to secure the contract concessionaires frequently agree to pay much higher rents than are economically feasible for typical restaurant operations. As much as 32 percent of sales may be paid on certain items as concession rent. Concessionaires may also agree to operate luxury restaurants to meet the tastes of the affluent sporting crowd, as well as to provide the traditional hot dogs and beer to the less affluent. An investment in the fixed concession plant is often required as well.

The range of products and the high costs, including rents, of providing them call for unusual merchandising and operating skills by the concessionaire. Low-cost items must be presented in such a way that patrons will be willing to pay a high price.

A strong management group must be retained, a group that is willing to travel and deal with the large numbers of temporary and casual employees who must be engaged. Staffing schedules must be flexible to meet the vagaries of weather and relatively popular and less popular events.

Strong and simple controls of revenue are advisable. Accountability of sales outlets, such as stands, on a retail price basis is usual. Employees are held accountable for the retail value of the products issued to them. The lowest possible prices for merchandise must be secured through national purchase contracts, and the suppliers made to bear the cost of storage. The bidding procedures and presentations made to arena owners are the product of sophisticated design and public relations departments of broad-based companies.

PART FOUR

Manpower Management

15

THE PERSONNEL FUNCTION

In recent years, the personnel function in the food service and restaurant industry has grown more complex. Factors such as rapid industry growth, the increasing scope of union activity in the industry, the passage of minimum wage legislation, and high levels of employment across the country have spurred the growth and development of the personnel administration function.

The purpose of the personnel function is the recruitment of employees to staff whatever number of jobs are necessary to service the present or anticipated volume of business. The responsibilities of the personnel department also include the development and administration of employee benefit programs, wage and salary policies, and employee training programs.

When necessary, unless outside counsel is used, the head of the personnel department may represent the organization in union contract negotiations and at meetings held to discuss employees' grievances. Maintaining a continuous check on compliance with the union contract is among the primary responsibilities of the personnel department.

The size of the personnel department is directly proportionate to the size of the organization and its operations. In a small organization, the personnel function is usually combined with some other function, such as the management of the operations.

In large organizations, personnel policies are established at the top corporate executive level and carried out at the unit operating level. In a multiunit operation, where the units are a considerable distance apart and cover a wide section of the nation, the regional personnel directors report to a national personnel director and are responsible for regional and local compliance with overall personnel policy.

Sources of Personnel

When it is necessary to hire employees, various sources are available. The personnel department must understand that hiring of personnel (either as replacement of the present staff or as an addition to it) must be authorized by management, which is responsible for operating results.

Recruiting

In general, when the employees sought are of the management trainee type, it may be advisable for the personnel director to recruit at a college or technical school. Compared with other methods of locating job candidates, on-campus recruiting is probably one of the most expensive in time and effort, but it can also be one of the most productive.

For on-campus recruiting, the person handling the personnel function should first contact the college or university and make preliminary arrangements. The arrangements should cover the college's approval of the plans for on-campus recruiting and the means provided for contacting those students who are likely to be interested in the jobs offered. At these interviews, such matters as employment and growth opportunities, salaries, and benefit programs should be thoroughly discussed with the interested students.

Good candidates for the management trainee positions are often invited to visit the company's office and places of operation and to meet the company's executive and supervisory personnel. Good prospects for executive positions are often worth waiting for, even though it may be some time before they graduate.

Trade shows are another source of prospective employees. There, the individuals who contact members of an organization having a personnel recruitment exhibit are frequently already employed but looking to improve their positions. There are many executives in the food service industry who feel that there is a direct connection between the dates of major trade shows and increases in the turnover of the types of employees who attend those shows.

Newspaper Advertising

The classified advertisement sections of newspapers are widely used for the recruitment of food service personnel. The organization placing the advertisement may choose to list its name, or it may decide to have résumés and letters directed to a box number of the newspaper. This arrangement offers the organization the opportunity to answer only those résumés or letters it selects for reply. The applicants whose letters are not answered do not know the identity of the company that did not select them.

Requiring a job applicant to write to a box number is not likely to elicit responses from those seeking positions as dishwashers, bus boys, and the like. For these positions, the address of the employment office where applicants can be interviewed in person should be given.

Employment Agencies

Private employment agencies charge a fee for their services that is paid by either the employee or the employer. Employment agencies build up lists of potential employees for a broad range of positions and usually can provide job applicants more quickly than any other source.

State Employment Agencies (Public Agencies)

Public agencies also maintain a list of workers available for numerous job categories compiled from those who have registered for unemployment benefits. Before referring individuals, these agencies require a brief description of each job that is open, including hours worked and hourly pay rate or the salary range. There is no charge for their services.

Walk-Ins

It is not at all uncommon for persons seeking employment merely to walk into an establishment and solicit employment, especially if there is a personnel office. Generally, an applicant who does this is applying at the suggestion of a friend or relative already in the organization's employ.

Other Sources

Executives in the food service industry and various industry consultants represent a limited source of personnel. They should be used only for the recruitment of executive personnel. One considerable advantage they can offer is knowledge of the qualifications and abilities of the job applicant.

Nearby schools and colleges, fraternal organizations, military installations, and residential areas may be sources of part-time employees who can effectively augment the regular staff during peak periods.

Institutions housing mentally retarded persons have recently become a source of employees for jobs requiring little or no skill. Mentally retarded persons have proved to be very satisfactory employees if care is taken to assign to them only work that they can handle.

Evaluation of Sources of Personnel

It is difficult to recommend any one particular personnel source because of the many variables involved. A large, multiunit food service organization generally will find it necessary to draw on many

Table 15-1. Data on Job-Seeking Methods

	Percentage of Total Job Seekers	
Category	Method Used	How Obtained
Applied directly to employer	66.0%	34.9%
Asked friends about jobs—		
Where they worked	50.8	12.4
Elsewhere	41.8	5.5
Asked relatives about jobs—		
Where they worked	28.4	6.1
Elsewhere	27.3	2.2
Answered advertisements in local paper	45.9	12.2
Private employment agency	21.0	5.6
State employment service	33.5	5.1
School placement office	12.5	3.0
Civil service test	15.3	2.1
All other methods	54.5	10.9

sources, including colleges and universities, to provide a steady flow of executive talent into the organization. On the other hand, a small restaurant would probably find other sources adequate.

An article that appeared in a recent issue of *Monthly Labor Review* (prepared by the U.S. Department of Labor, Bureau of Labor Statistics) provides some insights into the job-seeking methods used by various groups of unemployed persons. A survey covering white-collar, blue-collar, service, and farm workers indicated that 10,437,000 job seekers utilized one or more of the methods shown in Table 15-1 to seek employment.

It can be seen that job seekers use many ways to find work and that the most effective is applying directly to an employer. This result suggests that when an employer is known, applicants will come to him.

Employers should develop data regarding the efficiency of whatever methods are used to solicit prospective employees. When it is necessary to advertise for job applicants, to recruit on college campuses, or to use employment agencies or industry consultants, records of costs and results should be maintained. Then it can be determined not only which sources brought the most job applicants at the lower cost but also which sources provided the job applicants with the greatest skills and best adaptability to prevailing working conditions.

The Interview Process

When an interview is held, the job applicant meets with a representative of the personnel department or with the person assigned personnel recruitment responsibilities. Job applicants not deemed qualified should be informed quickly and courteously. Some organizations, as a matter of policy, help disqualified applicants by suggesting where job openings exist for their qualifications.

An employment application is filled out by the applicants who have been selected for further processing. Their applications are reviewed by the interviewer, and a face-to-face discussion then takes place.

The screening process is intended to eliminate those applicants who are unqualified or unsuitable in some obvious way; the interview is intended to determine if there are less obvious reasons why the applicant and the job may be incompatible. During the interview, the applicant is informed about the company with respect to its policies and goals relating to such matters as operations, employee relations, and advancements. Also the duties and responsibilities relating to the job are fully explained. If the representative of the personnel department is satisfied with the applicant and the position to be filled is for a management trainee, the next step is for the applicant to be interviewed by the executive for whom (or in whose department) the applicant will work. That executive decides whether to hire the applicant. One of the functions of the personnel department is to make sure that the executives spend their valuable time interviewing only well-qualified applicants.

Although it will be the executive and department heads, not the representatives of the personnel department, who do the actual hiring of management personnel and the more highly skilled employees, the policy may be more flexible with respect to other applicants. The department heads may not have the time or believe that it is necessary for them to interview the low-skilled employees such as dishwashers, potwashers, and kitchen porters. Experience has shown, however, that when employees are hired without being interviewed by the department heads under whom they are going to work, there is a greater likelihood of their proving unacceptable to the department.

It should be standard practice within the personnel department of a multiunit operation, where the units are concentrated in a relatively small area, that hiring for all the units be coordinated. Then an applicant found for a job opening that exists at more than one location can be interviewed by executives and department heads at selected locations and be placed where he will be most suitable.

The Hiring Process

After an applicant is offered and accepts employment, processing begins, and the new employee fills out the required forms. Practical processing controls for each applicant hired should provide the assignment of an employee number, processing an authorized employee requisition, designation of the cost center to which the salary is to be charged, and determination of the authorized starting wage or salary. These controls should also provide for preparation of a folder containing all processing information, which must be kept in the personnel department's file along with the filled-out employment application form. The records should be regularly updated and must always indicate the current hourly wage rate or salary, as well as performance evaluation.

Other Important Aspects of the Personnel Function

Other important personnel functions relate to retaining employees, helping them to acquire skills, maintaining an equitable wage and salary program, and evaluating work performance.

Training Programs

Employee training attempts to increase the level of workers' present skills and to teach new skills required for advancement. Training programs make it possible for a semiskilled worker to qualify for jobs that can be filled only by highly skilled workers, who are usually in short supply.

The personnel department is responsible for the establishment of training programs. However, the scope of the training and the number and type of programs to be given are determined by the operational needs of the organization and the status of the labor market. Many organizations in the food service industry have training programs that enable employees to acquire new skills necessary for advancement. Such training programs, coupled with a policy of promoting employees from within the organization, can greatly boost employee morale.

An experienced instructor is assigned to the formal training program and is made responsible for its development, execution, and the evaluation of the progress made by the individual employees. The skills to be taught are determined with the help of the heads of the operating departments. The objective is to fill as nearly as possible the needs of the organization. The instruction may be given in classrooms, or it may be in the form of on-the-job training. The latter could be given, for example, in a commissary, where an assembly-line type of operation provides an ideal arrangement for teaching certain skills.

The following is a summary of the method by which a job-instruction training program for trainee-employees is conducted:

1. *Prepare the Worker.* The instructor describes the job, explaining exactly what the trainee-employee will be expected

to do. The first part of the instruction will be given away from what is to be the employee's work station.

2. *Present the Job.*   The instructor and the trainee-employee move to the area where the employee is to do his work. The job will be presented to him by having him watch the performance of the duties by the instructor or trained employees.

3. *Tryout.*   The trainee-employee is given the opportunity to actually perform what are to be his duties and thus to show the progress he has made in acquiring the necessary skills.

4. *Follow-Through.*   The instructor, after a brief break-in period, lets the trainee take over the performance of the job. The instructor then makes several follow-up visits to ascertain if the trainee is handling everything well.

The advantages of the four-step training program are obvious. The new employee does not actually take over the responsibilities of a job until he knows how to handle them. He then continues to be watched to make sure he is carrying out his duties in the proper way.

On-the-job training, which is the more popular method of training, tries to have the employee learn everything on the job. With this type of training, the employee goes directly to his work station as soon as he reports for duty. He works alongside an experienced employee who is responsible for breaking him in. There are many advocates of this method of training, which appears to be less expensive than job-instruction training. One serious disadvantage, however, is that the trainee-employee too often is placed abruptly into an operating situation and is required or expected to maintain the pace of more experienced employees.

Training methods designed to teach new skills to employees so that they can be considered for better jobs in the same organization are probably closer to job-instruction training than to on-the-job training. Those who have completed such a program usually are placed on a list of employees ready for promotion as soon as the right job openings become available.

Employee Evaluations

As a rule, evaluations are not prepared for the unskilled categories of employees. Making periodic evaluations of executive and supervisory personnel is valuable, however, and should be done whenever possible. The personnel department is responsible for designing the evaluation forms and having them prepared by management and supervisory personnel whenever evaluations are required of the employees under their supervision.

A point-scoring method should be used to rate work performance. Sometimes, instead of using a point system, the evaluator is asked to comment on different aspects of the employee's work and also to give an opinion as to whether or not the employee is ready for promotion. Such evaluations usually are prepared prior to an employee's annual review and are an important factor in determining whether the employee is entitled to a salary increase or warrants a promotion. If the evaluation does not indicate that an increase in salary or a promotion is warranted, it should lead to a candid discussion between the employee and a designated executive (often the employee's superior) of ways in which work performance may be improved. For the sake of fairness, when possible, more than one evaluation of an employee's performance should be prepared, thus allowing several executives to participate in the evaluation.

Wage and Salary Administration

The establishment of a fair wage and salary program is an absolute requirement if any organization is to avoid a high rate of employee turnover. Needless to say, the wage scale must comply with federal and state minimum wage requirements and with collective bargaining agreements to which the organization is party. It is necessary to seek professional assistance from independent sources when a question arises regarding the interpretation of minimum wage legislation or the applicability of other regulations and agreements.

Wage and salary administration should extend beyond checking adherence to existing laws and union contracts. Wage and salary levels should be periodically evaluated by the personnel department or outside consultants. These evaluations should at least compare the salaries and benefits for selected positions in the organization with those for comparable positions in other organizations in the food service industry. Differences based on geographical location must be taken into consideration. Information relating to frequency and size of the salary increases given to the surveyed organization's employees should also be included with the comparison, as well as other employee benefits.

When completed, the wage and salary evaluation report should be studied by management to determine the strengths and weaknesses in the organization's salary and wage structure and related policies. This study can be used as the basis for future wage and salary policy decisions.

Labor Turnover Reporting

Regardless of the size of the organization, it is necessary to review periodically the reasons for employee terminations and voluntary resignations. Whether the employee was asked to leave or whether he left voluntarily is of equal importance. The fact that there was turnover indicates that there may be something wrong. Each time an employee leaves, advertising, screening, interviewing, processing, and training costs must be incurred to replace him. Aside from these direct costs, there are the possible indirect costs of having a large proportion of inexperienced personnel and low employee morale. High turnover also can result in poor quality operations.

For labor turnover reporting to be truly effective, it should be directly connected with an employee exit interview program. Such programs require that on or prior to the last day of work, the departing employee be interviewed by a designated member of the personnel department or management. The interviewer should endeavor to find the reasons for voluntary resignations. Such probing, when handled properly, may uncover reasons for leaving that may not have been completely explained when the initial notice of resignation was given.

All too often the reasons for terminating an employee—an employee released for a cause—are not given sufficient consideration to uncover the root problem. Closer scrutiny may alert the organization to conditions or situations that must be corrected to eliminate the problem of turnover. An evaluation report on the reasons for terminations and voluntary resignations should be prepared and widely distributed to all executives, including department heads. The following formula can be used in calculating employee turnover percentages:

$$\frac{\text{No. of terminated employees}}{\text{No. of employees on the payroll}} \times 100 = \text{Turnover percentage}$$

Job Enrichment

Traditional personnel practices and job concepts have been challenged somewhat by the concept known as "job enrichment," which is being discussed widely in industries that utilize mass production assembly techniques. Job enrichment is essentially an attempt to give the worker an opportunity to experience a feeling of real achievement, satisfaction, and motivation. This can be accomplished by giving an employee the following:

1. Greater responsibility.
2. Greater variety of duties.
3. Recognition for a job well done.

In the late 1960s a significant amount of publicity was focused on worker boredom and frustration in the automobile industry. High absentee rates and poor job performance were, according to some observers, a direct result of such dissatisfaction on the job. Admittedly the problem of boredom is more acute in the manufacturing and as-sembly-type positions, but the food service industry also has some employees who find their work monotonous. The problems of worker dissatisfaction, lack of advancement, and dead-end jobs can be as real in the food service industry as elsewhere. Some of the larger food ser-vice organizations have recognized this fact and have started to de-velop programs that provide as many workers as possible with some hope and opportunity for advancement. Because the job pyramid nar-rows toward the top, there will always be some employees whose chances for promotion to a better job are limited. To some extent, this is offset by less ambitious employees who may be entirely happy with their present jobs and ask little in the way of career advancement.

Those employees who do seek advancement and who through training programs can be helped to acquire new skills are an asset to any organization. They are valuable to the organization while they are holding their present jobs and should be even more productive after they gain advancement. Employees who have some hope for a better future are better motivated, have higher morale, and are much less likely to leave than employees in dead-end jobs.

Job Rotation

Because of the limitations of job enrichment program, a modification may be considered that tries to relieve the monotony generally associated with the type of work given to unskilled or semiskilled employees such as tableware washers, porters, and kitch-en cleaners. A program of job rotation can be developed whereby various not-too-complicated jobs are rotated at some predetermined interval among unskilled or semiskilled employees. Because the skills required for each job can be learned rather easily the employees holding them should be able to change easily from one to another. When the employees who would be rotated are covered by a union contract, the cooperation of the unions in implementing the program must be obtained.

It is obvious that a program of job enrichment and rotation has important limitations because it can cover only certain positions. There undoubtedly would be additional costs incurred by formulating and implementing such a program. The benefits to be realized, however, might outweigh the costs.

Labor turnover in the food service industry is extremely high compared with that of other industries. This suggests that some of the food service industry's personnel policies should be carefully exam-ined with a view toward changing them.

16

STAFF PLANNING
AND PAYROLL CONTROLS

Within recent years, salaries, wages, and fringe benefits have increased steadily in the food service industry. In many instances, they have risen faster than in other industries, and they now absorb a portion of the food and beverage sales dollar larger than any other individual item of cost or expense. The reasons for such a rise include greater unionization of the food service industry, federal and state minimum wage legislation, and a realization by large and small organizations that, in order to attract and hold employees, more competitive wages and benefits are necessary.

In the past, increasing selling prices was the most common means of offsetting the escalation of wages and other operating expenses (except during periods of government price controls). Consumer resistance to higher prices now usually limits this approach to maintaining profitability.

Although there have been varying degrees of unemployment in recent years, the labor market for qualified food service industry employees remains rather tight. Such a scarcity of labor decreases the ability to reduce staff levels during periods of low activity. In periods of ample labor supply, an organization can cut back its work force with the knowledge that when it will be necessary to increase its staff, labor will be available.

In view of the constraints imposed on management by labor unions, shortages in labor supply, and governmental regulations, management must become more innovative if it is to control labor costs effectively. Efficient labor utilization and payroll control procedures are avenues for keeping labor costs at a manageable level. Management personnel—down to the supervisory level—must be involved in planning, controlling, and implementing labor cost control systems.

342

The Control Process

One of the elements of control is a budget. Carefully prepared financial projections are necessary for profitable operations. Data on past levels of activity are also needed to project future work loads. For newly established operations, general standards or the experience of other operations must be used until the operation accumulates its own history. (See *Profitable Food and Beverage Management: Planning* for a more detailed discussion of budgets and pro forma preparation.)

Effective first-line supervision is also essential to a payroll control system, but this is frequently overlooked. Supervision includes the proper planning of work, scheduling of shifts, and the implementation of efficient work methods, which are discussed in more detail later in this chapter.

Job Analysis

A detailed job analysis can be helpful in identifying any inefficient operations and can also serve as the basis for preparing formal job descriptions. When a job is being analyzed, the worker should be observed performing each of his assigned duties under actual working conditions. Time-and-motion studies provide the most accurate evaluation of job performance. If time studies and actual observations are not possible, careful consideration of the job requirements and estimates of time requirements must be used.

The following questions are often used as a guideline in making a job analysis:

Why is the job done?
Why is it done at this station?
Why is it done at this time?
Why is it done by this employee?

The analyst should observe the performance of the individual components of the job in the proper sequence and determine if any time was lost between the components because of inefficient methods, poor workstation layout, or other hindrances.

Job Descriptions

Job descriptions are required for effective control of labor. To prepare job descriptions, it is necessary to study the information developed in the job analysis. A properly prepared job description should include the job title, department, classification, responsibilities, and qualifications. The duties and responsibilities of a head waiter, for example, are as follows:

1. Handle all reservations for seating in this room.

2. Direct and supervise all aspects of food and beverage service according to the standards established.
3. Ascertain by personal inspection prior to service periods that the service area as well as all utensils, condiments, supplies, and storage areas are clean, orderly, and properly set up, and that all scheduled personnel are on assigned stations.
4. Require musicians and entertainers to adhere to time schedules specified in their agreements.
5. Handle guest complaints courteously and diplomatically, reporting those of a serious nature to your immediate superior.
6. Endeavor at all times to promote sales and to operate this area in an efficient and economical manner.
7. Keep undesirable persons out of this area and maintain proper decorum at all times.
8. Approve all changes on guest checks; also approve all "house" or entertainment checks, and all gratuities on charge checks.
9. Require that established standards of housekeeping and sanitation be maintained at all times.
10. Provide adequate care over all furnishings, equipment, and utensils, including their appearance and condition. Report via prescribed channels any needed repairs, refurbishing, or replacement.
11. Maintain the prescribed degree of electrical lighting during the period the room is open to the public.
12. Hire and train all personnel assigned to this dining room to render proper service: to greet guests pleasantly, to seat them promptly, and to serve food and beverages in a prompt, courteous, pleasant, and willing manner.
13. Require proper dress, appearance, and conduct of all employees in the department, and maintain sensible discipline at all times.
14. Schedule all departmental personnel in accordance with prescribed staffing standards.
15. Develop and maintain a strong departmental organization with clearly defined areas of responsibility and lines of authority.
16. Prepare all records required by management.
17. Determine the quantities of sundry supplies required and see that they are on hand in advance of the time required.
18. Comply with all policies and approved practices, and comply with or execute promptly all orders and requests received from your immediate supervisor.
19. Follow all internal control procedures for revenue and expenses as established.

The prepared job descriptions must clearly state the duties and responsibilities in order to guide the employees in the proper performance of their jobs. Often in trying to cover the job fully, the job descriptions contain, in addition to minor details, methodology for performance of the duties, and thus they become inhibitive rather than guiding. The duties and responsibilities should be stated in broad terms that clearly convey the areas of responsibility.

Efficient Workstation Layout

The job analysis may show that a workstation is not properly designed, causing excessive reaching or walking by the worker. In addition to increasing operating costs, poor station layout causes worker fatigue. The job analysis may also reveal areas where labor-saving equipment should be installed.

Scheduling

The primary purpose of the schedule is to provide the right type and number of employees needed to serve the anticipated number of patrons in accordance with established standards of the operation. Failure to achieve this purpose can either incur excess labor cost or impair service because of insufficient staff. In either case, the operation is affected adversely.

In any operation there is a basic minimum or necessary, fixed staff. As the sales volume increases, a larger staff usually becomes necessary, although the increases are not necessarily proportionate to the sales increase. This is because some jobs are more affected by sales volume than others. Jobs may be classified as fixed, semivariable, and variable:

1. *Fixed.* Employees such as a manager, chef, bookkeeper, and so on whose workloads are hardly affected by changes in sales volumes.
2. *Semivariable.* Employees performing functions such as cooks, pantry men, dishwashers, and so on. Although fluctuations in volume affect their work loads, it is only when the fluctuations are substantial that consideration need be given to revising the numerical staff.
3. *Variable.* Employees performing functions such as servers, bus boys, and so on whose workloads are most sensitive to fluctuations in sales volume. Relatively minor fluctuations in sales volume require changes in staffing requirements.

In a large operation, scheduling of employees is the responsibility of a supervisor or department head. The preparation of the schedule may be delegated to a subordinate. In a smaller operation, the manager usually prepares the schedule. No matter who prepares it, the schedule should be adaptable to fit changing conditions.

Other Scheduling Requirements

In a six- or seven-day operation where employees work a five-day week, it is necessary to provide relief coverage for the sixth and seventh days. In general, employees who are covered by a union contract must be given two consecutive days off in a seven-day period. Sometimes, days off may be scheduled on normally slow days of the week, eliminating at least some of the need for reliefs. Usually, however, most regular full-time positions must have relief coverage. If the regular staff is flexible and the employees can perform several jobs, the problem of providing relief is greatly reduced. Too often, there is a separate group of relief employees, usually the least experienced members of the staff. These individuals must learn a number of jobs and become proficient in them even though they may perform them only once a week or even less frequently.

Problems sometimes arise when management permits employees to determine their days off, irrespective of the needs of the operation. This is particularly true in restaurants that have their peak days on weekends. The regular (nontipped) staff naturally want the weekends off to be with their families. If management is permissive in scheduling weekends off, the reliefs must be performed by less experienced and less productive employees. Such operations should hire employees on the understanding that they will be expected to work most weekends.

Shift Scheduling

When an operation serves more than one meal a day, shifts must be scheduled to provide coverage for the total period of operations. Staggered shifts usually permit staffing levels to be coordinated with the flow of activity in the operation. Figures 16–1 and 16–2 are bar charts showing the effect of staggered shifts on the staffing of dishwashers. At the bottom of Fig. 16–1 are the number of meals served for each hour of operation in this particular operation. In Fig. 16–1, six dishwashers are scheduled to start at 7:00 A.M. Other than setting up the machine, however, there are very few dishes to wash until sometime after 9:00 A.M., when the flow of business begins to approach a peak. Furthermore, most of the soiled dishes do not arrive at the dishwashing machine until after the guests have left. Soiled dishes may be stacked and accumulated until there are enough to warrant starting up the dishwashing machine. This bar chart also shows that two hours of overtime are built into the schedule each day to provide for late-night coverage.

The revised schedule (Fig. 16–2) shows staggered shifts. The need for "built-in" overtime is eliminated, and one dishwasher position is also eliminated. Coverage follows the flow of business more closely, and productivity is increased.

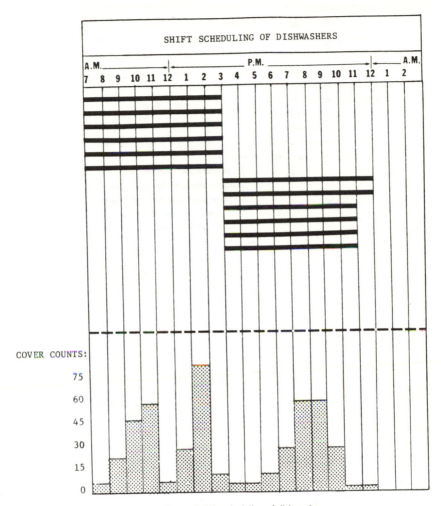

Fig. 16-1. Chart of shift scheduling of dishwashers.

Bar charts are excellent for determining schedule requirements. By plotting the scheduled hours against the amount of activity in each hourly segment, periods of low productivity can be seen immediately and schedules adjusted accordingly.

In scheduling days off, as well as in scheduling vacations, meeting the needs of the operation and the continuing need to hold the line on costs will require careful and thorough planning. To assist in the preparation of schedules, several forms are available. Among the more popular is a chart of standard man-hours (see Fig. 16–3). When prepared properly, it enables management to review the scheduling of an entire department or a component of it. For illustrative purposes, a 40-hour week is used in the scheduling plan.

Fig. 16-2. Chart of staggered schedule of dishwashers.

Forecasting Manpower Requirements

An important step in the payroll control process is forecasting expected volume for the purpose of planning the staffing requirements. Therefore, the forecast must be made as carefully and accurately as possible, and it should be reviewed and updated as needed.

Establishing Productivity Standards

To plan staffing intelligently, supervisors and department heads also need, in addition to accurate forecasts, productivity standards for each variable and semivariable job classification. With these standards and an accurate forecast, the required number of man-hours can be determined for each job classification and each meal period.

There are no general industry standards available that may be applied. Too many variables exist between individual operations to

CHART OF STANDARD MAN-HOURS

Name or Job Title	Sunday	Monday	Tuesday	Wednesday	Thursday	Friday	Saturday	Total Hours
Maitre 'D	12:00 P.M. 8:00 P.M.	S*	Off	Off	12:00 P.M. 8:00 P.M.	S	S	40
Head Waiter	1:00 P.M. 9:00 P.M.	S	S	Off	Off	Off	1:00 P.M. 9:00 P.M.	40
Captain	Off	12:00 P.M. 8:00 P.M.	S	S	S	S	Off	40
Captain	2:00 P.M. 10:00 P.M.	Off	Off	2:00 P.M. 10:00 P.M.	S	S	S	40
Captain	2:00 P.M. 10:00 P.M.	S	S	S	S	S	Off	40
Waiter	12:00 P.M. 8:00 P.M.	Off	Off	12:00 P.M. 8:00 P.M.	Off	12:00 P.M. 8:00 P.M.	S	40
Waiter	12:00 P.M. 8:00 P.M.	S	S	Off	S	S	S	40
Waiter	1:00 P.M. 9:00 P.M.	S	S	S	S	Off	Off	40
Waiter	Off	Off	1:00 P.M. 9:00 P.M.	S	S	S	S	40
Waiter	2:00 P.M. 10:00 P.M.	S	Off	Off	2:00 P.M. 10:00 P.M.	S	S	40
Waiter	2:00 P.M. 10:00 P.M.	S	S	S	Off	Off	2:00 P.M. 10:00 P.M.	40
Waiter	12:00 P.M. 8:00 P.M.	Off	Off	12:00 P.M. 8:00 P.M.	S	12:00 P.M. 8:00 P.M.	S	40
Waiter	12:00 P.M. 8:00 P.M.	S	S	Off	Off	S	S	40
Busboy	12:00 P.M. 8:00 P.M.	Off	Off	12:00 P.M. 8:00 P.M.	S	1:00 P.M. 9:00 P.M.	S	40
Busboy	1:00 P.M. 9:00 P.M.	S	S	Off	Off	1:00 P.M. 9:00 P.M.	S	40
Busboy	2:00 P.M. 10:00 P.M.	S	S	S	S	Off	Off	40
Restaurant Cashier	12:00 P.M. 10:00 P.M.	Off	Off	12:00 P.M. 10:00 P.M.	S	S	S	50
Restaurant Cashier	Off	12:00 P.M. 10:00 P.M.	12:00 P.M. 10:00 P.M.	Off	Off	Off	Off	20
Employees on Duty	15	12	11	12	12	12	13	
Employees off Duty	3	6	7	6	6	6	5	
Total employees	18	18	18	18	18	18	18	710

S* = Same hours as on the previous day.

Fig. 16-3. Chart of standard man-hours.

ANALYSIS OF COVERS SERVED AND DETERMINATION OF
EMPLOYEES' OUTPUT PERFORMANCE DURING A TEST PERIOD

	Sunday	Monday	Tuesday	Wednesday	Thursday	Friday	Saturday
Breakfast Covers Served:							
Week of:							
October 11-17	112	233	286	257	295	273	236
October 18-24	117	258	309	287	283	245	180
October 25-31	141	263	301	302	306	252	224
November 1-7	108	243	311	315	303	257	213
Total for test period	478	997	1,207	1,161	1,187	1,027	853
Average for test period	120	249	302	290	297	257	213
Cooks on duty	5	6	6	6	6	6	5
Average covers per cook	24.0	41.5	50.3	48.3	49.5	42.8	42.6
Luncheon Covers Served:							
Week of:							
October 11-17	247	262	264	291	318	285	259
October 18-24	261	277	325	303	293	285	253
October 25-31	328	253	254	285	286	245	272
November 1-7	276	314	314	326	299	272	231
Total for test period	1,112	1,106	1,157	1,205	1,196	1,087	1,015
Average for test period	278	277	289	301	299	272	254
Cooks on duty	10	12	12	12	12	12	10
Average covers per cook	27.8	23.0	24.0	25.0	24.9	22.6	25.4
Dinner Covers Served:							
Week of:							
October 11-17	135	230	224	227	235	223	175
October 18-24	124	205	216	211	222	206	184
October 25-31	142	193	182	225	195	190	189
November 1-7	194	223	257	243	219	203	197
Total for test period	595	851	879	906	871	822	745
Average for test period	149	213	220	227	218	206	186
Cooks on duty	8	10	10	10	10	10	8
Average covers per cook	18.6	21.3	22.0	22.7	21.8	20.6	23.2
Supper Covers Served:							
Week of:							
October 11-17	49	63	104	160	120	152	174
October 18-24	56	51	81	117	96	105	127
October 25-31	42	57	120	126	112	141	180
November 1-7	49	70	96	158	88	108	158
Total for test period	196	241	401	561	416	506	639
Average for test period	49	60	100	140	104	127	160
Cooks on duty	8	10	10	10	10	10	8
Average covers per cook	6.1	6.0	10.0	14.0	10.4	12.7	20.0

Note: The output figures are illustrative as to method only and are not to be considered a standard of performance.

Fig. 16-4. Analysis of covers served and determination of employees' output performance during a test period

permit their development. Each operation must develop its own standards, taking into consideration the following:

1. Ability of employees.
2. Effectiveness of supervisory staff.
3. Pattern of patronage.
4. Physical layout of facilities.
5. Complexity of menu items.
6. Hours of operation.
7. Provisions of union agreement.

Standards of employee performance may be determined in several ways as described below. Management must make the final decision as to which method to use, based on such factors as the cost of the various methods and the reliability and availability of the data.

Direct Analysis

In a direct analysis approach to establishing standards, the duties performed are observed in an operating situation. This method requires a trained analyst who spends considerable time observing employee performance during appropriate shift periods. Although expensive in terms of the analyst's time, it does provide accurate information when done properly.

Reviewing Historical Trends

Well-informed managers maintain reliable statistics about their operations, showing (among other things) the daily and cumulative volume of business. If these statistics are maintained on a per-meal basis, it is possible to calculate the seat turnover. This information, when used in conjunction with sales volume, serves as a basis for establishing trends in employee productivity. The data should cover several test periods to determine reasonable performance expectations.

For new operations without historical data, the experience of other similar operations or the experience of management gained elsewhere will have to be substituted until such time as a sufficient history is available. Figure 16–4 is an example of a performance analysis for a test period. Output is determined by the following computation:

$$\frac{\text{No. of covers served}}{\text{No. of employees}} = \text{Output per employee}$$

If the test period shows sharp fluctuations in sales volumes, their causes should be investigated, especially if they are unusual and do not follow the normal business patterns. If sharp fluctuations are due to nonrecurring events, then the abnormally low and high levels should be eliminated from the data. If they are recurring fluctuations, their causes should be determined and they should be considered in establishing the productivity standards.

Standards should not be set at peak levels of productivity. To do so is to invite problems. Employees will extend themselves for short periods of time on occasion, but they will not, nor should they be expected to, perform at peak levels at all times.

Translating the Data into Manpower Requirements

Using the established performance standards, a department head or supervisor can determine the staffing required to properly service the forecast volume.

Fig. 16–4 shows an analysis of productivity of cooks during a four-week test period. Except for the Sunday breakfasts, the productivity of the cooks (measured by the number of covers served per cook) is reasonably consistent by meal period. During the test period, 40 cook-days were used for breakfast, 80 for lunch, and 60 cook-days for dinner and supper. The average covers served per cook were:

Meal	Output
Breakfast	43.2
Lunch	24.6
Dinner	21.5
Supper	11.2

The noticeably low productivity of the supper cooks may indicate a problem in scheduling during the supper period. Or the low output may be due to a highly unpredictable pattern of patronage during this meal period and the need to be adequately staffed. Another cause of low productivity may be that the menu offered requires the complete staffing of a number of kitchen stations, even though the level of business is low.

On the basis of the test period, the current levels of productivity are about 43 covers per cook for breakfast, 25 covers for lunch, 22 for dinner, and 11 for supper. These may be established as the established standards, if it is felt that the cooks are currently working at or near capacity. This judgment may be made on the basis of personal observation. If, however, it is felt that a higher level of productivity is possible, a percentage factor may be applied. For instance, management may have determined, based on observation and experience, that the breakfast cooks are working at capacity but that there is some excess capacity in the schedule during lunch, dinner, and supper. An analysis of the supper operation might show that a minimum staff of four is required to man the required stations and produce the supper menu. During lunch and dinner, management thinks a 10 percent improvement is possible. This produces the following set of standards:

Meal	Covers per Cook
Breakfast	44
Lunch	28
Dinner	24
Supper	4 cooks plus one more for each 25 covers over 100 covers

The late supper standard provides for minimum coverage but requires the same productivity as at dinner over that minimum for higher levels of business.

Applying the Standards

To determine the number of cooks required to staff this operation under the revised standards, the supervisor divides the number of covers forecast for each meal period by the standard. This provides the theoretical staffing required for the forecast. However, other factors must be considered. First, the supervisor should plot out his bar charts to arrive at the right combination of full-time and part-time shifts in order to get the right combination of coverage in each job category for each meal period. For highly skilled positions, it may not be possible to employ part-time workers just to cover one meal period, and some adjustment must be made.

In addition, most employees are hired on a full-time basis and expect to work a full work week. Although there is usually some flexibility in the scheduling of days off, a certain basic staffing plan must be established. Therefore, the standards derived above may be used to determine a general plan rather than a day-to-day schedule. In the example given above, the test period and the revised standards indicate that the new staffing requirements for lunch are:

Sunday	10
Monday	10
Tuesday	10–11
Wednesday	11
Thursday	11
Friday	10
Saturday	9

Because of considerable fluctuations in the activity on Tuesdays, management may wish to staff the kitchen with all cooks on that day to ensure service, even though this reduces the productivity ratio.

This general pattern has been determined on a test period. Management should continue to measure the output per employee to be sure that the general staffing plan is still relevant to the current levels and patterns of business.

Other Means of Payroll Control

To this point we have discussed various methods of determining adequate and efficient levels of staffing. Staffing is adequate if the number of employees assigned provide the level and quality of service desired by management, and it is efficient if the level of productivity results in a reasonable payroll cost. There are, however, other elements of labor cost that must be controlled as rigidly as the staffing of an operation.

Control of Overtime

Another avenue of labor cost control is the control of overtime. Effective control of overtime can be achieved by management and supervisory personnel only when prior approval of contemplated overtime work is required. Although there are many instances in which overtime is necessary, an unnecessary amount of overtime is often incurred.

If inadequately controlled, overtime can become a wage subsidy to employees. If overtime is paid too frequently, employees soon get used to this increase in their take-home pay. Any subsequent reduction in their take-home pay is considered a reduction in the earnings to which they are entitled. Once this costly precedent is established in one department, it tends to spread to other areas of the operation and increase payroll costs substantially.

Control Elements

Control of overtime is based on the premise that a department head or supervisor can recognize in advance that certain employees will have to work overtime. He then prepares an overtime request (see Fig. 16–5) and forwards it to the designated management official for approval.

When several shifts are involved, requests for overtime should be submitted to management at a designated hour to allow sufficient time for review of the need for overtime prior to its approval. Having overtime requests submitted on a daily basis provides a degree of psychological control; the management review will quickly detect a request that is not justified by workloads or that might be eliminated by better supervision. In any event, prompt approval or disapproval of overtime will have to be given so that appropriate action can be taken. A properly authorized overtime request should be forwarded to the accounting department where the overtime hours appearing on the employees' time cards (or other record of hours worked) may be checked against the overtime authorization. This system is not designed to eliminate all overtime since there will usually be unexpected situations in which overtime is necessary. This system is also not applicable to every operation.

```
            OVERTIME AUTHORIZATION REQUEST

                              Date_____


    Department_____ Title_____

    Reason for overtime

    Explain in detail why overtime is necessary?


    Number of employees to work overtime _____
    Number of hours per employee _____
    Total hours requested_____

       Name and clock number of employees:
       1.                    5.
       2.                    6.
       3.                    7.
       4.                    8.

    Will employees be supervised?  Yes___ No___
    If yes, by whom?_____ Position_____

    Requesting Department Head _____

                    Designated Management Official:
                    Approved_____

    Total hours requested_____
    Approved_____    Disapproved _____

    Comments:
```

Fig. 16-5. Overtime authorization request.

In a small operation, it may be possible for the manager to determine personally when overtime is necessary, to approve hours worked whenever convenient, and to review personally the employees' time cards or reports prior to the preparation of the payroll. Although such informal procedure may be expedient, care must be taken that it does not get so informal that abuses go undetected.

Adhering to a formal procedure for the control of overtime should materially reduce it. The key elements in control are the review of the reasons for overtime and the requirement that overtime cannot be incurred unless it is approved by management beforehand.

Management Information

Timely management reports on manpower utilization are another part of the control procedures; they show the efficiency of the

DEPARTMENTAL COMPARISON OF
MAN-DAYS — ACTUAL VERSUS STANDARD

Department	Current Period						Cumulative Period		
	Average Number of Employees	Aggregate Hours Worked	Full-Time Employee Equivalents Man-Days Hours/8	Standard Man-Days	Man-Days Variance	Dollar Variance	Cumulative Man-Days Variance	Cumulative Dollar Variance	Average Cost Per Man-Day of Variance
Food Preparation	25	1,000	125	110	15	$375	75	$1,875	$25
Food Service	20	800	100	90	10	200	50	1,000	20
Beverage	10	400	50	50	-	-	-	-	-
Stewarding	15	600	75	65	10	200	50	1,000	20
Cashiering	3	120	15	15	-	-	-	-	-
Totals	73	2,920	365	330	35	$775	175	$3,875	$22

Fig. 16-6. Departmental comparison of man-days (actual versus standard).

control system and should be available as soon as possible after the close of business for the day, well in advance of the periodic financial statements. For some operations, weekly reports may be satisfactory. Weekly data can be easily compiled from that collected for payroll preparation.

Preparing Summary Reports

The caliber of the personnel given the responsibility for the preparation of payroll reports varies with the size of the operation. In a large operation, responsibility for the coordinaton of the program may be assigned to a payroll analyst, whereas in a small operation, report preparation may be an additional duty assumed by the manager, bookkeeper, or payroll clerk.

The proper choice of the individual to prepare these reports is important, particularly in a larger operation. It is obvious that the individual preparing payroll utilization reports will be in a sensitive position because his reports will reflect on the ability and perform-ance of supervisors, managers, and department heads. Accordingly, in the large operation, care should be taken to select a fair-minded individual. He should also not have to report on the person for whom he is working, and he should have sufficient poise and self-confidence to be able to handle himself well in this sensitive position.

Methodology

Timely reports on employee productivity are comprised mainly of a comparison of employee performance standards with actual performances for the period under review. They show the number of employees used for the number of covers served. For example, if 3,000 covers were served during the period under review, and 40 covers per cook per day is the established performance stand-ard, 75 cook-days would be required. If a review of the actual payroll hours indicates that for the period 600 cook-hours were required and the standard shift was eight hours, then $600/8 = 75$ cook-days were employed, indicating that the performance for the period was at stand-ard. If, on the other hand, the analysis reveals that 700 hours were worked by the cooks, then $700/8 = 87.5$ cook-days were employed, or 12.5 days over standard.

Often the value of the report to management and its impact upon operating personnel would be greater if the variance from standard were expressed in dollars. This can be done simply by determining the average daily wage and multiplying it by the number of man-day variations. In the example presented, if the average cook's wage is $25 per day, then the 12.5 man-day variance can be expressed in dollars as follows:

$25. $\times$ 12.5 = $312.50 (in overstandard labor cost for the period).

In the above examples, 40 covers per cook-day at a $25 per day rate are used for illustrative purposes. Actual standards will vary from one operation to the next as previously mentioned.

The analyst would logically follow the same procedure for all departments for which performance standards have been developed and for which a comparison of actual operating results with established standards would be meaningful. The completed report on employee productivity for the current period and the year to date would be submitted to management for review before being distributed to operating areas. Figure 16–6 shows a report on employee productivity based on a 40-hour week.

PART FIVE

Plant Management

17

HOUSEKEEPING AND MAINTENANCE

The housekeeping and maintenance functions in the food service business are as vital to the continuing success of an enterprise as food quality, good service, and cost controls. The level of housekeeping in front-of-the-house areas is an important measurement used by guests in forming their opinions of the restaurant. Second, the proper maintenance of the operation's assets is essential to its ability to continue to do business. In both areas, the food service operator must decide between using in-house staff and outside contractors to provide these important services. Each has advantages and disadvantages that are discussed below.

Housekeeping

Management in most industries considers housekeeping a necessary evil and has little interest in the costs and risks of poor housekeeping. Food service management has historically been somewhat more enlightened about this subject and aware of the significant damage a lack of attention to proper housekeeping can cause. However, many food and beverage managers continue to give housekeeping short shrift. They fail to define clearly the objectives and responsibilities of the housekeeping department, other than to "clean the place up." The function is not given the same status or supervision as other areas of operations. When times are tough, housekeeping budgets are among the first to be trimmed, in spite of the fact that there is no easier way to assure a sales skid. Housekeeping employees are often given additional tasks to perform (such as running errands) that are unrelated to their primary function and are often the least-trained employees in the business.

360

Proper housekeeping, like good sanitation practices, is no accident. It must be planned, and few employees are willing to take it upon themselves to follow proper practices without guidance and strong supervision. The establishment and continual monitoring of a housekeeping program is an important part of the food service manager's responsibility and one to which he must assign high priority in his daily routine.

Organization and Scheduling

The first step in organizing the housekeeping function is to make a top-to-bottom survey of the facility.

Starting at the front door of the establishment, the manager should study the outside of his building. Some of the things he should determine are:

1. Are there windows to be washed? How often, and by whom?
2. Are there sidewalks and driveways to be swept and kept free of debris? Is there shrubbery to be trimmed? Is there a parking lot to sweep and clean?
3. Are there outside lights to be changed? Does the sign need periodic cleaning and light maintenance?
4. Are there canopies or awnings to be washed?

The manager should then enter the operation and continue his survey of public areas thinking of how his guest will see things:

1. Does the front door need periodic cleaning, washing, painting, or polishing of hardware?
2. If there is an entrance foyer, how often should the floor be cleaned, and what methods should be used? What about walls, cleaning of mirrors or picture frames, dusting of artifacts and decorations? Light bulbs to be checked and changed if necessary?
3. In the bar or cocktail lounge, floor maintenance, cleaning of wall coverings, furniture cleaning and repairs, dusting of ceilings, and lighting checks must be scheduled. Who will clean behind the bar, and when? Everything from floor mats to piano keys should be listed and scheduled for regular cleaning. If there is a brass bar rail, how often must it be polished?

The survey then continues in the dining rooms. Reviewing all areas of housekeeping, the manager makes a detailed list of chores to be performed.

1. How are carpets or floor coverings to be cleaned, by whom, and how often?

2. Are walls to be washed, dusted, vacuumed, or painted? Are there mirrors to clean, pictures to be dusted and cleaned, light sconces to be polished and bulbs checked, shelves or mouldings to be dusted?
3. What about the ceiling? Air conditioning vents to be cleaned, light bulbs to replace, cracks to be patched, corners to be dusted?
4. Are there windows to be washed from the inside, or glass dividers between sections?
5. How will furniture be cleaned and maintained? Table bases must be dusted and occasionally washed. Upholstery must be cleaned and checked for burns, tears, and wear. Uncovered table tops need daily attention. Side stands and service stations must be cleaned thoroughly.

Back-of-the-house housekeeping is also studied on the scheduling tour and is to be included as part of the sanitation planning. At the back door, who will be responsible for clean-ups and housekeeping, including trash removal areas and containers? Rest rooms, both front and back of the house, must be cleaned several times daily and must be part of the regular schedule.

Following his survey, the manager should establish two things: (1) a detailed checklist to be used on a daily basis for performance and inspection of housekeeping duties, and (2) a detailed schedule of how often each task must be performed and who will do it. Only when this is done can the manager determine how large a housekeeping staff he needs and how large a budget is needed for this function. Once the schedule and budget are established, they must be followed to the letter, good times or bad, whether they can be "afforded" or not.

Selection of Materials and Cleaning Supplies

The housekeeping budget and the appearance of the operation will depend to a large extent on the materials selected in the construction and decoration of the restaurant. Silk brocade wall covering may be lovely at first, but how will it look in two years and what will it cost to maintain and replace? Certain paints may be cheaper than others, but how well do they wash and how long will they last? In the initial design of the operation and in any subsequent redecorating, the impact of materials selection on housekeeping must be a primary consideration. Significant savings in cost can be achieved by careful selection of materials for wall coverings, floor covering, ceiling treatment, and furniture upholstery with a keen eye on how they will be cleaned and maintained. Naturally, the aesthetics considerations are important. A world of plastic and steel may be long-lasting and easy to maintain but is unappealing to the eye and ear. With each selection of materials, the manager should consider how much wear it will get, how often he can afford to replace it, and what is required to clean and maintain it in addition to initial cost and decor factors.

Selection of cleaning supplies to be used in the housekeeping function is another important factor in the expense budget. For each housekeeping job, there is a wide variety of materials available from competitive supply manufacturers with widely varying prices. To select cleaning supplies, the manager must develop a set of specifications for the materials he will need. The specifications should include what material, fabric, or surface will be cleaned, how the cleaner will be applied, how often it will be used, and the size package in which it will be purchased. Fifty-gallon drums of floor wax are cheaper by the gallon than one-gallon jugs, but if only two gallons a month are used, the drum would not be a wise purchase.

The manager should also consider the level of training and expertise of the people who will be using the materials, as well as the labor cost implications of various cleaning supplies. For example, if one type of material must be measured and mixed while another is ready to use, the manager should consider potential waste and errors, as well as the labor required to do the mixing.

Once the specifications are developed, the manager should invite representatives of various cleaning supply manufacturers to submit proposals and make demonstrations of their products. These manufacturers can offer excellent advice and consultation if the manager keeps in mind that their motive is promoting their own brands. In addition, they offer training of employees as part of their service, and the manager should take advantage of this to assure that the supplies are properly used. Following manufacturers' instructions will often reduce costs by eliminating wasteful consumption of cleaning supplies by untrained personnel.

Selecting the proper equipment with which to perform housekeeping duties is important from both a labor-cost viewpoint and to assure a job well done. Having the proper equipment improves housekeeping productivity and safety. Equipment manufacturers also provide employee training on most major pieces of machinery.

Floor Care

The care of floors represents the housekeeping department's greatest single expense. The National Sanitary Supply Association has estimated that floor care consumes 40 percent of the housekeeping budget. Naturally, the cost and method of floor maintenance will depend on the floor material. The most commonly used materials for flooring in the food service industry are carpet, terrazzo, vinyl asbestos tile, quarry tile, ceramic tile, and wood.

Carpet should be checked daily for wear and fraying, which can cause a tripping hazard. Carpeted floors should be vacuumed thoroughly at least once a day to prevent soil from being ground in. Spot cleaning with a manufacturer-approved dry cleaning fluid should be performed as needed. Wet cleaning, or shampooing, should be performed at least quarterly or more often as needed by competent professionals using the proper equipment.

Terrazzo is a mixture of marble chips and cement that is poured and troweled out and allowed to dry for several days. When new, terrazzo should be mopped daily. After the floor has "cured," a sealer should be applied. When cleaning, neutral detergents or soaps should be used as strong acidic or alkaline cleaners will cause wear. A slip-resistant wax can also be used, and steel wool should be avoided in scrubbing or buffing.

Vinyl asbestos tile is usually laid in 12-inch squares and is relatively inexpensive in terms of initial cost. These tiles are available in a wide variety of colors and patterns and are resistant to alkalis, acids, soil, grease, and solvents. The floor should be dust mopped and swept and then mopped daily with any soap or detergent. Although some of the newer tiles need infrequent or no waxing, many existing floors require application of a wax regularly. Older floors also require application of a sealer to fill the pores. Waxed floors should be stripped periodically, and abrasive cleaners should be avoided on unwaxed vinyl asbestos floors.

Quarry tile floors are frequently used in kitchens and service areas, and many restaurants now use quarry tile flooring in the front of the house. Quarry tile is an unglazed ceramic tile, usually laid in six-inch squares with grouting. Although it is relatively expensive to install, quarry tile has long life and low maintenance costs. Quarry tile should be swept several times daily and mopped with a detergent solution. No waxes are required. Because of its slight porosity, occasionally an acid wash is used to remove ground-in soil, after which a sealer may be applied.

Ceramic tile is also frequently used in kitchen and rest room flooring and is a durable floor that is relatively easy to maintain. Ceramic tiles used in food service are generally glazed and laid with a grout or binding cement. The daily housekeeping should be accomplished by dust mopping and sweeping, followed by a wet mopping with a nonalkaline, nonacidic synthetic detergent. A seal is often recommended. Alkaline cleaners cause disintegration of the grout as do acids. Abrasive cleaners should also be avoided to prevent scratching of the surface.

The correct maintenance of wood floors is especially important because wood will show wear more quickly than other surfaces if it is improperly treated. Wood floors should be sealed with a penetrating seal and then waxed frequently. All wood floors should be swept, dust mopped, or vacuumed daily. A damp mop can be used on a waxed floor to remove excess soil. Avoid excess water as the wood will warp and buckle if saturated. A good stripper should be used periodically to remove old wax, and a new seal and wax coat applied.

Wall Care

As with floors, the maintenance and housekeeping of walls depends on the materials used. Among the popular wall finishes used in restaurants and institutions are ceramic tile, vinyl wall covering, paint, wood, and wallpaper.

Ceramic tile should be dusted daily and washed with a nonalkaline detergent as needed. Vinyl wall covering is extremely easy to keep clean with a damp cloth. Worn areas can be replaced easily with new pieces of vinyl. Different paints have varying maintenance characteristics. Latex paint is the least durable and is less easily washed. Enamel and latex enamel paints are more durable and can be cleaned by washing with a damp cloth and a mild all-purpose cleaner. Epoxy enamel paint is the strongest paint available and is easily maintained. Although more expensive initially, it has a significantly longer life than other paints and offers almost the same degree of protection for a wall as tile. Walls should be sealed with a primer before painting. Wallpapers, although attractive, have low durability and high maintenance costs. They are not easily cleaned, except by dusting and vacuuming, and often show wear and soil.

Ceilings and Lighting

Care of ceilings is a relatively easy housekeeping chore but an important one because ceilings are so readily visible to guests. Ceilings should be dusted frequently and painted when necessary. Nothing will detract from the decor of a restaurant quite as badly as a chipped, peeling, or cracked ceiling. The vents around air handling outlets should be cleaned at least weekly to prevent the accumulation of soot and grime. Light fixtures must be cleaned regularly as well. Recessed fixtures should have the diffusers removed and washed at least monthly. Chandeliers should be dusted several times a week and washed with a mild detergent periodically. Lanterns and sconces should be dusted and washed frequently as well. Burned-out bulbs should be replaced immediately in all light fixtures.

Furniture

One of the most important functions assigned to housekeeping is the maintenance and cleaning of furniture in the dining room. With upholstered furniture, this includes the periodic dry cleaning of fabrics, the repair of tears and worn spots, and the recovering of chairs and banquettes from time to time. Fabric selection will play an important role in durability and the cost of this care. Some fabrics, such as vinyls, are washable and can be cleaned daily with a damp cloth and an all-purpose cleaner. Other fabrics require spot cleaning with a dry-cleaning fluid as needed and periodic complete shampooing or dry cleaning of the furniture. It is wise to purchase a small supply of extra fabric when purchasing chairs or booths in order to be able to match fabrics when small repairs are needed.

Table bases should be cleaned weekly with a mild detergent and should be dusted daily. Chair bases, depending on the material, should be cleaned with the same regularity.

Cigarette burns on both tables and seats are a frequent problem in food service operations. On upholstered furniture, a patch or reweaving is required, if not replacement of the entire upholstery. Table tops can be refinished if they are made of wood, but plastic-base table tops must often be resurfaced entirely if burned.

Worn and frayed furniture is a sign to patrons that the operator takes little care in the running of his establishment. A regular inspection of furniture should be part of the manager's routine.

Exterior Housekeeping

Keeping the exterior of the restaurant clean is as important as interior housekeeping. The guest's first impressions are created on the outside, and an untidy exterior can have a serious effect on business. Sidewalks must be swept and occasionally washed down with a hose and detergents. Shrubbery must be kept free of debris and trimmed attractively. Lighting must be maintained, and signs must be freshly painted and clean. Maintenance of a parking lot is a time-consuming but important chore. Regular sweeping and picking up of litter is essential. Among the most important exterior chores is window washing, as windows show soil easily and are readily noticed by patrons. Cleaning windows with an ammonia solution should be scheduled twice monthly, or more often if necessary. Canopies and awnings should be washed regularly with a mild detergent and water spray. Even exterior woodwork must be washed with a hose periodically and repainted as needed.

In the back of the house, the area around trash dumpsters must be cleaned daily. The receptacle itself should be washed with a power hose, and the ground and docks should be hosed down daily after debris is picked up.

Contracts versus In-House Staff Housekeeping

In many operations, food service managers have decided to use outside professional housekeeping services rather than in-house staff for all or part of this function. These firms enter into contracts with the operator to perform a specifically listed number of chores on a regularly scheduled basis, often daily. In many cases, the outside service enters the restaurant at the close of business and performs housekeeping and heavy back-of-the-house cleaning chores at night. Each contract is individually negotiated for a specific list of services which typically includes all dusting, vacuuming, floor care, window washing, and restroom housekeeping.

The economic feasibility of this type of arrangment must be determined individually by the food service manager because each contract and each operation are so different as to preclude general conclusions about economics. There are, however, known advantages and disadvantages to use of outside cleaning and housekeeping services:

Advantages

1. The operator does not have to worry about housekeeping. He has a professional supervisor assigned to his account who supervises the work and monitors quality of performance.
2. The operator does not have to carry any housekeeping personnel on his payroll, with attendant costs of vacations, fringe benefits, lost time, and payroll processing.
3. The operator does not have to make any investment in housekeeping equipment. The equipment and supplies are provided by the contractor.
4. The operator does not have to spend time on housekeeping schedules, purchasing of materials, or supervision of staff.
5. A more professional job of cleaning may be done because the contractor knows modern methods, use of equipment, materials to use, and has trained personnel.

Disadvantages

1. The manager loses some degree of control over housekeeping. If he wants something special done, he has no staff on hand to perform the task.
2. The manager has "strangers" in his restaurant during times he is not there, and this sometimes leads to security problems. (In most cases, the contractor's employees are bonded.)
3. Most contractors bring a crew into the operation, work them there for several hours, and then go on to the next job. The one operation is not their only responsibility. Along the same lines, often a contractor supervisor is responsible for cleaning several places, and he is not on hand to monitor his crew at all times.
4. The contractor may not have the same standards as the operator.

To determine whether to use outside contracting, the food service manager must weigh these advantages and disadvantages, together with the economic factors involved. He must first prepare a detailed schedule of the work he wants done and how often it is to be performed. The next step is for him to determine how many man-hours of internal labor it would take to perform these tasks and apply appropriate costs to this labor, including all related payroll costs. These data should then be compared to proposals from a number of outside contractors to evaluate the comparative costs. The operator must remember that productivity among his own personnel may be lower than that of an outside contractor since once the work is done, the contractor moves the crew to another location. The operator must absorb the nonproductive time of his own crew. He must also evaluate the amount of time he personally devotes to supervision of house-keeping and take the value of this time into account when making the cost comparison.

Many food service operators, after performing this analysis, determine than for part, if not all, of the housekeeping duties, use of outside professional contractors presents sufficient benefits to warrant taking this approach.

Laundry and Linens

For a restaurant using full table linen, laundering and re-placement of linens and uniforms represents a significant operating cost. A complete laundry list for a first-class restaurant can include tablecloths of various sizes, napkins, table pads, uniforms for both the service staff and the back-of-the-house crew, aprons, side towels, and cleaning rags. Miscellaneous items such as mop heads, hot pads, table skirts, curtains, and draperies may also be included.

Laundry service may be managed in one of several ways:

1. Outside laundry service using rental linens and uniforms.
2. Outside laundry service using linens and/or uniforms owned by the business.
3. In-house laundry and owned linen and uniforms.
4. A combination of outside service and in-house laundry.

As a rule, the operation using an outside service will use rental linen unless its requirements are so specialized that the laundry cannot or will not provide it. Most large laundries will provide a selection of linens and uniforms and will purchase a stock of special items for a customer on a contractual basis. A two-year contract is often desired since this is the expected life span of the inventory. Laundry services and the manufacturers of laundry equipment both have listed the advantages and disadvantages of outside services and in-house laundries as follows:

Advantages of an On-Premises Laundry
(according to laundry equipment manufacturers)

1. Linen availability is not restricted by outside sources: strikes, truck breakdowns, and so on.
2. Labor can be performed by regular personnel in off hours. Highly skilled labor is not required.
3. Mangement has control over the quality and appearance of its linens.
4. Pilferage (at least by outsiders) is eliminated.
5. The life of the linens is increased.
6. The cost savings can be substantial.

Disadvantages of an On-Premises Laundry
(according to linen suppliers)

1. Managerial time is required to hire, train, and supervise the laundry operation and to deal with salesmen and service-men.
2. Technical knowledge is required: laundry techniques, equipment maintenance, supplies purchasing.
3. Breakdowns can be costly. Alternative sources of linen supply may not be immediately available.
4. Lack of quality control: Improper processing or poor quality fabrics can lead to linens with poor appearance.
5. There are hidden costs involved: energy costs (which may be substantial), administration, depreciation, rent for space, added payroll. Money is also tied up in inventories of supplies and spare parts.
6. Claims of worker productivity and linen life are often exaggerated.
7. On-premises laundries lack the flexibility to handle peak loads or to deal with absenteeism.

Permanent Press or No-Iron Fabrics

Much of the impetus for the trend toward in-house laundries has come from the availability of high quality permanent press fabrics. Such fabrics are blends of cotton and polyester that have been heat treated with a special resin process. Many of the past shortcomings of these fabrics have been overcome by improved fabrics and processes, by establishing proper laundering methods, and by the development of a reresin process to restore the original finish. In many cases, past dissatisfaction has been due to improper handling, which has led to wrinkling, graying or yellowing, and severe stains. (See Table 17–1 for a trouble-shooting guide.)

In addition to their labor-saving features, permanent press no-iron fabrics have the added advantage over pure cotton of reduced shrinkage, substantially longer life, less moisture retention for faster drying, and a softness that provides increased wearing comfort.

In-House Laundry Layout and Equipment

The basic equipment for an in-house laundry in a restaurant includes a combination washer-extractor, a dryer, an ironer, and a sink. An operation using all permanent press fabrics does not require the ironer. Additional equipment may include a hot water booster heater, folding equipment, storage shelving, and a scale for weighing.

A larger operation or a central laundry for several operations may find cost benefits from a form dryer or special drying cabinets for permanent press uniforms. In some cases, on-premises dry cleaning of service uniforms may be warranted. In addition, water-softening equipment is usually recommended to reduce the amount of detergent required and to prolong the life both of the fabrics and of the equipment.

For small restaurants, a large laundry space is not required. Small laundries have been successfully installed in 100 square feet or less. The space selected should be accessible to the linen storage areas and should permit direct venting from the dryer to the outside with a minimum of installation expenses. Floor weights and the effect of any vibrations should be checked in selecting a space and location for an in-house laundry.

Table 17–1. Trouble-Shooting Chart for No-Iron Fabrics

Problem	Solution
Wrinkling	1. Select equipment with a cool-down feature for rinse and dry cycles.
	2. Don't overload equipment.
	3. Don't overdry; remove from dryer when slightly damp.
	4. Fold at once.
	5. Allow to rest overnight before using.
Graying	1. Do not oversoap; use proper detergent and proper amount.
	2. Use correct water temperature and water level.
	3. Wash heavily soiled items separately.
	4. Separate white items from colored items.
	5. Use water softener in hard water areas.
Yellowing	1. Don't use bleach.
	2. Don't overdry.
Staining	1. Pretreat stains before washing.
	2. Wash heavily stained items separately.
	3. Use proper amount of detergent and proper water temperature.
Pilling or linting	1. Keep washers and dryers cleaned of lint.

The facility should be planned to provide a direct flow of laundry from sorting to folding and storage without backtracking. This flow consists of:

1. *Sorting and weighing.* Because sorting is often done on the floor, floors and walls should be of a material that will not cause stains. Unsealed concrete should be avoided for this reason. The sink should be located in this area for presoaking heavily soiled items. When laundering costs are to be charged to more than one department or operation, a scale may be used for determining the exact amount of laundry done for each department.

2. *The washer-extractor.* Fully automatic washers are now available that include extractors and automatic injection of detergents. Separate components are also available. In large operations the latter may require less investment because one extractor can service several washers; however, more labor is required to transfer the wet wash into the extractor.

3. *The dryer.* From the washer-extractor the laundry goes into the dryer, and from the dryer into the folding area. For no-iron fabrics, both the washer and dryer should be equipped for a gradual cooling down of the temperature to minimize wrinkling. For large operations, automatic folding equipment can reduce the amount of hand work required. In smaller operations or those using large banquet cloths, a simple clip device can permit one person to fold large cloths with a minimum of effort.

Manufacturers of laundry equipment can provide complete packages of services, including layouts and engineering drawings for the installation, recommendations as to linen selection and inventory controls, laundry operating procedures, and the training of laundry and maintenance employees. Some also provide regular servicing and inspection of machines, and they supply all materials. Independent consultants specializing in laundry operations can also be helpful in evaluating manufacturers' bids and proposals.

Uniforms

Labor contracts and labor laws in some areas require that employees' uniforms be furnished and laundered by the employer. In addition to the union and legal aspects of providing uniforms, clothing supplied to the employees can improve staff morale.

Some operators of very informal operations permit their service employees to wear their own clothing on the job. Although this may contribute to a relaxed atmosphere, it does represent some loss of management control over the employees' appearance, including the cleanliness and condition of the clothing. In fact, such a policy may be in violation of local health department regulations and for preparation personnel may present a safety hazard.

For front-of-the-house personnel, a middle-ground policy is the use of "career clothing" such as that developed by the airlines. A coordinated line of sportswear is selected in styles and colors that harmonize with the decor of the operation. A selection of dresses, skirts, slacks, jackets, shirts, vests, and blazers is usually offered in combinations of several colors and patterns. From this line, the employee selects the particular combinations he prefers. The formal look of traditional uniforms is thus avoided, and the employees are permitted to select their own clothing. In all cases, however, the operator must consider the image of his service personnel in relation to the total operation and decor.

Maintenance

Although the maintenance function usually has a relatively low level of visibility, it can affect a food service operation in many ways. First, the ability of the business to function can be severely restricted by a lack of physical plant maintenance over a period of time. Insufficient attention to maintenance can also affect the efficiency and the life span of the physical assets. Poorly maintained equipment can lower the quality, the quantity, and even the safety of the products being made. Working conditions for the employees may become unsafe because of a lack of proper maintenance of the equipment or the building. This can result in violations of federal safety regulations or local health laws, with accompanying fines and adverse publicity for the business. The risk of loss by fire may also be increased, resulting in increased fire insurance costs. Last, poorly maintained equipment can be costly to operate and waste substantial amounts of energy.

Inadequate maintenance has a multiplier effect. Equipment that does not operate properly can cause employee frustration and poor morale, which in turn can lead to misuse of the equipment by the employees and even greater loss of equipment effectiveness. Poorly maintained public areas create a poor image of the business in the minds of the customers and thereby discourage repeat business. Reduced sales volume may lead management to make further reductions in maintenance expenditures, putting the business on a downward spiral.

Maintenance work can be divided into different functions:

1. Routine repair work, such as stopping leaky faucets, changing light bulbs, repairing broken chair rungs, or replacing a cracked pane of glass.
2. Preventive maintenance, including inspection of machinery, cleaning, oiling, and making adjustments.

3. Emergency breakdowns—situations that must be dealt with immediately, such as burst pipes, inoperative elevators, or refrigeration breakdowns.
4. Special projects, including seasonal jobs such as the starting up of air conditioning in the spring or closing down an outdoor operation at the end of the season. One-time special projects may include installing a new piece of equipment or a major rehabilitation project such as the overhauling of an older piece of equipment.
5. Fabrication, such as the custom construction of a special item for use in the operation.
6. Correction of unsafe conditions, such as applying skid-proof finish to floors where falls may occur and inspecting the premises for fire hazards.
7. Monitoring and controlling energy usage, including the operation of heating, ventilating, and air-conditioning equipment.

In a large operation, the maintenance manager must supervise all these functions as well as maintain an adequate inventory of spare parts, supplies, and tools; keep adequate records of maintenance expenses, warranties in effect, and energy consumption; keep files of manufacturers' brochures and parts lists, up-to-date building plans, and drawings. He must also plan and control the workflow through his department, provide training and supervision for his staff, and control his labor and inventory costs.

Preventive Maintenance

A preventive maintenance program is essential in controlling maintenance costs and preventing critical breakdowns. It goes beyond the mechanical aspects of checking, adjusting, cleaning, and oiling machinery. Preventive maintenance begins with the selection of the proper piece of equipment for the job. Forcing a machine to perform a task for which it was not designed is asking for a maintenance problem.

Proper installation of the equipment with adequate wiring, ventilation, and plumbing connections in a location where the equipment can function properly is important. Once the equipment is selected and installed, employees must be trained—and retrained—to use the equipment properly. Such training includes not only the operation of the machinery but also the use of proper cleaning procedures.

Management must be alert to the possibility of intentional or accidental misuse of equipment. Unintentional misuse indicates a need for increased training and supervision; intentional damage requires disciplinary measures.

The maintenance department's role in the preventive maintenance program involves regular inspections according to an established written schedule, routine cleaning, adjusting, and oiling, minor parts replacement as required, and keeping proper records. The frequency of inspections should be determined from records of past work performed and manufacturers' recommendations.

To enforce thoroughness of inspections and to maintain records, checklists with spaces to mark off each point as inspected and to record any work performed are often used. Some manufacturers provide checklists or inspection procedure forms with their equipment brochures.

The Maintenance Function in Food Service Operations

Few food service operations are large enough to warrant a separate large-scale maintenance department such as described above. In institutional food services, maintenance services are usually provided by an on-premises staff, and a large individual restaurant or localized chain of restaurants may have general handymen to take care of routine repair work that does not require a skilled craftsman. In large complexes or office buildings, the landlord's maintenance staff may provide electrical, plumbing, painting, or carpentry work for tenants that is then billed on some basis according to the terms of the lease agreement.

Most restaurant operators must rely on outside services for most of their maintenance needs. Larger operations may have a general handyman on the payroll to perform minor routine and preventive maintenance chores, but when necessary, they call in specialized tradesmen for electrical or plumbing jobs or for large, infrequent jobs such as repainting of large areas.

For work of a specialized or highly technical nature, many operators purchase a service contract. For a fixed fee, a local service shop or manufacturer's representative will provide regularly scheduled preventive maintenance service and will be available for any necessary repairs or emergency breakdowns. The service contract is, in effect, an insurance policy. The service shop is betting that, with proper preventive maintenance, the occurrence of breakdowns and the need for repairs will be greatly reduced. The cost of a service contract will vary with the age and condition of the equipment to be serviced, on the frequency with which inspections are to be made on the reliability of the machine and how complicated it is to repair, and on the distance the service shop's representative will have to travel to the customer.

Some manufacturers designate certain service shops as "factory authorized"services. This usually means that those dealers or service shops carry a required level of inventory of the manufacturer's spare parts and supplies and have received some training from the manufacturer through short seminars or home study courses, or has been supplied with special technical literature. Frequently, equipment still under warranty must be repaired by an authorized service shop for the warranty to be in effect.

Service contracts for air conditioning and refrigeration are often a good idea. Air conditioning is virtually mandatory for operation in any warm-weather area. Being without air conditioning in hot weather can be devastating to the business. A loss of a major refrigerator can also be costly, both in spoilage and in lost storage capacity. If an ice machine is out of service, ice can be purchased from an outside vendor; however, in any volume operation this can be extremely expensive.

Another piece of equipment is the dishwashing machine. Because of its complexity and the low level of employee skills in operation, dishwashers are probably subject to breakdowns more than any other piece of restaurant equipment. Furthermore, for a table service restaurant, a breakdown in the flow of clean tableware can create a serious disruption in the operation, result in reduced sales volume, and possibly create a health hazard if improper manual washing procedures are used as a substitute for machine washing.

Service contracts can also be made for all general kitchen equipment (including scales), electrical signs, vehicles, office equipment and cash registers, public address and music systems, and various housekeeping functions such as extermination, snow removal, flue and exhaust duct cleaning, wall washing, rug shampooing, window washing, heavy kitchen equipment cleaning, and waste removal.

The Unit Manager's Responsibility for the Maintenance Function

With the help of outside craftsmen and contracted services, the manager of many food service operations must be his (or her) own maintenance manager. Although his inventory of spare parts may be limited to a few fuses and screws and his tools to a screwdriver and a pair of pliers, he still must perform most if not all the maintenance functions described above. He should maintain records on the amount of expenditure and the frequency of inspections of various pieces of equipment. If a service contract is in force, he should note when the service representative comes, and that the terms of the contract are being carried out. He should make his own inspections of major equipment and learn to make minor adjustments as required. He should learn to identify signs of trouble, such as noises of motors off balance, compressors going on and off too frequently, and so on, and he must be alert to the condition of the premises when making regular rounds.

Proper training and supervision of the staff in the use of the equipment is also vital, and this function can be performed *only* by line management.

Record keeping is very important. A file should be maintained of all records and brochures for each piece of equipment, including servicing instructions and spare parts lists. Records of warranties in force should be kept current and easily accessible. Warranty cards on new equipment should be filled out and mailed promptly. Many operators spend a lot of money needlessly for repairs on equipment still covered by warranties.

When calling a repair service, the manager should have some idea of what is wrong with the equipment so that the repair man can come properly equipped to deal with the problem. Even before calling for service, the manager should check to be sure that there is a bona fide need for service. Some manufacturers provide a trouble-shooting guide for their equipment that may include such vital points as "be sure the appliance is properly plugged in, and that there is power in the lines." The electric appliance may also be equipped with an automatic cut-off in the case of an overloaded circuit. All that may be required is that the overload be removed and a "reset" button pushed. Calling a repair service for this type of problem can be very costly.

There is a checklist, prepared by the National Restaurant Association, which provides a basis for planning routine and preventive maintenance on dishwashing machines, refrigerators, and other types of kitchen equipment.

18

SANITATION

No area of food and beverage operation commands more public attention than sanitation. A restaurant may serve the most delicious cuisine and service may be performed at the highest level, yet if sanitation standards are not acceptable, the public will stay away from the door. A poor reputation spreads like wildfire through a community. The food and beverage operator must never forget this fact, for it is a justified customer reaction and one that is now getting prominent attention from consumer groups and the news media. The public expects—and every operator has a legal and moral obligation to provide—safe, clean, and sanitary conditions where food and beverages are handled and served.

A large body of information on this subject is readily available to the operator. Local, state, and federal health authorities publish laws, standards, and guidelines, and numerous books, pamphlets, and trade magazine articles are in print on sanitation. Yet some operators continue to give minimal attention to this very important aspect of their operation.

What Is Sanitation?

A dictionary definition of sanitation gives the origin of the word as *sanitas*, or health. The primary objective of any sanitation program is to prevent the transmission of diseases and to protect good health. The sanitation program must encompass all aspects of the food and beverage service cycle, from selection of raw materials through storage and preparation, to cooking and service, to the washing of dishes and utensils. Food, beverages, utensils, serviceware, equipment, and people must be free from concentrations of harmful bacteria, toxins, and other contaminants. An active, continuing sanitation program is one of the primary duties of food and beverage management and is a public responsiblity that cannot be avoided.

Contamination: What/How/When/Where

Contamination of food and beverages can take many forms. Among these are those discussed below.

Bacteria

Bacteria are microorganisms that are found in all foods. Not all bacteria are harmful to humans, and in fact some play an important role in various physiological functions. Contamination occurs when harmful bacteria multiply and grow, either forming toxins (poisons) or masses of bacteria harmful to health. Bacteria, in addition to being naturally present in foods, are introduced to food products by handling, contact with contaminated surfaces, or exposure to air-borne contaminants. Some of the more common types of bacteria that occur in food handling are as follows.

1. *Staphylococcus:* "Staph" bacteria are present on skin and often cause the infection of skin wounds. They are also prevalent in the noses and mouths of humans. Staph bacteria are transmitted by sneezes, coughs, scratches, cuts, and sores. When allowed to multiply, they form staphylococcus enterotoxin, a poison. The staph bacteria themselves can be easily killed by disinfectants and heat. However, once the enterotoxin is formed, the poison is not affected by disinfectants or heat. Therefore, food handlers with colds or coughs must not be allowed to work (see Personnel and Training, p. 385), and food handlers with cuts or scratches must be given plastic gloves with which to work.

2. *Salmonellosis:* There are over 800 varieties of salmonella bacteria capable of producing gastrointestinal illness. These bacteria are found naturally in the intestinal tracts of humans, many warm-blooded animals, and poultry. Salmonella are transmitted to food in several ways: fecal contamination by food handlers, contaminated raw meats and poultry, and contaminated utensils or equipment on which salmonella have been placed or allowed to grow. Rodents and flies are also frequent carriers of salmonella bacteria. Salmonella bacteria do not produce a toxin as do staph bacteria but are themselves harmful when found in large concentrations. Prevention of contamination from this source is best accomplished through enforcement of strict personal hygiene habits by food handlers and by thorough inspection of sources of supply. Elimination of flies and rodents is also an important preventive measure.

3. *Streptococcus:* Strep bacteria are prevalent in certain nasal and oral infections and are transmitted to food or equipment by sneezing and coughing. There are several varieties of strep bacteria, all of which are introduced into food by humans. Exclusion of persons

with strep infections from the food handling process is the major method of prevention.

4. *Clostridium perfringens: Clostridium perfringens* are natural contaminants of meats and fish. When allowed to grow, these bacteria form a toxin that can cause severe gastric upset. They grow especially rapidly in meat, stews, and the like that have been partially cooked and allowed to cool at unsafe temperatures. Growth of this bacteria to a toxin-forming level can be prevented by rapid refrigeration of meats between cooking and use.

5. *Clostridium botulinum:* Botulism, a sometimes fatal disease, is caused by toxins formed by *Clostridium botulinum* in improperly processed or unrefrigerated foods of low acidity. Swollen cans are a danger signal. The bacteria grow only in the absence of air and form spores that can resist boiling. However, the toxin produced by these spores can be inactivated by boiling the food for 20 minutes before serving. The operator should never use food from a swollen can, and all home-canned foods should be boiled thoroughly.

For all the above and other bacteria, the important factor is prevention of growth to harmful levels. Under "Food Handling," p. 380, we discuss methods of prevention.

Trichinosis

The larvae of *Trichinella spiralis* are found in some pork and pork products from hogs fed uncooked, infected garbage. Trichinosis can be prevented by thoroughly cooking all pork products to 160° F.

Pesticides

Insecticides and rodenticides used in food production centers sometimes contain arsenic, fluoride, or lead, which can be poisonous. Thorough washing of all fresh fruits and vegetables when received and proper storage of pesticides can prevent contamination from this source.

Hair and Insects

One of the most frequent contaminants found in food is human hair from food processors or servers. This causes a most unpleasant experience for the customer and can be easily prevented by use of hairnets or caps by all employees. Flies are most undesirable in a food and beverage environment for two reasons: (1) they are often carriers of bacteria, and (2) they indicate to the guest a lack of sanitation in all respects. Flies can be eliminated from the operation by proper handling of garbage and trash, installation of fly fans or screens at every door and window, installation of fly-killing devices, and general good housekeeping outside the building. Cockroaches are other insects that seek out the food and beverage environment if the operator lacks vigilance. There are many types of roaches, but all have one thing in common: They are repellent to the consumer. Roaches carry disease on their legs and bodies and also give off an unpleasant odor. The best prevention is to seal doors and windows, pipes and conduits, and other possible entrances into the building. Good housekeeping discourages roaches. Scheduled periodic treatment by a professional exterminator is part of this housekeeping and will help eliminate many types of insects. Cockroaches hide during the day and forage at night. Therefore, the fact that they are not seen during the day should not be taken to indicate their absence.

Rodents and Animals

Rodents will invite themselves to the restaurant if conditions extend a "welcome." Proper handling of trash is of primary importance since rodents are attracted to uncovered or overflowing trash receptacles. Doors and other entrances should be kept closed at all times. The outside of the building, especially at the delivery entrance, should be hosed and swept daily. No live animals other than humans should be permitted to enter any food and beverage operation with the exception of seeing-eye dogs. Animals can carry disease on their fur and feet and are not to be welcomed.

Prevention of Contamination

Good sanitation practices and prevention of food-borne diseases are no accident. They require an organized, consistent effort on the part of the food and beverage operator. A program of training, scheduled cleaning, proper food handling procedures, personal hygiene practices, and good housekeeping standards should be established and carried out. In the food and beverage operation, good sanitation starts with proper attention to building design, equipment, materials and finishes, lighting, and space allocation. The remaining areas in the prevention program are food handling, housekeeping (back of the house), personnel and training, warewashing and equipment handling, housekeeping (front of the house), and pest control.

Food Handling

Proper food handling starts at the beginning, on the farm or ranch where the food originates. The food producer has the same obligation as the restaurateur; his product must be wholesome and free from contamination. As the food flows through the processing, manufacturing, and distribution channels, each firm or individual handling the food is responsible for its safety. As a food and beverage operator, one has an obligation to continue and preserve this chain of safety.

Sanitation safeguards and procedures for purchasing, receiving, and storage are discussed elsewhere; preparation and food handling procedures are considered below.

The Time/Temperature Syndrome. All food handling techniques and procedures must be developed with the time/temperature syndrome in mind. Simply expressed, this means that time and temperature are basic ingredients for dangerous bacterial growth and formation of toxins. The operator must structure his food production procedures to avoid allowing too much time to pass at the wrong temperatures.

Temperature: Temperature is both the principal friend and the feared enemy of bacteria. Under proper temperature conditions, bacteria will prosper and multiply. Under adverse temperature conditions, bacteria will either "hibernate" (and not multiply) or will be killed. Bacteria prosper best between the temperatures of 40° and 140° F. Below 40° F, the growth rate slows until it stops completely at freezing temperature (32° F), although the bacteria remain alive. Above 140° F, bacterial growth also slows, and most harmful bacteria are killed at temperatures above 160° F. The temperatures mentioned are expressed in terms of the *internal* temperature of the food, not the air surrounding the food. Bacteria grow fastest at temperatures ranging from 70° F to 120° F. Unfortunately, this is within the temperature range of most kitchens in which food is prepared and handled.

Time: Because of human temperature requirements, food cannot always be handled under safe temperature conditions. Many food sanitation problems would be solved if all food could be handled and prepared in huge refrigerated rooms held at under 40° F. Therefore, the important factor is to *limit* the amount of time any food spends in the danger zone (40° to 140° F).

Research has shown that a cumulative time of four hours is the outside safe limit on exposure to danger zone temperatures. Cumulative time means, for example, that if food is exposed for 30 minutes when received, then placed under refrigeration, then taken out and trimmed or sliced for one hour, then placed into an oven for roasting for two hours, then removed and allowed to "cool" at room temperature for one hour, then refrigerated, then placed on a room temperature buffet for two hours, the food has had cumulative exposure to danger zone temperatures of 4½ hours and should be considered unsafe for consumption. The combination of the 30 minutes, one hour, another hour, and two hours, each period separated by periods of safe temperatures, adds up to too much time in the danger zone. Therefore, food must be moved through the danger zone as quickly as possible. To avoid dangerous time/temperature conditions, follow a few simple guidelines: (1) work with small quantities of food while in the danger zone, (2) move food through the danger zone quickly and don't let it sit out unnecessarily, and (3) in planning production methods and schedules, keep one eye on the time/temperature syndrome to avoid recipes or procedures that are dangerous.

The Finished Product. All the efforts expended in avoiding contamination in receiving, storage, and preparation are for naught if food and beverages are not served to the customer in a sanitary and safe condition. Contamination engendered in the serving process is not as frequent as that in the previous stages but is equally dangerous. Personnel involved in the serving of food must take certain precautions and observe certain rules and procedures to avoid this last-minute contamination.

Bacteria on the hands of service personnel can be easily transmitted to freshly prepared food. For example, if a waitress handles silverware improperly while clearing used dishes from a table, she can transmit bacteria from one guest to another. Therefore, all silverware, whether used or clean, should always be touched by the handle, not the service end. The same is true of glassware. Service personnel should *never* handle glassware by the rim. They also should not be allowed to pick up several glasses at once by placing their fingers inside them. Sneezes and coughs by service personnel are additional sources of contamination. All service personnel should carry disposable tissues (not handkerchiefs) to "catch" these sneezes and coughs. The tissues should be discarded immediately after use, and hands must be washed too. Every waitress, waiter, bus boy, or bartender should be made to wash hands frequently. This is especially true of bus boys or waitresses who handle soiled dishes and then reset tables with clean serviceware.

Too often, in an effort to promote a certain image or appeal, operators permit waitresses to work without hairnets. However, finding hair in a salad will do a lot more to affect a customer's opinion of a restaurant than a waitress's hair style.

Another common method of contamination in the service area is the towel used to wipe tables. Often, one towel is used all day long to wipe tables, clean up spills, clean ashtrays, and so on. This practice leads to huge concentrations of bacteria on the towel and must be prohibited by the operator. Inexpensive, disposable cloths are available that can be used for an hour or two and discarded.

Sanitation at the bar is often far below the standard the operator requires in the kitchen. Most small bar operations involve glass washing by the bartender, but how often does the manager check the procedures in use? Cold water, brush-type machines are available that use a germicidal detergent solution. In larger operations, bar glassware may be washed with the china and silver or in separate glasswashing machines. Behind the bar, bottle wells are often sources of accumulated spillage and dirt. Dishes used to hold fruits and garnishes must be taken to the kitchen daily for a run through the dishwasher. Pourers should also be run through the dishwasher frequently, as should bar spoons, strainers, blender jars, and other bar equipment. The bar should get sanitation attention equal to that observed in food production areas.

Housekeeping (Back of the House)

In addition to the food handling aspects of sanitation mentioned above, proper housekeeping plays an important role in prevention. General housekeeping in storage and refrigerated areas has already been discussed. Generally, housekeeping in food preparation areas can be easily accomplished by preparing and sticking to an organized schedule of cleaning. The schedule can take the form of a monthly calendar prepared at the beginning of each month and then used as a check list. Naturally, some housekeeping/sanitation chores must be performed daily, and these daily tasks can be incorporated on a separate check list.

Generally, each employee should be responsible for the sanitation at his or her workstation. This includes cleaning equipment used in the course of food preparation, such as slicers, choppers, and mixers. When the responsibility for cleaning all equipment is left to the steward's department, food preparation employees often take a poor attitude toward sanitation. Therefore, the operator should insist that each employee clean each piece of equipment, table, or work station at which he works, and time should be allowed during the shift for this purpose. Heavy cleaning, such as that required for exhaust filters, fryers, the area behind stoves, hoods, ceilings and air outlets, and so on can be performed in off hours and should be part of the monthly schedule. The operator should make a list of important heavy-duty cleaning items and plan for them either weekly, twice monthly, or monthly.

Some general trouble spots deserve constant scrutiny by the manager and should be checked daily on his tour of the facility. Among these are can openers and can opener blades, which should be run through the dishwasher at least daily; drawers and undershelves, which accumulate crumbs and dirt if not cleaned regularly; range drip pans, which are too often forgotten in the daily clean-up routine; overshelves, which accumulate dust and dirt if not cleaned daily; reach-in refrigerators and pans inside reach-ins; condiment bins, which are a lot of trouble to empty and sterilize but which must be cleaned regularly; tops of refrigerators, cabinets, ovens, and other equipment, which are not looked at too often, except by the health inspector; hoods and vents, especially the inside lip on a hood enclosure, which tends to collect grease if not drained daily; the area behind tables, ovens, ranges, refrigerators, and sinks where it is difficult to clean and employees will avoid cleaning if you let them; and last but not least, under everything. A hands-and-knees inspection with a flashlight will provide a new perspective on an operation's sanitation program.

Included in the back-of-the-house areas are support rooms, including boiler rooms, compressor rooms, storage areas for furniture, tools and equipment, work shops, mechanical equipment areas, and other nonproduction spaces. These rooms are often dark, sometimes moist, and are favorite hiding places for roaches, other insects, rodents, and similar contaminants. These areas should not be forgotten on the regular extermination tour and should be kept clean and dry as a part of the regular housekeeping schedule.

Employee locker rooms and restrooms require top sanitation priority. In the initial design, these rooms should never open into food preparation areas. Once in use, they should be scheduled for twice daily sanitation visits. Obviously, toilet facilities must be kept sanitized, as should floors, walls, mirrors, sinks, showers, and so on, with the help of a good commercial disinfectant cleaning solution. Paper disposable towels should be provided for employees to use, not cloth roll towels or individual cloth towels. Of course, employees must be instructed to wash hands thoroughly after using toilet facilities and before starting work, and a surgical quality disinfectant soap is recommended for employee washrooms. This soap should be liquid or leaf soap to avoid contamination of bar soap in common use. No food, beverage, or other similar item should be permitted in either restroom or locker room areas. Regular locker inspections should be scheduled but performed unannounced for both sanitation and security reasons.

The trash removal area also requires constant attention. Trash cans, dumpsters, compactors, or other receptacles must remain closed at all times. Open-top trash receptacles provide a welcome to flies, insects, rodents, and other pests. The area around, under, behind, and adjacent to trash receptacles must be hosed down daily to avoid collection of odorous liquids that sometimes leak from these containers. Plastic can liners are recommended for all trash cans used throughout the kitchen, but cans must be washed after being emptied even when liners are used.

An often neglected area in the back-of-the-house area is the janitor's closet, or slop sink. This room, or closet, must be maintained in the same manner as the kitchen itself. Mops should never be stored with their heads on the floor. A rack should be provided to hang them, as well as brooms, squeegees, and other sanitation equipment. The slop sink must be kept clean. Mop buckets should be kept clean, inside and out, and have an assigned storage place when not in use. Hoses should not be coiled on the floor but should be hung on a rack to dry.

Floor mopping is often given as a task to the least skilled employee in the operation, someone with little or no training and not much supervision. However, this is a vital function in the sanitation effort and requires a little time on the part of the operator to assure that it is being done properly. First of all, mop heads should be clean. How often do we see a floor supposedly being cleaned with a mop head that is filthy, smelling, and full of bacterial concentrations? Replace mop heads frequently, and keep those in use clean. The steward, or porter, must be provided with a double-tank mop bucket with wringers on both tanks. One tank holds a detergent solution, the other clear warm rinse water. The porter must be trained in how much detergent to use in each bucket of water. Too often he just throws in a handful, which may be too little and ineffective or too much and wasteful. The floor should be swept before mopping. It should be rinsed thoroughly after washing with the detergent solution and allowed to dry before traffic is allowed on the floor for both safety and cleanliness. Small areas should be mopped at one time, not the whole kitchen. The mop tanks should be changed frequently during the mopping; one bucket will not do the job for the whole kitchen. When the job is finished, the mop must be rinsed out thoroughly in the mop sink (not in a food production sink!) and hung on the mop rack, head up, to dry.

Personnel and Training

People are the key to the success of any sanitation program. Without proper training and motivation, the program will be worth no more than the paper on which it is written, for the people involved will not understand its importance or care enough to follow through.

Training in sanitation must become a key part of the orientation and training of each new employee. Retraining of old-timers is also important, for people tend to overlook things as they settle into a routine on a job. Numerous materials from a number of sources are available for employee training. Literature and training materials are available from governments, associations, cleaning supplies manufacturers, and equipment manufacturers.

Personal Hygiene. A major subject in employee training must be personal hygiene. Personal hygiene in the food preparation and service area consists of two basic areas: (1) prevention of the spread of the illness of an employee, and (2) prevention of contamination caused by the poor personal habits of an employee.

The first category of prevention is more easily handled by the operator. He can prevent spread of illness by removing the ill employee from the production process. An enlightened sick-leave policy is a good investment for the operator. No employee with a cold, flu, or other illness should be economically penalized for his illness and therefore encouraged to work when sick. All employees should receive a physical examination at least once a year, and a health certificate should be on file for all employees. An apparently healthy individual can be a carrier of any one of a number of diseases. In many areas, health certificates are a legal requirement for food handlers but the operator should make them mandatory in any case. Employees should be sent home when they become ill, start coughing or sneezing, or otherwise present a health hazard. When an employee is unable to work because of illness (other than a common cold or flu), the manager should require a doctor's certificate of permission to return to work before allowing the employee to return.

The second area of personal hygiene involves transmission of bacteria or contaminants due to poor personal habits. Most of the critical areas of concern are matters of common sense but do require constant scrutiny and training by management. Examples include washing of hands after using toilet facilities; preventing scratching of head, wiping nose, touching own mouth, and so on, and then handling food; prohibiting smoking or use of any tobacco in food storage, production, or service areas; insistence on hairnets, hats, and other hair-containing gear on *all* food service employees; providing plastic disposable (single-use only) gloves for employees with cuts, scratches, or other skin problems; prohibition of any jewelry on hands (except plain wedding bands); requiring short clean fingernails on all employees (and no nail polish); providing a clean uniform every day for each employee, or other similar provision, and clean aprons when needed; prohibition of using cooks' towels and cloths to wipe perspiration from face; prohibition of spitting in both sinks and on floors in all areas; training in how to handle serviceware, glasses, and silverware to avoid spreading contamination; and setting a general example on personal appearance, conduct, and cleanliness. Regular training on personal hygiene should be scheduled for all employees, old and new.

Motivation. Motivation of employees to follow and actively participate in the sanitation program should not be left to chance. It should be an active effort on the part of the operator. The motivation program can include regularly scheduled meetings, cleanliness awards, bonuses for best appearance, best cleaned work station, and so on, and many other "gimmicks." Each employee must thoroughly understand the risks involved if sanitation levels are allowed to fall. This should not imply motivation through threat but rather an awareness of the importance of the program. Each member of the operation should have a sense of pride in the cleanliness and appearance of the operation, and it is the job of the manager to instill this feeling of pride.

Warewashing and Equipment Handling

The warewashing area is of prime importance in the overall sanitation program. A combination of proper equipment, space, and trained personnel must be brought together to perform this function in an efficient manner. Equipment must be sized properly to handle the volume of material being processed. Purchase of undersized dishwashing equipment is a false economy that will result in higher long-range operating costs and inefficiencies. Adequate support space must be provided for the warewashing function including space to stage and sort soiled serviceware and space to stage, sort, and hold clean ware. Most important is the personnel training function for warewashing. As with floor care, too often the least able, and least trained personnel are placed in the warewashing area with little or no formal training and little or no supervision. This is akin to putting an unlicensed driver behind the wheel of a new Cadillac, since the dishroom probably represents the largest investment in equipment in the kitchen. The operator should take advantage of the training program and outlines prepared by the detergent manufacturers and dishwashing machine manufacturers. These people are the experts in this field and have spent a great deal of time in preparing training programs for food service operators.

The Dishwashing Machine. Commercial dishwashing machines come in all sizes, shapes, and styles, but all have one thing in common: They all use a combination of water under pressure and detergent to remove soil and food from dishes, glasses, and silverware. Care of this piece of equipment should be part of the daily management routine in any food service operation. Dishwashing machines will perform well for many years when maintained and operated properly. When neglected, no other piece of equipment in the kitchen will cause the operator more problems and headaches. Therefore, in self-defense and for good economic reasons, the following rules should be insisted upon by the manager:

1. Change water after every meal period.
2. Remove all spray arms and spray heads daily to flush and clean. Brush water ports as part of this routine.
3. De-lime machine as needed in hard water areas (a water softener is an excellent investment and will prolong the life of the dishwashing machine, reduce detergent consumption, and improve cleaning performance).
4. Keep outside of the machine clean, including the floor under-

neath and around the machine. Do not let spilled detergent or water accumulate.

5. Check detergent dispensing equipment to assure that proper levels are being maintained and that excess detergent is not being used. Also check rinse injectors.
6. Check temperatures to assure that proper water temperatures are being maintained. Wash tank temperature should be between 140° and 160° F. Rinse temperatures should be between 170° and 180° F (the higher temperature being required by some health authorities).
7. Check hoses, gaskets, joints, doors, and tanks for leaks or signs of wear.
8. At the end of the day, drain and clean the machine thoroughly. Do not leave water tanks full and heaters on during periods when the machine will be idle.
9. If the machine is equipped with a conveyor, the gears and belt should be kept clean and free from obstructions at all times.
10. For the dishwashing machine as for any machine, lubricants are required on a regular basis.

The Dish Room. Above all, the dish room must be well organized. Equipment, serviceware, and other materials should not be scattered about in a haphazard manner. Designated spaces should be assigned for specific functions and items. Bus pans of soiled dishes should not be placed near clean serviceware. Racks should be sorted and stacked on dollies by type, not mixed together. Nothing, whether clean or soiled, should be placed on the floor. Mobile racks should be provided for stacking serviceware and equipment at both ends of the machine.

Washing (Silverware, Glassware, Dishes). Silverware should be presoaked before washing. It should be placed unsorted into flat racks, loosely packed, for washing. After going through the machine, the silverware should be sorted into silver cylinders with the handles down. These cylinders should then be run through the machine again to sanitize the "heads." After the second washing, the ware is turned handles up by placing an empty container over the top of the full one and turning them over. This will put the handles up without touching the blades, tines, or bowls of the silver.

Glassware should be sorted into racks before washing and run upside down through the machine. Glasses should remain in the racks in which they are washed to prevent breakage and to avoid excess handling.

Dishes should be scraped before washing and should be washed as soon after use as possible. Occasionally, they will have to be soaked before washing as well, when a particular type of food presents difficult problems. Dishes should be sorted at the "dirty" end of the machine, not at the clean end. This prevents excess handling after washing and improves the dishwashing machine's operating speed; it can be accomplished by having personnel at the scraping table sort dishes by type into various bus pans. When a pan is filled, its contents are run through the machine.

Care must be taken to separate dishes properly in racks or on the conveyor in order to allow a good flow of water on all dish surfaces. Two bowls stuck together will not get cleaned if the water cannot get to all surfaces.

The dishwashing area should be designed to permit an adequate "run" on the clean end of the machine. This is to allow the ware to air dry. The use of a rinsing agent will aid in drying by permitting water to "sheet off." This also avoids water spotting. Wet dishes may also be an indication that the rinse water is not hot enough. Towel drying of ware should be avoided as it is a potential source of contamination.

Pot Washing. Pot washing often takes place in a scullery separated from the dish room. The pot-washing function is a key to food production; the best chefs in the world need clean pots in which to cook and are helpless without them. A pot washer must have a three-compartment sink in which to work. The first compartment contains a detergent solution in 140° F water. The second compartment contains 160° F rinse water, and the third compartment contains 180° F final rinse water. Sometimes a presoak compartment is provided. The pot washer should be provided with heavy-duty rubber gloves because the water temperatures must be high and the detergent is more caustic than dish detergent. When food production levels are high, the pot washer often has a machine especially designed for this function.

Cleaning the Dish Room. The dish room can easily become untidy and a source for potential contamination if time and effort are not provided for housekeeping. At the end of each shift, the machine should be cleaned, floors mopped and dried, walls wiped down, tables and racks organized and cleaned. Floor mats should be cleaned and allowed to dry. Carts should be emptied and cleaned thoroughly. Racks and shelves should be cleaned carefully. Everything should be stored in its place. In this way, the room is left in clean condition ready for the next crew or the next day's work.

Personnel in Warewashing. There is no reason why warewashing personnel cannot be given the same respect and encouragement as a skilled chef or bartender. However, it seems to have been the practice in the industry to afford second-class status to warewashing crews in both wage scales and management attention. High turnover and low productivity in this area will continue unless working conditions, salaries, and social status are improved for personnel in warewashing. The smart operator will encourage professionalism in this crew and will give recognition to the importance of this role in the overall operation. Training, motivation, and psychology are all involved.

Although personnel at the "dirty" end of the machine should not handle clean dishes, and vice versa, employees should switch positions at specific times during the shift to help alleviate boredom (washing hands between changes). All other employees should be trained to treat the warewashing crew with the same respect they desire for themselves. In fact, when possible, each waitress, cook, and bartender should be given a four-hour turn in the dish room occasionally to remind them of what it is like on the other side of the fence.

The detergent manufacturer will provide regular inspections of the dishwashing equipment and will help in training personnel. Take advantage of this service as an extra pair of eyes in the operation. Above all, give this area of the operation as much attention as any other area.

19

SAFETY AND SECURITY

One of the primary duties of management in any business is the protection of the company's assets against various types of losses, including fire, theft, vandalism, embezzlement, and fraud. In addition, any employer has both a legal and moral obligation to protect employees against injury from unsafe working conditions. In the hospitality industry, there is ongoing concern for the safety of guests and for the security of their property.

Therefore, the subjects of safety and security are important areas for the food and beverage manager to study and know. The two primary areas in which the operator must be trained and knowledgeable are *prevention* and *contingency planning*.

Extensive published material is available from a variety of sources to assist the operator in prevention and contingency planning. At the end of this chapter, a list of some sources of information is presented to allow the reader to acquire more detailed information and assistance regarding these subjects.

The safety of employees and guests is of primary importance and should be the subject of thorough, continuous training of all food and beverage personnel. Productive time lost by employees injured in the course of their duties involves heavy expense to the operator and disrupts the effectiveness of the operation, to say nothing of the pain and suffering the employee experiences. In 1971, the Occupational Safety and Health Administration act (OSHA) became part of the national labor law. The full implications of the OSHA with regard to employers' responsibilities and reporting requirements will be discussed later.

Accidents and Prevention

The prevention of accidents involving either employees or guests requires the continual training of the former and the removal of all potential hazards to both groups. A comprehensive self-inspection program is an essential part of the food service manager's daily routine. This program, to be effective, should include:

1. An inspection of equipment and physical facilities throughout the operation.
2. A review of the physical fitness of employees to perform their duties safely.
3. A review of actual operating practices of employees to assure that equipment is being operated safely and that work practices are performed without hazard.

The National Restaurant Association in 1973 published a booklet entitled, *A Safety Self-Inspection Program for Foodservice Operators.* This program gives comprehensive details of potential hazards and provides the operator with an excellent check list to be used during the self-inspection tour.

The food service industry, although relatively safe compared to some heavy construction and manufacturing industries, involves a number of hazards to employees that result in frequent injury. Employee accidents can be avoided in large measure by following the four basic principles of accident prevention:

1. Correction of physical hazards.
2. Formulation of rules.
3. Instruction of all employees in these rules.
4. Enforcement of the rules.

Virtually all employee accidents are caused either by physical hazards in the food service operation or by violation of basic safety rules by the employee. Instruction and enforcement of these rules is a continuing responsibility of management in the day-to-day conduct of the business.

The principal employee accidents may be categorized as follows:

1. Slips and falls.
2. Lifting strains.
3. Burns.
4. Cuts.
5. Food machine injuries.

Contributing to such injuries are the relatively high turnover rate of employees and the rushed conditions associated with preparing and serving foods to order.

Slips and Falls

Good planning and the procedures outlined below can greatly reduce falls.

1. Plan and design the layout to avoid congestion, cross-traffic, and blind spots. Floors should be of a material that allows proper cleaning and drainage and inhibits skids.
2. Avoid congestion in aisles caused by boxes, trash containers, food equipment, and other tripping hazards.
3. Establish a regular schedule of floor washing and enforce it. Mop up all spills immediately. When mopping floors, rope off or block the wet area until dry. Post "Wet Floor—Caution" signs. Avoid use of cleaning and polishing materials that cause slippery conditions.
4. Forbid running, rushing while carrying, or any type of horse-play.
5. Maintain flooring materials in top condition at all times. Replace broken or cracked tiles. Repair tears in carpeting immediately. Replace broken duck boards. Remove any protrusions or similar tripping hazards.
6. Keep stairs and steps in good condition. Stairs must be dry, free from obstacles, well lighted, and in good repair. Use non-skid materials on stairs and steps.
7. Provide ladders for reaching shelves and for other similar purposes. Do not allow standing on boxes, equipment, or on shelving. Maintain ladders in good condition with nonskid feet and steps.
8. Keep docks, walkways, driveways, and outside stairs dry, free from snow and ice, clear of obstacles, well lighted and in good repair.
9. Clean and dry floors in walk-in coolers and freezers regularly to avoid build up of moisture, ice, or other slippery conditions.
10. Suspend warewashing activity in dish room areas for a five-minute period each hour to allow cleaning and mopping of floors, duck boards, and removal of obstacles causing congestion.

Lifting Strains

Lifting strains are relatively easy accidents to prevent. The key to prevention of this type of injury is common sense. Employees should be trained to avoid lifting things that are too heavy for them to manage. Some basic rules should be enforced:

1. Do not assign lifting duties to employees who are physically unable to perform such tasks.
2. Provide the proper materials-handling equipment for movement of goods. These include carts, dollies, and bins of the proper configuration, with the proper casters.

3. Do not buy raw materials in packages that are too bulky or too heavy for the employees to handle, even if a cost savings is involved. One-hundred-pound sacks of sugar are fine for those who can lift them for dumping into a bin, but 25-pound bags cause a lot fewer strains. It doesn't take many days of lost time to pay for the difference in price.

4. Instruct waitresses and bus boys not to overload trays and bus pans. Two safe trips to the kitchen are better than one trip to the hospital.

5. Instruct cooks to consider what will happen to a stock pot after it is full. Will it have to be moved before it is emptied? If so, use a smaller size pot and cook in batches.

6. Keep floors dry and clean. Many lifting strains and back injuries are caused by near falls when an employee carrying something slips on a wet floor but doesn't actually fall.

7. Do not put heavy goods on high shelves in the storeroom. Save these shelves for light paper goods or similar items.

8. Instruct employees to ask for help if they need it. Four hands are better than two in lifting almost anything.

Burns

Cooking involves high temperatures and burns are the natural result of carelessness in such situations. Training, enforcement of rules, and common sense play an important role in avoiding potentially serious burns in the food service operation. The basic rules may be stated as follows:

1. Provide employees with the proper cloths and pads to protect their hands in picking up hot pots, pans, and utensils. Instruct employees to use dry towels for pot holders, as wet cloths can result in steam burns. Instruct cooks to assume that all pots containing food are hot.

2. Do not allow handles from pans, utensils, or stock pots to project out into walking aisles or off the range.

3. Insist that cooking personnel be dressed properly, in long-sleeved heavy jackets that protect the employee from hot spills and from range heat, and in proper shoes.

4. Provide the pot-washing area with a cool-down rack on which hot pots can cool before being handled by the pot washer. Instruct the cooks to warn the pot washer when placing hot equipment in his area for washing.

5. Maintain cooking equipment in good condition. Discard or repair pots and pans with weak or broken handles. Assure that hot tops, broilers, friers, steamers, and all other equipment are

in good operating condition before being used. Do not allow untrained personnel to use this equipment.

6. Instruct employees in proper handling of hot oils when filtering or changing frier fats.
7. Provide proper equipment for handling disposable convenience food pans, as these are often weak and require special handling.
8. Use caution in opening drums or containers containing caustic agents such as detergents and cleaning compounds. These occasionally are under pressure and can cause burns or eye injuries. Provide employees who regularly work with caustic agents with heavy-duty rubber gloves.
9. Install splash guards on steam-jacketed kettles and other pieces of equipment where hot liquids could splash when being emptied.
10. Make sure that dish room employees are properly trained in cleaning and operation of dishwashing equipment to avoid burns from heating elements, rinse water, and detergent compounds.

Cuts

Preparation of food requires sharp instruments that can cause severe injuries if improperly used. Virtually all employee accidents involving cuts can be traced to improper training or carelessness. The basic rules governing use of sharp tools are very important:

1. Keep knives sharp. A dull knife is more likely to slip and cut the person using it than a very sharp knife. Employees should be trained in the proper method of sharpening knives and safe use of sharpening instruments.
2. Never attempt to catch a dropped knife. As simple as this rule sounds, such attempts constitute a frequent cause of cutting injuries.
3. Never place a knife in a sink to be washed. Never place a knife in a drawer with other tools. Never place towels, boxes, or other items on top of a knife.
4. Store knives properly when they are not in use. Preferably, this storage should be in the vertical position, handle up, in a slotted cabinet, magnetic knife holder, or similar device.
5. Transfer food from open cans with sharp edges into other containers.
6. Remove broken glass immediately following breakage.
7. Remove or cover with protective materials sharp edges on equipment, fixtures, and furniture.

Food Machine Injuries

A great number of very serious injuries in the food service industry are caused by improper use of food machinery. Almost all food processing machinery is potentially dangerous since it is designed to slice, chop, saw, mix, or heat. All these actions can cause injury to the operator of the machine if he is careless, improperly trained, or if safety devices are ignored. The importance of thorough, continuous training in use of food machinery cannot be overemphasized. Often, manufacturers and distributors of such equipment are more than willing to assist the manager in training employees in proper and safe use. Complete training of employees in operation, cleaning, movement from place to place, and maintenance of food machinery is essential to save them from injury.

1. Never let an employee operate, clean, move, or repair any piece of food machinery on which he has not been trained and checked out.
2. Do not attempt to remove (except for cleaning) or otherwise disturb safety devices installed by the manufacturer for the protection of the employee. Never let an employee operate any machinery without all guards in place.
3. Never clean a piece of electrically operated food machinery such as slicer, buffalo chopper, grinder, saw, vertical cutter, or mixer unless the machine is unplugged or a circuit breaker is opened. The same rule pertains to maintenance and repair.
4. Do not allow employees to wear loose clothing, jewelry, long hair, or anything else that could possibly get caught in a piece of food equipment. Rings, necklaces, scarves, braids and the like are extremely dangerous around cutters, mixers, grinders, and the like.
5. Never use hands or fingers to guide food into a slicer, grinder, chopper, or other similar equipment. Use tampers, paddles, and other tools recommended by the manufacturer.
6. Post all instructions and safety rules for each piece of machinery next to the machine. Some operators have these instructions sealed in plastic and mounted on the machine or near it.

Handling of Emergencies

When an injury occurs, the most important rule is to avoid panic. It is always preferable to have at least one employee or member of management trained in first aid. Many YMCA facilities and other such organizations offer inexpensive courses that can often save a life in emergency circumstances. The operator should be prepared to handle emergencies in the following ways:

1. Keep the phone number of ambulance, police, fire, and hospital posted next to every telephone in the operation.
2. Know the location of the nearest hospital. Know the quickest route to that hospital.
3. Keep a fully equipped, approved first aid kit on the premises and available for use. It won't do any good if it's locked in the manager's desk and he's on his day off.
4. Know how to treat shock, which can result in more serious damage than the injury itself. Apply first aid as required to any accident victim or critically ill guest or employee.

The Occupational Safety and Health Administration (OSHA)

In 1971 the Williams-Steiger Occupational Safety and Health act of 1970 became effective, creating the Occupational Safety and Health Administration as an agency of the U. S. Department of Labor. OSHA was charged with administration of the act, which Congress enacted to "assure so far as possible every working man and woman in the Nation safe and healthful working conditions and to preserve our human resources."

The act covers every employer in a business affecting commerce that has one or more employees. Specific health and safety standards have been adopted by OSHA, as well as a general duty requirement which states "that each employer shall furnish to each of his employees employment and a place of employment which are free from recognized hazards that are causing or likely to cause death or serious physical harm to his employees." In addition to the federal OSHA act, states are permitted to establish their own plans and guidelines "at least as effective" as the federal program.

The act provides for an inspection program to be conducted by an occupational safety and health compliance officer. An inspection can be conducted at any place of business for any one of the following reasons:

1. If a catastrophe or fatal accident has occurred.
2. When OSHA has received a valid employee complaint.
3. If it is a "target industry" or involves a "target health hazard."
4. If it has been randomly selected by either state or federal officials.

The act generally prohibits advance notice of an inspection visit. The operator and an employee representative may accompany the compliance officer on his inspection tour of the facility. The officer will announce the reason for his visit and may ask to review safety and health records required by the act. He may also interview employees.

In addition to the safety and health standards specifically applicable to an operation, the officer may cite any hazard under the general duty clause. After the inspection, the compliance officer will hold a closing conference with the operator and discuss what he has seen and review any violations. When the officer returns to his office, he writes a report and discusses it with his superiors. The area director determines what citation will be issued, if any, and what penalties will be proposed. These are sent to the operator by certified mail. The compliance officer may not issue any citations on his own nor may he "close down" a food service operation on the spot.

There are four types of violations that can be cited in the event a food service operation is found to be not in compliance with OSHA standards:

1. *De minimis:* A violation in which there is no direct or immediate relationship to job safety and health.
2. *Nonserious:* A violation that does have a direct relationship to job safety and health but probably would not cause death or serious physical harm. A proposed penalty of up to $1,000 is optional. A nonserious penalty may be adjusted downward by as much as 50 percent, depending on the severity of the hazard, the employer's good faith and his history of previous violations, and the size of the business. This penalty can be reduced an additional 50 percent if the employer corrects the violation within the prescribed abatement period.
3. *Serious:* A violation where there is substantial probability that death or serious physical harm could result and that the employer knew, or should have known, of the hazard. A proposed penalty of up to $1,000 is mandatory, but may be adjusted downward by as much as 50 percent based on the employer's good faith, history of previous violations, and size of business.
4. *Imminent danger:* A condition where there is reasonable certainty that a hazard exists that can be expected to cause death or serious physical harm immediately or before the hazard can be eliminated through regular procedures. If the employer fails to abate such conditions immediately, OSHA can go directly to the federal district court for legal action as necessary.

If the operator disagrees with the citation, a proposed penalty, or a period set for the abatement of a hazard, he may first meet with the area director for an informal discusson of the case. If, after the meeting, he decides to contest the case, he must within 15 days of receipt of a notice of proposed penalty in writing notify the OSHA area director stating what he contests. The case will then be heard through various levels of appeal until a final decision is made at the U.S. Circuit Court of Appeals level.

In addition to the maintenance of proper standards of safety and health conditions, the operator who employs 11 or more employees is required to keep certain records of job-related fatalities, injuries, and illnesses. There are three basic forms required, none of which must be submitted to OSHA but which must be made available to the compliance officer when an inspection is made. These record-keeping requirements are an important part of the act, and failure of the operator to maintain the required records can result in citation for violation of the OSHA act. The forms, copies of regulations, standards, and other assistance are available from any office of OSHA and through the operator's workmen's compensation carrier.

Information regarding both the legal aspects of safety and security and the various insurance coverages required by the food service operator is presented in *Profitable Food and Beverage Management: Planning*.

Fires and Fire Prevention

Information from the National Fire Protection Association indicates that during 1972 one out of 10 restaurants had some sort of fire. Although the average loss was only $2,500, many losses were in excess of $250,000.

The NFPA has also found that over 50 percent of all restaurant fires occur when the business is closed and no one is present. Aside from those restaurant fires of incendiary or suspicious origin, the majority of food service fires are caused by kitchen equipment or from the ignition of grease in exhaust ducts.

The frequency and severity of restaurant fires has led some insurance underwriters simply to stop insuring this type of business. However, the conscientious manager, by implementation of a care-fully planned prevention program, can significantly reduce the possibility of fire in his food service operation.

The first line of defense against fire is the proper design and installation of cooking equipment, ventilating systems, and building electrical and mechanical systems. Twenty-three percent of all restaurant fires in 1972 were caused by faulty wiring and electrical appliances. Addition of new equipment is often done without consideration given to the electrical loads imposed on the building system. Circuits are often overloaded, defeating the purpose of the fuse and circuit-breaker apparatus designed to prevent fires. Motors, compressors, pumps, and other mechanical equipment used in food service operation are often improperly maintained, creating fire hazards. The operator should set up a schedule of preventive maintenance and checks on all equipment to assure that it is not overloaded and is operating efficiently. Compressors, pumps, and similar equipment should be installed in properly vented areas, allowing sufficient air circulation to prevent overheating. No wiring should be installed by personnel other than those licensed and trained according to the National Electrical Code.

Hoods, ducts, and exhaust systems should be designed and installed with automatic fire protection equipment. This equipment takes a variety of forms but is all designed either to stop fires from igniting in these systems or to extinguish fires already started. There have been new systems designed recently that automatically wash and clean all ducts and hoods daily to prevent build-ups of dangerous grease. In systems without automatic wash-down equipment, it is essential that ducts be designed with access doors to allow regular manual washing and cleaning. Hoods should be equipped with grease filters that trap grease particles before they enter the ducts. These filters should be washed with detergent and water at least weekly, or their effectiveness is diminished. Most duct fires are started when a small fire starts on a piece of cooking equipment under the hood, such as a flare-up of broiled meat. This ignites any grease that has been allowed to build up in the hood and ducts and can result in a major fire of catastrophic proportions. The key to prevention is to stop grease from accumulating in the exhaust system by regular cleaning and maintenance, a job often performed by an outside firm with the proper equipment for it. Even when cleaning is performed on a scheduled program, it is possible for a fire to be ignited in exhaust systems. If automatic extinguishing equipment is installed, such fires are usually put out immediately and do not cause extensive damage. The automatic systems can be dry chemical, carbon dioxide, or water spray and are activated by fusible link assemblies that react to temperatures above a safe level. The major advantage of a carbon dioxide system is the absence of a residue that must be cleaned up following activation of the system.

Fires caused by smoking materials accounted for over 14 percent of restaurant fires in 1972. Such fires are started primarily by careless disposal of smoking materials by either guests or employees. Employees should be instructed not to empty ashtrays into tablecloths while clearing tables. Ashtrays and cigarettes should also never be emptied into trash containers that include dry refuse. Separate, covered, fireproof containers should be provided for disposal of smoking materials. It is virtually impossible to prevent restaurant guests from dropping smoking materials onto carpets or seats. The best prevention against fire from this source is to specify fire-retardant fabrics and materials. The initial investment in these materials is relatively inexpensive when compared to the devastating effect of a major fire. Of course, safe ash trays should be provided in all areas.

Training of employees in fire prevention and in an action plan in case of fire is an essential management duty. The proper fire extinguishing equipment must be provided and employees trained in its proper use. The insurance underwriter of the restaurant and the local fire company are often more than happy to assist the operator in training employees in use of extinguishing equipment. Portable carbon dioxide extinguishers should be available in cooking areas in addition to the automatic system in exhaust hoods. In dining areas, an approved Class A extinguisher should be available for each dining room.

Employees should also be trained in the evacuation of guests in case of fire. Several employees should be selected to form a fire brigade with specific duties in case of fire. For example, one employee should be responsible for notification of the fire department. Another should be responsible for seeing that all employees have evacuated all areas of the building, and another group should oversee guest evacuation to prevent panic and disorder. The operator should conduct occasional fire drills with employees to assure calm, organized action when an actual fire occurs. This fire brigade should also be trained in the proper use of extinguishing equipment and first aid practices.

The operator should check regularly that exit doors are not blocked or locked in a manner to prevent egress. He should also check emergency lighting and exit lighting to assure its proper functioning in case of fire.

One of the major dangers in a major fire occurring in a public building is smoke inhalation by occupants. Smoke is often spread through the building by air-conditioning and ventilation equipment. Installation of smoke detection equipment that automatically shuts down air-conditioning and ventilation fans can be a worthwhile addition to loss-prevention equipment.

Of course, an automatic sprinkler system throughout the restaurant or food and beverage operation will add significant protection in case of fire. This equipment will also result in lower fire insurance premiums for the operator, since historically, losses from sprinkler-equipped buildings are substantially lower than those not so protected.

Highly inflammable decor should also be avoided whenever possible, and the designer should be required to consider both the flammability and smoke-generating characteristics of the materials chosen for the restaurant.

In a matter of minutes, a fire can wipe out the years of effort taken to build a restaurant's reputation and possibly injure or even involve loss of life. The smart food and beverage operator constantly monitors his facility to assure that adequate protection is provided, that employees are properly trained, and that risks are reduced through proper housekeeping and operational practices.

Fire Insurance Rates

The cost of fire insurance for a restaurant or food service operation can vary widely. According to the Insurance Information Institute, the rates are based on fire safety and risk of loss. The basic factors affecting fire insurance rates are:

1. The fire protection capability of the community in which the business is located. This takes into consideration the local fire department's location, equipment, and capability, and the available water system.
2. The materials used in the construction of the building, including the type of walls, floors, and roof.
3. The presence of an automatic sprinkler system. Fully sprinklered buildings present a much smaller degree of risk than nonsprinklered buildings.
4. The "occupancy hazard" or the inherent fire hazard involved for a particular type of business. With food service operations, fire rating organizations have established three general categories. The lowest rating is given to "food service with no cooking." The second category is "food service with limited cooking," which includes counter-type appliances such as are found in coffee shops or snack bars. The third type is "restaurant with commercial cooking," which involves cooking processes that produce substantial smoke or grease-laden vapors. The last category involves considerably more risk than the first two.
5. Within the last category, several other factors are considered, including the relative expense of the decor, whether entertainment is provided, as well as the hazards of cooking. Costly decors require higher insurance rates, and underwriters have found that losses in night club and cabaret fires are also higher than in restaurants without entertainment.

Although the individual restaurant owner or operator has little control over the capability of his local fire department and probably has no control over the construction materials used in his building, he can still take steps to minimize his fire insurance costs by installing good fire protection systems and by maintaining good housekeeping practices.

Fire insurance is an important part of the loss prevention program in a food and beverage operation. Not only does adequate fire insurance protect the owners of the facility in case of its physical loss but also for liability arising from injuries, loss of life, and other losses as well. Business interruption insurance can also be purchased to allow the operator to recover some of the losses of revenue and profit he experiences while rebuilding after a fire. The operator's insurance carrier should be included in the planning procedure for any new restaurant; he can show the operator how to minimize premium costs through installation of loss prevention devices at the design stage. Once the restaurant is operating, the insurance counselor can play an important role in advising the operator regarding employee training, extinguishing equipment, and similar areas. The operator should also be aware of the inflating replacement cost for his restaurant and increase his insurance coverage periodically to reflect this fact. Numerous restaurants have never reopened after a fire because the owner failed to increase his coverage adequately as the cost of construction rose over the years.

Security

Security for the food and beverage operator involves protection of a wide variety of assets against a broad variety of potential losses. His inventory consists of highly desirable food and liquor, both quite easy to pilfer. There are often large amounts of cash on the premises. Employee turnover is often high, and the historical record of employee theft in the industry is not good. Since restaurants are open to the public, physical security of facilities is difficult; the very things that attract large numbers of customers also attract potential thieves. Therefore, security in a food and beverage operation cannot be left to chance. A continuing program of carefully planned management activity consisting of a combination of physical controls, accounting controls, and people management is required.

Physical Facilities

Security over physical areas is accomplished in two ways: (1) by manning the area with authorized personnel who are responsible for the security of the area, and (2) through physical barriers such as locks, fences, doors, and cages. During operating hours, the front door of every food and beverage operation must naturally be open, but the back door may be closed and locked. Storerooms can be locked up at night after closing but should be manned with a storekeeper or kept locked during the day. Several basic principles apply to the security of the food service facility and should be observed by the operator.

Storage Areas. Access to all food and beverage storage areas should be limited at all times. Only those personnel having a legitimate need to be inside these areas should be permitted access. If bus boys, waiters, bellmen, or porters are seen in storerooms or walk-in coolers, it is essential to question their need to be there. Some large operations have installed systems of color-coded identification badges by which a management employee can determine whether a person is authorized to be in a specific area. In smaller operations, limiting access is a matter of both physical barriers and management observation. Storage areas should be locked at all times the operation is closed. Although the doors to the kitchen may be locked, all storerooms, walk-in coolers, reach-in coolers, and storage cabinets should also be locked every night to prevent unauthorized access. Again, in larger operations, a closed stores system may be feasible, in which all food and beverages are issued on a written requisition basis by stores personnel to various departments. Under this system, only stores employees are permitted access to any storage areas, and records are kept of all movements of goods in and out of storage. When this is not feasible, the principle of limited access should be maintained. Even in smaller operations, it is often possible to limit general access to one day's inventory of food and beverage. Through use of locked cages, screens, and dividers, the manager can separate the "in-production" inventory from general stores, limiting potential losses or improper usage of inventory.

Key Controls. Any system of locks is virtually ineffective unless there are adequate controls over keys from the day the locks are installed. Unfortunately, in most operations, no records exist of to whom keys were issued, how many copies are in existence, or when the locks were last changed. When this situation exits, the operator is exposed to substantial losses since the very devices he thinks are protecting him are actually a *carte blanche* to the potential thief. Keys must be controlled and secured as thoroughly as the cash and inventories to which they give access. The following steps should be taken:

1. Issue keys only to those personnel who absolutely need them.
2. Record to whom each key has been issued and which locks the key fits.
3. Do not identify any key with its lock by a mark.
4. Make sure the submaster, master, and grand master keys are in the hands of a very limited number of management employees only.
5. Make sure discharged employees turn in every key issued to them.
6. Do not allow keys to be left on counters, on desks, or in

desk drawers, or otherwise left available for potential duplication.

7. Never loan keys to an employee to fetch goods from a storeroom or other area (the manager should open the room for the
employee and close it when the job is done).

8. Keep originals of keys in a locked key cabinet with numbered
tags (the key to the key cabinet and the list identifying each
key should be in the hands of a very limited number of management personnel).

9. Change all locks periodically and destroy all old keys.

10. Change any lock for which the key is missing.

11. Never hide keys for delivery men or other outsiders to gain
access to the building.

12. Impose strict discipline upon any employee abusing the
established key controls, including dismissal if the key controls are flagrantly violated.

Liquor and Bars. Security over liquor is especially significant in view
of the high desirability of this commodity and the relative ease with
which it can be removed from the premises if adequate controls are
not in effect. All liquor and beer must be kept under lock and key at all
times the bar is not in actual operation. If a service bartender leaves
his station to go on a coffee break, his bar inventory should be locked
up or his bar manned even for those few minutes. Each night after
closing, all liquor should be put into locked storage until opening the
next day. Whenever possible, control over the liquor inventory should
be in the hands of a management person other than the bartender. The
bartender should not be given access to the bulk liquor storage but
should be limited to the stock issued to him each day. One person
should be responsible for the keys, and they should never be left in a
cash register drawer or lying about the bar. Of course, adequate
beverage cost controls should be in effect, as described in earlier
chapters. These controls will point up any discrepancies that require
further investigation.

Parking Lot and Guest Cars. Although liability for protection of
guests' automobiles varies with the circumstances under which the
car was parked and the applicable state laws, the food service operator
should nevertheless act to prevent vandalism and theft from parking
lots. This is best accomplished by provision of adequate lighting to
discourage these acts and by regular patrols of parking areas by
restaurant personnel. In cases when the operator provides valet
parking, he is indeed responsible for the security of the automobiles
and should provide adequate training and supervision of parking lot
personnel. These employees should be carefully screened to assure

that they will act in a responsible manner and not participate in any acts of theft or vandalism.

Guard Services

Use of outside security agencies is warranted in a number of circumstances and should be carefully considered by the food service operator as part of his overall security program. Management personnel within the organization are often either unqualified or too preoccupied with operational problems to give adequate attention to the security program. Outside security experts also can provide methods and modern techniques that the restaurant operator is not familiar with. A professional security force can be expected to accomplish a number of tasks for the food service operator, including: (1) physical control of facilities such as storage areas, entrances, and exits, (2) checks on equipment and patrols of outside areas; (3) preventing access by unauthorized persons and checking packages and parcels; (4) control over keys; (5) traffic control; (6) fire prevention and checks of extinguisher equipment; (7) first aid; (8) police relations; and (9) handling unruly or intoxicated guests. Guards also can assist in the movement of cash to banks for deposit and in physical protection of cash within the operation. Often the food service operator will engage an outside security contractor to provide one or two of these functions, handling the others internally. When an outside security agency is engaged, the operator should carefully study the proposals offered, check references from other clients of the firm, and insist on the right to approve the personnel assigned by the agency to that account.

Police Relations

Maintenance of proper relations with law enforcement agencies is quite important if the food service operator expects to rely on their prompt action in time of need. This does not mean that the restaurant operator must provide free meals, or even coffee, to every cop on the beat as some do; it does mean that the manager should get to know the police officials having jurisdiction over his neighborhood and should work together with them in the performance of their duties. The cocktail lounge manager should not expect the police department to act as a "bouncer" for him. Handling unruly guests is the role of the manager or security man until such time as a law is violated as a result of assault or property damage. The principal rule governing police relations in food service is as follows: If you do not expect to prosecute or press charges, do not call on the police for help. This rule applies to employee theft, guest theft, or handling unruly guests. The operator should be prepared to press charges in situations requiring police assistance. He will have to testify and fill out numerous forms. If the police discover that the operator "cries wolf" too often—telephoning for help and then dropping charges in the morning's light—they will not respond as quickly when the manager really needs help. The operator should also give full cooperation to police officials in conduct of investigations by vice squad, fraud and bunko detectives, and others with whom he is likely to come into contact. If proper relations with law enforcement authorities are maintained, the authorities can be a valuable ally when the operator discovers fraud, prostitution, or theft going on within his establishment.

Cash Security

Like a number of retail industries, the food and beverage establishment handles a relatively large amount of cash during the course of each business day. Unlike many other retail outlets, though, the restaurant often conducts business well after banking hours and must maintain cash on the premises late into the night. The amount of cash on hand should be minimized by making frequent bank deposits, using the night depository when required. The amount of cash on hand at cashier stations, at the bar, and other publicly accessible locations should be minimized by having the manager collect cash from these locations several times during each shift. This cash, following audit, should be placed in a secure safe prior to the bank deposit. All auditing and counting of cash should be done in a locked room, away from public view. If possible, this room should be equipped with a one-way mirror so that personnel inside can see who is outside without being seen. The room should be equipped with a telephone and an alarm buzzer that rings a bell at another location in the event of attempted robbery. The safe selected for the operation can be selected from a number of designs and sizes. When a combination safe is selected, the combination should be changed periodically, and the numbers to the combination should not be recorded in writing anywhere. When a key safe is selected, control over the keys should be in the hands of one or two persons only. All safes should be bolted or welded to the floor and should include a slot so that deposits can be made without opening the safe.

Movement of cash to the bank for deposit requires common sense security precautions. If the operation can justify the cost, armored car service provides the best security. In the absence of this method, the operator can use other techniques to minimize the chances of robbery. The movement of cash should not be done at the same time each day. A different person should be used, on a rotation basis, from day to day to take the cash to the bank. A different route should be taken, selecting from three or four alternate routes on a random basis. All these things are intended to avoid establishment of a daily routine that can be observed by a potential thief. If cash is moved at random times by random personnel using varying routes, the likelihood of a robbery is significantly reduced.

All cashier locations should be equipped with a telephone. In addition, it is wise to provide an alarm button that cannot be heard by a robber and that the cashier can activate without arousing suspicion.

Shoppers' Services

From time to time, the operator may engage the services of an outside agency known as a shoppers' service to assist him in security. These services are primarily geared toward apprehension of dishonest employees handling cash or valuable inventory. Many methods are used by the shoppers' service, but they all basically involve a person acting as a customer who observes how the employee handles transactions: the practices of bartenders, waitresses handling cash, clerks, cashiers, and so on. When food and beverage controls reveal a problem that the operator cannot routinely solve or trace, the shoppers' service is a valuable security tool. If charges are to be brought against dishonest employees, evidence from a shopping service may be essential.

Walk-Outs (Theft by Customers)

All retail businesses face the threat of theft by customers, and the food service industry is no exception. Where the clothing store must reduce shoplifting risks, the restaurant operator must eliminate walk-outs who eat or drink and leave without paying. The physical design of the operation is an important factor in reducing the number of potential walk-outs, and consideration should be given to this factor in layout and design stages. The policies and systems installed for cash handling, such as using cashiers instead of having waiters and waitresses handle cash, should be designed to reduce the risk of walk-outs. Accurate control of serially numbered guest checks is the important first step in reducing this problem. State laws vary on the amount of responsibility that can be placed on hourly employees for missing checks and walk-outs, and the operator should consult local legal advisors prior to establishing policies in this regard.

Bad Checks, Bad Credit Cards, Counterfeiting

In our nearly cashless society, the risk of theft by bad checks, stolen or bad credit cards, and counterfeit currency or travelers checks is increasing daily. For those operators whose type of clientele and service permits, the surest way to avoid this risk is to accept cash only for payment. However, from a marketing viewpoint, the number of food services that can successfully adopt this policy is declining rapidly. Therefore, the operator must instruct his employees in several rules that will reduce the potential losses:

1. Establish and enforce a check-cashing policy. This policy can include some or all of the following rules:
   (a) accept checks only for the amount of purchase plus tip.
   (b) no out-of-town checks.
   (c) no third-party checks.
   (d) no post-dated checks.
   (e) no checks from intoxicated guests.
   (f) no checks above a certain limit in amount.
   (g) checks with preprinted name and address of maker only.
   (h) checks written and signed in the presence of a managerial employee only.
   (i) two forms of identification with name, address, and signature should be presented.
   One very effective way to discourage the professional bad-check passer is to use a thumb-print recording device on the back of the check. These are inexpensive and an excellent security addition.
2. Train employees to examine credit cards thoroughly for (a) expiration date and (b) signature matching with voucher.
3. Check all credit cards against the cancellation bulletin published by the issuer. In high-volume operations, use of an automatic verification device connected by telephone to the credit card company's computers is often a worthwhile security investment.
4. Instruct employees handling cash what to look for in the way of counterfeit currency or travelers checks. The local police and law enforcement agencies will offer assistance in this type of training.

Armed Robbery

As previously mentioned, several physical precautions should be taken to reduce the risk of losses by armed robbery. However, in spite of these precautions, restaurants and bars are increasingly becoming targets of robbery owing to the relatively large amount of cash on hand.

There are two primary rules in which employees should be thoroughly instructed regarding armed robbery:

1. Do not resist. Do not threaten the robber in any way, either physically or verbally. Make no sudden movements. Give the robber all monies he can see and follow his instructions exactly and calmly. Do not panic.

2. Observe anything you possibly can about the robber: height, weight, race, color of hair and eyes, scars or other marks, clothing, and speech. As soon as the robber leaves, write these things down so you won't forget when questioned later.

Employees should be completely aware that the management does not expect nor want them to attempt to be heros. Above all, they should do nothing to force the robber to act violently. In virtually all cases, the robber is nervous and wants to escape as quickly as he can without using any force. Allow him to do so, observing his actions as much as can be done without physical risk. He should never be confronted, threatened, chased, or otherwise encouraged to protect himself through use of force. Following any robbery or attempted robbery, call police immediately and report as many details to them as possible. Be prepared to make identification of any suspects and to testify in court.

Employee Security

Prevention of employee theft and similar internal security problems begins at the employment office. This is the place to screen out potential security risks to the operation. In hiring, the food service operator should take several precautions:

1. The employment application form should be designed to obtain as much information about the applicant's background as is permitted by law.
2. In examining the application form, the operator should be on the lookout for several things: unexplained gaps in employment, similar gaps in residences, dishonorable discharges from military service, frequent job changes without adequate explanation, and similar suspicious facts.
3. The interview should be detailed and penetrating. The applicant should be able to describe in detail the previous places he has worked and be able to give names as references. Ask if he would object if you called these references to check on him.
4. Any background facts discovered in the application or interview that cause the operator to have any doubts should warrant a background check. This can be as simple as a few phone calls or as extensive as credit bureau reports and police checks if cash or vulnerable inventory is to be handled. On occasion, written reference checks are required. If your employees are to be bonded, the insurance carrier will outline requirements for thorough background checks.

Although discharge for cause, a brief police record, or other negative factors in a person's background should not necessarily disqualify him from employment opportunities, the operator should carefully weigh the risks to his operation by employing personnel with questionable histories. Fairness to the applicant and fairness to the investors in the enterprise should be considered in making any such decisions.

Handling Dishonest Employees

Every food service operator eventually is faced with the situation of dealing with a dishonest employee whom he has caught embezzling cash, stealing inventory, giving away drinks, or stealing from customers. These situations are invariably unpleasant and uncomfortable for the manager but must be dealt with professionally and firmly.

In such cases, there are very few instances in which disciplinary action less than termination is a satisfactory solution. When a dishonest employee is fired, the question arises whether to prosecute. Often the operator will not do so for many reasons: He doesn't want to be troubled testifying, he feels the theft wasn't too serious, he doesn't want to "ruin someone's life," and so on. However, once word gets around town that the most serious penalty for stealing at that restaurant is termination, it can become a haven for internal thieves. If all the potential thief risks is loss of job, there is no risk at all for him. Therefore, the operator who vigorously prosecutes dishonest employees will acquire a reputation, both internally and externally, as a person not to be thought of lightly.

Sources of Information
on
Safety and Security

Following is a list of organizations (and their addresses) that may be contacted for further information on the subject of safety and security in business operations:

The National Restaurant Association
Suite 2600
One I.B.M. Plaza
Chicago, Illinois 60611

National Fire Protection Association
470 Atlantic Avenue
Boston, Massachusetts 02210

National Safety Council
425 North Michigan Avenue
Chicago, Illinois 60611

National Sanitation Foundation
NSF Building
3475 Plymouth Road
Ann Arbor, Michigan 48106

Underwriters' Laboratories
207 East Ohio Avenue
Chicago, Illinois 60611

Occupational Safety and Health Administration (OSHA)
Regional Offices in Boston, New York, Philadelphia, Atlanta,
Chicago, Dallas, Kansas City, Denver, San Francisco, and
Seattle

Liberty Mutual Insurance Company
175 Berkley Street
Boston, Massachusetts 02117

Chamber of Commerce of the United States of America
1615 H Street N.W.
Washington, D.C. 20006

BIBLIOGRAPHY

Operations Management

General Books on Commercial and Noncommercial Food Service

Cloyd, Frances (ed.). *Guide to Food Service Management.* Cahners Books, Boston, Mass. 1972.

Coates, Dennis. *Industrial Catering Management.* Cahners Books, Boston, Mass., 1971.

Drive-In Management Magazine. *Drive-In Management Guidebook.* Harbrace Publications, New York, N.Y. 1970.

Dukas, Peter. *How to Plan and Operate a Restaurant.* Hayden Book Co., Rochelle Park, N.J., 1973.

Dyer, Dewey. *So You Want to Start a Restaurant?* Cahners Books, Boston, Mass., 1971.

Eshbach, Charles. *Food Service Management.* Cahners Books, Boston, Mass., 1974.

———. *Food Service Trends.* Cahners Books, Boston, Mass., 1974.

Gardner, Jerry. *Contract Food Service/Vending.* Cahners Books, Boston, Mass., 1973.

Kahrl, William. *Food Service on a Budget for Schools, Senior Citizens, Colleges, Nursing Homes, Industrial, Correctional Institutions.* Cahners Books, Boston, Mass., 1974.

———. *The Food Service Productivity and Profit Idea Book.* Cahners Books, Boston, Mass., 1975.

———. *Meeting Challenges in Food Service.* Chain Store Age Books, New York, N.Y., 1974.

———. *Planning and Operating a Successful Food Service Operation.* Chain Store Age Books. New York, N.Y., 1973.

Keister, Douglas, and Wilson, Ralph. *Selected Readings for an Introduction to Hotel and Restaurant Management.* McCutchan Publishing, Berkeley, Calif., 1971.

Kotschevar, Lendal. *Food Service for the Extended Care Facility.* Cahners Books, Boston, Mass., 1973.

Miller, Edmund. *Food and Beverage Management and Service.* Educational
    Institute of the American Hotel & Motel Association, Kellogg Center,
    East Lansing, Mich., 1964.
Soloman, Kenneth, and Katz, Norman. *Profitable Restaurant Management.*
    Prentice-Hall, Inc., Englewood Cliffs, N.J., 1974.
Stokes, John W. *Food Service in Industry and Institutions.* Wm. C. Brown,
    Dubuque, Iowa, 1973.
————. *How to Manage a Restaurant or Institutional Food Service.* Wm. C.
    Brown, Dubuque, Iowa, 1974.
U.S. Department of Commerce. Small Business Administration. *Starting and
    Managing a Small Drive-in Restaurant.* U.S. Government Printing
    Office, Washington, D.C., 1972.
U.S. Department of Commerce. *Starting and Managing a Small Restaurant.*
    U.S. Government Printing Office, Washington, D.C., 1964.
Warner, Mickey. *Industrial Food Service and Cafeteria Management.*
    Cahners Books, Boston, Mass., 1973.
West, Bessie et al. *Food Service in Institutions.* John Wiley & Sons. New York,
    N.Y., 1966.
Zaccarelli, Herman and Maggiore, Josephine. *Nursing Home Menu Planning,
    Food Purchasing and Management.* Cahners Books, Boston, Mass.,
    1972.

Menu Planning

Eckstein, Eleanor F. *Menu Planning.* Avi Publishing Co., Westport, Conn.,
    1973.
Kreck, Lothar. *Menus: Analysis and Planning.* Cahners Books, Boston, Mass.,
    1975.
Morris, Maurice, and Outland, John G. *Rotating Seasonal Menus.* Hayden
    Book Co., Rochelle Park, N.J., 1966.
Restaurant Business, Inc. *Menu Planning and Foods Merchandising.* ITT
    Educational Publishing Co., Indianapolis, Ind., 1972.
Seaberg, Albion G. *Menu Design, Merchandising and Marketing.* Cahners
    Books, Boston, Mass., 1973.
U.S. Department of Agriculture. *Food Selection for Good Nutrition in Group
    Feeding.* Government Printing Office, Washington, D.C., 1972.
Visick, Hubert E. and VanKleek, Peter E. *Menu Planning: A Blueprint for
    Better Profits.* McGraw-Hill Book Co., New York, N.Y., 1974.
Waldner, George. *65 Quality Menus for Quantity Service.* Hayden Book Co.,
    Rochelle Park, N.J., 1965.

Institutional Menus and diet manuals

American Hospital Association. *Diet and Menu Guide for Extended Care
    Centers.* AHA, Chicago, Ill., 1967.
American Hospital Association. *Diet and Menu Guide for Hospitals.* AHA,
    Chicago, Ill., 1969.
Iowa State Department of Health. *Simplified Diet Manual.* Iowa State
    University Press, Ames, Iowa, 1969.
Lindauer, Lois. *Diet Workshop Restaurant Manual.* National Restaurant
    Association, Chicago, Ill., 1972.

Reference Books

Dahl, Crete. *Food and Menu Dictionary.* Cahners Books, Boston, Mass., 1972.

Escoffier, Auguste. *Escoffier Cookbook* (originally published as *Guide Culinaire).* Crown Publishers, Inc., New York, N.Y., 1969.

Gancel, J. E. *Gancel's Culinary Encyclopedia of Modern Cooking.* Radio City Bookstore, New York, N.Y., 1970.

Hering, Richard. *Hering's Dictionary of Classical and Modern Cookery.* (trans. by Walter Bickel.) Radio City Bookstore, New York, N.Y., 1972.

Montagne, Prosper. *Larousse Gastronomique* (ed. by Charlotte and Nina Froud.) Crown Publishers, Inc., New York, N.Y., 1961.

Ranhofer, Charles. *The Epicurean.* Dover Press, Inc., New York, N.Y., 1971.

Saulnier, Louis. *Le Repertoire de la Cuisine.* Radio City Bookstore, New York, N.Y., 1970.

Simon, André L. and Howe, Robin. *Dictionary of Gastronomy.* McGraw-Hill Book Co., New York, N.Y. 1970.

Food Purchasing, Receiving, and Storage

American Can Company, Home Economics Section. *Purchase and Use of Canned Foods.* American Can Company, New York, N.Y., 1957.

————. American Canners Manual. E. L. Judge, 79 Bond St. Westminster, Md. (Annual).

American Frozen Food Institute. *Code of Recommended Practices for the Handling of Frozen Food.* AFFI, Washington, D.C., 1970.

American Home Economics Association. *Handbook of Food Preparation.* AHEA, Washington, D.C. 1971.

American Hospital Association. *Food Purchasing Guide.* AHA, Chicago, Ill., 1967.

Axler, Bruce. *Focus on: Buying and Using Convenience Foods.* ITT Educational Publishing Co., Indianapolis, Ind., 1974.

Beau, Frank N. *Quantity Food Purchasing Guide.* Cahners Books, Boston, Mass., 1974.

Kotschevar, Lendal H. *Quantity Food Purchasing.* John Wiley & Sons, New York, N.Y., 1975.

Maizel, Bruno. *Food and Beverage Purchasing.* ITT Educational Publishing Co., Indianapolis, Ind., 1974.

National Canners Association. *Canned Foods Tables.* NCA, Washington, D.C., 1959.

National Frozen Food Association. *Frozen Food Institutional Encyclopedia.* NFFA, Hershey, Pa., 1973.

Ross, Lynne, and McHenry, Roberta M. *Food Purchasing: Study Course.* Iowa State University Press, Ames, Iowa, 1971.

Sexton, John & Co. *Volume Feeding Buying Guide.* John Sexton & Co., Englewood, N.J., 1970.

United Fresh Fruit and Vegetable Association. *Buying, Handling and Using Fresh Fruits. Buying, Handling and Using Fresh Vegetables.* UFFVA. Washington, D.C., 1967.

U.S. Department of Agriculture. *Food for Us All. Yearbook of Agriculture,* 1969.

————. *Shoppers Guide. Yearbook of Agriculture, 1974.*

————. *Food Purchasing Guide for Group Feeding.* Agriculture Handbook No. 284.

————. *Food Storage Guide for Schools and Institutions,* 1959.

————. *How to Use U.S.D.A. Grades in Buying Food,* 1972.

————. *Meat and Poultry. Standards for You,* 1973.

————. *U.S.D.A. Grade Standards for Food—How They Are Developed and Used,* 1973.

————. *U.S.D.A. Yield Grades for Beef,* 1968.

————. *U.S.D.A. Yield Grades for Lamb,* 1971.

————. *U.S.D.A. Standards for Food and Farm Products,* 1972.

————. *Federal and State Standards for the Composition of Milk Products,* 1971.

————. *Federal Standards for Food Products,* (by item). From Code of Federal Regulations. Superintendent of Documents, Washington, D.C.*

Regular Reports on Market Conditions

American Institute of Food Distribution. *Report on Food Markets* (Weekly). Fair Lawn, N.J.

————. *Washington Food Report* (Weekly). Fair Lawn, N.J.

————. *Weekly Digest.* Fair Lawn, N.J.

National Provisioner. *Hotel, Restaurant, Institutional Meat Service Report.* (Weekly). Chicago, Ill.

U.S. Department of Agriculture. Agricultural Marketing Service. *Food Marketing Alert.* U.S. Government Printing Office, Washington, D.C.

United Fresh Fruit and Vegetable Association. *Monthly Supply Letter.* Washington, D.C.

Meats

Club Managers Association of America. *Meat Purchasing Guide for Private Clubs.* CMAA, Washington, D.C. 1968.

Fabbricante, Thomas, and Sultan, William. *Practical Meat Cutting and Merchandising: Vol. I, Beef.* Avi Publishing Co., Westport, Conn., 1974.

————. *Practical Meat Cutting and Merchandising: Vol. II, Pork, Lamb, Veal.* Avi Publishing Co., Westport, Conn., 1975.

Levie, Albert. *The Meat Handbook.* Avi Publishing Co., Westport, Conn., 1970.

National Association of Hotel and Restaurant Meat Purveyors. *Meat Buyer's Guide to Portion Control Meat Cuts.* NAHRMP, Chicago, Ill., 1967.

————. *Meat Buyer's Guide to Standardized Meat Cuts.* NAHRMP, Chicago, Ill., 1965.

National Live Stock and Meat Board. *Meat Evaluation Handbook.* NLSMB, Chicago, Ill., 1969.

---

*All of these publications of the U.S. Department of Agriculture are available from the U.S. Government Printing Office, Washington, D.C.

Food Production

Amendola, Joseph, and Berrini, James. *Practical Cooking and Baking for Schools and Institutions.* Hayden Book Co., Rochelle Park, N.J., 1971.

American Dietetic Association. *Standardizing Recipes for Institutional Use.* ADA, Chicago, Ill., 1967.

American Hospital Association. *Food Service Manual for Health Care Institutions.* AHA, Chicago, Ill., 1972.

American Institute of Baking. *Modern Sandwich Methods.* AIB, Chicago, Ill., 1964.

Axler, Bruce. *Focus on: Adding Eye Appeal to Foods.* ITT Educational Publishing Co., Indianapolis, Ind., 1974.

———. *Focus on: Breakfast Cookery.* ITT Educational Publishing Co., Indianapolis, Ind., 1974.

Hardwick, Geraldine, and Kennedy, Robert L. *Fundamentals of Quantity Food Preparation: Desserts and Beverages.* Cahners Books, Boston, Mass., 1975.

Hospitality Magazine. *The Guide to Convenience Foods.* Patterson Publishing Co., Cleveland, Ohio, 1968.

Kaplan, Aaron. *Elements of Food Preparation and Baking.* ITT Educational Publishing Co., Indianapolis, Ind., 1971.

Keister, Douglas C. *How to Increase Profits with Portion Control.* Hayden Book Co., Rochelle Park, N.J., 1966.

Kotschevar, Lendal H. *Standards, Principles, and Techniques in Quantity Food Production.* Cahners Books, Boston, Mass., 1974.

Kotschevar, Lendal H., and McWilliams, Margaret. *Understanding Food (Programmed).* John Wiley & Sons New York, N.Y., 1969.

Kramer, Mary A., and Spader, Margaret. *Contemporary Meal Management.* John Wiley & Sons, New York, N.Y., 1972.

Litton Systems, Inc. *An Exciting New World of Microwave Cooking.* Pillsbury Publications, Minneapolis, Minn., 1971.

Mok, Charles. *Practical Salad and Dessert Art.* Cahners Books, Boston, Mass., 1973.

Paul, Pauline et al. *Food Theory and Applications.* John Wiley & Sons, New York, N.Y., 1972.

Pinkert, Michael S. *The Ready Foods System for Health Care Facilities.* Cahners Books, Boston, Mass., 1973.

Pyke, Magnus. *Catering Science and Technology.* Avi Publishing Co., Westport, Conn., 1974.

Rietz, Carl A. *A Guide to the Selection, Combination and Cooking of Foods. Vol. I.* Avi Publishing Co., Westport, Conn., 1961.

Rietz, Carl A., and Wanderstock, Jeremiah. *A Guide to the Selection, Combination and Cooking of Foods. Vol. II.* Avi Publishing Co., Westport, Conn., 1965.

Rogers, John L. *Production of Precooked Frozen Foods for Mass Catering.* Avi Publishing Co., Westport, Conn., 1969.

Simpson, Jean I. *The Frozen Food Cookbook and Guide to Home Freezing.* Avi Publishing Co., Westport, Conn., 1962.

Smith, Evelyn E., and Crusius, Vera. *A Handbook on Quantity Food Management.* Burgess Publishing Co., Minneapolis, Minn., 1970.

Smith, Laura Lee, and Minor, Lewis J. *Food Service Science.* Avi Publishing Co., Westport, Conn., 1974.

Terrell, Margaret E. *Professional Food Preparation: Techniques and Equipment for Large Quantity.* John Wiley & Sons, New York, N.Y., 1970.

Thorner, Marvin E. *Convenience and Fast Food Handbook.* Avi Publishing Co., Westport, Conn., 1972.

Thorner, Marvin, and Herzberg, R. J. *Food Beverage Service Handbook.* Avi Publishing Co., Westport, Conn., 1970.

Tressler, Donald K. (ed.). *The Freezing Preservation of Foods: Vol. I. Principles of Refrigeration. Vol. II. Factors Affecting Quality in Frozen Foods. Vol. III. The Freezing of Fresh Foods. Vol. IV. The Freezing of Precooked and Prepared Foods.* Avi Publishing Co., Westport, Conn., 1968.

VanZante, Helen. *The Microwave Oven.* Houghton Mifflin, Boston, Mass., 1973.

Baking

Amendola, Joseph. *Bakers Manual for Quantity Baking and Pastry Making.* Hayden Book Co., Rochelle Park, N.J., 1972.

Amendola, Joseph, and Lundberg, Donald E. *Understanding Baking.* Cahners Books, Boston, Mass., 1971.

Indiana Bakers Association. *Baker Boy Manual.* National Restaurant Association, Chicago, Ill., 1969.

Sultan, William J. *Practical Baking.* Avi Publishing Co., Westport, Conn., 1969.

Quantity Recipes

Asmussen, Patricia. *Simplified Recipes for Day Care Centers.* Cahners Books, Boston, Mass., 1974.

Caviani, Mabel, and Urbashick, Muriel. *Simplified Quantity Recipes. Nursing/ Convalescent Homes and Hospitals.* National Restaurant Association., Chicago, Ill., 1974.

Cornell University, School of Hotel Administration. *Tested Quantity Recipes.* Ithaca, New York, N.Y., 1967.

Folsom, Leroi. *The Professional Chef.* Cahners Books, Boston, Mass., 1974.

Fowler, Sina F. et al. *Food for Fifty.* John Wiley & Sons, New York, N.Y., 1971.

Iowa State University, Institution Management Department. *Standardized Quantity Recipe File for Quality and Cost Control.* Iowa State University Press, Ames, Iowa, 1971.

Snider, Nancy. *Professional Chef's Soy Protein Recipe Ideas.* Cahners Books, Boston, Mass., 1971.

Sonnenschmidt, Frederic, and Nicolas, Jean. *The Professional Chef's Art of Garde Manger.* Cahners Books, Boston, Mass., 1973.

Terrell, Margaret E. *Large Quantity Recipes.* J. B. Lippincott, New York, N.Y., 1975.

Treat, Nola, and Richards, Lenore. *Quantity Cookery.* Little, Brown & Co., Boston, 1969.

U.S. Department of Agriculture, Agricultural Research Service. *Recipes for Quantity Service.* U.S. Government Printing Office, Washington, D.C., 1972.

U.S. Department of Defense. *Armed Forces Recipe Service.* Superintendent of Documents, U.S. Government Printing Office, Washington, D.C., 1969.

Operating Cost Controls

Albers, Carl H. *Food and Beverage Controls.* Educational Institute of the American Hotel & Motel Association, Kellogg Center, East Lansing, Mich., 1964.

Coffman, James P. *The High Payroll Low Profit Syndrome.* Cahners Books, Boston, Mass., 1970.

Keiser, Ralph J., and Kallio, Elmer. *Controlling and Analyzing Costs in Food Service Operations.* John Wiley & Sons, New York, N.Y., 1974.

Maizel, Bruno. *Food and Beverage Cost Controls.* ITT Educational Publishing Co., Indianapolis, Ind., 1972.

Service

Axler, Bruce. *Focus on: Showmanship in the Dining Room.* ITT Educational Publishing Co., Indianapolis, Ind., 1974.

————. *Focus on: Profitable Catering.* ITT Educational Publishing Co., Indianapolis, Ind., 1974.

————. *Focus on: Tableservice Techniques.* ITT Educational Publishing Co., Indianapolis, Ind., 1974.

Cornell University, School of Hotel Administration. *Essentials of Good Table Service.* Ithaca, N.Y., 1971.

Dahmer, Sondra, and Kahl, Kurt. *The Waiter and Waitress Training Manual.* Cahners Books, Boston, Mass., 1974.

Forster, August. *American Culinary Art.* Hayden Book Co., Rochelle Park, N.J., 1958.

Finance, Charles. *Buffet Catering.* Hayden Book Co., Rochelle Park, N.J., 1975.

Fuller, John. *Gueridon and Lamp Cookery.* Hayden Book Co., Rochelle Park, N.J., 1964.

Gilbert, Edith. *Let's Set the Table.* Jet'Iquette, 510 Michigan Ave., Charlevoix, Mich., 1972.

Hirsch, Sylvia. *The Art of Table Setting and Flower Arrangment.* Thomas Y. Crowell Co., New York, N.Y., 1967.

Huebener, Paul O. *Gourmet Table Service: A Professional Guide.* Hayden Book Co., Rochelle Park, N.J., 1968.

Lang, Howard F. *Catering.* Hayden Book Co., Rochelle Park, N.J., 1975.

Lehrman, Lewis. *Dining Room Service.* ITT Educational Publishing Co., Indianapolis, Ind., 1971.

McCrory Corp. *Cafeteria Guide to Customer Service.* National Restaurant Association, Chicago, Ill., 1973.

Waldner, George K., and Mitterhauser. *Professional Chef's Book of Buffets.* Cahners Books, Boston, Mass., 1968.

Mulcahy, Cherie, and Corbin, Robert. *It Pays to Be a Pro.* Foodcraft Management Corp., 3147 Far Hills Ave., Kettering, Ohio, 1971.

————. *Today's Busboy.* Chain Store Age Books, New York, N.Y., 1971.

————. *Today's Cocktail Waitress.* Chain Store Age Books, New York, N.Y., 1974.

————. *Today's Waitress.* Chain Store Age Books, New York, N.Y., 1971.

Weiss, Edith, and Weiss, Hal. *Catering Handbook.* Hayden Book Co., Rochelle Park, N.J., 1971.

Vending

Gardner, Jerry. *Contract Food Service/Vending.* Cahners Books, Boston, Mass., 1973.

Haberl, F. J. *Profitable Vending.* National Restaurant Association, Chicago, Ill., 1971.

National Automatic Merchandising Association. *The Vending and Foodservice Management Market.* NAMA, Washington, D.C., 1971.

Rogers, John L. *Automatic Vending: Merchandising—Catering.* Avi Publishing Co., Westport, Conn., 1958.

U.S. Department of Commerce. *Starting and Managing a Small Automatic Vending Business.* Small Business Administration, Washington, D.C., 1967.

Bar Operation and Wine Service

Axler, Bruce. *Focus on: Practical Wine Knowledge.* ITT Educational Publishing Co., Indianapolis, Ind., 1974.

Bar Server Magazine. *Pouring for Profits.* Hiram Walker, Inc., Detroit, Mich., 1969.

Duffy, Patrick G., and Beard, James. *The Bartender's Guide.* Pocket Books, New York, N.Y. (Originally pub. by Doubleday, 1956).

Grossman, Harold J. *Grossman's Guide to Wines, Spirits and Beers.* Charles Scribner's Sons, New York, N.Y., 1974.

————. *Practical Bar Management.* Hayden Book Co., Rochelle Park, N.J., 1959.

Haims, Oscar. *Cocktail and Wine Digest: The Barman's Bible.* Oscar Haims, 252 E. 61st St., New York, N.Y., 1974.

Haszonics, Joseph, and Barratt, Stuart. *Wine Merchandising.* Hayden Book Co., Rochelle Park, N.J., 1963.

Lichine, Alexis. *New Encyclopedia of Wines and Spirits.* Alfred A. Knopf, New York, N.Y., 1974.

Liquor Store Magazine. *Knowing Alcoholic Beverages.* Schenley Imports Co., New York, N.Y., 1971.

Trader Vic. *Bartender's Guide.* Doubleday & Co., Garden City, N.Y., 1972.

Personnel Administration and Staff Planning

Bryan, John R. *Managing Restaurant Personnel.* Chain Store Age Books, New York, N.Y., 1974.

Club Managers Association of America. *Job Descriptions for Club Operations.* CMAA, Washington, D.C., 1972.

Elliott, Travis. *Profitable Food Service Management Series.* (9 pamphlets.) National Restaurant Association, Chicago, Ill., 1966–1968.

Kazarian, Edward. *Work Analysis and Design for Hotels, Restaurants and Institutions.* Avi Publishing Co., Westport, Conn., 1969.

Leslie, C. E. et al. *Human Relations for Hotel-Motel Supervisors.* Educational Institute of the American Hotel & Motel Association, Kellogg Center, East Lansing, Mich., 1970.

Lundberg, Donald and Armatas, James. *The Management of People in Hotels, Restaurants and Clubs.* Wm. C. Brown, Dubuque, Iowa, 1974.

National Restaurant Association. *Career Ladders in the Food Service Industry.* NRA, Chicago, Ill., 1971.

———. *How to Invest in People: A Handbook of Career Ladders.* NRA, Chicago, Ill., 1973.

Ross, Lynne N. *Work Simplification in Food Service: Individualized Instruction.* Iowa State University Press, Ames, Iowa, 1972.

Siegel, Laurence, and Lane, Irving. *Psychology in Industrial Organizations.* Richard D. Irwin, Inc., Homewood, Ill., 1974.

Spriegel, Schulz, and Spriegel. *Elements of Supervision.* John Wiley & Sons, New York, N.Y., 1957.

U.S. Department of Agriculture, Agricultural Research Service. *Labor Utilization and Operating Practices in Commercial Cafeterias,* U.S. Government Printing Office, 1969.

———. *Labor Utilization and Operating Practices in Table Service Restaurants.* Superintendent of Documents, U.S. Government Printing Office, Washington, D.C., 1971.

Wilkinson, Julie (ed.) *Increasing Productivity In Food Service.* Cahners Books, Boston, Mass., 1973.

Zabka, John R. *Personnel Management and Human Relations.* ITT Educational Publishing Co., Indianapolis, Ind., 1974.

INDEX

INDEX